THE GREEK STONES SPEAK

Athens, Acropolis and environs, air view. (Greek National Tourist Bureau)

THE GREEK STONES SPEAK

SECOND EDITION

THE STORY
OF
ARCHAEOLOGY
IN
GREEK LANDS

PAUL MacKENDRICK

W. W. NORTON & COMPANY
NEW YORK · LONDON

Copyright © 1981, 1962 by Paul MacKendrick

Published simultaneously in Canada by George J. McLeod Limited, Toronto.

Printed in the United States of America

Second Edition

Library of Congress Cataloging in Publication Data
MacKendrick, Paul Lachlan, 1914–
The Greek stones speak.

Bibliography: p.
Includes index.
1. Greece—Antiquities.   2. Excavations
(Archaeology—Greece.   I.   Title.
DF77.M18   1981   938   81–4349
ISBN 0–393–01463–0   AACR2

W. W. Norton & Company, Inc., 500 Fifth Avenue, New York, N.Y. 10110
W. W. Norton & Company Ltd. 37 Great Russell Street, London WC1B 3NU
1 2 3 4 5 6 7 8 9 0

To the
faculty and members
of the
American School of Classical Studies
in Athens

FOREWORD
TO THE SECOND EDITION

The first edition of this book appeared in 1962. Since then, excavation has gone on so actively in Greece and Greek lands that extensive updating and revision, both of text and of photographs, have been necessary. Since then I have also published five other books in which, as in this one, my aims have been twofold: to write cultural history based on a selection of archaeological evidence, and to illustrate archaeological inference at work. In these books I have dealt with Greek (and Roman) 'sites in Spain, Germany, France, Romania, and North Africa, supplementing the final chapter here, which presents a selective account of Greek art and architecture under the Roman Empire.

The obligations recorded in the foreword to the first edition still stand: to Harvard University, the Fulbright Commission, the Trustees of the American Academy in Rome, the Guggenheim Foundation, the Research Committee of the University of Wisconsin Graduate School, and the Librarian of the American School of Classical Studies in Athens. Now it is a pleasure to add my philhellene publisher, George P. Brockway. To my colleagues E. L. Bennett, Jr., and Kenneth Sacks I am indebted for skilled proofreading. The dedication is in deep thanks for kindnesses—including the donation of heart's blood—showered upon me while I was recovering from a broken leg in Athens in the summer of 1980.

CONTENTS

ILLUSTRATIONS

NOTE

The legends under each illustration give references to sources, either in full or by short title. The key to the short titles is in the list of *Books and Articles Consulted*. Where no reference is given, the source is assumed to be in the public domain. For permissions to reproduce photographs, warmest thanks are due to the holders of copyright.

THE GREEK STONES SPEAK

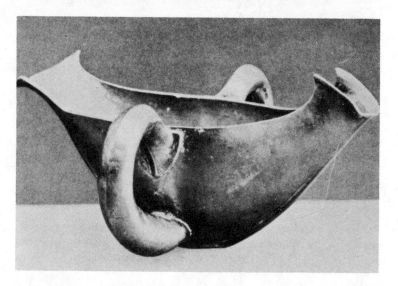

FIG. 1.1 Troy II, "Priam's treasure." Two gold cups and a gold "sauce-boat," actually 1000 years older than Priam. Formerly in Museum für Vor- und Frühgeschichte, Berlin; abstracted by Russians, presumably destroyed: gold reproductions in Schloss Charlottenburg, Berlin. (F. Matz, *KMT*, Pl. 5)

1

The Aegean in Prehistory

(to 1900 B.C.)

On May 31, 1873 Heinrich Schliemann, far on the lofty plains of windy Troy, wrote in his journal, "Eight or nine meters down I laid bare the stretch of the circuit wall of Troy by the Scaean Gate and discovered, in a room of the House of Priam adjoining this wall, a copper container . . . filled with great silver vases and with silver and gold cups (Fig. 1.1). To keep these from the workmen's greed, I had to extract them, hide them [in his wife's shawl], and send them off in such haste that I neither know their number nor am in a position to describe their form."

The excavations that uncovered this treasure, begun three years before, opened a new and fascinating chapter in ancient history. Later investigation showed that the treasure, the house, and the wall were not Priam's, but a thousand years older; that the findspot was not a room in a Trojan house, but a hiding place in the wall itself. But for all his error and amateurishness, Schliemann was a pioneer, the founder of the new science of archaeology, which by now has revolutionized our ideas of the origins of Greek civilization. He began in a new spirit. His enthusiasm was not simply for treasure in gold and silver, but for evidence: evidence, now universally accepted, that the Trojan war as described in Homer was historic fact. To establish this thesis, he learned to depend on what have been the archaeologist's most reliable indicators ever since, potsherds (Fig. 1.2) which, he wrote in 1876 to his friend Gladstone, "are far more indestructible than all the city or fortress walls in the world. The strongest wall in the world can easily be removed, but no mortal man can remove the potsherds with which the site of every ancient city is covered."

In an age when Greek scholars scorned everything preclassical, Schliemann devoted his efforts entirely to prehistory, and most of what we know about the Aegean since the third millennium B.C. we owe to beginnings made by him. When in 1882 he persuaded the twenty-nine-year-old William Dörpfeld, a trained architect who had already dug at Olympia, to join him at Troy, the combination of Schliemann's enthusiasm and wealth (derived from judicious profiteering in the Crimean War) with Dörpfeld's precision, clarity, sound method, and sobriety made possible a genuinely scientific contribution to the understanding of the history of Troy. This understanding was still further refined by the University of Cincinnati excavations (1932-38) under C. W. Blegen. The whole dramatic story of prehistoric archaeology in the Aegean area, bound up as it is with strong personalities, is as full of human as it is of scientific interest.

Schliemann's earliest report on his excavations at Troy is dated April 21, 1870, and is addressed to the president of the Institut de France. In it he expresses his conviction that the eighty-five-foot mound of Hissarlik, some three and a half miles back from the sea, is Homer's Troy. He describes with impatience his difficulties in getting authori-

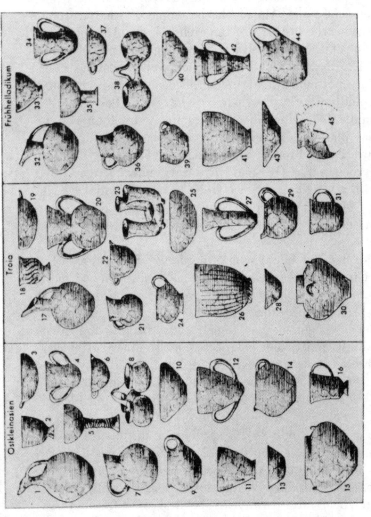

Fig. 1.2 Troy I-II, pottery shapes (Nos. 17-31) compared to those of eastern Anatolia (1-16), and early mainland Greece (32-45), to show how archaeologists determine cultural relations between sites. (Schachermeyr, 1955, p. 155, by permission of the publishers, W. Kohlhammer, Stuttgart)

zation to dig from the Turkish government, records his decision to dig without permission, and tells how within an hour of first striking spade into Trojan earth, he came upon ancient walls. Already he has some of what we now recognize as the instincts of the archaeologist. He notes the depths of finds, records strata (including evidence of burning and earthquake) and fortification walls, mentions finds of coins, potsherds, and unidentified clay objects (they were spindle whorls, of which Troy has yielded an astonishing number). He identifies as a temple a building of rectangular plan that later turned out to be a megaron, the standard Early Bronze Age upper-class dwelling. Schliemann's megaron at Troy had when it was new a long narrow hall with a weighty roof of cypress beams, a central hearth thirteen feet wide, an open porch, and a single door. Some scholars claim it to be the ancestor of the classical Greek temple.

In this first dig Schliemann often drew inferences as if by instinct from the very objects that have since proved most useful to archaeologists in their work of reconstructing a culture from mute stones and clay. But in 1872, in his impatience to get at the Homeric city, he dug the great north-south trench that ruined so much—almost a quarter —of the precious stratification of his beloved city. The damage was not irreparable, however, for he left "islands" in the midst of his trench from which Dörpfeld and Blegen were later able to recover the history of the site. By 1879 he knew his business and was able to distinguish seven superimposed citadels on the hill of Hissarlik. His findings would have been more precise had not the Turks, for military reasons, forbidden all measuring and drawing on the site. In 1880, after two years of desk-work at fourteen hours a day, he published his findings in *Ilios,* a landmark in the history of Greek archaeology.

Of all his finds, the most thrilling and spectacular was "Priam's treasure" (see Fig. 1.1). Besides vessels and weapons in bronze and copper, which proved the hoard to belong to a civilization that has already emerged from the Neolithic age, the treasure included vessels and jewelry in precious metals: a golden flask and a "sauce-boat," a golden diadem, earrings, and necklaces, in which he arrayed his lovely Greek wife, Sophie, and had her picture taken; six golden armbands, bar silver, many vessels in silver, and in the alloy of gold and silver called electrum, and 8700 miscellaneous golden objects: granulated gold earrings, buttons, and beads. The earrings mostly were not matched pairs, and were therefore probably the spoils of Trojan raids; if they had matched, there would have been more reason to believe that they came from a Trojan princess' jewel box. Though humble potsherds are often more informative to the archaeologist than much fine gold, he would not be human if he did not rejoice in the occasional discovery of valuable hoards. These include an astonishing variety of objects: double axes, scales, daggers, anvils, swords, talent-weights (in bronze, shaped like ox-hides), spears, mirrors, vases, bronze handles, diadems, calipers, harness-bits, fibulae (the ancient safety pins), hammer heads, seals, beads, cauldrons.

Though "Priam's treasure" was only one of nineteen such hoards found by successive excavators on the site, it was the one that captured the public imagination and established Schliemann's fame overnight. Apart from its intrinsic value and the romantic circumstances of its discovery, the treasure has another, deeper interest. After Dörpfeld's careful work had established that the treasure belonged not to Priam's Troy, but to Troy II, over a thousand years earlier, it became clear that this early Troy's wealth was princely, derived from war, but perhaps also from profitable trade with inner Anatolia, the Aegean Islands, and the Balkans, for all these regions have yielded to the archaeologist's spade objects comparable to those which make up the treasure. The "sauce-boat" is Aegean, the granulated gold technique is Mesopotamian (there is a Mesopotamian cylinder seal among the finds to reinforce the connection), and the handsome "parade ax" in lapis lazuli which forms part of another treasure of the same date has parallels in Bessarabia. Finds of Baltic amber, too, point to connections with the north.

When Schliemann died in 1890, he had dug at Mycenae, Ithaca, Orchomenos, and Tiryns, and had negotiated, unsuccessfully, for excavation rights in Crete, but the plan and dating of the various levels at Troy were still not entirely clear. That Dörpfeld was able to draw and date

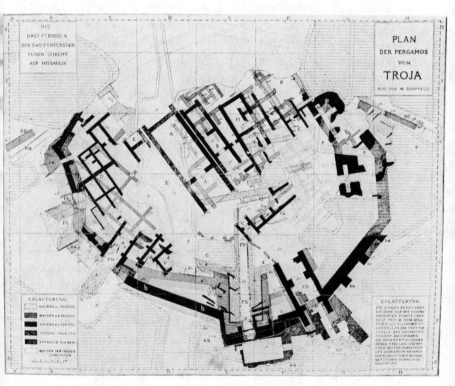

FIG. 1.3   Troy, Dörpfeld's plan, distinguishing three subdivisions of Troy II. The darker the wall-line, the earlier the level. Blegen added four subphases, but Dörpfeld's pioneer work has stood up well. Dörpfeld, 1902, fac. p. 16)

Fig. 1.4 Troy VI, fortification wall. Built in segments, with a pronounced batter (receding slope) to support mud-brick superstructure. (F. Matz, *KMT*, Pl. 114)

a plan was due largely to funds generously provided by Schliemann's widow, and later by Kaiser Wilhelm II, to whom Dörpfeld's two great volumes on Troy are dedicated. His trained architect's eye was able to distinguish nine superimposed levels on the citadel, and his plans of 1902 are still authoritative (Fig. 1.3). Among his 120 workmen were many named after Homeric heroes, who proudly answered, "Here!" as the names Agamemnon, Odysseus, Achilles were called at muster. On the evidence of the technique of the walls (Fig. 1.4), and of the pottery, which resembled that found at Mycenae, he identified the sixth level from the bottom, which had not been completely excavated at Schliemann's death, as that of Homeric Troy. This conclusion remained unchallenged until Blegen's more meticulous techniques modified it in 1937. Dörpfeld and his colleagues distinguished building materials of different dates, dated fortification walls, recorded the pottery care-

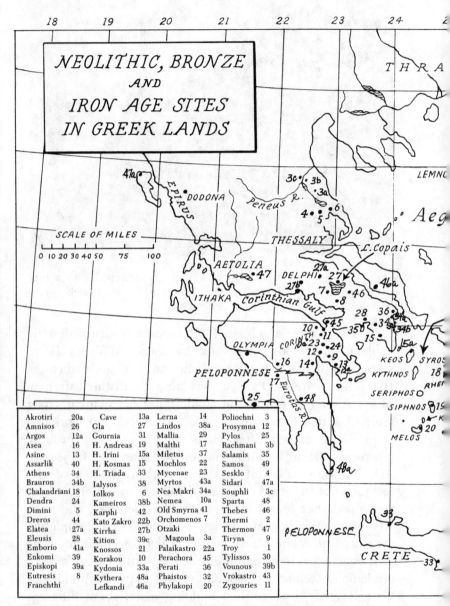

Akrotiri	20a	Cave	13a	Lerna	14	Poliochni	3
Amnisos	26	Gla	27	Lindos	38a	Prosymna	12
Argos	12a	Gournia	31	Mallia	29	Pylos	25
Asea	16	H. Andreas	19	Malthi	17	Rachmani	3b
Asine	13	H. Irini	15a	Miletus	37	Salamis	35
Assarlik	40	H. Kosmas	15	Mochlos	22	Samos	4
Athens	34	H. Triada	33	Mycenae	23	Sesklo	49
Brauron	34b	Ialysos	38	Myrtos	43a	Sidari	47a
Chalandriani	18	Iolkos	6	Nea Makri	34a	Souphli	3c
Dendra	24	Kameiros	38b	Nemea	10a	Sparta	48
Dimini	5	Karphi	42	Old Smyrna	41	Thebes	46
Dreros	44	Kato Zakro	22b	Orchomenos	7	Thermi	2
Elatea	27a	Kirrha	27b	Otzaki		Thermon	47
Eleusis	28	Kition	39c	Magoula	3a	Tiryns	9
Emborio	41a	Knossos	21	Palaikastro	22a	Troy	1
Enkomi	39	Korakou	10	Perachora	45	Tylissos	30
Episkopi	39a	Kydonia	33a	Perati	36	Vounous	39b
Eutresis	8	Kythera	48a	Phaistos	32	Vrokastro	43
Franchthi		Lefkandi	46a	Phylakopi	20	Zygouries	11

FIG. 1.5 Neolithic, Bronze, and Iron Age sites in Greek lands, to illlustrate Chs. 1-3.

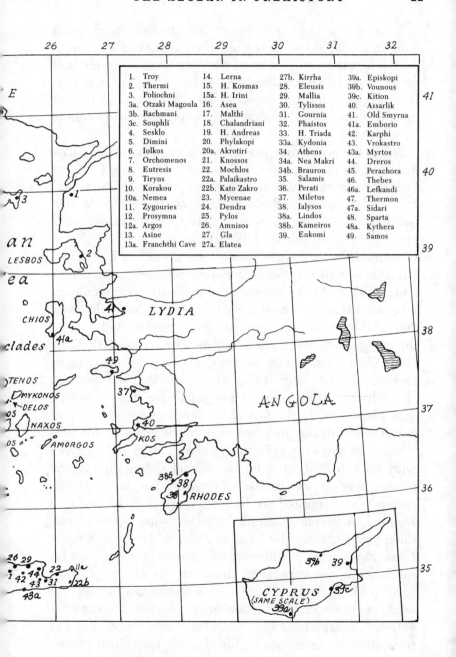

1.	Troy	14.	Lerna	27b.	Kirrha	39a.	Episkopi
2.	Thermi	15.	H. Kosmas	28.	Eleusis	39b.	Vounous
3.	Poliochni	15a.	H. Irini	29.	Mallia	39c.	Kition
3a.	Otzaki Magoula	16.	Asea	30.	Tylissos	40.	Assarlik
3b.	Rachmani	17.	Malthi	31.	Gournia	41.	Old Smyrna
3c.	Souphli	18.	Chalandriani	32.	Phaistos	41a.	Emborio
4.	Sesklo	19.	H. Andreas	33.	H. Triada	42.	Karphi
5.	Dimini	20.	Phylakopi	33a.	Kydonia	43.	Vrokastro
6.	Iolkos	20a.	Akrotiri	34.	Athens	43a.	Myrtos
7.	Orchomenos	21.	Knossos	34a.	Nea Makri	44.	Dreros
8.	Eutresis	22.	Mochlos	34b.	Brauron	45.	Perachora
9.	Tiryns	22a.	Palaikastro	35.	Salamis	46.	Thebes
10.	Korakou	22b.	Kato Zakro	36.	Perati	46a.	Lefkandi
10a.	Nemea	23.	Mycenae	37.	Miletus	47.	Thermon
11.	Zygouries	24.	Dendra	38.	Ialysos	47a.	Sidari
12.	Prosymna	25.	Pylos	38a.	Lindos	48.	Sparta
12a.	Argos	26.	Amnisos	38b.	Kameiros	48a.	Kythera
13.	Asine	27.	Gla	39.	Enkomi	49.	Samos
13a.	Franchthi Cave	27a.	Elatea				

fully level by level, catalogued the thousands of small finds in metal, stone, bone, and clay, described the sculpture, inscriptions, and coins of the post-Homeric levels, and drew masterly conclusions about the history of the pre-Homeric and Homeric cities. In 1902 it seemed as though the definitive archaeological history of Troy had already been written.

But in the next thirty years new excavation on the Greek mainland, in the Cyclades, and in Crete (see map, Fig. 1.5) had raised new problems about the history, culture, and trade relations of prehistoric settlements in the Aegean basin, so that when in 1932 the Taft family made funds available to Professor Carl W. Blegen of the University of Cincinnati, he eagerly reopened the excavations at Troy. His aim was to use the information collected since Dörpfeld's book to fix a chronology and clarify Troy's cultural relations by means of artifacts from which he could draw dependable inferences because their precise findspots in the complicated levels were known. The terms of the Taft grant placed him under no compulsion to be startling or sensational, or to court publicity, and indeed the contents of his four massive volumes (1950-58) are more scientific than glamorous. In the first of his seven campaigns he dug over three miles of trenches in a fruitless search for preclassical tombs; in 1935 he dug in eleven areas and removed with his light railway 3000 carloads of debris; in 1937 he moved over 10,000 carloads of earth. His finds, chiefly pottery, he deposited in the Archaeological Museum in Istanbul, reserving a sample collection—400 boxes of certified potsherds—for the local museum in Troy's port town, Chanakkale, while a still more select sampling was kept for exhibition in the Excavation House on the site.

Blegen's methods, a model of scientific archaeology at work, are the envy of his fellow archaeologists. They involve patience, persistence, and controlled imagination. He had to remove the enormous dump of earth from Schliemann's excavations, first making sure that the site chosen for the new dump was archaeologically sterile. He had to assure the continuity of his staff, so that the same scholar could be in charge of the same area for season after season. He had to train his workmen; to issue them, for example, only small picks, so that the delicate pottery would not be damaged. He had to make sure that the excavation daybooks were meticulously kept. He dug trial trenches to determine strata, being careful to dig always at right angles to walls, not parallel to them, so as to record the contiguous strata. He took levels carefully with a surveyor's transit. He saw to it that the expedition's architect kept up with the dig, drawing stone-for-stone plans. Every find, however insignificant, had a wooden label attached, recording the area, section, and level in which it was found, assigning it a number and a date, with a cross-reference to the notebook where its detailed description was recorded. The earth was sieved, as though the excavators were panning for gold; and indeed from the historical point of view their conclusions were more precious than gold. The smallest finds were placed in pillboxes, cushioned with cotton wool. Sherds were cleaned in a dilute solution of hydrochloric acid, pots were mended with shellac, gaps in them filled with plaster. Inventories were kept, the finds numbered by categories, thousands of photographs taken.

Dörpfeld's nine settlements stood up well under Blegen's more refined analysis, but each was broken down into subphases, so that in the end forty-six subdivisions were distinguished. The criteria used for setting up the nine phases were sweeping shifts in orientation (Fig. 1.6), changes in implements, artifacts, and pottery. Careful type-charts drew distinctions, vital for dating, in pot shapes and decoration (the pots of Troy I were handmade and incised), and in types of pins, idols, bone awls, and spindle whorls. Blegen found copper in the lowest level: Troy I was already on the way to the Bronze Age in 3000 B.C. Molds in stone and terracotta show that the artifacts were made on the spot. None of the pottery in this earliest level could be matched elsewhere: this settlement was not yet sophisticated or important enough to have much of an import trade. A surprising and unique find was a sandstone slab or stele with a representation of a human face, the earliest such monument known from the Aegean area.

And Troy I was fortified. What was excavated was a citadel, a place reserved for the king and his nobles, with no evidence throughout its ten subphases of any of the humble dwellings or artifacts which would have indicated the presence of a lower class. Yet the finds revealed that there were Trojan farmers, fishermen, potters, stonemasons, and builders. These must have lived in the lower town, as yet unexcavated, below the hill of Hissarlik. Between this lowest level and Troy II was the evidence, in a burnt layer, of the destruction of the earliest settlement by fire.

In Troy II Blegen, carefully observing the pottery, and with the help of the stratification in the "islands" left by Schliemann and Dörpfeld, was able to distinguish seven subphases, compressed into two meters vertically. Most of these subphases in most places belonged to the final phase. Within this level the culture developed rapidly: wheel-made pottery now first replaced handmade ware; excavation of the fortification walls showed that the citadel was expanded and remodeled on a grand scale, with massive double-roomed gateways and a double megaron surrounded by a colonnade. Late in this level falls Schliemann's "treasure"; the finds, in gold, silver, and crystal, and abundant pottery show, as we have seen, contacts with and imitations of neighboring cultures, to the north, in the hinterland of Asia Minor, and in the Aegean islands, and the ratio of imported to local ceramics increases from phase to phase.

Troy II ended in cataclysm, as Schliemann's treasure shows: no survivor returned to recover it. In one room of a private house, the excavators report, the "orderly rows

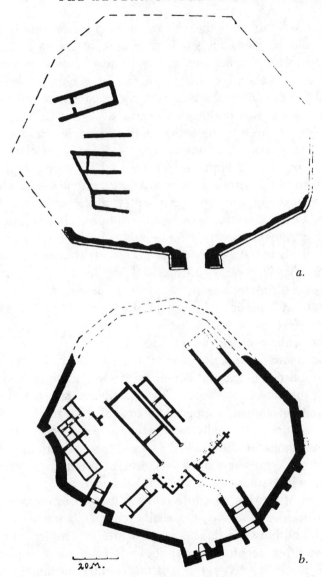

FIG. 1.6 *a*. Troy I. *b*. Troy II, to illustrate criteria for distinguishing phases. Note difference in orientation, and, in II, more sophisticated plan: larger megaron, portico, double gates. (Schachermeyr, 1955, Figs. 42 and 144)

of loomweights, and the 189 small gold beads found scattered on the floor, suggest a wife busy at the loom, summoned to flee for her life; in her haste to escape, we may suppose she abandoned her bracelet or necklace, perhaps caught in the fabric she was weaving, or taken off and hung up while she was performing her task."

The next three levels, while they yielded less impressive finds, were more than mere villages; Troy VI, richer still than Troy II, and apparently destroyed by an earthquake, brings us to the threshold of Priam's city, discussion of which is best postponed to the next chapter. Since the lowest five levels yielded no frescoes or inscriptions, the prehistoric twilight remains nearly impenetrable, but the evidence is clear of aristocratic prosperity, derived from trade; of distinction between class and mass; of life lived with a certain elegance: drinking vessels in precious metals, shaded porticoes to walk in, heated houses, but with a certain insecurity too; the Trojan princes felt the need to protect themselves behind walls over thirty feet thick.

The relative chronology of artifacts found on a site can be established if careful attention is paid to the levels in which objects are found. Stone artifacts are, normally, earlier than copper, copper than bronze, bronze than iron. Incised pottery is usually earlier than painted ware. Similar objects found at different sites establish synchronism between the corresponding levels. But in prehistoric archaeology, where most sites were inhabited by a population ignorant of writing, absolute chronology, expressed in years B.C., is harder to arrive at. Usually it depends on equations established between finds on such a site as Troy, where no early written records exist, and finds from more sophisticated places such as the Hittite country in inner Asia Minor, or Egypt, where dated written records were kept from very early times. Where there is no writing, pottery is very important. Thus sherds from Troy II resemble closely in fabric and decoration a sherd from Asine, on the

Greek mainland. in the Argolid (see map, Fig. 1.5), which is stamped with a swastika seal identical with some found in Egypt in a context dated to the Vth Dynasty. Written records date the Vth Dynasty between 2500 and 2350 B.C. Such is the complicated set of equations by which a fixed point can be established within Troy II (see table, Fig. 1.7).

Chronological Chart for the Aegean Bronze Age
and the earlier Dark Age

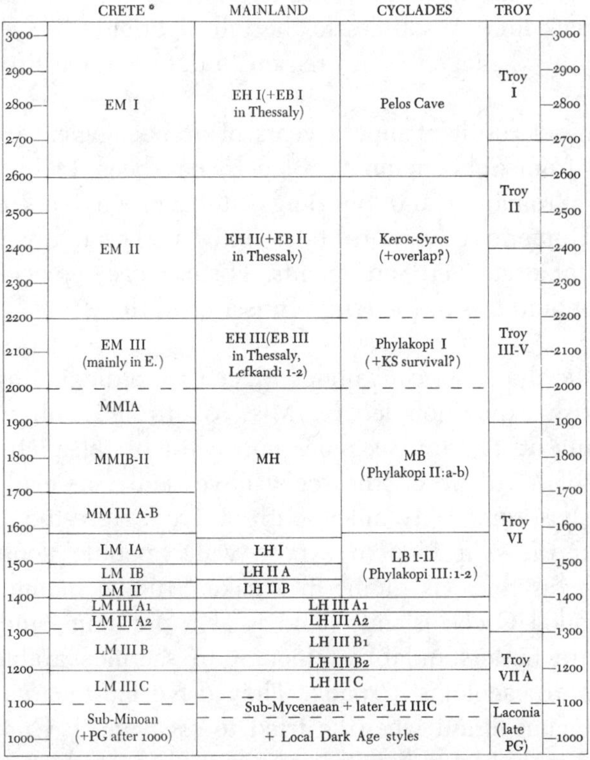

	CRETE [*]	MAINLAND	CYCLADES	TROY	
3000					3000
2900				Troy I	2900
2800	EM I	EH I(+EB I in Thessaly)	Pelos Cave		2800
2700					2700
2600				Troy II	2600
2500					2500
2400	EM II	EH II(+EB II in Thessaly)	Keros-Syros (+overlap?)		2400
2300					2300
2200			— — — —	Troy III-V	2200
2100	EM III (mainly in E.)	EH III(EB III in Thessaly, Lefkandi 1-2)	Phylakopi I (+KS survival?)		2100
2000	— — —		— — — —		2000
1900	MMIA				1900
1800	MMIB-II	MH	MB (Phylakopi II:a-b)		1800
1700					1700
1600	MM III A-B			Troy VI	1600
1500	LM IA	LH I	LB I-II (Phylakopi III:1-2)		1500
	LM IB	LH II A			
1400	LM II	LH II B			1400
	LM III A1		LH III A1		
1300	LM III A2		LH III A2		1300
	LM III B		LH III B1		
1200			LH III B2	Troy VII A	1200
	LM III C		LH III C		
1100	— — — —	Sub-Mycenaean + later LH IIIC		Laconia (late PG)	1100
1000	Sub-Minoan (+PG after 1000)	+ Local Dark Age styles			1000

[*] Peter Warren (*AJA* 84 [1980] p. 499) prefers the following dates for EM and MM: Final Neolithic: pre-4000-3500; EM I: 3500-2900; EM II: 2900-2300; EM III: 2300-2150; MM IA: 2150-1930; MM IB: 1930-1800; MM II: 1800-1700.

FIG. 1.7 Synchronisms: Crete, Cyclades, mainland, Troy. R. Hope Simpson, *SMA* 52 (1979) p. 130

Once this date is firmly established, all stratified objects found at Troy below the level of our eloquent potsherds are obviously earlier, and all stratified objects found above it are later than this date. Some notion of the duration in time of a given level results from the thickness of the strata. Thus the date accepted by most scholars nowadays for Troy I is 3000-2700 B.C.; for Troy II, 2700-2400; for Troy III-V, 2400-1900; and for Troy VI, a deep stratum, 1900-1300. This still does not bring us down to the date assigned by Greek literary sources to the fall of Priam's Troy, which is 1184 B.C.; Blegen found reason to date it some fifty years earlier.

The net result of ninety years of archaeological study of Troy, from Schliemann to Blegen, has been to change it from a romantic and puzzling source of golden treasures and Homeric adventure tales into a thoroughly known series of organized settlements. History has replaced false glamor, and this in the long run is a good thing.

While the Americans under Blegen were digging at Troy, a British expedition led by Miss Winifred Lamb was excavating at Thermi, six miles northwest of the picturesque town of Mytilene on the rocky olive- and vine-clad island of Lesbos, some sixty miles south of Troy. Here the sea had eroded the cliff face to expose walls, pebble floors, and sherds "as thick as plums in a cake." In the mountainous, thin-soiled Greek islands, land is at a premium, and peasants are understandably reluctant to sacrifice arable land to the archaeologist's spade. They drive hard bargains, as Schliemann found when he tried to excavate in Crete. But Miss Lamb had difficulty only with one landowner, and managed to dig at Thermi for five seasons, unearthing five superimposed towns, each distinguished by different houses, differently oriented, and separated by sterile strata indicating gaps in the occupation of the site. Miss Lamb's work was in the best tradition of modern scientific archaeology.

A gun emplacement on the site supplied a bench-mark from which levels could be taken; she drew stone-for-stone maps of each of her five towns, dividing them into areas lettered in Greek so that the workmen could read the labels attached to the finds, and understand the importance of recording the findspot of each artifact exactly.

Her most important conclusion was negative. Of the 604 pots she catalogued from all five towns, not one was wheel-made. All can be matched in shape and decoration from Troy I or other Anatolian sites known to be contemporary with Troy I. This means that the history of all five towns at Thermi is embraced within the 300 years (about 3000-2700 B.C.) assigned to Troy I.

Among artifacts, weapons are rare, and Thermi I was unwalled: this suggests a peaceful agricultural community without fear of aggression. Bones found in the houses show that animals—goat, pig, and ox—were domesticated, and Miss Lamb was able to report that there had been a local breed of prehistoric dog "about the size of a fox-terrier." The earliest settlers of Thermi were fishermen, too, as their descendants still are. Bone fishhooks and terracotta net-sinkers were found, and shells of limpets, oysters, sea urchins, and cuttlefish show that seafood was part of the diet. The site yielded vegetable seeds, but no grain; yet, since the houses have ovens, grain must have been raised and used for bread. Spindle whorls, loomweights, and spools found beside the hearth present a pleasant if dullish picture of the domestic occupation of women.

Beginning with Thermi II, Miss Lamb found molds, some containing a cupreous deposit, which on assay proved to contain an amount of arsenic appropriate to Anatolian copper; she also found whetstones of emery, the nearest deposits of which occur on the mainland coast opposite Lesbos, but not on the island itself; from these facts the inference is warranted that Thermi's earliest trade relations were with Asia Minor. But over 100 terracotta figurines or idols,

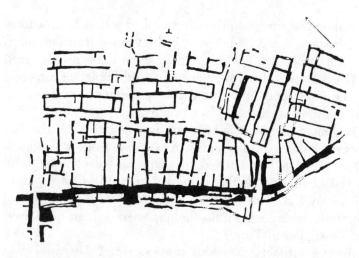

FIG. 1.8   Thermi V, showing double or triple circuit wall and long, narrow houses with common party walls. (Schachermeyr, 1955, p. 167)

crudely representing big-breasted, fat-bottomed women—the "Mother Goddess"?—have hybrid parallels, ranging from Thessaly to the Cyclades and south and central Anatolia.

Thermi's developed town plan (Fig. 1.8) presents long narrow houses of the megaron type familiar from Troy. They are equipped with built-in benches, sleeping alcoves, an altar, an oven, and a well. The lower courses of their walls are built in the herringbone fashion also found in Troy I. The houses are close together and were probably flat-roofed. They radiate from an open space which is the ancestor of the classical agora or market place. Beginning with Thermi II, the streets are paved—with beach pebbles —and Thermi V has a double or triple circuit wall, the innermost of which is thick and equipped with towers. The walls, like early Troy's, must have been built to meet a threat from the Hittites or some other rising power in central Anatolia. Miss Lamb found no evidence of violent destruction: the site appears simply to have been abandoned for a thousand years. When it revived, its pottery shows the influence of Mycenean Greece. A final cataclysm destroyed the site about 1200 B.C. What destroyed late Thermi is what destroyed Troy VIIA: the Achaean expedition immortalized by Homer. Achilles sleeps with one woman of Lesbos, spoils of a raid; and is promised others, similarly acquired, by Agamemnon, when he tries to persuade him to renounce his wrath and rejoin the battle.

American and British activity at Troy and Thermi was matched between 1930 and 1936, and has been matched again since 1951, despite the imminent danger of being blown up by land mines, by Italian excavation at Poliochni, on the east coast of the island of Lemnos: in mythology, the seat of the forge of the lame smith-god Hephaestus. The early work at Poliochni trained a generation of young Italian archaeologists, but the original excavator died without having produced a final publication. Recent work has been complicated by the vandalism of German troops in World War II. They robbed the walls of building stone, dug trenches through the prehistoric settlement's main street, and dumped into meaningless heaps the pottery finds from 150 carefully labeled cases. Old notebooks proved incomplete: no drawings, sections, or restorations, and no complete site plan. This is a pity, for Poliochni was a vast Neolithic and Bronze Age town, one of the most advanced in the Aegean. It had (Fig. 1.9) a towered and gated circuit wall, regular wide streets and squares, sometimes paved; blocks of houses bounded by alleys; public wells, stone baths, storm sewers, warehouses backed against the circuit wall—all giving evidence of a strong central authority and a high degree of civic organization and social progress. Separate rooms for artisans show division of labor, and one large chamber is identified by the excavators as an assembly room for the town elders. The Italians distinguished seven levels, which they designate by colors. (This is a sensible way of meeting a difficulty; namely, that at the outset of a dig an excavator

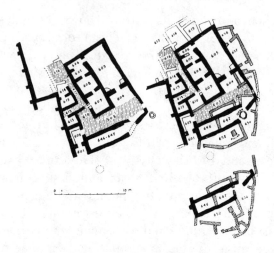

FIG. 1.9 Poliochni, Yellow level, house blocks. Note oven, and wells marking two public squares. (Bernabò Brea, 1955, p. 150, by permission of Prehistoric Society of England and Wales)

cannot be sure that the lowest level in his first trench is really Level I, the next above Level II, and so on; another trench may reveal an earlier level.) The oldest or Black level is thirty feet down; since it contains oval huts, known elsewhere to be older than houses of rectangular plan, it is presumed older than Troy I, but though it had stone baths, it has emerged from the Neolithic, since bronze was found in it. The three levels above this, Blue, Green, and Red, are dated by pottery to the time of Troy I and early Troy II. The upper levels, Yellow and Brown, span the years 2400-1900, with gaps corresponding to Troy III and V. The Yellow level, which corresponds in its earliest part to the height of Troy II, had the most impressive buildings; no princely houses, but complexes of twenty rooms or more are evidence for a prosperous bourgeoisie. In one of these, in the summer of 1956, workmen clearing away roots pulled to the surface a buried jug containing a gold treasure comparable to "Priam's," and of the same date. It included a soldered filigree gold pin with two animal figures, gold earrings, buttons, torques, and necklaces; the technique is Anatolian. Pots knocked to smithereens from falling walls, but with the fragments still fairly well united, give evidence of a violent and unexpected destruction of this level, about 2000 B.C. or a little after. This ended Poliochni's prosperity, for this is the best period of conspicuous architectural remains. The destroyers may have been invaders not from Anatolia, but from mainland Greece, themselves refugees from intruders from the Balkans who were probably the first true Greeks, in the linguistic sense, to enter European history.

Though the earliest modern work on the prehistoric Greek world was not done on the mainland, it inspired work there, especially by Greek, German, and American archaeologists, and what they found proved to be earlier than Troy I; in fact, Neolithic. (Thus far palaeolithic discoveries in Greece have been few, but they are well attested and fairly widespread. Fourteen graves and stone implements of the Mousterian period [ca. 130,000 B.C.] were reported in 1959 from the Peneus valley in Thessaly. A small cave in Boeotia [Seidi near Haliartos] has also produced palaeolithic implements. Between 1967 and 1977 American excavations in the vast Franchthi cave—six kilometers long—on the Gulf of Argos some twenty miles southeast of Nauplia, revealed in four meters of deposit traces of human habitation from the late Palaeolithic to the Neolithic eras (with carbon-14 dates of 19,530 to 4300 B.C.), bones of deer, boar, wild cattle, and fox, seeds of vetch, emmer, barley, and pistachio nuts, obsidian imported from Melos, and many burials, including the skeletons of two children interred in a contracted position, without a trace of funeral offerings except a few pebbles under the head of one.) Among the earliest and best work was that published in 1908 by the pioneering Greek archaeologist Chrestos Tsountas at Sesklo and Dimíni in the rich farming land of Thessaly (see map, Fig. 1.5). Sesklo—the name means "beet" in modern Greek—

lies two and a half hours' walk northwest of Volos, now the third port of Greece; in antiquity it was called Iolkos, and was the port from which sailed Jason and the Argonauts after the Golden Fleece; an important palace of Mycenaean date has recently been discovered there, with fresco fragments, 90 feet of foundation wall, and a sherd with a representation of a ship that might be Jason's *Argo*.

At Nea Nikomedeia, in Macedonia, ten kilometers northeast of Beroea, were found two Neolithic settlement phases, the earlier going back to 6200 B.C. The site yielded stone and clay figures of a fertility goddess.

Sesklo is of unique interest because Tsountas found there a stratum nearly ten feet deep, far, far below the levels of pottery that matched Troy I. This stratum contained sherds in context with stone weapons, in jadeite, granite, and jasper. These must belong to a developed Neolithic age: Tsountas called it Neolithic A. This period, to judge by the thickness of the deposit, must antedate the founding of Troy by 200 years or more. Nowadays over 150 Neolithic sites are known in Thessaly, but of these Sesklo and Dimini are still among the best recorded. Tsountas' great virtue was an analytic mind combined with a sharp eye. He laid down over fifty years ago categories of Neolithic pottery which, though expanded in the youthful work (1912) of the great English archaeologist A. J. B. Wace, have never been superseded, and which have proved valuable for producing order out of chaos wherever Neolithic ware has appeared in northern Greece, and for providing certified parallels with Neolithic pottery elsewhere. The most interesting Neolithic A ware is painted, not incised, with geometric patterns. With the next level above, Neolithic B, restraint disappears, and the pottery (Fig. 1.10), while still not naturalistic, is of a truly barbaric lavishness and undisciplined exuberance, in two or three colors, involving meanders, checkerboards (sometimes in different fields on the same pot), spirals, chevrons, ripples, zigzags, hatched circles, bowed curves, executed with great

Fig. 1.10 Dimini, Neolithic B, two patterns on the same bowl. (Wace, *Prehistoric Thessaly*, p. 76, by permission of Cambridge University Press)

freedom and variety, at its best anticipating and outdoing in stylistic technique the Geometric ware that was to be the fashion in Greece many millennia later.

This pottery came mostly from Sesklo's acropolis (Fig. 1.11), strategically located, with water for man and beast, in a secluded mountain glen between two rivers, 650 feet above sea level. There are traces of what is perhaps a double circuit of Neolithic B walls in the southwest. It encloses twenty to twenty-five acres, and would hold 3,000. The largest house has a porch, a main room with three postholes and a fixed hearth, an inner room with two ovens, and a back apartment, divided into three small rooms, which Tsountas thought was made over for the eldest son when he married. (There was some provision for privacy; one house had a device for locking the bedroom door from the inside.) There is some evidence that the houses were built to a standard measure, the unit being 0.30 cm. (about a foot). Chunks of dried mud, with an imprint of reeds, preserve the traces of a pitched roof; Tsountas saw in the houses, with their porches and inner rooms, the prototype of the classical Greek temple.

In the houses Tsountas found fifty-nine idols in clay, stone, and bone, mostly exceptionally well-padded females, with

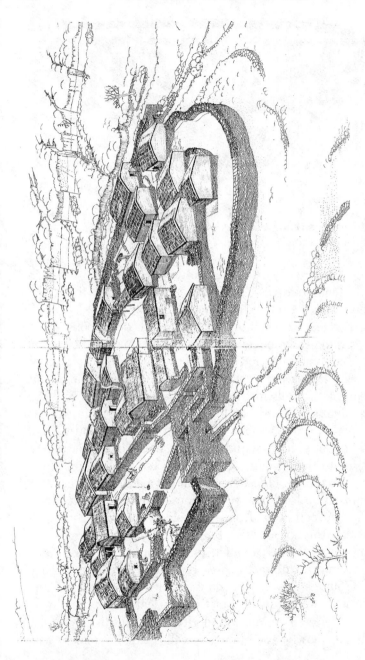

FIG. 1.11 Sesklo, reconstruction drawing. (Demetrios Theochares, *Neolithic Greece* (Athens, 1973) Fig. 178, by permission of Dr. N. Chourmouziades, Volo

their hands on their breasts, and with rolls of fat at the hips. There was one Neolithic madonna and child, and one male statuette two and a half inches high, grasping his private parts with both hands. Obviously fertility was an abiding interest, if not an obsession, with the Neolithic inhabitants of Sesklo. Among other artifacts might be singled out knives of flint (imported from Albania and Epirus), and obsidian (imported from the island of Melos). Neolithic B footstuffs included wheat, barley, peas, acorns, almonds, and figs.

Prehistoric Dimini (Fig. 1.12), an hour seaward (east) of Sesklo, was first discovered in 1901 during excavation of tholos or beehive tombs of later, Mycenaean times nearby. The acropolis is noteworthy for at least six concentric circuit walls in stone, much spoiled by the plow; pottery dates them to Neolithic B, about 3250 B.C. They enclose an area of over 10,000 square yards. Since the innermost area, with a hearth or altar in the middle, is not all built over, it is clear that the outer walls were not added to enlarge living space, but to act like watertight bulkheads, providing protection in emergencies for refugees from the countryside. The building technique shows great skill and much experience of sieges. The various entrances or gates in successive circuit walls are in a straight line; the series on the southwest, on the axis of the impressive megaron and against the innermost circuit wall on the northeast, is impressive enough to have seemed to Tsountas a prehistoric ancestor to the Periclean Propylaea or monumental entrance to the Acropolis at Athens. All the gates but one are planned to be too narrow to permit two invaders to charge abreast; the one in the outermost circuit on the northwest was perhaps left purposely wide to let refugees bring in their chattels. The walls are too narrow (two to four and a half feet thick) to stand on and still leave room for battlements; the defenders must have stood behind them, but the ground level must have been lower outside the walls than inside; otherwise they would have been too easy for the invader to

climb. The third wall, counting from within, must be contemporary with the inner two, since the second was never
a complete circuit: it is finished with squared ends on east
and west, while houses, which would have needed protection, lie outside it to the north. The open space around
the megaron, in the middle of the acropolis, was probably
surrounded by a portico or stoa; at all events a manger-like
structure on the west has walls too thin to have been left
unprotected from the weather. The whole plan suggests
monarchy, control literally central. This has been described
as the first major fact in the political history of Europe.

Multiple circuit walls like Dimini's were known in
Tsountas' time from Herzogovina and Transylvania, so that
the results from Dimini were used to infer direct Danubian
or Illyrian influence on Neolithic Greece, but Tsountas had
excavated others on the island of Syros in the Cyclades;
and he knew of still others from Phylakopí on Melos. Others
have been excavated since, as we saw, at Thermí on Lesbos
and Poliochni on Lemnos, so the question of origins
remains open, with Anatolia a distinct possibility. The
megaron house, too, is known in the Danube area, and is
suitable for a cold climate, but whether the influence runs
from Anatolia to central Europe, or the other way about, is
also an unsettled question.

But the relation to mythology and the Argonauts is interesting. Why, Tsountas argued, should not the later beehive tombs of Dimini be the graves of real Argonauts, as
Troy VIIA is the city of a real Priam, and Mycenae, rich in
gold, the stronghold of a real Agamemnon? These tomb
builders, the "Minyans," would be invaders—from Asia
Minor, on the evidence of Anatolian parallels with "Minyan"
pottery found in Greece—who drove out the inhabitants
of Sesklo and Dimini; the refugees will have moved south
and taught their southern neighbors to build fortification
walls, megara, stoas, and public hearths. These notions
seem less fantastic now than they did when Tsountas first

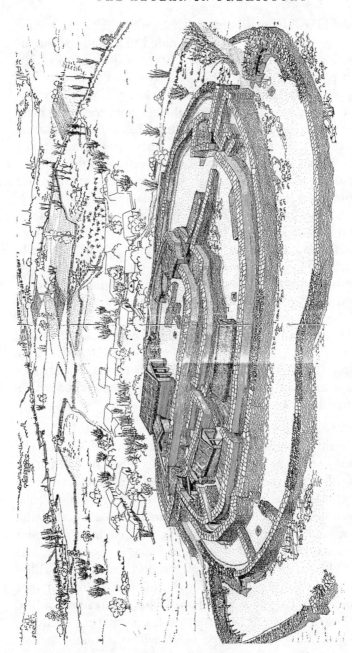

FIG. 1.12 Dimini, reconstruction drawing. (Theochares, *op cit.*, Fig. 187, by permission of Dr. N. Chourmouziades, Volo)

published them in 1908, especially since the palace at Iolkos, discovered by Tsountas, has been dated to a time contemporary with Achilles' father Peleus. It lies on a 25-acre hill within the periphery of modern Volos, its site marked by twenty feet of deposit. It flourished from 2500 to 1200 B.C., with continuity into Protogeometric times; in the classical era its primacy passed to nearby Pagasae (map, Fig. 6.21). The excavators note a copper crucible of 2200. Iolkos increased in importance in Late Helladic I and II (1550-1400), perhaps under Minoan influence, or at any rate through sea-borne commerce: vessels are figured on the pottery. In Late Helladic III (1400-1200), kylikes, many local, some from the Peloponnese (Mycenae?), abound, bespeaking a palace, as at Pylos. Timbers strengthened its four-foot-thick walls (but the circuit-wall appears to be medieval). The rooms were large—up to 36 feet long—with white stuccoed floors. Eumelos, son of Admetus who let Alcestis die for him, could have lived here; a lower stratum could be the palace of Pelias, wicked uncle of Jason the Argonaut. A still lower stucco floor bore soapy-textured Minyan ware (first discovered at Orchomenos) of Late Helladic II (fifteenth century). This was no mere Minoan or Mycenaean colony, but an important pottery center with a long tradition.

A beehive tomb of the Mycenaean period led to the discovery of pre-Mycenaean remains elsewhere than at Dimini. In 1870 the villagers of Skripoú, the ancient Orchomenós, in Boeotia, in central Greece, heard the hollow echo of something like an explosion from inside a nearby hill. They ran and found that the ceiling of a chamber adjacent to a beehive tomb, which had held for over 3000 years, had finally yielded to the weight of the earth above it. Schliemann excavated the tomb in 1881, and restored on paper the handsome rosettes, spirals, and lotus blossoms of the ceiling decoration, but it was left to his compatriot H. Bulle, in 1903, looking for a palace to go with the tomb, to find the round buildings that are apparently the oldest evidence of habitation on the excavated part of the site of Orchomenos. Bulle worked under difficulties: when he began, the only communication with Athens, less than ninety airline miles away, was by wagon, two days over deplorable roads; when the railroad was put through in 1905, he congratulated himself that the journey took only five hours. A scientific staff of two was inadequate to supervise eighty to a hundred workmen, who, left for a short time unwatched, triumphantly dismantled the entire walls of two unique prehistoric round buildings. The workmen never learned—it is not easy—to distinguish prehistoric mud-brick walls from the surrounding earth. An iron nail and a Turkish shoe in a deep stratum proved how thoroughly Schliemann's deep trenches had upset the levels. The villagers refused, quite reasonably from their point of view, to sacrifice their vegetable gardens to let the excavators extend their trenches, and the village cemetery lay directly in the midst of what proved to be the most promising area for excavation. Under these circumstances, it is no wonder Bulle's results were equivocal.

He discovered three superimposed building levels (Fig. 1.13). The lowest buildings, on bedrock, were round, with lower courses in stone. While he was digging, a winter colony of nomadic Vlachs (from Romania) had settled on a nearby hillside, and he triumphantly compares their round huts with what he was excavating. The Vlach huts had a frame of pliant boughs, overlaid diagonally with twigs and then interwoven with reeds. They were rain- and windproof, but let smoke escape. On St. George's Day (May 6) the Vlachs would dismantle their huts, store the reusable wood, burn the reeds, and strew the ashes where the floors had been. This is a nice analogy, but it is damaged by the fact that some of the round buildings excavated by Bulle were too small for even two people, and in none of them was any trace of a doorway found: hence they are more likely to have been granaries or silos than dwellings.

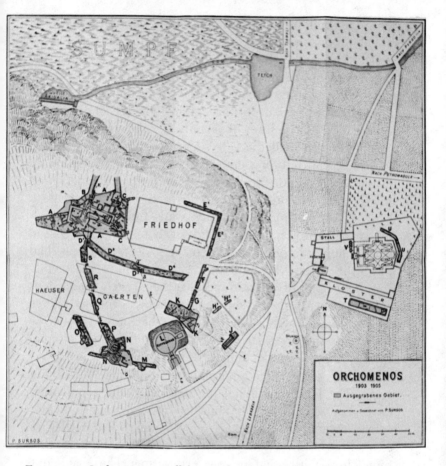

Fɪɢ. 1.13   Orchomenos, Bulle's trenches. Note plans of mysterious round buildings in K, N, and P, apsidal buildings in A and N. L is the later beehive tomb. The site would repay further digging, especially under the cemetery (Friedhof) and in the swamp (Sumpf) to the north. (Bulle, Pl. II)

In the level next above them, the typical building plan (the two lower courses, in stone, alone survived) was horse-shoe-shaped, with pits (*bothroi*) in the floor, sometimes more than one to a room. These were filled with ashes, animal bones, sherds, and plant fibers. Between this and the next higher level were the traces of burning that indicate the overthrow of a settlement by violence; above the burned stratum, the house plans are rectangular.

Orchomenos is a prime example of a site whose intelligibility is much reduced because no proper track was kept of the pottery. Over twenty years and a major war intervened between the publication of the site and the publication of the pottery: in the interval, the scanty reports of levels had been lost. The pottery could still, by analogy with that from other sites, be grouped and distinguished as Neolithic, Early Bronze, and later, but no connection was any longer possible between the pottery and its precise findspot. However, one of Bulle's trenches (K), reopened, yielded at bedrock a type of burnished ware everywhere typical of the Early Bronze Age, of the period called Early Helladic, corresponding on the mainland south of Thessaly to Troy I-V and datable 3000-1900 B.C. This means that neither of Bulle's two lower levels, neither the round nor the horseshoe-shaped buildings, is Neolithic; rather they are both Early Helladic (see Fig. 1.7), and pre-Greek. The burnt layer is the mute evidence of the same invasion of Greek speakers that we met in Thessaly, and the rectangular (megaron-type) houses are like theirs. The fact remains, however, that though the excavated buildings are Early Helladic, Bulle found plenty of Neolithic pottery, in enough variety to suggest a long development. Unfortunately, no one knows exactly where it came from. Some of it may have been thrown into the round buildings when they were covered up to make level ground for the village of horseshoe-shaped houses, some of it may have come from Schliemann's dump. The Neolithic settlement at Orchomenos adjoins the beehive tomb L; it has apsidal houses in adobe on stone foundations. Above this level lay the Early Helladic city of 3000-2000 B.C.

Twenty miles southeast of Orchomenos, and about seven miles southwest of Thebes, at Eutresis, a site much visited in antiquity because on it the Thebans beat the Spartans in the Battle of Leuctra (371 B.C.), Miss Hetty Goldman excavated under American auspices, in four campaigns (1924-27). She was attracted to the site because the very surface of the rolling plateau was strewn with sherds she recognized as prehistoric; the visible traces of an extensive circuit wall (Fig. 1.14) proved on excavation to be Late Helladic, otherwise known as Mycenaean (thirteenth century). In the lowest level of twenty-one feet of deposit, she found traces of what she describes as "round tepees or huts," which sound not unlike Bulle's mysterious round buildings in the lowest level at Orchomenos, but she was not able to tell whether these formed a sequence with later settlements at higher levels, or whether they had been deserted by previous inhabitants. Later American work, reported in 1959, established that the site was occupied in Neolithic times; Neolithic pottery was found effectively sealed off under tight pebble pavements of Early Helladic I. In the level above, the houses were close built, as at other pre-Greek sites, such as Thermi; a house containing a broken copper—not bronze—chisel, and therefore belonging to a period transitional between the Neolithic and the Bronze Age, contained spiral-decorated pottery with relations both to Sesklo and to the island of Amorgos in the Cyclades, where the favorite motif was the spiral. (Eutresis lies only six miles from a port in the Gulf of Corinth, so import would be comparatively easy.) Miss Goldman dated it Early Helladic (carbon 14 date 2496 B.C. ± 69 years). Outside the later House L was found a puzzling circular building, twenty feet across and with a stone surround, within a funnel ten feet deep, perhaps to facilitate contact with underworld deities. Excavation had shown that Early Helladic could be divided into three subperiods. In the second of these (carbon 14 date 2481 ± 58), the level above the house of the broken chisel,

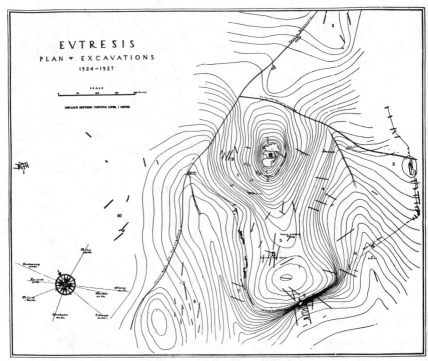

FIG. 1.14 Eutresis, plan, showing excavator's trenches. EH houses H and L are on the summit, near the medieval tower. House 1 is an inch south of this on the plan. Circuit wall on east, probed properly by trenches perpendicular to it, is Mycenaean. (Goldman, Pl. I, by permission of Harvard University Press)

belongs House L, of roughly megaron type. It bore evidence— stacked bowls crushed by fallen walls—of having been destroyed by violence, but this time natural, not man-made: what did the damage was an earthquake. In the level above this again, which would be Early Helladic III, containing for the first time at Eutresis some wheel-made pottery, an equation with Troy III-V, House H had the roof of its large room supported by a brick column, the oldest known from mainland Greece. The Early Helladic III phase of House H was destroyed by burning: the third piece of evidence we have

noted of the cataclysm that overwhelmed Greece about 2000
B.C., when the Greek-speaking invaders came. A later phase
of House H contained so many high-stemmed goblets that
the excavators nicknamed it the House of the Tippler. An
outbuilding, belonging to the Early Helladic III phase, was
horseshoe-shaped and clearly served for stabling animals;
perhaps this is a way to explain Bulle's horseshoe-shaped
structures at Orchomenos. Many of the small finds from
Eutresis are typical of Early Helladic sites: clay loom weights,
spools, figurines, buttons, spindle whorls; bronze of an Anatolian alloy; tool handles of red-deer horn; obsidian (always
a sign of trade connections with Melos in the Cyclades, the
prehistoric source for this dark volcanic glass, used for sharp-
edged tools and weapons); boars' tusks pierced for sewing
to leather helmets. By custom, or from poverty, the graves
contained few objects; in those of the levels after the invasion
as at other sites of the same date, the bodies were buried in
a cramped position, with the head pillowed on the hand. At
the Middle Helladic level was found a community bake-
oven: the defensive wall was built or strengthened in Late
Helladic IIIB (thirteenth century).

Eutresis is one site in which the ubiquitous Schliemann
never set spade. On the acropolis of Tiryns in the Argolid, on
the other hand, (traditionally Heracles' city, and the surviving walls (Fig. 1.15) are certainly Herculean), he dug
first in the late summer of 1876, noticing prehistoric pottery,
which he carried away to Athens without recording just
where it was found. He found house walls, too, but, as at
Troy and Orchomenos, he destroyed some evidence with
one of his enormous trenches. He dug again, more carefully, with Dörpfeld in 1884 and 1885; the resulting book
(1886) treats the architectural remains with Dörpfeld's
characteristic and marvelous clarity. After the turn of the
century, as more and more was learned from Evans at Knossos, from Tsountas in Thessaly, from the British in the Cy-

FIG. 1.15 Tiryns, air view, from east, showing northern loop added in Phase III (see Ch. 2) as place of refuge. (University of Wisconsin Geography Department).

clades (at Phylakopi on Melos) about earlier levels of culture, Dörpfeld encouraged promising young German archaeologists to dig again, and their final results appeared in publications that were models of constructive scientific archaeological method, the volume on architecture in 1930, that on pottery in 1938. The sherds from earlier digs stored in nearby Nauplia, partly in a mosque, partly in a windowless cellar, proved very difficult to work with, and their findspots had mostly not been recorded. The massive citadel proved to be Late Helladic; it falls beyond the limits of this chapter. The search for older levels proved to be difficult, since the important and impressive Late Helladic (Mycenaean) remains had to be preserved, but to the east of the megaron, beneath the citadel's first phase, the excavators re-examined deep strata that Dörpfeld in 1884 had called "chaos," out of which by 1930 they had made sense. They distinguished twelve levels: in the lowest some sparse

Neolithic pottery, and an idol. More striking were the footings of houses, oval, apsidal (horseshoe-shaped), and rectangular, in three levels, dated by the potsherds they contained to the Early Helladic period. The pottery included narrow-spouted ware, almost certainly used as babies' nursing bottles; a double-walled wine-cooler; and a vase with an impression made in the wet clay with an engraved cylinder, showing a dog in full cry after a hare. The pottery, thin-walled and with sophisticated décor, is clearly the tableware of an aristocratic class. Its settlement must once have extended over the whole area later occupied by the citadel, and perhaps over the level ground around it, though excavation here is limited and levels disturbed by the installations of an agricultural experiment station. Still more important are the stone-built remains, footed on bedrock, of a massive round building (Fig. 1.16), perhaps a granary, 286 feet around, which underlies the center of the later palace. It must have been a lofty structure, for traces of buttresses remain. If its height matched its diameter, it was over eighty-six feet tall, a most impressive tower, perhaps domed, or like the Sardinian watchtowers called *nuraghi* (see *Mute Stones Speak,* pp. 15-18), but much older; the excavators deduce that it was destroyed by fire (possible evidence, unique in Tiryns, of the Greek-speaking invaders) before the beginning of the Middle Helladic period about 2000 B.C. Burnt tile found in its remains comes either from its pavement or its roof. This is the first monumental building on Greek soil; the excavators, with pardonable exaggeration, compare it with the Pyramids.

Sesklo and Dimini, Orchomenos, Eutresis, and Tiryns are typical Neolithic and Early Helladic sites on the Greek mainland. They are not the only ones; new, important, and interesting excavations go on every year. Brief mention of a few key sites will suggest what all of them have added to our knowledge. Many of them are interesting precisely because they are humble, the villages of nameless prehistoric

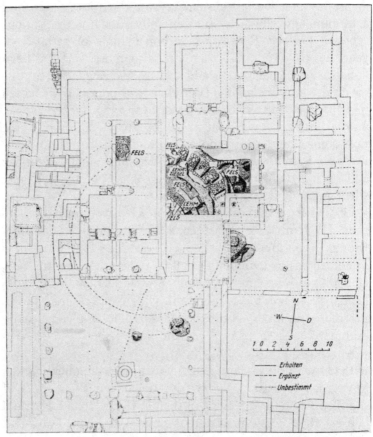

FIG. 1.16   Tiryns, round building, plan, showing concentric foundation walls, buttresses, and burnt tile (Lehmziegel) from pavement or roof. (Matz, *Hdbh*, p. 198, by permission of C. Beck,
Munich)

men and women, whose exploitation made possible the later
brave displays of Mycenae, rich in gold, and Agamemnon,
king of men.

Among them are Korákou and Zygouriés near Corinth
(see map, Fig. 1.5). Here Blegen excavated in the twenties.
At Korakou he dealt with 100,000 sherds. They enabled him

to propose an over-all chronology for the Bronze Age and a terminology which is still generally used for the various types of pottery. Recently a carbon-14 date of 2262 ± 56 years has been reported from here; also, more work has been done on Mycenaean IIIB and C ware. At Zygouries he discovered a potter's shop (later than the period with which this chapter deals) with a stock of over 1330 stacked pieces, unused. At Prosymna, near Argos, he excavated tombs, some rich, some plundered, some poor, ranging in date from Neolithic to Late Helladic. They yielded fine animal figurines and bronze daggers (of Mycenaean date) with a gold and silver inlay of dolphins and birds.

Off the mainland, at Vounous on Cyprus, an Early Cypriote III tomb (of 2000-1900 B.C.) produced evidence of Bronze Age ritual: a spirited clay model (Fig. 1.17) of a sacred enclosure, containing bulls in pens, a figure enthroned, and another carrying an infant. Still others, wearing bull's heads, stand holding hands, from which snakes hang down. Six more stand or sit on benches, while one, apparently excluded, tries to climb over the wall.

At Asine on the coast of the Argolid a Swedish expedition, with Crown Prince (later King) Gustav as a member, worked from 1920 to 1924. The Swedes unearthed thirty tons of sherds (two to three million of them), Early Helladic apsidal houses, the Egyptian seal that helped to date Troy, and evidence (fire) of the violent break frequently found between Early and Middle Helladic. Recently, Swedes and Greeks have found evidence here for unbroken occupation from Early Helladic through Geometric, the bulk of the sherds being Middle Helladic Gray Minyan and Matt-Painted ware.

At nearby Lerna, a series of American campaigns uncovered the complex plan of the rich and sophisticated House of the Tiles (published 1954–58), a palace or administrative center in which farm products were stored under seal (the

Fig. 1.17 Vounous, Cyprus, Early Cypriote III model of sacred
enclosure, now in Nicosia Museum. (*Archaeologia* 88 [1938],
Pl. 7, by permission of Professor Einar Gjerstad)

carbon-14 date is 2283 B.C. ± 66 years); and even more important, a towered Early Helladic double ring wall; with the
House of the Tiles, it is an impressive monument of the period
in Greek prehistory when Anatolian influence dominated,
though pottery gives evidence of contacts also with the Balkans and with Crete. The excavator, J. L. Caskey, uses the
evidence from Lerna to suggest that the violent cultural break
in the Bronze Age occurred between Early Helladic II and
III. The inhabitants reduced the debris of the House of the
Tiles to a low tumulus, ringed with stones and regarded as
taboo. The appearance, without signs of violence, of new pottery styles and new burial customs at a carbon-14 date of

1948 B.C. ± 117 *may* mark at Lerna the transition from Early to Middle Helladic, and the arrival of a new people from the far northeast. Of later levels, Lerna VI is coeval with the Shaft Graves at Mycenae (1580 B.C.). Level VII matches Mycenaean IIIB and contained a horse-burial, as at Marathon (Vrana) in Attica. At least thirty-seven mourners toasted the beloved animals.

At Hagios Kosmas on the Attic coast, Mylonas excavated (1930-31, 1951) an Early Bronze Age settlement, possibly of islanders from Melos trading in obsidian. It died out, according to the excavator, in the Middle Bronze Age, but if Caskey's analysis of the pottery from Lerna is sound, the matching pottery from Hagios Kosmas must be dated earlier, so that the destruction will have occurred at the close of Early Helladic II. At all events the settlement revived in Mycenaean times.

At Asea in Arcadia another Swedish expedition (1936-38) unearthed Neolithic and Early Helladic remains, followed, after the customary evidence of conflagration, by later levels. On the rocky hilltop of Asea the accumulations of pottery are thin and subject to confusion by erosion and human activity, so that the evidence is equivocal, and Asea may (or may not) have been sacked after Early Helladic II, as were Lerna and Hagios Kosmas. The important thing is that Caskey's conclusions from Lerna will require a complete re-thinking of the accepted chronology of the Early Helladic period in the Argolid and Arcadia. His results, published in 1960, sixteen years after Asea, will illustrate the tentative nature of all attempts at chronology and the need for caution in drawing categorical conclusions from them. About Neolithic pottery from Asea there is no doubt; it shows close cultural connections with Thessaly, the Early Helladic with Anatolia. At Malthi, the ancient Dorion, in Messenia, still another group of Swedes dug (1933-35) five superimposed town-levels, the bottom two unwalled (and destroyed at the end of Early Helladic), the top three walled, and centering around an unimpressive "palace" which has been held to reflect the strong will of an invading ruler. No classical Greek city plan is so centralized, so schematically neat. The 320 houses have common party walls, as at Thermi and Poliochni. Six miles west of Malthi, the Middle Helladic village of Peristeria sprawls across its hilltop, overlooking fertile wooded country. The villagers worked bronze and obsidian, wove, and buried their dead under their house floors: one house had nine children buried under one room. In Late Helladic I a large tholos tomb was ruthlessly cut into the village houses; by IIIb there were three, surrounded by a precinct wall. They have so far yielded frail flowers and flying wasps in gold, and three gold cups.

A remarkably well-stratified Middle Helladic site, rich in Minyan and Matt-Painted ware, is Kirrha, in classical times the port for Delphi. (The excavators describe as a totem, and connect with Delphi, a dolphin motif [*delphinos* in Greek] frequent on the pottery.) Kirrha presents a unique sequence, unbroken from Early through Late Helladic times. Though Middle Helladic begins with invasion, the town quickly recovered, reaching its acme in the late 1600s and ranking in importance with Orchomenos, Malthi, Asea, and Lerna: the Middle Helladic deposit is four meters deep, and yielded, from 59 tombs and a number of megaron houses, arms (including an ivory-hilted dagger), bronze and a little gold jewelry, and tools. After Middle Helladic IIIb there is a noticeable decline: most of the inhabitants moved to the nearby acropolis of Krisa. The total impression of all these sites is a of a unity of culture in Neolithic and Helladic times that Greece was not to know again until Roman days.

To that prehistoric cultural unity a major contribution was made by the Cyclades, the group of Aegean islands clustered around the sacred isle of Delos. The Cyclades are lovely: blue sea, tawny sand, mountains bare or clad in gray-green olive, harbor towns where the spotless white

of the houses vies with the spotless white of the windmill
sails. They are lovely, and they are remote. Consequently,
the archaeological richness has hardly been tapped, though
Greek excavations on Naxos since World War II have revealed a site as rich as anything hitherto known in the
Cyclades. A dozen others, Middle Cycladic (dated close to
Middle Helladic) or earlier, await the spade. Greeks better
than barbarians bear the rigors of travel by small sailboat
to the outlying islands. It is not surprising, therefore, that
some of the earliest and best work in Cycladic archaeology
was done before the turn of the century by Tsountas. He
excavated hundreds of tombs on Amorgos, Paros, and neighboring islets; tombs and citadels on Syros and Siphnos. The
190 graves on Paros yielded bronze, but so scant as to indicate a date very early in the Bronze Age, corresponding to
Early Helladic on the mainland: for this culture Tsountas
coined the name Early Cycladic. The scanty remains of
houses with apsidal and megaron plans, containing incised
and painted pottery of the same type as that found in the
tombs, some of it wheel-made, showed that the Cyclades
had reached the same stage of development as Troy II.
The equation $EC = EH = Troy\ II = 2700\text{-}2400$ B.C. is therefore possible and even probable. Tsountas' richest site was
Chalandrianí on Syros, where he found some 500 graves,
and an acropolis with a double wall of which the inner was
towered. At Hagios Andreas on Siphnos he excavated 250
yards of another acropolis wall, later in date, but also double,
cunningly contrived, the gates few and narrow, and access
to them made ingeniously difficult. The graves on Syros
yielded two kinds of objects of unique interest. The first
is a series of clay artifacts shaped like a frying pan (Fig.
1.18), incised with spirals, a triangular symbol probably
representing the female sex organ, and a likeness of a ship
with a fish figurehead. Tsountas conjectured that they were
intended to be filled with water and used as mirrors. The
second is a series of violin-shaped marble idols, whose

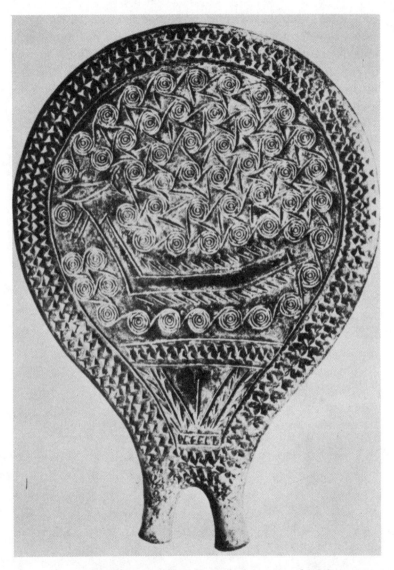

FIG. 1.18 Syros, Cycladic "frying pan," clay, incised with running
spirals, a ship with high prow and figurehead, and possible fertility symbol. Laid this side down, and filled with water, it
might serve as a mirror. Athens, National Museum (Matz,
KMT, Pl. 12)

cool severity appeals strongly to modern taste. In the same style, though not from Tsountas' dig, are some handsome marble statuettes of musicians (Fig. 1.19) rivaling the best of the archaic Greek sculpture of 1600 years later; the one illustrated here is from Amorgos, and stands about nine inches high.

FIG. 1.19 Amorgos, Cycladic marble statuette (ht. 8¾ inches) of lyre player. The simplicity of line appeals strongly to modern sculptors. Athens, National Museum (Emile Séraf)

But the best known and best published site in the Cyclades is Phylakopi on Melos, excavated by a British team between 1896 and 1899, the first important prehistoric dig since Schliemann, and again by another British group in 1911. The prehistoric town owed its prosperity to an obsidian factory, from which were shipped, all over the Aegean world, cores and blades of the glass-like stone which flakes to so sharp an edge that knives, razors, arrowheads, harrow teeth, and sickles made with it were prized beyond metal well down into the Bronze Age. Out of this site came, for four seasons, until excavation was suspended in favor of Evans' epoch-making dig at Knossos in Crete, 10,000 to 20,000 fragments a day, providing a unique, orderly pottery sequence extending over the whole Bronze Age. The excavators distinguished three phases of the city, of which the first (Fig. 1.20; typically Anatolian in being small, unwalled, self-contained, with minimal commerce) was overwhelmed, about the same time as the cities of mainland Greece, by the same kind of catastrophe, caused no doubt not by the Greek-speaking invaders but by refugees from them, who fled to Melos and ousted the original settlers of Phylakopi.* After the catastrophe the city was rebuilt on much the same plan, with double fortification walls as at Chalandriní, stepped rectilinear streets with drains, close-packed houses, numerous private baths, and a palace quarter with a mega-ron like those of Troy VI, Tiryns, Mycenae, and, as we shall see, Pylos. The spirited wall-painting of flying fish (see Fig. 2.17) is in the Minoan tradition; it may belong to a later period. The increasing use of metal for spear points, arrowheads, and tools caused a fall-off of the obsidian trade, and the third city gradually declined, finally falling prey to invasion from the mainland. In its time of prosperity its

---

* The Minoan settlement of Kythera, just off the southeast corner of the Peloponnese, was abandoned about 1450 B.C., and not reoccupied for a century, by which time its connections were with the mainland.

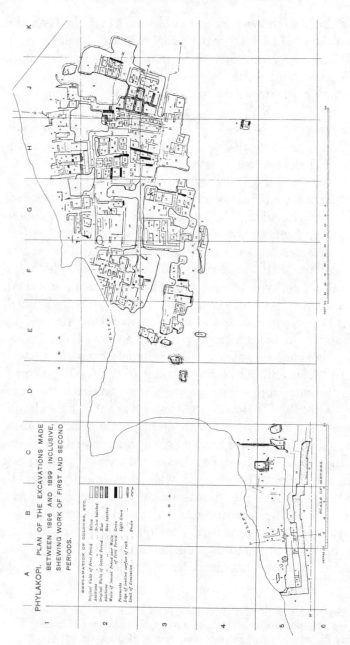

Fig. 1.20   Phylakopi I and II, plan. The darker walls are later. Note resemblance to Poliochni (Fig. 1.9). The massive circuit wall, lower left, belongs to Phylakopi III. X, in G3, marks findspot of Flying Fish Fresco (p. 91). (Atkinson, Pl. II)

aesthetic taste and the passion for cleanliness evinced by the baths and drains show that its main cultural connections were with one place, Knossos, the metropolis of Crete.

If Knossos shares with Troy the glamor among prehistoric sites in the Aegean basin, it is because it, like Troy, was excavated by a rich and flamboyant character, Sir Arthur Evans. He succeeded, where Schliemann had failed, in breaking through the local landowners' "almost inexhaustible powers of obstruction," and bought outright the site he was to name the "Palace of Minos." From 1900 until his death in 1941, Knossos was his whole life, and upon it he lavished the considerable resources of his energy, his imagination, and his fortune. As his half-sister Joan wrote, he "had come to the site in hope of finding a seal impression and a clay tablet, and Time and Chance had led him to discover a civilization." As early as 1900 he had identified Neolithic levels there, as well as three subsequent strata, which he christened Early, Middle, and Late Minoan. His reconstruction, largely at his own expense, of the Palace of Minos, while not always accurate in detail, makes the site the easiest to recreate in the imagination of any in the prehistoric world. It is vivid to the modern traveler because it was vivid to Evans: "out of an inchoate mass of pottery and stone, metal and faience, clay tablets and seals, walls and pavements," writes his half-sister, "he had to achieve a synthesis." And he did, in four massive and sumptuous volumes (1921-36), which have become the Bible of prehistoric Greek archaeology, and, like the Bible, the prey also of the Higher Criticism.

Of the thirty-eight feet (Fig. 1.21) of deposit which Evans records under the west court of the Palace at Knossos, the bottom twenty-four feet belonged, on the evidence of pottery, to a Neolithic settlement, one of the largest and most important known in Europe or the Near East. The coarse, undecorated, handmade earthenware is more primitive and therefore older than Neolithic A at Sesklo; it

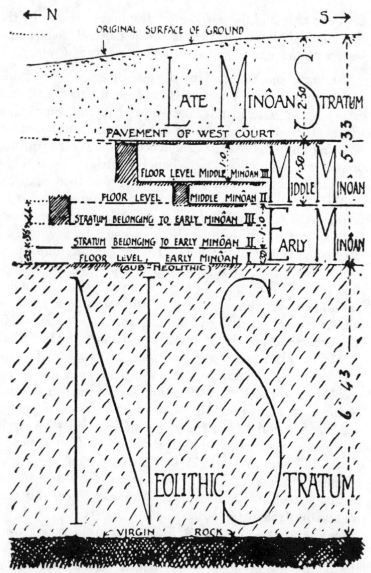

FIG. 1.21 Knossos, Palace of Minos, levels below West Court, schematic drawing. The extraordinary depth of the Neolithic stratum (shown in meters), shows long habitation. (Evans, *BSA* 10 [1904] p. 17)

probably goes back to 6100 B.C. Higher up in the Neolithic level comes incised ware like that of Troy I, figurines and obsidian from the Cyclades. The houses are rectangular, their lower courses of stone, their floors of pebbles; their plan involves a number of small rooms clustering around a main one: already in miniature the labyrinthine plan that the Palace was to make famous as the home of the Minotaur, the fabulous monster, half-bull, half-man, slain in his lair by the heroic young Theseus, prince of Athens.

The Early Minoan levels, distinguished by the first appearance of copper, and by kiln-fired and painted pottery, were much destroyed when the site was leveled off for the Middle Minoan I Palace. Characteristic of this early level is mottled ware, produced by uneven firing. There is also a number of stone vases—the best come not from Knossos but from an American dig at Mochlos—where the striations of alabaster or steatite make patterns extraordinarily pleasing because of the tension between the rectilinear décor and the curve of the pot. Such vases have parallels in Egypt, and make possible the dating of Early Minoan (somewhat shakily, for stoneware may endure long after the period of its making) from 3000 to 2000 B.C., but Evans identified the craftsmanship as local. At the end of Early Minoan, the art of engraving on gems and seals flourished: a lens found in a Knossos grave may have been a magnifying glass used by a craftsman in intaglio. The most impressive architectural survival of this age is the great *hypogaeum* or underground vault under the south porch of the Palace. It is twenty-six feet wide and twice as high, curving up to a beehive vault. Access to it was by a winding stair round the outside, with windows at intervals opening into the vault, or alternatively by an elaborate tunnel. All this implies something worth guarding, and hints already at the prosperity enjoyed by the rulers of Knossos, and attested by the contents of the storerooms of the later Palace.

The transition from Early to Middle Minoan (about 2000

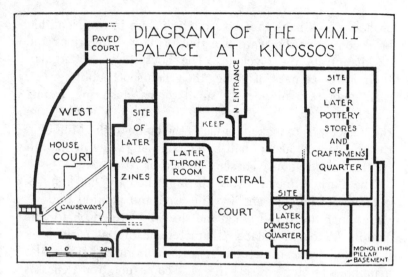

FIG. 1.22   Knossos, Palace of Minos, Middle I phase, simplified plan
showing relation to earlier and later phases. (Pendlebury, 1939,
p. 96, by permission of Messrs. Methuen, London)

B.C.) is marked by wheel-made polychrome pottery with
charming plant motifs ("Kamares ware"), by the emergence
of an as yet undeciphered hieroglyphic script, and by the
consolidation of the house-blocks of the Early Minoan settlement into the earliest palace (Fig. 1.22). This is the period
also of the earliest palace levels discovered by the French
at Mállia east of Knossos and by the Italians at Phaistós near
the south coast. At Knossos the debris of the Early Minoan
settlement was used to make a terrace for the palace, which
was approached on the west by a ramp and causeways,
from the north by an entrance protected by a keep, one of
the fortified blocks which made up the first palace. The
provisions for drainage were elaborate. At this time too
(Middle Minoan I, *ca.* 1900 B.C.) the old trade route from
the south was improved by the construction of a great via-
duct: it was by this route that Egyptian artifacts arrived.
The inscribed statue of an Egyptian ambassador or pur-

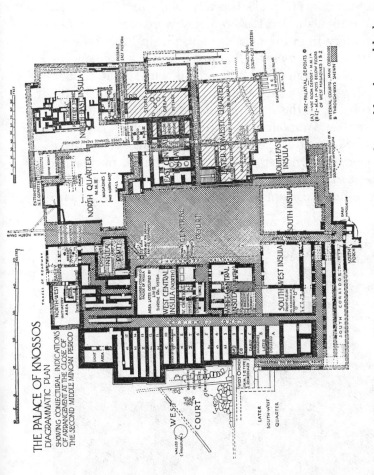

FIG. 1.23 Knossos, Palace of Minos, late MM II phase, plan, showing how older house-blocks were consolidated. The wealth of the palace was stored in the long, narrow magazines on the west. (Evans, 1921, Fig. 152, by permission of Messrs. Macmillan, London, and the Trustees of the Sir Arthur Evans Estate)

chasing agent in XIIth Dynasty style (1991-1786 B.C.), found in a Middle Minoan II level, belongs to the next phase of the palace (Fig. 1.23), when the fortified blocks were consolidated into a homogeneous whole. In the process, three deep round pits, called locally *koulouras* (Fig. 1.24), sunk under the west court as granaries, were used to contain broken pottery from the palace rubbish heaps. Fifteen long, narrow storerooms were built on the west to contain the tribute received from vassal cities, in oil, wine, grain, copper, bronze, silver, and gold. A new ramp gave access to the central court from the south; to the northeast rose the royal pottery store and a roomful of giant *pithoi*, storage jars taller than a man. To the east the hillside was later cut away to make a great Domestic Quarter, the private apartments of the king and queen. The whole complex was elaborately drained, with stone-built, cement-lined conduits, and a latrine with

FIG. 1.24 Knossos, Palace of Minos, circular, lined rubbish pits, and remains of earlier houses, under West Court. (Pendlebury, 1954, Pl. I.2, by permission of Max Parrish, London)

gypsum-lined walls, wooden seats, and provision to prevent the escape into the room of noxious odors. To this period is dated the first real piece of mural decoration, the feature that, as restored, makes later phases of the palace colorful today. This is the "Saffron Gatherer" (Fig. 1.25), a grayish-blue figure picking crocuses and putting them in vases set among rocks, against a red background. Evans had the figure restored as a boy, but since something very like a tail is waving in the air above him, it is more probably a monkey.

Some idea of the appearance of less palatial houses of the period is provided by a series of plaques in faience (earthenware with an opaque metallic glaze), the "Town Mosaic" (Fig. 1.26). The houses are windowed, two or more stories high, flat-roofed, with an attic or clerestory above. The construction indicated is of stone alternating with squared beams, or round beams with the ends showing. Red-painted window panes imply the use of something like oiled parchment instead of glass.

Middle Minoan II ended in an earthquake, followed by the great period of the palace, to be described in the next chapter.

Archaeological excavation of Neolithic and Early Bronze Age sites in the Aegean basin has made it possible to reconstruct ground plans, analyze pottery, and—sometimes—assess works of art. No archaeologist would deny that this work of reconstruction, analysis, and criticism has a fascination of its own. But such archaeologists as Schliemann, Dörpfeld, Tsountas, Evans, and Blegen are not satisfied with catalogues of mute stones, broken pottery, fragmentary sculpture, and bits of fresco. What they have dug up is history, especially cultural history, and cultural history means—at least to the archaeologist with imagination—not chronological tables, categories of vases, catalogues of works of art—though these are indispensable starting-points—but the inferences from these. And these inferences are about

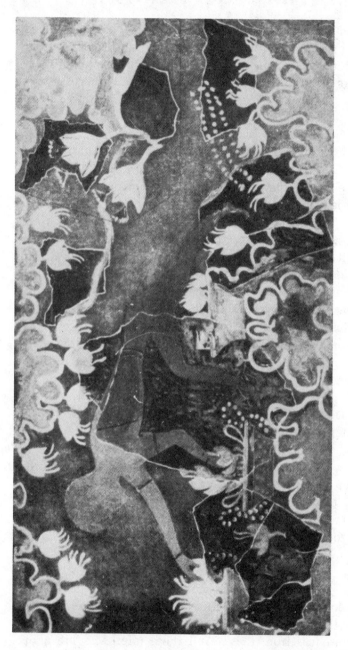

FIG. 1.25 Knossos, Palace of Minos, Saffron-gatherer fresco (actually monkey). Heraklion, Museum. (Pendlebury, 1954, Pl. XI, by permission of Max Parrish, London)

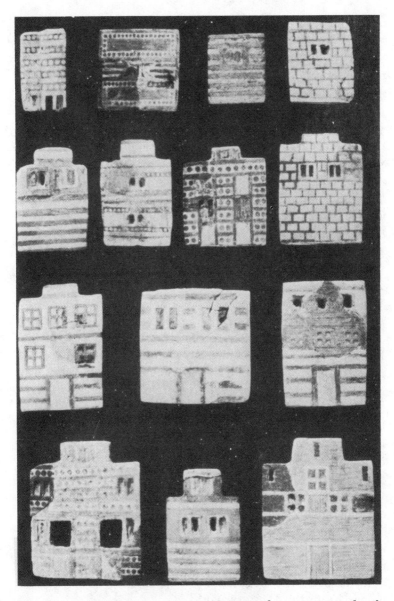

FIG. 1.26   Knossos, Town Mosaic. Faience plaques, giving details of Minoan houses. Heraklion, Museum. (Matz, *KMT*, Pl. 45, by permission of the British School in Athens)

people. The development from the primitive ground plan
of Troy I to the sophisticated buildings of Troy II implies
the material growth of a people from subsistence living to
prosperity, and their spiritual growth from savagery to civilization. But the burnt layer between Troy I and Troy II
implies further that the growth was not peaceful. Troy I
yielded only local pottery; Troy II imported some of its
earthenware. The inference is a broadening of cultural as
well as commercial horizons: contacts with Hittites, norther-
ners, islanders. This means not only mercantile profit, but
the mental stimulus that comes from seeing the cities of men,
and knowing their minds. The fall of Troy I is far from
the only evidence of violence: "Priam's treasure" is probably loot, which leads to the melancholy reflection that for
4300 years civilization has meant war. Troy VIIA fell, which
leads to the even more melancholy reflection that in 3300
years man has not learned that they that take the sword
shall perish by the sword.

The close-packed plans of Thermi V, Poliochni, Sesklo,
Dimini, and Phylakopi may have been evolved out of the
necessity for protection, but they came to be the way
Mediterranean people preferred to live, as in many villages
they still do: close together, with common party walls to
their houses, but finding their livelihood outside the villages,
in the fields or on the sea, and returning after labor to the
intimacy of their close-knit neighborhoods, and the friendly
gossip of their outdoor living room, the town square. There
is a lesson of continuity here, as there is in the controlled
excitement of Dimini's geometric pottery, to which the
descendants of Dimini's people seem to have returned for
inspiration after 1600 years. We have seen, too, how the
unity of the plans implies a centralized government of kings
and subjects, the beginning of the checkered history of
monarchy in the Western world.

At Orchomenos, the evidence of the silos with the burnt
layer above enables the archaeologist to reconstruct the

pathetic picture of a peaceful agricultural people overwhelmed by invaders. We know from Miss Goldman's excavations that the people of Eutresis, though poor, domesticated animals, were not averse to a convivial cup of wine, and were rich enough to import bronze from Asia Minor and obsidian from Melos. The babies' nursing bottles from Tiryns humanize the site; the massive remains of the round tower monumentalize it. Most of us find the former more interesting than the latter. The potter's surplus stock from Zygouries prompts reflection on the pathos of the small proprietor ruined by invasion. The figure trying to get over the wall of the sacred enclosure from Vounous may cause us to ponder on how old and shameful the human tendency to exclusiveness is. Asine's Early Helladic trade with Egypt, Lerna's unique Early Helladic palace give us a new view of the prosperity and sophistication of Greek mainland peoples in the third millennium B.C. The traders from Melos who ran the station at Hagios Kosmas traveled in the sort of boats pictured on Cycladic "frying pans," and helped to provide the wealth to support the sculptor of the Cycladic harper, whose work does not suffer from comparison with Henry Moore's.

But the most eloquent archaeological evidence for the way people lived in the Early Bronze Age comes from Knossos. The first impression a visitor to Knossos gains, as I see from my own journal for Easter, 1936, is of the profound difference in tone and atmosphere from the culture of classical Greece. This is not surprising, for the Middle Minoans were probably not Indo-Europeans, as the classical Greeks were. The very name of Knossos is earlier than the arrival of the Indo-Europeans (possibly Anatolian), and so are the names of Corinth, Athens, and Tiryns. Other words in classical Greek that are survivals from the older language give a surprisingly accurate picture of the culture: the word for the sea itself, *thalassa*, which made Minos' commercial fortune; names for trees and plants: cypress, terebinth (turpentine-tree), arti-

choke; chestnut, absinth, cherry; flowers: narcissus, hya-
cinth; herbs: mint, oregano; articles of luxury or leisure:
purple mussel, bathtub, chessboard, lyre. This gifted people
gave to the classical Greeks many of the softer and more
attractive aspects of their nature. The later taste for city
life is already clear in Troy and Thermi, Poliochni and Sesklo.
The talent for sculpture, the joy in color and design, is
visible in Cycladic statuettes and Kamares pottery. The
exalting of the female principle over the male is suggested
by the "idols," which hint in turn at the importance of
women. The love of gardens, music, and leisure is implied in
the pre-Indo-European vocabulary itself. This civilization
came to its flowering at Knossos. It was the civilization that
Sir Arthur Evans loved: "set in beautiful Mediterranean
country, aristocratic and humane in feeling; creating an art
brilliant in color and unusual in form, that drew inspiration from the flowers and birds and creatures that he loved.
It provided him with enigmas to solve and riddles to interpret, and opened a new world for eye and mind to dwell in:
a world which served to isolate him from a present in which
he had found no real place."

The Greek-speaking invaders who upset all this added
some stiffening, vigor, directness, and adventurousness to
this charming pursuit of pleasure, and Greeks retained to
the end some of the superstition, coarseness, passion, and
cruelty of their non-Greek Neolithic ancestors as well; but
our Greek heritage would seem far less attractive to us
without the contribution of the prehistoric people who were
not, linguistically speaking, Greeks at all.

2

"Mycenae, Rich in Gold":
Greece in the Late Bronze Age (1900-1125 B.C.)

In about 1900 B.C. or a little earlier the culture of the pre-historic non-Greek Aegean, as archaeology reveals it, was destroyed. Many settlements were violently overwhelmed by the invasion of a people who, there is some reason to believe, were the first Greeks. About that time Troy emerged from the doldrums of Troy III-V into the prosperity of Troy VI. It was in this period, as study of animal bones from all layers of Troy showed, that the horse began to be used here. Blegen found that this settlement was destroyed by a disastrous earthquake about 1300 B.C. Its circuit walls were patched, the stones of its fallen houses reused for much less pretentious new buildings. Imported pottery is no longer found: the inference is that prosperity has sharply declined. This settlement, Troy VIIA, lasted for about a generation; then it in turn was violently destroyed by fire and looted. Blegen thought this was Homer's Trojan War;* he

* A relief krater, of about 675 B.C., delightfully naïve, but with a tragic theme, turned up on Mykonos in 1961. It portrays the end of Troy. Seven Greeks look out of square portholes in a Trojan horse on wheels; two of them hand sword and helmet to others, bristling with weapons, who have already

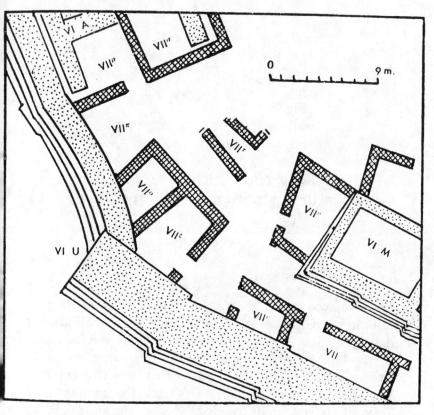

Fig. 2.1   Troy VIIA, house walls built against circuit wall of Troy VI
(Page, p. 72, by permission of the University of California
Press)

dates it about two generations earlier than is usual, about
1240 B.C. The survivors tried to pull their town together
again (Troy VIIB1) only to have it taken over, without
signs of violence, by a people, perhaps from Thrace, whose
barbarity is clear from their ugly pottery. By 1125 B.C. this

disembarked. Nineteen metopes show the fate of Trojan women and children, including Astyanax, son of Hector and Andromache, who is brained by
Neoptolemos, son of Achilles.

culture fades, and Troy never rises to prominence again.

From Troy VIIA, the Troy of Priam and Helen, Hector and Andromache, Blegen's excavation has stripped most of the glamor. Houses, accurately described as "a series of sheepish cubicles," are jammed together, close against the circuit wall (Fig. 2.1). The danger of siege apparently drove many nearby villagers into the citadel, where crowding created slums, and food was stored and dispensed under emergency conditions. Blegen found much evidence of burning and violence: scraps of human bones in the streets, a skull in a doorway, a skeleton of a man, struck down in flight and left unburied. But Priam's Troy, though patched, was still powerful: the beetling walls are still impressive. To breach them took ten years of siege and, in myth, one final piece of ingenuity (ruse or siege-engine), the Trojan Horse.

Troy fell before Agamemnon, King of "Mycenae, rich in gold." The citadel of Mycenae, under the shadow of crystalline mountains, overlooking the rich Argive plain, had early attracted Schliemann. He went there to dig in the autumn of 1876. With his usual luck he hit, within the walls, in less than seven weeks of digging, upon a grave circle. It was crammed with gold diadems, cups, and masks (Fig. 2.2). It contained, too, the pathetic bones of royal children, their hands and feet wrapped in gold leaf. There were inlaid bronze daggers, portraying lion hunts not native to the Peloponnese; and bones which his imagination enlarged to giant size. On November 28, 1876 he sent his famous telegram to King George of Greece (a Dane), congratulating him on the discovery of the graves of his ancestors. Soberer work was done between 1877 and 1902 by Tsountas, the excavator of Dimini and Sesklo; in 1920-23, 1939, and 1950-55 by that Nestor among Englishmen, A. J. B. Wace, and in 1952-54 by the Greek Archaeological Society with the coöperation of the dynamic Greek-American, George Mylonas. Their excavations made it clear that Mycenae was

Fig. 2.2 Mycenae, Shaft Grave V, gold death mask. Schliemann thought it was Agamemnon, but the grave is much earlier. Athens, National Museum. (Matz, *KMT*, Pl. 87, Foto Marburg)

destroyed, luckily for us (unluckily for the Mycenaeans) while it was still fairly prosperous. The thousand yards of its twenty-foot-thick fortification walls, long concealed under Schliemann's dump, proved to be as monumental as the walls of Tiryns. Pausanias, who saw those great stones in Roman times, said that a pair of mules could not budge the smallest of them. The existence of Mycenae's walls, palaces, and rich tombs implies prosperity, derived from territorial expansion, trade, and dynastic intermarriages like that of Mycenaean Menelaus to Spartan Helen.

The entrance to the citadel of Mycenae is through the

FIG. 2.3 Mycenae, Lion Gate, with Schliemann and Dörpfeld. (DAI, Athens)

famous Lion Gate, surmounted by the oldest piece of monumental sculpture in Europe (Fig. 2.3). The noble beasts face each other heraldically in the relieving triangle over the lintel. Between them is a tapering column, anticipating Frank Lloyd Wright. No doubt they symbolize the power of the lords of the Mycenaean palace. Sherds under the threshold, each, as always, a page of history, place the gate and the adjacent curtain wall in the period which Blegen and Wace named Late Helladic IIIb (about 1250 B.C.), Agamemnon may have driven through the gate in his chariot on his way to the ships to embark for Troy. (Late Helladic, or Mycenaean, IIIa is dated by Emily Vermeule 1425-1300; IIIb, 1300-1210; IIIc, 1210-1125, involving a slight alteration in the dates on the chart, Fig. 1.7.) But there is evidence of earlier occupation of the site, and a place so rich would always have had need of walls. Mylonas found an earlier phase in the northern circuit (see plan, Fig. 2.4). To yet a third phase belong casements on the north, and the eastward extension, which nowadays overlooks a shady grove of wild olives. It is equipped with an awe-inspiring ninety-three steps, which run underground to a cistern outside the wall. Outside the walls, the ridges are covered with thyme and asphodel, and today are loud with bees. Here, where the nightingale sings in the plane trees, lay the lower city. There Wace in 1952 excavated the House of the Oil Merchant, containing thirty-eight clay tablets inscribed in the script called by Sir Arthur Evans Linear B.

The center of the citadel was occupied by the palace, whose excavation is chiefly due to Tsountas. It was approached by a ramp and, in a later phase, by a grand staircase, recently restored (Fig. 2.4, 21). Its most impressive surviving room is a megaron, facing west on a court (Fig. 2.5). The megaron had a raised central hearth, a gaily painted floor, walls covered with frescoes of warriors, horses, chariots, and women, and a roof supported by four tall slender wooden columns. Sherds date the megaron as contemporary with the

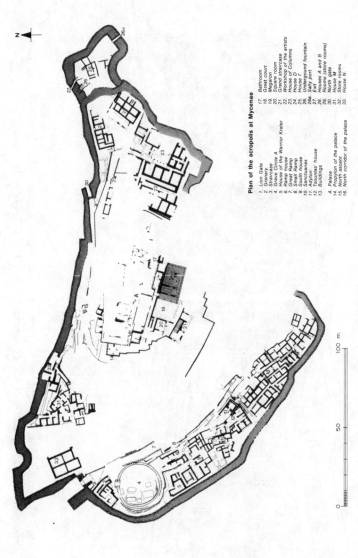

Plan of the acropolis at Mycenae

1. Lion Gate
2. Granary
3. Staircase
4. Grave Circle A
5. House of the Warrior Krater
6. Ramp house
7. Great Ramp
8. Small Ramp
9. South house
10. Sanctuaries
11. Adyton
12. Tsountas' house
13. Buildings

A. Palace
14. Propylon of the palace
15. North ascent
16. North corridor of the palace

17. Bathroom
18. Great court
19. Megaron
20. Square room
21. Grand staircase
22. Workshop of the artists
23. House of Columns
24. House Γ
25. House Δ
26. Underground fountain
26a. Sally port
27. Exit
28. Houses A and B
29. Rooms (store rooms)
30. North gate
31. House M
32. Store rooms
33. House N.

Fig. 2.4 Mycenae, citadel, plan. A, Lion Gate; D, Grave Circle A; L, Palace; S, stair to cistern. (Prof. G. E. My-lonas, by permission)

FIG. 2.5 Mycenae, court in front of megaron, reconstruction drawing. For details of construction, compare Knossos Town Mosaic, Fig. 1.26. (Kenneth Schaar, U. of Texas, Arlington)

Lion Gate. North of the megaron is a bath, whose blood-red stuccoed walls have led the modern Mycenaeans to identify it as the very room in which Agamemnon was murdered. In a palace storeroom was treasured up a divine triad, two women and a child in ivory, beautifully detailed in its rendition of embroidery and jewelry. It is perhaps of the fourteenth century B.C. Both east of the palace, by the circuit wall, and also westward, within the Lion Gate, near Schliemann's grave circle, are remains of houses grand enough to have belonged to palace officials: the House of the Columns (23 on the plan), is one of the most impressive Mycenaean *houses* (as opposed to palaces) yet excavated. Some rooms in it must have been artisans' workshops, as in Crete: they contained ivory chips, gold leaf, fragments of flawed opal, steatite, quartz, copper slag, a broken rock crystal bowl, chunks of blue paint, painted stucco fragments, and bits of solder. The House of the Warrior Vase (5) is named from a famous find of the late thirteenth or early twelfth century (Fig. 2.6) now in the National Museum in Athens, along with the other objects from this area. On the vase six unidealized warriors, all different, with provision bags on their spears, march off leaving a woman grieving behind them. The Ramp House (6) yielded a fresco of bull-leaping. Tsountas' House (12) provided a fresco of masqueraders wearing asses' heads; it may have been for the high priest. Southeast of it, recent excavation has revealed a cult center, with altars, a slaughtering stone, horns of consecration, frescoes, and statuettes, including intentionally ugly demons, perhaps Erinyes. This was destroyed in an earthquake (Mycenaean IIIB) and abandoned a century later. The Granary (2), so called from the carbonized grain found in jars within it, produced a pottery style that has given its name to a late phase of Mycenaean ceramics. These houses were looted and fired while Late Helladic IIIc pottery was in use, perhaps about 1125 B.C.

A hundred yards north of Grave Circle B, Petsas excavated more private houses: one contained a store of 500 unused

FIG. 2.6 Mycenae, Warrior Vase. Athens, National Museum. (Schuchhardt, *Schliemann's Excavations*, Fig. 285)

vases, closely packed. West of the citadel, Wace explored the House of the Oil Merchant, with its huge storage jars, each in its alcove, its inscribed tablets, already mentioned, to which more has been added by more recent excavating of further foundations discovered in widening the modern road for tourist buses. If these are private houses, and not quarters for palace staff, the tablets suggest a wider range of Mycenaean literacy than had hitherto been suspected. Wace found, too, the buildings he christened the House of Shields and the House of Sphinxes. They yielded an unmatched series of exquisite carved ivories, probably all that is left of inlaid wooden furniture. From the West House came fragments of chariot- and lily-frescoes. These houses were destroyed in the twelfth century B.C. by the cataclysm called the Dorian invasion, perhaps from the northwest, which destroyed Bronze Age civilization. The Warrior Vase would then portray the kind of men who vainly tried to ward off the destruction. There is evidence for invasion but not for invaders; i.e., the artifacts found in and above the destruction levels do not differ from Mycenaean. This observation led the late Vincent Desborough to write, "The balance of probability must be that [the Dorians] were in no way connected either with any of the disasters of the end of the thirteenth century or with the further decline in the twelfth."

Outside the citadel, too, are chamber tombs—Tsountas published fifty-two of them—where broken pottery found above suggests a final toast drunk to the dead, and the goblets smashed afterward. Figurines found in these tombs may represent either nurses (in children's graves) or goddesses. Limited pottery sequences warrant the inference that these tombs were violated a century before catastrophe befell the city proper. More interesting, among the architectural remains outside the citadel, are the beehive or tholos tombs, of which nearly eighty are now known on the Greek mainland and adjacent islands. Of the ones near Mycenae only one, at Dendra some seven miles southeast,

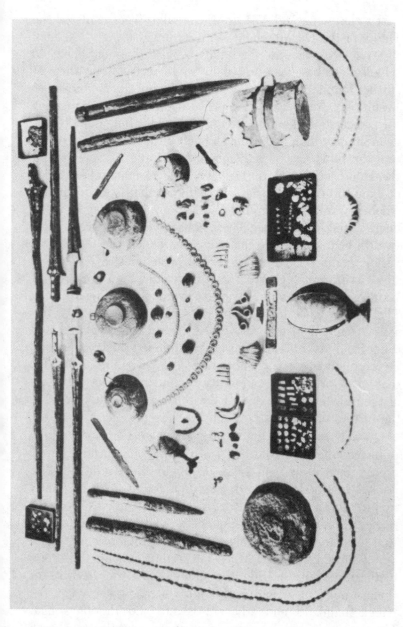

FIG. 2.7 Dendra, tholos tomb, finds. Note especially the ostrich egg, bottom center. (Persson, 1931, Pl. 8; by permission of C. W. K. Gleerup, Lund)

was found unplundered. From its treasures, as displayed in the National Museum in Athens, we can get some idea of the richness of the Mycenaean tholos tombs before the ancient grave-robbers did their work.

The Dendra tholos tomb was discovered by an American, Dorothy Burr, now the wife of Homer Thompson, long-time director of the American excavations in the Athenian agora. Out for a mule ride one April Sunday in 1926, on a bus-man's holiday from Blegen's dig at Prosymna, she noticed some farmers trying to remove from a field some large flat blocks, among which she recognized the lintel of a tholos tomb. Three pits in the tomb floor, excavated by the Swede Axel W. Persson, yielded treasures as exotic as they were valuable (Fig. 2.7): a massive gold ring; a great Mycenaean

FIG. 2.7a Dendra, bronze cui-rass. (Nauplia, Museum)

necklace; an ostrich egg, probably an import from Egypt, with a silver neck, gold-edged bronze banding, and glass paste appliqué; a gold cup with an octopus motif; bronze swords (of a type in use after 1400 B.C.), with gold-mounted hilts and ivory or agate pommels; and a gold-and-silver cup decorated with bulls' heads. This cup, filled with red Nemean wine and passed round the company, prompted Demetrios, the innkeeper of La Belle Hélène nearby, to exclaim, "Twice God has let me drink from gold cups: in Vaphió in '89 when I was with Tsountas, and again today. Now I can die content!" The dig ended on the fiftieth anniversary of Schliemann's first setting spade into his grave circle at Mycenae. In 1960 another Dendra tomb yielded a unique find, now in the Nauplia museum: a complete bronze cuirass (Fig. 2.7a), contemporary with the fall of Knossos, and with it a pair of bronze greaves (shin guards), and the remains of a shield.

Such treasures must once have filled the romantically named "Treasury of Atreus," the "Tomb of Clytemnestra," and the other seven tholos tombs near Mycenae, but nowadays what awes the visitor is their size and the obvious skill of the great architect who built them. The Treasury of Atreus is the largest and the most famous. Today its name seems less fantastic than it used to; for it certainly once contained a treasure, and its date, established by pottery under the entranceway or *dromos*, and by the style of building, is contemporary with the Lion Gate, and not far from the traditional date (which is about 1300 B.C.) of Atreus himself. It is one of the most impressive monuments of the Mycenaean world, nearly fifty feet in diameter, over forty-three feet high to the top of the beehive (Fig. 2.8), and with a lintel block weighing 120 tons. The beehive shape is built up in thirty-three courses of stones. Above the foundation course, each ring of blocks is cantilevered to overlap the one below, until finally the circular top block is set to crown the whole and give the impression of a vault, a false impression, since the top

FIG. 2.8 Mycenae, Treasury of Atreus, interior, showing twenty-two of the thirty-three courses. Note enormous lintel block. (Saul Weinberg)

block is nonfunctional as a keystone. On both sides of the lofty entrance were half-columns in a green stone, perhaps from Sparta; they are decorated with chevrons and spirals.

Only slightly smaller and slightly later than the Treasury of Atreus is the "Tomb of Clytemnestra," some 150 yards west of the Lion Gate. Here, in October, 1951, in the course of repairs, workmen stumbled upon some pieces of a grave monument on its original base. Soon after, the Greek archaeologist Dr. John Papadimitriou and the Greek-American George Mylonas discovered three more worked stones, set on a curve. It looked to them as though they had hit upon another grave circle, like the one Schliemann had discovered within the wall seventy-five years before. Excavation proved them right: there was a circle, and within it twenty-four graves, of which fourteen yielded highly significant finds, dated by pottery to Middle Helladic III, about 1580 B.C. These included bronze swords with alabaster pommels, ivory-handled bronze daggers, and the remains of a leather scabbard in gold appliqué. There were vases in silver and bronze, a death mask in electrum, and quantities of gold leaf. Jewelry included gold and silver earclips and gold diadems strengthened with bronze wire. Mylonas was particularly touched by the discovery of a child's gold rattle and thin gold curlers. He found, too, boars' tusks which had once covered helmets, and a belt in gold appliqué. The masterpiece of the collection was an exquisite rock crystal bowl in the form of a duck (Fig. 2.9). A fluted silver cup, bags of obsidian arrowheads, and an Egyptian scarab in lapis lazuli complete the selection from the rich roster of finds. They are now in the National Museum in Athens. Skeletons from two of the graves revealed macabre medical details: one had a fractured skull, neatly trepanned, the earliest such operation known in Europe; between the lower right ribs and the iliac crest of the other were two green-brown, faceted and polished stones: they

FIG. 2.9   Mycenae, duck vase in rock crystal from Grave Circle B, now in National Museum, Athens. (Mylonas, 1957, Fig. 61, by permission of Princeton University Press)

FIG. 2.10 Mycenae, Grave Circle A, reconstruction drawing. Visible, from the top down, are the triangular back of the Lion Gate relief, the Granary, the *stelai* over the Shaft Graves, the Ramp House, and the House of the Warrior Vase. (Wace, *op. cit.*, Pl. 22)

were gallstones, suggesting a rich diet, worthy of a Homeric hero. This unfortunate seems from his gnarled joints to have suffered also from arthritis.

These are fabulous finds, belonging either to newcomers or to a local elite. Three quarters of a century earlier, Schliemann, excavating *his* grave circle (Fig. 2.10), had brought mythological Greece within the orbit of early Greek history. Within the circle he and his Greek colleague Stamatakis found six shaft graves containing nineteen burials; their rich contents made this, until the 1951 finds, the outstanding single discovery in Greek archaeological research. Schliemann, mistaking the disorder of fallen grave roofs for Aegisthus' guilty haste, thought Agamemnon was buried here, but the pottery dates the graves far earlier, between 1580 and 1500 B.C. Metalwork technique suggests that the craftsmen of Circle B worked also in A. All the Mycenaean burials, shaft graves, chamber tombs, and *tholoi* belong to one unbroken tradition: all are family graves, all are furnished for the journey to Hades (including sometimes the occupant's favorite hound), all are burials, not cremations; all are heaped with earth, all marked with gravestones engraved or plain, all involved a funeral meal and libation or pouring of liquid offerings. Construction techniques show that the beehive shape is only an extension of the grave-circle principle. The exciting discoveries at Mycenae caused many a heightened heartbeat among the excavators, an excitement that seldom shows in their factual reports. Indeed, one archaeologist writes of the Grave Circle finds as an indiscriminate accumulation of *objets d'art* and showy trinkets of shoddy workmanship and deplorable taste. But all the excavators of Mycenae, from Schliemann to Mylonas, were humanists, keenly aware that they were digging up not things but men: these weapons, wielded 3500 years ago, brought victory or defeat to real men, the vases once held priceless ointment for real women, the bones are of real people. Not the least reward of archaeology, as Mylonas says, is to infer from withered flowers the hour of their bloom.

Eight miles south-southeast of Mycenae lies the sister citadel of Tiryns, whose pre-Mycenaean history as archaeology reveals it we have already traced. Its remains, dated after 1900 B.C., are even more impressive than the massive round tower described in the last chapter. The pottery reveals, in Late Helladic II and III, between 1500 and

1230 B.C., a vigorous, ambitious building period which produced in three phases the most monumental Mycenaean fortification walls known (Fig. 2.11) and the surviving palace. Tiryns in mythology is Heracles' city: do his victories over local beasts symbolize Tirynthian victories over local barons?

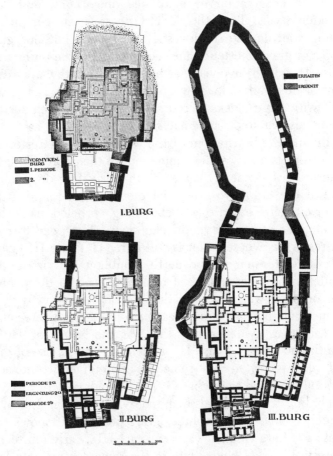

FIG. 2.11 Tiryns I, II, III Phases. The walls of Phase I are jogged, as in Troy VI (Fig. 1.4). For Phase III, cf. Fig. 1.15. (Müller, 1930, Pl. 4, by permission of DAI, Athens)

Kurt Müller, the excavator of Tiryns, learned his archaeological techniques from Dörpfeld, and his results are a model of interpretation, acute, accurate, scrupulous, and thorough. Since most of but not quite all the pottery was cleared away either when the top of the acropolis was leveled off to build the palace or when Schliemann excavated in 1884, the relative dating had to be done mostly by acute observation of materials, dimensions, and construction styles. Thus the earliest phase, best seen in the citadel wall on the southwest, used sizable but not giant blocks of gray limestone, finished smooth on the outer face. Phase II, which involved northward and southward extensions of this wall and a new eastern approach by ramp, was built with large blocks of red stone. Phase III includes the great false-vaulted "casemates" (galleries) on east and south, and the bowing out of the west wall (now restored). This protects a new stair, reminiscent of the approach to the cistern at Mycenae: it has a pitfall thirty feet deep and a gate at the top. Two others have since been found in the lower citadel. They are 30 meters long, corbeled, have sloping stepped roofs and yellow clay floors. They lead to rock-cut reservoirs whose water is still pure. To Phase III belong the vast extension to the north, doubling the size of the citadel to provide a place of refuge at need to the population of the lower city; and the frescoed megaron with its throne, painted pavement, hearth, columns, and forecourts. All this gives evidence that this was the height of Tiryns' wealth and power. Phase III is identified by its use of gray and red stones, mixed, some of them gigantic, none as smoothly finished as in Phase I. Just enough pottery survived (including a few sherds painted with signs in Linear B script), to make an absolute dating possible. It shows that Phase I is Late Helladic (Mycenaean) IIIA, early fourteenth century. Phase II begins late in the same century and lasts well down into the thirteenth. The magnificent Phase III is dated a little later than the Lion Gate at Mycenae (i.e., after 1250, on the evidence of a new east gate, like the Lion Gate in material, dimensions, and plan, but showing slight improvement in detail). This is the phase whose Herculean ruins astonish the modern visitor. Its existence implies friendly relations with Mycenae, which must have regarded Tiryns' walls not as a menace, but as merely a legitimate defense of Tirynthian treasure.

The approach today is by the same route that would have been taken by a visitor in Mycenaean times: up the ramp, a sharp right turn at the east gate, a sharp left along a narrow passage between massive beetling walls to yet another gate, the twin to the Lion Gate at Mycenae; then on to a forecourt, keeping the casemates on the left. All this time the right or shieldless side of the visitor was exposed to defenders on the walls, but from this point on the architecture changes, from a closed and forbidding to an open and welcoming mood. From the forecourt another right turn takes the visitor through the palace entrance gate or propylon, into a stucco-paved court; from its northwest corner opens, off-center, the entrance into the main court in front of the megaron. This court was porticoed on three sides, and contains an altar. The contrasting red and gray of the stonework, the brightly painted front of the megaron entrance (Fig. 2.12), the carpetlike painted floor of the inner propylon, its alabaster frieze, with its elongated rosettes, in Cretan style, bordered with spirals picked out with beads of blue glass paste, made the whole ensemble strikingly colorful. The megaron itself closely resembles those of Troy VI, the palace at Mycenae, and, as we shall see, the Palace of Nestor at Pylos. It had a painted floor, in which octopus and dolphin motifs alternated with geometric patterns; a stripe like the border of a carpet shows where the throne-dais stood against the east wall. Frescoes of a boar hunt, a chariot race, a festal procession of demure women with offerings, and bull-leaping enlivened the palace walls in one phase or another with a range of seven colors:

Fig. 2.12   Tiryns, court and megaron entrance, reconstruction water
color. The details (tapering columns, portico, figure-eight shield)
show Minoan inspiration. (Müller, 1930, Pl. 42)

white, black, blue, two tones of red, yellow, and green.

West of the megaron are suites of apartments, one with
a red-trimmed bright blue floor enlivened with painted
dolphins; and a bathroom floored with one single colossal
limestone block. East of the main megaron is a smaller one,
perhaps for the Queen Mother, or Crown Prince, since it,
too, had a throne; the floor was painted with rosette-embel-
lished stripes. In an adjoining room, north of the stairwell,
the dolphin-octopus motif recurs in the painted pavement.
Both megara face south, the quarter from which in summer
the cooling sea-wind blows across the Argolid from the
Gulf of Nauplia. The sleeping rooms have an eastern ex-
posure, for coolness in the evening. Wooden beams built
into the stone courses of the walls provided a cushion
against earthquakes, but also a hazard of fire. The roofs
were flat; their height has been calculated from the diameter

of column-bases and the height of stairwells; some inner rooms must have been lit by clerestories, others by light-wells. The whole palace complex gives evidence of great technical competence and architectural skill in the manipulation of space. There were private houses on three sides of the citadel, and on the spur below the palace, within a circuit wall of after 1250, with towers every 38 feet. One house, destroyed in the Dark Ages, contained a graverobber's hoard of gold, bronze, amber, and weapons. But Tiryns in its prime was the appropriate seat of a considerable kingdom, related to or at least on friendly terms with Mycenae, prospering no doubt on the spoils of the destruction of the Palace at Knossos and the fall of the Minoan Empire. But it too fell to violent assault by the Dorians and perished in flames. The blocked drains in the bath give evidence of a lower cultural level in the Sub-Mycenaean age. Tiryns, like Mycenae, never regained its former grandeur. Refugees from it settled, in 479, at Porto Cheli (ancient Halieis) not far from the southern-most tip of the Argolid, where American excavators have examined the acropolis and traced part of the circuit wall, now under water.

By 1939 the discovery in the southwest Peloponnese, near classical Pylos, at the north end of the Bay of Navarino in Messenia, of more "royal" tholos tombs than anywhere else except Mycenae led Greek archaeologists to invite Blegen to join them in more extended excavation. (Since then, more tholoi have been found, dated in the 1400s and by their richness reinforcing Blegen's identification of the neighboring palace as Nestor's. One, about 100 yards north-east of what proved to be the palace hill, contained a griffin sealing, two small owls in gold; amethyst and amber beads, and fragments of bronze weapons. Another to the south yielded four skeletons in jars, twenty-two swords and daggers, bronze vessels, and a wild-boar sealing. About 600 yards down the road toward the plain, another tholos, though looted, produced bits of carved ivory, gold beads, semiprecious stones, and faïence. Chamber tombs 550 yards to the west, for ordinary citizens, contained pottery.)

On the height of Epanò Englianós, three miles north of the beach of sandy Pylos on a steep plateau, crowned by magnificent olives, Blegen, in association with K. Kourouniotis of the National Museum, Athens, found the ruins of an extensive complex of buildings, calcined and fused by an intense conflagration, which sherds established as a palace of late Mycenaean date. It is identified by Blegen as the Palace of Nestor, the aged, garrulous king of Pylos in Homer's *Iliad,* and host in the *Odyssey* to Odysseus' son Telemachus as he searches for his father. The excavation,

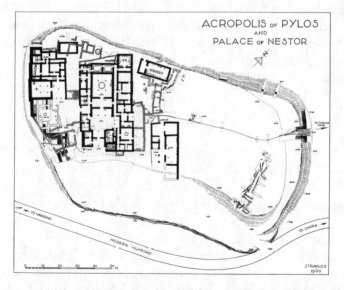

FIG. 2.13 Pylos, palace, plan. The Archives Room, where the Linear B tablets were found, is in the lower left corner of the central block, where megaron with central hearth can also be identified. Artisans' quarter to the right, older palace to the left. Note circuit wall and gate discovered in 1960. (Blegen, 1961, Pl. 53.1)

interrupted by World War II, was reopened in 1952 and was continued through 1966. Successive campaigns have revealed (Fig. 2.13) a central palace block with at least forty-six rooms on each floor, including forecourt, main and subsidiary megara, and storage rooms; an older southwest block, with throne room, hearth, painted pavements, and toilet facilities; and an artisan's quarter with armory, winecellars, and storerooms to the south and east. Out of one of these very storerooms Nestor's maid may have broached the eleven-year-old wine in honor of Telemachus' visit, as described in the *Odyssey:* "They took their places on the settles and chairs, and the old man prepared a bowl of mellow wine for his guests, from a jar that had stood for ten years before the maid undid the cap and broached it." In 1960 innumerable fragments and chips of ivory were found in this area, as well as 500 diminutive bronze arrowheads. The plan closely resembles that of the palaces at Mycenae and Tiryns. No less than eight pantries were found, filled to overflowing with orderly nests of unused pottery. One set of 850, found right beside the front door, suggests the need for instant hospitality for visitors, attested by the Homeric poems. Beside the throne room was found a kind of bar, with provision for setting large wine jars to cool, for the refreshment of those awaiting audience. Over 8000 whole pots in all were found, of which all but a dozen are Late Mycenaean IIIB and c: they date the destruction about 1200 B.C., a generation after Blegen's date for the destruction of Troy VIIA. Earlier ware in deeper levels, going back to Middle Helladic, proves that the site had been occupied since about 1900 B.C. by modest houses, which were swept away in Late Mycenaean IIIB to make room for the palace.

The main megaron has a magnificent version of the usual Mycenaean round central hearth, thirteen feet across, edged with a flame pattern and with painted spirals running horizontally round the raised rim. The floor has a chessboard design, as at Tiryns, with abstract and octopus patterns,

and a space marked out for the throne, which was flanked
by a frescoed griffin on one side, a lion on the other. Many
colorful fresco fragments found fallen from above show
that all the important rooms were gaily decorated, with
figures of gods, tanned men in spotted white tunics, women
(one with a superb feather headdress), panthers, lions, boars,
deer, sphinxes, dogs, horses, marine creatures; processions,
duels, sieges, a lyre player perched on his own colorful private mountain: he may be Apollo, Orpheus, or a nameless
bard playing at a banquet (Fig. 2.13a). A fresco of two
sphinxes facing each other heraldically over a gate invites
comparison with the Lion Gate at Mycenae; the griffin on
the megaron wall is like the one in the "Throne Room" at
Knossos. A bathroom with a built-in bath and a kylix or
footed shallow drinking cup smashed in the tub may either
imply that Mycenaeans drank wine while bathing, or it may
have contained oil for anointing, as Nestor's daughter
anointed Telemachus on his visit: "She bathed him and

Fig. 2.13a Pylos, fresco from Throne Room: the lyre player (reconstruction in water color by Piet de Jong).

rubbed him with olive oil; she gave him a tunic and arranged a fine cloak around his shoulders, so that he stepped out of the bath looking like an immortal god." One pottery kylix, excavated in 1957 (and now in the National Museum in Athens), is a foot high and a foot wide, the largest ever found: it reminded Blegen of Nestor's gold cup in the *Iliad*, which was the size of a soup tureen. The 1959 campaign revealed at last traces of an early (fifteenth century) fortification wall with gate and tower, abandoned in the thirteenth. An open raised wooden aqueduct supplied the palace with water from a spring 600 yards away. Trial trenches below the citadel uncovered the house walls of a lower town, which supplied the last features necessary to make the palace and its environs perfectly parallel to those of Mycenae and Tiryns, and to clinch it as, like them, the seat of a powerful and wealthy dynasty and, like them, doomed to fall, not long after the siege of Troy, to the merciless and uncivilized Dorian invaders, who took advantage of an area overpopulated, torpid with bureaucracy, and overdependent on an agricultural economy.

All this is important, but another Pylos find, dating from the very first week of the first campaign, made possible the most important breakthrough in the history of early Greek archaeology. In *The New York Times* of April 28, 1939 was announced Blegen's discovery, in an Archives Room in the south corner of the central palace, of over 600 fragments of clay tablets, inscribed in a script identical with the one identified by Evans at Knossos a generation before, and named by him "Minoan Linear B," to distinguish it from an earlier "A" script with some different characters, and from still earlier hieroglyphs. In 1936, when Evans lectured in London on this tantalizing writing, in his audience was a fourteen-year-old English schoolboy, Michael Ventris, who vowed to take up the challenge of this undeciphered script. Sixteen years later, with the aid of the Pylos tablets and techniques of cryptanalysis learned in World War II, he had cracked it.

Both Evans and Blegen had observed, from the pictorial nature of some of the signs of the script, that they were dealing with lists, catalogues, or inventories of persons, domestic animals, cereals, and other commodities, with numbers or quantities recorded in a decimal system. Since the Pylos deposit was the first one found in mainland Greece, Blegen was able to conclude, without being able to read the script, that the Mycenaeans were not illiterate, that they were capable of orderly methods of administration, and that the strikingly similar palaces of Mycenae and Tiryns must also have contained such tablets, and hence their bureaucracy must also have been literate. The failure of the excavators to find the evidence there must have been due to sheer chance or to the fact that the conflagrations which destroyed those palaces did not always bake the clay of the tablets hard enough to preserve it. (Even the better-baked Pylos tablets had to be dried for days on specially constructed wire-mesh frames before they could be handled.) Wace in fact did, as we have seen, later find Linear B tablets at Mycenae. The finding of tablets on the mainland in the same script as those known since 1900 at Knossos created the strong presumption that all the tablets, Pylian and Cretan alike, were written in some early form of Greek. This justified the further inference that the Palace at Knossos in the level at which the tablets were reportedly found (Late Minoan I-II, fifteenth century B.C.) was occupied by Greek-speaking invaders. Evans went to his grave in 1941 denying this, but Ventris proved it true.

Ventris began by distinguishing on the tablets some eighty-eight signs, uniform on the mainland and on the Cretan tablets. Eighty-eight signs are too many for an alphabet, too few for such a system of ideographs as Chinese, or Egyptian hieroglyphs. Therefore the system must have been a syllabary, in which the signs might stand for *ba, be, ka, ke,* etc. With some 2500 tablets to deal with, Ventris was able to find which signs were statistically frequent, average, or infrequent; initial, medial, or final; to determine which signs were regularly paired or linked, and which never associated. On the assumption, rendered safe by the mainland finds from Pylos, that the language of the syllabary was Greek, he could guess that the most frequent initial signs were *a* and *e,* as they are in classical Greek. Earlier work by an American, Alice Kober, had established that the word-endings (ascertained by noticing the upright strokes, or dividers, marked in the clay) involved vowel variation, and showed that certain signs shared the same consonant, others the same vowel, and that there were characteristic inflectional vowels, as in the Greek or Indo-European inflections for gender, case, and number. Thus a series (called "Kober's triplets") might run 〖signs〗, 〖signs〗, 〖signs〗, or 〖signs〗, 〖signs〗, and 〖signs〗. The way in which certain sign-groups were used suggested that they referred to certain categories: places, persons, trades or occupations, and commodities. Ventris had available nearly 1700 tablets from Knossos; place names near Knossos survived down into classical times; he could play some hunches. For example, in the first series above, which comes from Knossos (where Linear B may have been invented by Minoan scribes at the order of Mycenaean masters), the initial sign had already been noted as high-frequency, and therefore a vowel. Now the name of the harbor town of Knossos was known to be Amnisos. These four syllabic signs were therefore guessed to represent *a-mi-ni-so.* Another very frequently occurring Knossian sign-sequence, also cited above, shared one sign with this: - - *so;* why should this not be *ko-no-so* = Knossos? The other final signs would be adjectival case-endings, to be extrapolated from Greek: *ja, jo.* The first syllable of *ko-no-so* occurred often together with one of two signs, either 〖sign〗 or 〖sign〗, together with pictorial ideograms clearly meaning *MEN* and *WOMEN*. The classical Greek for "boy" is *kouros* (involving a lost digamma or *w*-sound); "girl" is *kore*. These two pairs of signs might then be transliterated *ko-wo* and *ko-wa*, and the final signs in each could then be substituted, as a pair of case endings, in another of "Kober's triplets."

Another sign, ⊙ , occurred with high frequency in the final position. These are lists: the sign might be an enclitic (tacked-on) *and*, like -*que*, "and," in Latin, *te* in classical Greek; Ventris assigned it the value -*qe*. Already Ventris had possible equivalents for twelve of the eighty-eight signs, and each verified hunch would produce a chain reaction substituting knowns for unknowns in more tablets. It was time to systematize these relationships in the form of a grid.

Ventris' grid (Fig. 2.14) provided space for five vowels across the top and twelve or thirteen consonants down the sides; i.e., equivalents for up to sixty-five out of the eighty-eight signs in the syllabary. It will be noted that there is no *b*, *c*, *f*, *g*, *h*, *l*, *v*, or *x*: *b* and *f* ($= ph$) are labials, for which *p*- does duty in the syllabary; *c* and *g* are gutturals, for which *k*- does duty; *h* is not an expressed consonant but a rough breathing; *r* and *l* both seem to be represented in the syllabary by *r*, as when a Chinese speaks English; *v* is not a letter in the classical Greek alphabet; and *x* is a double letter ($= ks$). How to find more clues? Among Blegen's tablets found in 1939 at Pylos was one where the signs 𝖬𝟮, 𝟢𝟢 were repeated with the *WOMAN* ideogram. In the Greek dialects the word for "mother" is *mater*; suppose 𝖬𝟮 $=$ -*ma-te*; then 𝟢𝟢 $= pa-te = pater$ "father," and two more syllables are added to the grid. Pairs of words identical except for one sign were helpful, too; the variation would indicate alternative spellings, and a relation could be established between pairs of signs which

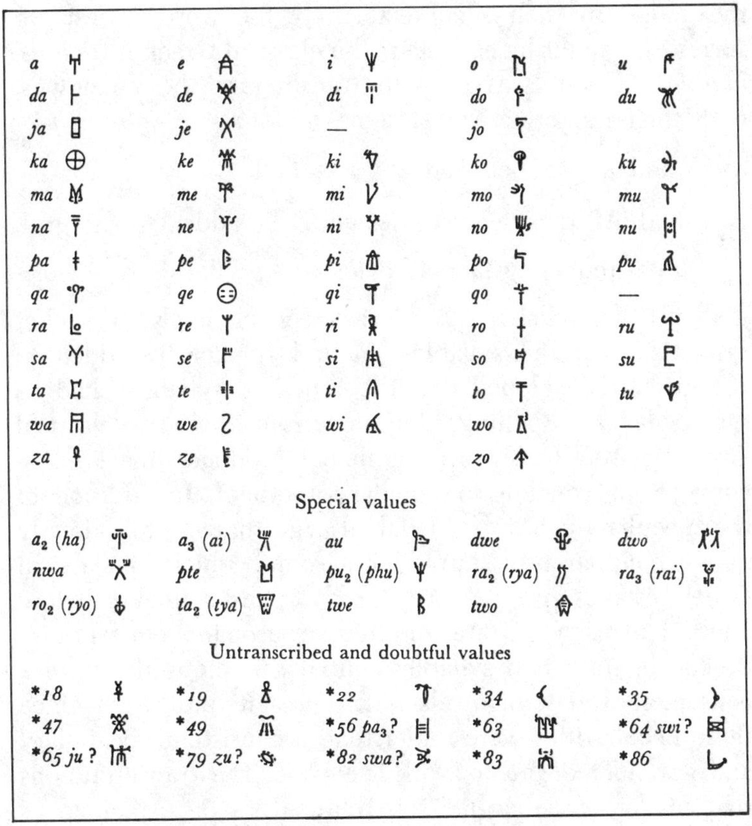

a	e	i	o	u
da	de	di	do	du
ja	je	—	jo	
ka	ke	ki	ko	ku
ma	me	mi	mo	mu
na	ne	ni	no	nu
pa	pe	pi	po	pu
qa	qe	qi	qo	—
ra	re	ri	ro	ru
sa	se	si	so	su
ta	te	ti	to	tu
wa	we	wi	wo	—
za	ze		zo	

Special values

a_2 (ha)	a_3 (ai)	au	dwe	dwo
nwa	pte	pu_2 (phu)	ra_2 (rya)	ra_3 (rai)
ro_2 (ryo)	ta_2 (tya)	twe	two	

Untranscribed and doubtful values

*18	*19	*22	*34	*35
*47	*49	*56 pa_3?	*63	*64 swi?
*65 ju?	*79 zu?	*82 swa?	*83	*86

FIG. 2.14   Linear B grid. (Ventris-Chadwick, 1973, p. 385, by permission of the Cambridge University Press)

would differ by only one letter. Thus a Pylos tablet read 〈symbols〉, a Knossos one 〈symbols〉. Frequency tables showed that 〈symbols〉 were vowels. Another Knossos tablet contained the sequence 〈symbols〉 along with 〈symbols〉. The *pater* deduction had established 〈symbol〉 as *pa*, 〈symbol〉 as *-te;* The Amnisos-Knossos deduction had established 〈symbol〉 as *-si*, *Pa- si te-?-?* might be *pasi theois*, classical Greek for "to all

the gods." In such a context surely the word "priest" or
"priestess" might be expected: the classical Greek is *hiereus,
hiereia.* Thus it was easy to transliterate the unknowns,
with their numerous vowel signs, as *i-e-re-u, i-je-re-u, i-je-
re-ja,* and a link between $\stackrel{.}{A}$ = *e* and $\nmid$ = *je* was established. All these new values could be added to the grid.

A high-frequency pair at Pylos is fil : if this is "Pylos,"
and in the syllabary *r* = *l*, as seemed likely on other
grounds, then the syllables *pu* and *ro* can be added to
the grid. It developed that the Linear B syllabary had its
own rules for spelling, different from those of classical
Greek (naturally, since an alphabet produces one kind of
conventional spelling, a syllabary another). In addition to
the peculiar behavior of labials,. gutturals, etc. already
noted, *q* apparently stands for a sound which in classical
Greek resolves into *k, p,* or *t; l, m, n, r,* and *s,* final or before
another consonant, are omitted; consonant clusters are
broken up into two syllables; initial *s* is omitted before a
consonant; the semivowels *j-* and *w-* are indicated. Once
these peculiarities were understood a consistent vocabulary
and grammar began to work itself out. The transliterations
that made sense became too frequent to be explained as
coincidence, and the language was established as Greek.
Chadwick illustrates how the guesses became virtual cer-
tainties, by postulating that work on an English cipher might
establish the combinations XYZ and ZYX as nouns, XY and
ZY as verbs, XYYZ and YZZ as adjectives; *G, O,* and *D*
then become the only possible equivalent for *X, Y,* and *Z.*
Ventris announced his provisional results in June, 1952. In
May, 1953, Blegen found a tablet at Pylos with a picture
of a tripod on it, and beside it a sign-series which by Ventris' grid worked out as *ti-ri-po-de* (Fig. 2.15). The decipherment was an accomplished fact, and the Greek language
was proved to have a 3300-year history, which only Chinese

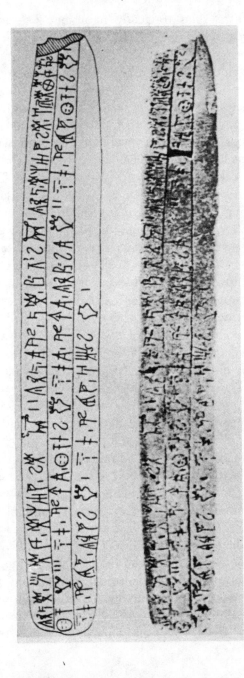

FIG. 2.15 Pylos, tripod tablet. The four signs to the right of the second tripod in the top line read, according to Ventris' grid, *ti-ri-po-de*, thus clinching the soundness of his decipherment. (Ventris-Chadwick, 1956, fac. p. 111)

can rival. Ventris died tragically in a motor accident in September, 1956; his work is being carried on by John Chadwick (Cambridge), Emmett L. Bennett, Jr. (University of Wisconsin), and many other scholars from many countries. countries.

The decipherment yielded at once a vast number of personal names and names of occupations. Personal names make up 65 per cent of the vocabulary of what we must now call Mycenaean Greek. They include some that recur in classical Greek mythology and history, such as Theseus and possibly Alkmaion; god-names, Athena, Poseidon, and Dionysus: enough to suggest strongly the Mycenaean origin of Greek myth. Over 100 names of occupations were deciphered in the first report. They show a sophisticated division of labor and interest in luxury goods, and include goldsmiths, shipwrights, masons, bakers, cooks, woodcutters, messengers, longshoremen, oarsmen, coppersmiths, fullers (dry cleaners), saddlers, shepherds; as well as the Homeric names for King and Leader of the Host. Later, Ventris and Chadwick were able to add the words for doctor, herald, potter, forester, carpenter, bowmaker, flaxworker, carder, spinner, weaver, bath attendant, and unguent-boiler.

At Pylos the tablets included inventories of inlaid furniture and costly objects in ivory, gold, silver, and lapis lazuli. They revealed that the palace controlled an area halfway in size between Attica and Boeotia, or about 3500 square kilometers, organized as a bureaucracy, working down from King and court through military leaders, administrative officials, charioteers (146 pairs of chariot wheels), mayors of surrounding villages, craftsmen, and landworkers. It was this palace bureaucracy that fell when the Dorians invaded; with it Greek literacy disappeared for centuries. The tablets established religion, too, as involving offerings of agricultural produce, precious objects, men, and women, to named gods: Poseidon, Zeus, Hera, Hermes, Dionysus, and perhaps

Artemis. They tell us what Greek was like 500 years before Homer; what elements in Homer are Mycenaean and what late; what the origins of classical Greek mythology, religion, and art are. They prove (because Linear B was derived from the still-undeciphered but non-Greek Linear A in Crete) that there was communication, verbal and cultural, between Greeks and Minoans. If Greeks could communicate with Cretans, they could presumably communicate with other cultures; e.g., the Hittites, who used tablets at this time. Thus One World in the Near East in the thirteenth century B.C. becomes an established fact.

When in the fall of 1953 I excitedly announced the news of Ventris' decipherment to a colleague, he asked drily, "What is the poetry like?" The answer is that so far there is none; nothing but inventories and prosaic documents of that kind. But they are enough to bring the Mycenaean world out of the darkness of prehistory into the light of historic documentation, and there is good reason to believe that the Homeric poems as we have them derive ultimately from Mycenaean oral epic.

Neleus, founder of Nestor's dynasty at Pylos, took to wife a princess from Orchomenos in Boeotia; the tholos tomb there, Schliemann's so-called "Treasury of Minyas" (mentioned above, Chapter 1) is to be dated as contemporary with the Tomb of Clytemnestra at Mycenae. Besides the tholos tomb, bits of fresco showing architectural details and bull-leaping (which involved catching the bull's horns and somersaulting onto his back and off again) hint at the Mycenaean palace, or at any rate an upper-class house, at Orchomenos, which the tomb presupposes, and so does a stirrup-vase (a squat, flat-bottomed container for liquids, named from the shape of its handles) painted with Linear B signs. The palace, of Mycenaean IIIB, has since been found, complete with canonical frescoes (depicting chariots and the hunt), megaron, and round hearth. The wealth, prosperity, and sophistication which these finds imply clearly resulted from the draining of the nearby Lake Copais. When this operation was repeated in the late nineteenth century of our era, the contractors found the dikes that bounded the ancient drainage canals. Since these are built of polygonal blocks in the same technique as the later phases of the circuit walls of Mycenae and Tiryns, a late Mycenaean date is established for them. On the tiny rocky island of Gla near the lake's east shore, French and German excavators discovered a citadel larger than Mycenae and Tiryns together, walled in salients like the southwest side of the acropolis of Tiryns, with a main gate that probably boasted a relieving triangle in the Mycenaean manner, though nothing above the lintel is preserved. Against the inner north face of the circuit wall at its highest point, with a fine view over the lake or the rich fields, was built an L-shaped palace or villa whose plan (Fig. 2.16) strongly resembles, as we shall see (Fig. 2.26), the villa excavated by the Italians at Hagia Triada in southern Crete. South of the palace stretched a deep rectangular agora flanked by buildings. The surrounding area was very efficiently drained in Mycenaean times by dikes, and the palace itself has traces of drainage conduits, as well as painted pavement and frescoes. Unique finds include clamps or lead for joining the wooden door jambs to the walls, and pilasters and half-round columns in stucco, apparently used as moldings to frame frescoes or relieve the monotony of solid-painted walls. Like Mycenae, Tiryns, and Pylos, Gla came to a violent end by fire, probably in the twelfth century B.C.

Athens and Demeter's holy city of Eleusis also flourished, apparently without falling before the Dorian invaders who destroyed many Mycenaean sites. Eleusis, some fourteen miles west of Athens, was from Mycenaean times a holy city. The evidence is Megaron B, a Late Helladic II building beneath the archaic level of the Hall of Mysteries (Telesterion) there. The Mysteries celebrated the resurrection from

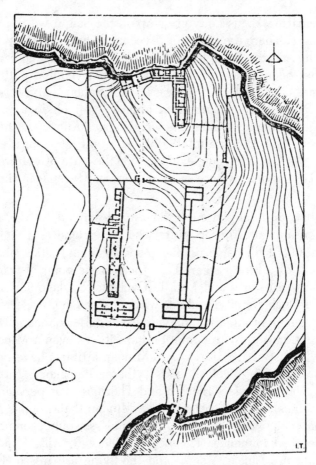

Fig. 2.16 Gla, palace, plan. Recent excavation has revealed an en-
trenched camp with long walls south of the palace. (Pl. XXIIA.
Reprinted from *The Greek Bronze Age* by Emily T. Vermeule,
by permission of The University of Chicago Press. © 1964 by the
University of Chicago)

the dead of Persephone, young goddess of flowering things,
and the joy after sorrow of her mother Demeter. Initiation
into the Mysteries, always secret, involved things done, said,
and shown (by the hierophant), and gave one happiness in

the hereafter. Eleusis city grew up on the height west of the sanctuary. There are traces of Mycenaean houses behind the museum and the Panaghia's chapel, and a Mycenaean cemetery has been excavated still farther west, yielding pottery, figurines, and stelae. A Linear B inscription (Mycenaean IIIc) painted on an amphora appears to include a place name and a personal name known also from Knossos. Athens' story can be told more intelligibly as a unit later on. Meanwhile, the Cyclades give evidence for the state of culture at Phylakopi and elsewhere in the islands in Mycenaean times.

Phylakopi I, a phase of the city described in the last chapter, appears from its pottery to have come to a violent end, at about the same time as many mainland cities, about 1900 B.C. or a little earlier. This, then, is the point of transition between Early and Middle Cycladic. Phylakopi II is a Middle Cycladic city, walled, with frescoed houses, streets crossing at right angles, and evidence of close connections in trade and culture with Crete; perhaps it was even a Minoan colony. A list of 121 sites where Minoan artifacts have been found (including Delos, Kea, Kythera, Phylakopi, Naxos, Thera, Vaphio, Asine, Eleusis, and Thorikos) has persuaded some scholars of the existence of a Minoan thalassocracy, or colonial sea power. Others, more cautious, see only economic, not political influence. The best evidence for this Minoan influence are Linear A signs and the flying fish fresco (Fig. 2.17), found in association with Cretan Kamares ware, but dated about 1600 B.C. It is a gay freehand piece, in marine blue, yellow, red, and black; in it the fish dart now up, now down, with wings now closed, now outspread, against a background of rocks, sponges, and fish eggs. Phylakopi III centers around a new palace (no trace of earlier phases below) with a megaron in the mainland style and a central hearth. There is a Mycenaean shrine with frescoes, dated 1360 B.C. With the palace goes mainland, not Cretan pottery. The style is Late Mycenaean III, and the finest piece is the

FIG. 2.17   Phylakopi, flying fish fresco. Athens, National Museum.
(Émile Séraf)

Fisherman Vase, on which four men with Picasso-like eyes
walk on a pebbly beach carrying miniature dolphins by the
tail in each hand. Some scholars would assign the flying fish
fresco also to this phase. The style is close to that of the
Warrior Vase from Mycenae. One sherd, otherwise undated,
bears syllabic signs which, interpreted as Linear B, apparently comes from Lyktos in Crete; if the language is Greek,
the pottery was imported after mainland invaders had taken
Crete over. Phylakopi III declined with its mainland neighbors, and about the same time, under the stress of the Dorian
invasion of about 1125. Other islands, Naxos, Kea, Delos,
Kythnos, Seriphos, Amorgos, Paros, Siphnos, Tenos, Kimo-
los, yield late Mycenaean wares, including ivory, which
cease after the mainland palaces were sacked, but there has
been little or no systematic excavation and cultural details
are lacking. It is a moot question whether there was ever a
Mycenaean political as opposed to commercial "empire." A
computer-produced map shows "principalities," presumably
independent, at Iolkos, Delphi, Orchomenos, Thebes, Athens,

Mycenae, Tiryns, Sparta, and Pylos. A ship with a cargo of nearly a ton (scrap bronze, and ingots of copper and tin), which sank about 1200 B.C. in 100 feet of water off Cape Gelidonya, southwest Turkey, probably came from a Semitic port. Cretan influence ceases after the mainland folk sacked Knossos, and mainland influence ceases after the Dorians sacked the Mycenaean palaces. Thereafter the Cyclades, like the rest of the Aegean world, lapse into the poverty-stricken "Dark Ages" that yield little to the excavator.

Crete remains. We left it, at the end of the last chapter, in the midst of the Middle Minoan period, before the prime of the palaces at Knossos, Mallia, Gourniá, and Phaistos. The culture to be described is as on the mainland of vast extent in time, nearly 800 years. An earthquake at the end of Middle Minoan IIB, about 1700 B.C., gave the architects of the New Palace at Knossos a free hand for expansive plans. Prosperity resulting from sea trade, piracy, and tribute provided the means. Knossos, archaeology tells us, was for about a century (1580-1480 B.C.) the center of an international power, the first in European history.

The wealth, enthusiasm, and imagination of Sir Arthur Evans reconstructed chiefly this phase of the palace (Fig. 2.18), not always, it is to be feared, with complete fidelity to the archaeological data, but the result is vivid, picturesque, and colorful enough to satisfy the most jaded tourist: the bright frescoes; the famous downward-tapering painted cypress-wood columns; the huge storage jars, taller than a man, have been restored or left *in situ* to lend the Palace of Minos more human interest than any other prehistoric Greek site. The palace as reconstructed is a great six-acre square, 400 feet on a side, built around a central court, and dominating a flourishing city (almost entirely unexcavated) with a population estimated by Evans at 82,000 (100,000 if we include the port town, Amnisos, three miles away, with its lily-frescoed Late Minoan I villa. Its state entrances and public rooms were on the south and west. In the rich store-rooms beneath them Evans found the lead linings of chests that had once contained objects of value. From the west porch a dog-leg corridor, frescoed with a processional scene, led first south, then east. Out of the middle of its eastern leg opened northward a propylon, not unlike the one at Tiryns, decorated with a fresco of cupbearers. From this, one ascended a broad staircase to an audience hall on the upper story. Opening out of the northwest corner of the central court is a suite of rooms belonging to a late phase of the palace, including one with a ceremonial seat in gypsum

FIG. 2.18   Knossos, Palace of Minos, air view. 1, grand staircase to audience chamber; 2, Throne Room; 3, Theatral Area; 4, Central Court; 5, magazines of great *pithoi*; 6, 15, horns of consecration; 8, Hall of the Double Axes; 9, Northeast Magazines; 10, Pillar Hall; 11, Propylon. (Scullard, *Atlas*, Pl. 14, by permission of Elsevier, Amsterdam)

flanked by frescoed griffins. Evans called this the "Throne Room," but the lustral area and kitchens adjoining make it more likely that it was used for some cult ceremony requiring a high priest (perhaps the King) to live here for several days running. This "Throne Room" may have been the seat of the power of the Mycenaean invader who took over the palace late in Late Minoan I, a greater feat than the taking of Troy. There is certainly a close resemblance to the throne rooms of Mycenae, Tiryns, and Pylos. When the room was excavated, vases for anointing oils were found on the floor as they had fallen. Perhaps—it is all conjecture—the final catastrophe (about 1400 B.C., a pillage, massacre, burning, and withdrawal, due to rebellious Cretans, earthquake, or other Mycenaeans; e.g., Theseus of Athens, perhaps taking advantage of an earthquake) overwhelmed the palace at the very moment when an anointing ceremony was going on. The southeast block, Evans found, belonged almost entirely to the New Palace (Middle Minoan IIIb). It contained the Domestic Quarter, the private residence of the king and queen, approached by the Grand Staircase, whose five flights, embellished with a fresco of shields, open out of the eastern side of the central court. Evans' reconstruction of the Grand Staircase is one of the major feats of modern archaeological rebuilding. It gave access to the airy Hall of the Double Axes (so called from the masons' marks cut in the building blocks). That in turn opened, through seven of its eleven doorways, on an L-shaped portico and terrace with a view over the valley below, where, Evans believed, was the bull ring where Theseus and his Athenians performed before King Minos and his daughter Ariadne. (It is equally possible that the bull-leaping was done in the central court.) South of this hall, and isolated from it by a dog-leg corridor, are the charming apartments centering on what Evans called the Queen's Megaron, with its vivacious fresco of blue dolphins (cousins of the flying fish of Phylakopi), with bubbles flying off their fins, set in a border of coral and sponges. Although this megaron has five doors and seven windows, it does not open on the eastern terrace: its blank eastern wall was painted, in compensation, with a landscape. Adjoining it on the west was a bath and (a comfort to those who equate civilization with plumbing) a flush toilet. A room to the south has been called the "Nursery" because its entrance has a low gypsum barrier which might have been a gate across the door of a baby's room.

The northeast wing was the artisans' quarter, where Evans identified the laundry and small cells with grooves for sliding doors, which he thought were kennels. In the north-south corridor of this wing he found an elegant gaming board in rock crystal, blue glass paste, silver, ivory, and gold. North-westward is the impressive stepped "Theatral Area," over-looked, Evans thought, by a "Royal Box." It could hardly have been used for bull-leaping, since it offered spectators no protection; perhaps it was used for ceremonial dances, or for hearing lawsuits. From the "Armoury," which faces the road leading west from the Theatral Area, comes a tablet recording in Linear B numerals 8640 arrows. Sealings with the Linear B ARROW ideogram were found here attached to the charred remains of two boxes containing arrowheads and their carbonized shafts.

Middle Minoan is the period of the undeciphered Linear A script, many of whose signs anticipate Linear B, but the Linear B tablets belong to a later and prosperous period when Mycenaean invaders occupied the palace. Another earthquake, about 1580 B.C., destroyed the magnificence, but the restored palace and its dependent houses show frescoes of very high standard, depicting scenes from nature and wild life; blue monkeys, partridges, hoopoes. There are also proud human figures: the Priest-King or Lily Prince (found near the entrance from the Processional Corridor into the central court) with his swelling chest, powerful muscles, and lean thighs, wears a coronet of lilies and peacock plumes. The cupbearers, lining the south propylon walls, wear silver

FIG. 2.19 Knossos, La Parisienne, fresco fragment. Heraklion, Museum. (Evans, 1921-36, IV. 2, Pl. XXXIE, by permission of Messrs. Macmillan and the Trustees of the Sir Arthur Evans Estate)

earrings, necklaces, bracelets, and anklets; silver belts inset with gold pinch in their waists. The masterpiece of this period is the "Parisienne" (Fig. 2.19), the very type of elegant, slightly decadent young Cretan womanhood, with her ivory-white skin, big, bold dark eyes, dark curly hair falling in unrestrained ringlets over a low forehead, retroussé nose, full coral-red lips, and delicate chin. The so-called "Harvester" Vase of the same period from Hagia Triada (Fig. 2.20) probably portrays a riotous festival at sowing time. The participants, led by a priest, carry hoes bound with willow shoots, and have bags of seed strapped to their

FIG. 2.20 Hagia Triada, Harvester Vase. Heraklion, Museum.

thighs; they bellow and stamp, not in drunkenness, but in religious ecstasy. Just about this time (*ca.* 1450 B.C.) the Linear B tablets begin, the palace adds its throne room of the mainland type, and tombs and pottery in the Knossos area become strongly Helladic; i.e., Mycenaean. Pretty clearly the Minoan kingdom and palace were now taken over by a mainland prince. Perhaps mythology reflects this in the story of the slaying of the Minotaur in the Labyrinth by the Athenian prince Theseus. Thirty Mycenaean sites in Attica may have been among the places which he allegedly re-united in peaceful coexistence (*synoikismos*) under Athens. There are Mycenaean beehive tombs at Marathon (with a horse burial), Menidi (with an ivory lyre), and Spata (with an ivory plaque of about 1300 B.C. showing a lion attacking a goat).

Evans spent a fortune restoring the Palace of Minos, not always—to repeat—with complete accuracy. But the vivid reds and blues of the columns, the fresh colors and lively motifs of the frescoes, the giant vats in the storerooms make it one of the most rewarding sites to visit in the entire ancient world. It is all too easy to forget that there are other sites in Crete, not as accessible, not as well publicized, not as boldly restored, but vitally important for an under-standing of Minoan culture as a whole. Arkhanes, five miles south of Knossos, was perhaps the summer palace of the kings. It yielded an elaborate model of a two-storied house. At nearby Phourní, an ossuary of 2500-2150 B.C. held 196 skulls; in the beehive tomb of a princess (of about 1400) was found a sealed larnax containing 140 pieces of gold jewelry; a horse, no doubt her favorite, was sacrificed at her death. The discovery, on an altar, of a skeleton, a bronze knife be-side it, has led the excavator to posit human sacrifice, which, though rare in historical Greece, occurs in myth (Iphigenia), and in fact (before the battle of Salamis). At Nirou Khani, eight miles east of Knossos, the Villa of the Captain of the Port contained so much religious gear—including forty to fifty altars—that it has been labeled a center for the dissemination of the faith. Even more important are five more complexes: the palace of Mallia (a French dig, since 1922); the town of Gournia (American, 1901), both east of Knossos; the palace of Phaistos and the villa of Hagia Triada (Italian, since 1901), near the south coast, and the palace at Kato Zakro to the east.

Mallia, eighteen miles east of Knossos, proved, since its walls were stuccoed but not frescoed, to be a provincial palace, smaller and less elegant than Knossos, but very like it in general plan, with its complex of *insulae* grouped about a central court (Fig. 2.21). Its ancient name *may* have been Milatos, and it may have been the mother city of Miletus in Asia Minor. The French excavators found numbers of Minoan sherds at the first stroke of the pick: the site had not been inhabited since the catastrophe, perhaps the result of local rivalries, which overwhelmed it earlier than the other Cretan palaces, early in Late Minoan I, about 1600 B.C. Here, as at Knossos and, as we shall see, at Phaistos, the main entrance is on the west. Here it is in a recess protected by bastions. It opens into a narrow corridor, narrowed still further by a door at its east end, which connects with a wider north-south corridor with storerooms opening off it, as at Knossos. The thick buttressed walls of some of these were planned to bear the heavy weight of a story or more above. Bits of gold leaf were found in the storerooms, but clandestine diggers had long ago carried off nearly everything of intrinsic value. Potsherds remained, in which, as always, the history of the site could be read; and in the Domestic Quarter opening off the northwest side of the central court was found a stone votive ax splendidly worked into the shape of a leopard, the hide rendered with running spirals; and a bronze sword a yard long with a gold-plated hilt and rock crystal pommel, bearing in gold leaf on its underside a figure arching its back in acrobatics. A series of eight

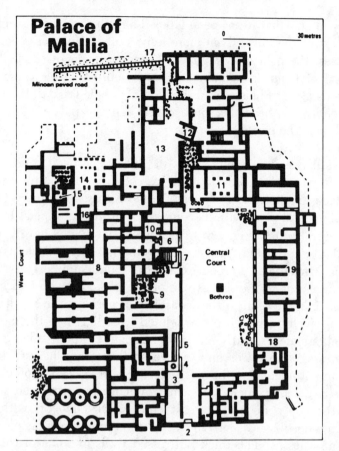

FIG. 2.21   Mallia, palace, plan. Note resemblances to Knossos; magazines (19), central court, pillar hall (11). 1, granaries; 2, main
entrance; 5, 7, staircases; 9, pillar crypt; 10, Hall of Leopard;
13, N. Court; 14, megaron; 15, lustral basin; 16, archives; 17,
n. entrance. (*Blue Guide, Greece*, London, 1977, p. 734. By
permission of E. Benn, Ltd.)

circular granaries was built in the southwest corner. In the
northwest quarter the rooms, grouped around their own
stucco-paved court, included a sunken lustral area like the
one adjoining the throne room at Knossos. In a room just
south of the court a number of clay tablets was found, in-

scribed in early Cretan hieroglyphic. Its signs recur at Knossos, and in the same grouping, which warrants the inference that the language used was the same in both places. Some Linear A was found, but no Linear B, which is Greek. The *insula* west and southwest of the stuccoed court was for artisans: one room had so many fragments of ivory in it that it may have been a workshop. The block south of this contained a potter's shop under the monumental stair. South of the stair the open, naturally well-lit vestibule facing on the central court is the largest room in the palace: it was perhaps the entrance to the rooms of state.

The central court had an altar in the center, and porticoes on its north and east sides, and possibly all the way round. Since dowel holes in the blocks between the columns show that this space was barricaded part way up, it may be that the court (and by inference those in other Cretan palaces) was used for the dangerous sport of bull-leaping, in which as we saw, acrobatic athletes vaulted between the horns of the bull, turned a somersault, and vaulted off over his tail, a feat that Spanish bull-fighters have declared impossible, but which is portrayed on Minoan frescoes and in ivory statuettes.

East of the central court are more storerooms, with low platforms in which oil-jars are set; channels led the overflow to collecting jars (*pithoi*) sunk in the floors. A seat in the northeast corner enabled a guard to keep watch over the stores. Measures and weights were found here, and traces of carbonized wheat and lentils. The pillared hall north of the central court was full of incense-burners: it was the crypt of an important room, perhaps a banqueting hall, above. The block north of this contained more storerooms, one of them a pantry, crammed with broken pottery, which could be pieced together. (It is a useful archaeological principle that where masses of sherds can be pieced together, they represent a deposit; where they cannot, they represent a dump.) The rooms in this block, too, are grouped around their own court. One of them contained two-part molds of imported stone, for bronze-casting. A paved causeway led up to another entrance, on the northwest.

The French have also dug trenches in the area round the palace, Mallia town, which, they calculate, would hold a population of 12,000, probably protected, uniquely, by a wall. Some fifty yards north of the palace, an open area, larger than the palace central court, may be the town marketplace or agora; opening onto it a hypostyle crypt has been interpreted as a meeting place for the town council, unique evidence for a bourgeoisie beside the palace aristocracy. West of this (in Area M) was found a hieroglyphic archive of Middle Minoan I and II, and the earliest sunken lustral basin yet found; nearby to the northeast a signet-seal workshop. In the rich necropolis 500 yards north of the palace, where the pottery shows the burials to be of the inhabitants of an earlier phase of the palace than the one described above, the chief find, from what may have been the royal burying ground, was a gold pendant (Middle Minoan I) whose motif (Fig. 2.22) is a pair of bees, wasps, or hornets, arched round a honey-cake, with a gold bead in a gold cage above. The jewel is soldered, and the granulated work is very fine. One of the villas has been restored as a small museum of Minoan daily life.

Another series of villas, excavated by the Greeks, published by the French, at Tylissos, eight miles west of Knossos, ranges in date from Early Minoan to Late Minoan III. All the villas showed similar ground plans. Among the finds were a bronze talent, three huge bronze cauldrons, one weighing 110 pounds, vases containing pigments (red and yellow ocher, copper oxide), Linear A tablets, tables of offering made of steatite, fine-toothed saws for work with ivory, and a cylinder seal, an import from Hittite Anatolia. The Tylissos villas were more elegant than those of Mallia town: some rooms were frescoed, with crocus and lily motifs. The Tylissos houses, together with Mallia palace and town, are of particular interest as showing that neither the palace

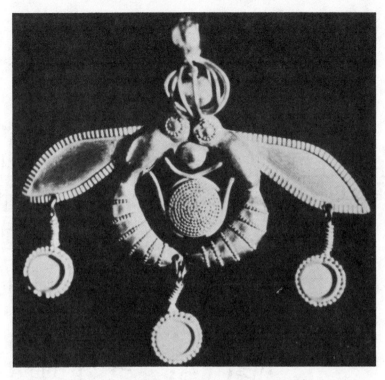

FIG. 2.22 Mallia, necropolis, gold bee pendant. Heraklion, Museum.

nor the domestic architecture of Knossos is unique; it is all part of a common Minoan architectural language, of which Mallia represents a provincial phase.

The best excavated and most interesting Minoan *town* is Gournia, near the coast, twenty-five miles southeast of Mallia. It was dug in 1901-03 under the direction of an American woman, Harriet Boyd Hawes, who compared its steep, stepped streets and crowded multistoried house blocks (Fig. 2.23) with Naples; it also presents analogies with Phylakopi III and with Dorion IV (Malthi). The palace (plan, G), is one-tenth the size of Knossos, and does not enclose a central court, as elsewhere; the court (H)

FIG. 2.23   Gournia, town plan. (Hawes, 1908, plan at back)

is rather the agora or market place of the whole town. This petty king kept his vassals at no greater distance than would a medieval lord. A vast quantity of weapons, tools (a carpenter's set of eight), eight potter's wheels, and utensils in bronze, stone, and clay gives a full and lively picture of the life of a minor Cretan city of the second half of the sixteenth century B.C. (Late Minoan IA); unwalled, it was destroyed about 1450 and reoccupied, probably by Mycenaeans; there is some reason to believe that toward the end Gournia was an important center for the production of an elegant pottery that rivaled the late "Palace Style" at Knossos.

Five kilometers southeast of Gournia lies Vasiliki, an agglutination of Early Minoan II to Middle Minoan II houses, which amounts in sum to a small palace, two-storied in some places.

Another major Cretan palace site is Phaistos, covering two acres, near the south coast, thirty-six difficult miles by road southwest of Knossos. The Italians under Luigi Pernier began to excavate it in May, 1900, as Evans was ending his first campaign at Knossos, but the final publication did not appear until 1951, and digging, under Doro Levi, continued to 1967. The 1960s were also a time of British activity at Knossos under Sinclair Hood and Mervyn Popham of the British School at Athens. The excavators of Phaistos claim it gives, because here restorations have not exceeded the evidence, a better and clearer idea than Knossos of a palace dating from the height of Minoan civilization. Reconstruction at Phaistos has been limited to rebuilding a few vertical walls to no great height, leaving a groove between the genuine Minoan stonework and the modern reconstruction; and roofing over a few rooms to preserve stratification, pavements, or artifacts left *in situ*. Clarity at Phaistos results from a fixed line of stratification between an earlier and a later palace, provided by a concrete-hard second-palace pavement laid down over the leveled remains of the first palace,

whose foundations had inadequate footings, so that an earthquake toppled it in Middle Minoan III, about 1700 B.C., to
judge by the pottery. This pavement (which incidentally
suggested to Pernier that the palace-dwellers went barefoot
indoors, oriental fashion) provides as clear a baseline as the
marks of the Persian fire of 480 B.C. on the Acropolis at
Athens, or the layer of Vesuvian ash over the Pompeii of
A.D. 79. Beneath this pavement the first palace stratum
averages about five feet thick; below that again, trial pits
have yielded over nine feet of sub-Neolithic and Neolithic
deposits with traces of huts, bones of boar, hare, and wild
goat, obsidian flakes, stone weapons and tools. The absolute
dating of Palace I depends indirectly on Egyptian artifacts.
None was found in the first palace level, but first-palace
pottery presents exact analogies with sherds found at nearby
sites in association with Egyptian scarabs and amulets of
the XIIth Dynasty (after 2000 B.C.). The synchronism is
clinched by imported pottery of the Phaistos first-palace type
found in a XIIth Dynasty stratum at Kahun in Egypt. In
both places archaeology has revealed this to be a period of
great prosperity and ambitious building.

Parts of the first palace were reused in the second. In
the first palace the excavators distinguished forty rooms,
including a shrine and sacrificial trench in the west court.
The façade projected farther west into the west court than
did the façade of the second palace, and the entrances were
less monumental, but otherwise the plans of the two were
much the same: the central court measuring 170 by 80
Minoan feet, was common to both. The most famous find
from the first palace is the Phaistos Disk, discovered in 1908
together with a number of Linear A tablets, in a Middle
Minoan IIIB context in the basement of an archives room at
the west end of the northeast block. It contains (Fig. 2.24)
forty-five different hieroglyphic symbols, impressed on both
faces with separate stamps like movable type, in a spiral
running from the outside in, with vertical word-dividers. The

FIG. 2.24 Phaistos disk. Heraklion, Museum. (Evans, *Scripta Minoa*, I, Pl. XII, by permission of Clarendon Press, Oxford)

Disk has never been deciphered. Its symbols include men standing or running, women and children, heads feather-crowned, like that of the Lily Prince at Knossos, fish, birds, insects, vases, shield, boughs, ships, tools, and parts of animals. Guesses as to its meaning include lists of soldiers, a hymn to the rain lord, an astronomical chart, the king speaking about the construction of the palace, and a genealogy, possibly in verse.

The plan of the second palace (Fig. 2.25) presents many analogies with Knossos, whose power may have reduced

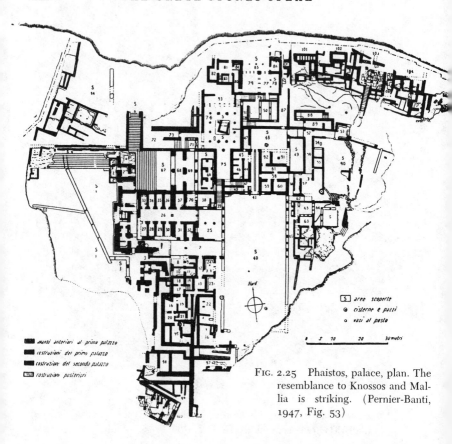

FIG. 2.25   Phaistos, palace, plan. The resemblance to Knossos and Mallia is striking. (Pernier-Banti, 1947, Fig. 53)

the lords of Phaistos to peaceful coexistence. It nearly equals in size the Palace of Minos; like it, it includes a "theatral area" (the steps in the northwest); west and central courts; *insulae,* functioning either as storerooms, or as living quarters, or as rooms of state. The west court is dominated on the north by a magnificent flight of steps with a wall at the back. If the area was used for bull-leaping, these steps were unsafe for spectators, and in any case would not hold many: in a posed excavation picture, fifty-three persons overcrowd them. We may suppose the spectators used the north terrace (94 in the plan) above, or the windows of the palace façade on the east of the court or the central court itself, which has a "mounting block" in its northeast corner. The main entrance to the palace was by a splendid fifty-foot-wide flight of steps, built convex, to shed water, or to make a figure parading up its center look taller; its blocks are up to nine feet long. It leads east, out of the northeast corner of the west court; the excavators describe it with pardonable pride as the most monumental thing in Minoan architecture. Across a broad landing at the top is a double propylon (monumental entrance), its outer portion supported by a single column, as at Pylos later. But the whole ambitious plan leads not to a great audience hall, as at Knossos (the Italians doubt Evans' reconstruction) but to a light well and a blank wall. (Beneath the light well is a labyrinthine store-room of Palace I.) Entrance to the rooms of state was not straightforward, as in later classical architecture, but by a devious, pure Minoan dog-leg corridor leading to the left out of the inner propylon and into a peristyle (74) with traces of an Early Minoan house in the middle, and lower levels going back to Neolithic times. Minoan dog-legs make possible (a) contrasts of light and shade, (b) checking visitors' credentials, (c) preventing influx of rioters. The whole palace is built on terraces, and this is the highest of them all, with a breath-taking view across the Geropotamos Valley to snow-capped Mt. Ida, the throne of Zeus, beyond, and, on its flank, the Kamares cave, from which the stunningly beautiful Middle Minoan pottery is named. The peristyle has an entrance, again divided by a single central column, from the south as well, whence a vestibule and a choice of stairs lead to the central court (40) below. North of the peristyle, six double-leaf doors opened into a lozenge-paved reception hall. North of this again, and not opening directly upon it, is a suite of isolated small rooms, with stuccoed walls painted with marine plants. The suite includes a sunken bath and latrine, reminiscent of the Queen's Megaron at Knossos. East of the peristyle, and deviously connected with it by a dog-leg stair, is another luxurious suite (50) with double porticoes and stuccoed walls painted with four-petal red rosettes within white disks. Particularly elegant pottery was found here. It is unlike the contemporary Palace Style at Knossos, and Luisa Banti, Pernier's immediate successor at Phaistos, thought it might come from a center at Gournia. South of this suite is a small open court (48), out of which opens a corridor (41) open to the sky (it has an open gutter down its middle), which leads to the central court. Looked at from the court, it is monumentally framed by half-columns (like the Treasury of Atreus at Mycenae), and frescoed niches. In the northwest corner of the central court is the platform that may have had something to do with bull-leaping. The porticoes on each of the long sides of the central court were supported by an alternation of pilasters and columns as at Mallia and, as there, may have been barricaded part way up to protect spectators of the dangerous sport. The southern end of the central court together with the whole southeastern corner of the palace has slipped into the ravine, but ruts in the surviving open space suggest that the court had a south entrance for wheeled traffic.

Near the northwest corner of the central court a vestibule (25) leads into a series of storerooms symmetrically ópening on a central corridor. Their thick walls suggest a story above, with a room of state like the one over the crypt at Mallia. One of the storerooms (33) contains storage jars so tall a terracotta stool was needed for peering into them. They once contained the tribute, in oil, wine, or grain, of the vassals of the prince of Phaistos. The southwest block must have contained living quarters, perhaps for guests: it has at least two sunken baths (19, 21). A later building in the extreme southwest, differently oriented, is an archaic Greek temple, dedicated, as we know from an inscription, to Rhea, a fertility goddess lineally descended from the Cretan Mother Goddess herself, a nature goddess, Mistress of Animals, fostering fertility. Her statuettes, sometimes in ivory and gold, represent her in a high tiara, a bodice revealing her breasts, and a flounced skirt, with snakes coiled around her.

The palace area east of the central court contained more living quarters, perhaps for the heir-apparent: they are intermediate in elegance between the crowded rooms on the southwest and the sumptuous suites on the north. There is a sunken "lustral area" (63) in which the excavators found nine bronze double axes, handsome vases, and "horns of consecration"; a latrine adjoins. This suite opens eastward onto an L-shaped portico strongly reminiscent of the portico on the east of the Domestic Quarter at Knossos. It, too, enjoys an extensive view, across the rich plain of the Mesará. North of this is an industrial quarter, centering on a trapezoidal court (90) with a smelting furnace in the middle: slag was found in it. A gatehouse, differently oriented, marks a northeast entrance. From it a flight of steps led down to the dependent houses in one of which (101) the Disk was found. Like the other Cretan palaces, the second palace at Phaistos was destroyed all at once in Late Minoan Ib by a surprise raid, as vases found on floors all over the palace and lamps *in situ* show.

What was destroyed embraced altogether 104 rooms, grouped into *insulae* differentiated in function. The architectonic aim is not grandiosity, as in Egypt, or subordination to a central megaron, as at Mycenae or Tiryns, but variety of line and color, achieved by façades with setbacks, terraces and flat roofs of various heights, the play of light and shadow on white gypsum stucco, blue-gray local stone, red cypress beams and columns; the alternation of light and darkness in propylons, light wells, peristyles, porticoes, and open courts of various shapes and sizes. If color is the key at Knossos, line is the key at Phaistos. To many modern tastes its cool restraint will seem preferable to the baroque extravagance of Evans' restorations.

A pleasant two-mile walk west of Phaistos, reached by ford-

ing the Geropotamos, is the sumptuous and elegant villa of
Hagia Triada, perhaps the summer home of the lords of Phaistos. Pottery dates it contemporary with or slightly later than
the second palace, and it was destroyed at the same time,
though a megaron-shaped room (9 on the plan, Fig. 2.26)
show that it was reoccupied by the Mycenaean invaders.
In post-Mycenaean times it was not in use (whereas
the archaic temple shows the Phaistos palace was), and
therefore it is richer in frescoes, tablets (150 in Linear A
were published in 1945),* seals, gems, bronze (including
nineteen hide-shaped copper ingots from Cyprus, each
weighing a talent: were they innovations of the Mycenaean
invaders?), and such rarities as the famous painted sarcophagus. Though it was excavated in 1903-05 and 1910-14,
the final publication has not yet appeared. Its L-shape anti-

---

* Since Hagia Triada has supplied the largest number of Linear A tablets
yet found, the Swede Arne Furumark has been emboldened to try to
decipher them (in a Berlin lecture of 1956). The tablets, like Linear B, are
inventories, under headings, by categories, totaled. Though the ideograms
are often different from those of Linear B, those for men, looms, textiles,
vases, tripods, axes, grains, figs, honey, wine, fish, and miscellaneous tools and
equipment are clear. The signs for whole numbers closely resemble Linear B;
those for fractions are different, but their interpretation is still in doubt. The
categories of words dealt with are place names, personal names (individuals
and groups), commodities, and vocabulary words. Furumark distinguished
categories by a method of exclusion; e.g., headings with subheadings in fractions cannot refer to persons. Like Miss Kober, he used spelling variants to
detect what signs are closely related. He claims to have distinguished gender,
vowels, and syllables, and, without using Linear B, to have established that
the nineteen signs in Linear A identical in form with Linear B are identical
also in sound. On this basis he sets up a grid, and offers decipherments of
place names corresponding to known sites; e.g., Alasija (Cyprus), Samos,
and Kydonia, Dikte, and Sitia in Crete; commodities (coriander, sesame,
figs), and words corresponding to those used in Linear B for deficit, total,
grand total, and "warehoused." The place names and an alleged third person
singular verb ending in -ti point, he claims, to an Anatolian origin for the
language: he apparently thinks, though he does not say, that Linear A's
affinities are with Luvian, an Anatolian Indo-European language. A rival
attempt at decipherment, by the American Cyrus Gordon, concludes that
Linear A is a Semitic language. Both cannot be right, so the question remains
open, and other large finds of Linear A tablets have not settled the matter.
Only 500 are so far known, though they come from 27 different sites.

cipates the fortified palace or villa at Gla. Its northwest corner presents the same combination of propylon, airy main room, and L-shaped portico that we have seen in the Domestic Quarter at Knossos and in the eastern *insula* at Phaistos; this time the view is of the sea. East of the propylon, behind a room lined (as sometimes at Phaistos) with benches whose risers bear a triple groove like the triglyphs of classical Greek temples, is a small room with a raised slab which, spread with animal skins, would make a bed. North of the proplyon is an elegant room frescoed with a fine naturalistic cat stalking a pheasant. South of this block, and in the north wing, are pantries and storerooms; beyond them on the east another small but elegant signorial suite. To the south is a

Fig. 2.26   Hagia Triada, villa plan. 1, Mycenaean shrine; 3-7, sig-norial suite; 10, room with benches; 12, room with cat frescoes; 16, treasury, with ingots; 20, porticoed market. (*Blue Guide, Greece*, p. 726)

paved courtyard. Opening on it at the northeast, and independently oriented, is a Mycenaean shrine paved with stucco painted with marine scenes like those at Pylos and Tiryns. To the north is a Minoan village, rebuilt in Mycenaean times with a porticoed and perhaps awninged market anticipating Hellenistic plans, and Trajan's market of a millennium and a half later in Rome. About 150 yards north of the village is a necropolis, where in a stone-lined trench was found the famous painted limestone sarcophagus, in a context with Late Minoan III sherds, and perhaps dating from the Mycenaean occupation. It portrays (Fig. 2.27) a cult of the dead, in which the double axes are Minoan, the offering of a curve-prowed boat Egyptian, and the deified deceased rising from the tomb at the right, Mycenaean. A lyre-player like one on the sarcophagus appears on the Pylos fresco, Fig. 2.13a. This pomp and circumstance, this heroizing of the great dead, has more in common with the implications of a Mycenaean bee-hive tomb than with the comparative simplicity of a Minoan burial; the inference is that we are faced with a Minoan artist's attempt to cope with portraying the strange funeral cult practices of his new Mycenaean masters. Recent excavation at Gephyra, near Tanagra, thirty-eight miles northwest of Athens, has revealed a number of other sarcophagi (called *larnakes*), whose scenes of mourning women (as on the Warrior Vase), chariots, and bull-leaping show a mixture of Mycenaean and Minoan motifs.

David Hogarth, excavating in east Crete in 1900, missed by a few yards a fourth palace, the only one unrobbed, at Kato Zakro, which Nicholas Platon, partly subsidized by the American Leon Pomerance, discovered in 1961. Its central court, which contains an altar, measures 40 by 100 Minoan feet; its overall dimensions are over 7,000 square yards. Its state dining room (Fig. 2.28, 1), had paneled floors and spiral-frescoed walls. The royal apartments (14-15), on the east, open on a circular, originally roofed swimming pool 23

FIG. 2.27 Hagia Triada, sarcophagus, *ca.* 1400 B.C. Heraklion, Museum. (Pernier, *Monumenti Antichi* 19, Pl. I)

feet in diameter. The east block, with its state apartments
(2-4), one of which yielded eight wine jugs and ten amphoras,
its shrine (6), archive (7), and treasury (8), shows how
God, Mammon, and art were linked in Minoan palaces. A
rhyton shows a peak-sanctuary with goats bounding about;
the archive held Linear A tablets in boxes whose hinges survive; in the treasury were six 65-pound copper ingots from
Cyprus, four elephant tusks from Syria, and a rock crystal
rhyton now in the Heraklion Museum, put together from 300
pieces. Here, as at Knossos, elaborate plumbing was provided.
The goods were under the control of the king in Knossos or
his viceroy here; here, as at Knossos, some piers bear double-

Fig. 2.28   Kato Zakro, palace, plan. (S. Hood, *Minoans*, London,
1971, p. 66. By permission of Thames and Hudson, Ltd.)

ax masons' marks. The road net, centered on Knossos, shows centralization of a trading empire prospering from the export of stone and clay vases and purple-dyed cloth. The prosperous Kato Zakro complex was destroyed about 1450 B.C., possibly by an eruption on the Island of Thera 75 miles to the northwest, volcanic lumps from which were found on the site. Saws found in the state apartments show that these rooms were under construction as the catastrophe struck.

Controversy rages as to whether the catastrophe which overwhelmed most Cretan sites (except Knossos) about 1450 B.C. was due to Mycenaean invasion, natural causes, or foreign invaders taking advantage of natural causes. The most devastating natural disaster recorded for the period was the volcanic eruption on Thera. Since 1962, excavation at Akrotiri, seven airline miles southwest of the island's capital, Phira, has revealed the buildings of a large town, with one- or two-storied houses and richly frescoed walls. It flourished about 1550 B.C., was destroyed by an earthquake about 1500, reoccupied, and finally overwhelmed a few months later by an eruption which deposited thirteen feet of pumice upon it. Cretan pottery and Linear A writing identify the place as a Minoan colony. A gap of about fifty years between destruction here and on Crete is best explained by the hypothesis of invaders taking advantage of the natural disaster to take over the island, from a base at Knossos.

The Akrotiri frescoes are rich and varied: the themes include dolphins (as in the Queen's Megaron at Knossos, and at Phylakopi), swallows, lilies, blue monkeys (as at Knossos) robbing an orchard, a fisherman (as at Phylakopi) with his catch, naked, bejeweled, and bewigged boys boxing (Fig. 2.29), a bare-breasted woman, and a long narrative piece depicting a sea expedition, with seven pentekonters, including a full-dressed flagship, making for an expectant (not fearful) city—Akrotiri—with multistoried houses and a circuit

FIG. 2.29   Akrotiri, boy boxers, fresco. (C. Doumas, ed., *Thera and the Aegean World*, London, 1976, Pl. F)

wall bearing horns of consecration. Presumably the house with this fresco on its walls belonged to the admiral. One interpreter sees a joint expedition: Mycenaean officers, Minoan crew; another sees Therans.

The archaeological sites and finds described in this chapter, at Troy and on the mainland, in the Cyclades and on Crete, are our main historical documents for a span of time as long as from the coronation of Charlemagne in 800 to Shakespeare's birth in 1564, or from Magna Carta (1215) to our own day. It all adds up to a coherent picture of the material, social, religious, artistic, and intellectual life of the Aegean peoples of 1900-1125 B.C., upon whose cultural heritage the classical Greeks drew. Knossian frescoes reveal the small, wiry, brunette Minoan physical type; Mycenaean gold masks show the broad-faced, mustachioed men whose descendants fought at Troy. Tombs, frescoes, and tablets make clear the richly colored dress and costly gold adornment of the ruling classes. Storerooms, shaft graves, and again the invaluable tablets make real for us the inlaid bronze swords and daggers, the boars' tusk helmets, the scabbards in gold-appliqué of these ancient warriors. Patient, intelligent excavation has fixed the ground plans of palace, villa, citadel wall, and town. For social life our most valuable evidence comes from the tablets and the pottery, though the tombs, too, betray the wide cleavage between classes. The tablets show that the government was monarchical, with a literate bureaucracy; that the division of labor was sophisticated, with many luxury trades; imported pottery shows the extent of international trade relations, between mainland and Cyclades, between both and Crete, Egypt, and Anatolia. As to religious life, the frescoes supply evidence of anthropomorphism; games such as bull-leaping are connected with cult, and double axes and horns of consecration found in Cretan palaces suggest fetishism, being inanimate objects obviously regarded with awe as containing a potent spirit or magical powers. The Hagia Triada sarcophagus and the tholos tombs suggest among the Mycenaeans if not a cult of the hero dead, at least a solicitude for his welfare on his journey to the other world. Names of gods and goddesses on the tablets show that classical Greek religion and mythology had Mycenaean origins. A highly developed artistic sense is amply revealed by the frescoes, statuettes, goldwork, gems, seals, and painted pottery; Minoan art and architecture is clearly the work of a "wild, irregular, venturesome, colorful" people. While recognizing Minoan charm, we ought also to give the Mycenaeans their due; their culture was, at its best, "adventurous, clean, spare, emblematic and poetic," as Emily Vermeule has so well said. The decipherment of Linear B has revealed literacy. Only poetry is lacking; it must have been oral or recorded on perishable materials. Archaeology and the tablets make clear that the first great Greek poet, Homer, when he began to compose in the ninth or early eighth century B.C., drew upon Mycenaean memories; but between him and the great towns and palaces of the Mycenaean-Minoan world stretches the great blank—blank partly because they yield little to the excavator—of the Greek Dark Ages. The Dorian invasion brought that darkness; from that invasion the only major city that escaped was Athens.

3

Mycenaean Athens, the Dorian Invasion, Protogeometric, Geometric

(1250-700 B.C.)

The story of prehistoric Athens, as archaeology reveals it, has been postponed to this point in order to treat it as a unit. Italian excavations on the south slope of the Acropolis and American on the northwest slope have revealed Neolithic pottery and a Neolithic house, and there is evidence that Athens has been continuously inhabited since the fourth millennium B.C. Unfortunately, investigation of the Acropolis itself was undertaken before the era of scientific archaeology, so that basketfuls of precious prehistoric sherds were unexamined; and classical buildings effaced earlier ones, but enough remained to make certain that Athens, like Mycenae, Tiryns, and Pylos, was a fortified citadel in Mycenaean times. The palace (Fig. 3.1) lay south of the classical Erechtheum; a ground plan with megaron and forecourt, as at Mycenae, Tiryns, and Pylos, is most likely.

The first clear light thrown upon Mycenaean Athens resulted from the Swedish-American Oscar Broneer's excavations in the 'thirties on the north slope of the Acropolis.

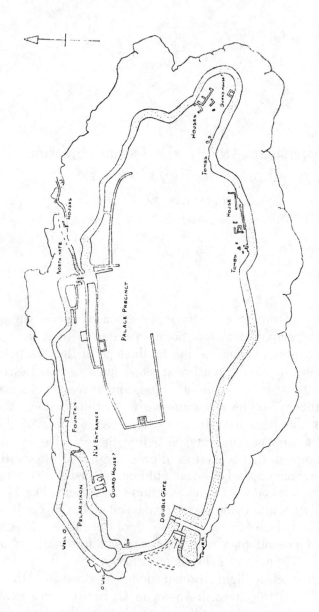

FIG. 3.1 Athens, Acropolis, thirteenth- and twelfth-century state, showing Mycenaean palace precinct. (Reprinted from *The Greek Bronze Age* by Emily T. Vermeule by permission of The University of Chicago Press © the University of Chicago)

His intent at the start was to illuminate the classical cult of Eros and Aphrodite, a spring fertility festival in which the goddess' statue was ritually washed and her sacred bird, the dove, sacrificed. Broneer located the cult sanctuary by spotting two hitherto unnoticed inscriptions carved in the rock, but when he had removed the dump, sometimes more than three meters deep, from nineteenth century excavations of the Acropolis, he found, nearby, traces of a stair leading down from a postern gate defended by towers (Fig. 3.2). This discovery was interesting in itself, but Broneer was able to fit it fascinatingly into prehistory because he could identify and date the potsherds he found in association with it. They were of a pattern well known in Mycenae, called Mycenaean IIIB, and datable 1300-1225 B.C. From the postern a stair (wrongly shown in Fig. 3.2 as

FIG. 3.2   Athens, Acropolis, Mycenaean postern and tower, restoration drawing. (Holland, 1924, p. 147)

a path) led down; it was abandoned before the end of the Mycenaean period (potsherds again), and houses built over it. These in turn were abandoned, and in a hurry, for Broneer found coarse household pottery scattered over the floors. But there was no burnt layer, and the pottery goes on without a break. What historical inferences are warranted? Surely that within the seventy-five years covered by the pottery the postern was abandoned (for a reason which will emerge in the sequel) and covered over by squatters' houses ("squatters," because their pottery is so poor), which in turn were hastily deserted, surely in the face of a threat of invasion, presumably of the Dorians. Athenian history proudly recorded that the Athenians successfully stood the Dorians off, and Broneer's excavations have proved the truth of the boast. Their mythical king Codrus, who sacrificed himself for victory, would fit into twelfth-century history. They could thank good planning more than luck: the "Pelasgic" wall of the Acropolis yielded sherds that matched Broneer's, and when the little Nike temple that flanks the Propylaea (the present west approach to the Acropolis) was dismantled for rebuilding in 1936, the bastion on which it stands revealed, under archaic and fifth-century phases, a "Pelasgian" core, again dated by potsherds to the same period as the rest of the wall and Broneer's postern. So the whole of the Acropolis defenses were strengthened at the same time and against the threat of the Dorian invasion. (The date matches that assigned in the traditional Athenian genealogies to Theseus, the Attic Heracles, whose heroic exploits included the voyage to Crete and the slaying of the Minotaur.)

But the tale of Broneer's exciting discoveries is not yet all told. Once some modern squatters' houses were demolished in 1937-38, he was able to return to work on the north slope. Re-exploring an underground passage west of the Erechtheum, which had been known since 1897, he discovered a stairway (Fig. 3.3) leading down, seven flights through a cleft in the rock, to a fountain 130 feet

Fig. 3.3   Athens, Acropolis, north slope, stair to Mycenaean fountain, restoration drawing of flights III-V. (Broneer, 1939, p.
338)

below. He was at once struck by the parallel with the
underground stair that gave access to a water supply at
Mycenae, and to the stairs protected by the west bastion
at Tiryns. And sure enough the sherds, this time Mycenaean IIIc (after 1210 B.C.), proved the staircase to be of
Mycenaean date; presumably it was after this staircase
was constructed that the earlier postern was abandoned.
That it was an emergency measure is proved by the fact
that it was built partly of wood, which in the damp cleft
in the rock would hardly last more than twenty-five years
unmended, and when this portion collapsed it was left
where it fell. When the Dorian menace was past, the
Athenians could get their water more simply and openly.
The pottery is all of one style: the period of the stair's

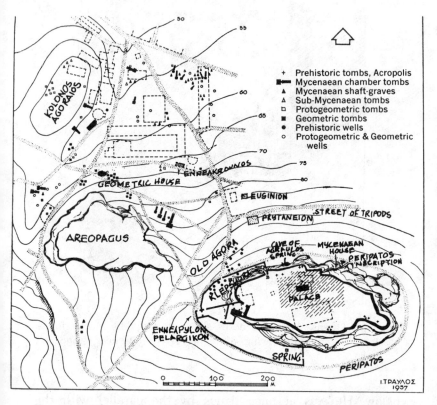

Fig. 3.4   Athens, plan of prehistoric finds. The chamber-tomb under
the temple of Ares is between the 50- and 55-meter contours;
the oval between contours 65 and 70 is the Geometric House;
the "Princess" Tomb is the largest south of the 80-meter contour.
The Acropolis (lower right) shows in black the palace and the
Mycenaean bastion under the Nike temple. Broneer's stair led
to the spring marked by arrow in the middle of the Acropolis
north slope; the right-hand arrow marks the squatters' houses
over the postern stair. (after Travlos, 1960, p. 23)

construction and abandonment was so short that the pottery style did not have time to change.

The American excavations in and around the Athenian
Agora or market place have hit upon enough burials (Fig.
3.4) to prove that the area was a cemetery in Mycenaean

and Sub-Mycenaean times. One of the richest of these is a chamber tomb discovered under the Temple of Ares in 1951. It contained fourteen to sixteen interments, and the accompanying pottery shows that the tomb was in use from 1450 to after 1200; the later burials, here and elsewhere in the Agora, containing the uninspired plain-banded Sub-Mycenaean and Protogeometric pottery, tell the same story as Broneer's staircase: Athens survived the Dorian invasion without a cultural break. A rich chamber tomb on the north slope of the Areopagus contained an ivory box carved with deer and griffins; at least 100 gold ornaments; fine Mycenaean IIIB pottery; and a bronze ladle, mirror, and hairpins. Clearly its occupant was a woman, perhaps royal, to judge by the gold; perhaps she had lived in the palace on the Acropolis in the generation before the Dorians came: some excavators call her final resting place the Princess Tomb. Her dog was buried with a large beef bone within sniffing distance.

For twelfth-century Athens the archaeological evidence is slight indeed: only enough to prove that the Athenians hung on through troubled times. (The excellent volume in the Agora final reports devoted to the Mycenaean age distinguishes six phases: [1] the shaft grave period; [2] the Early Palace; [3] the peak period, 1450-1380; [4] a period of overseas commercial expansion, 1380-1240/30; [5] retrenchment, with elaborate walls (1250-1200); [6] a period of regional styles, contemporary with the legendary King Codrus.) The date when the evidence begins to be copious again, about 1100, is the date ascribed by Greek historical tradition to the Dorian invasion. How can this date be reconciled with Broneer's archaeological evidence, which dates the passage of the Dorians a century earlier? The answer may be that the Dorians came not in a single assault but in a series of waves. Herodotus supplies a clue with his story of Hyllos son of Heracles (another name for the Dorian invasion is the Return of the Sons of Heracles) who fell in a duel at the Isthmus of Corinth, after which his men promised not to return for three generations. This story shows that the ancient Greeks were at least as aware as any modern archaeologist that the Dorian invasion took time. Where it passed, the evidence is cist tombs and single burials, at Vergina, *Iolkos,* Lefkandi on Euboea, Orchomenos, Thebes, *Athens,* Perati, *Salamis,* Mycenae, *Argos,* Tiryns, *Asine,* Skyros, Kameiros on Rhodes, and Olous (the port of Dreros) in Crete. The tombs are especially numerous at the italicized places. The invention to fill the gap masks a historical fact: the unrest caused by these migrations of Greek-speaking clansmen from the northwest lasted a hundred years. The traditional date of the invasion marks the end of that time of trouble. And Broneer in 1957 found a towered fortification wall at the Isthmus with Mycenaean pottery dated 1250-1200 in the fill, which proves that it was not the Athenians alone who put up a fight against the invader. But Athens was bypassed; the Peloponnese beyond the Isthmus bore in the end the full brunt. Tiryns, Pylos, and finally Mycenae fell. The invaders swept on, into the south Aegean islands, southwest Asia Minor, and Crete. Wherever they established themselves, the language in historical times was Doric—Greek with a broad *a.* Meanwhile, Athens survived to become a haven, according to tradition, for refugees, especially from Pylos.

The archaeological evidence for this was provided by German excavations (1927-1938) in the cemetery in the Ceramicus, the ancient Potters' Quarter of Athens, where three roads diverged: one to the port of the Piraeus; a second, the Sacred Way westward to Demeter's holy city of Eleusis; and a third, the road to the grove of Akademe, which Plato was to make famous. This cemetery yielded an uninterrupted 500-year sequence of pottery. The graves that concern us were found in clearing between and under the foundations of the Pompeion, a building in which gear used in processions and festivals was stored between

times. Under and around this building the Germans excavated 108 graves, laid out in eleven uneven rows, and cut
as deep as a man can shovel. They judged by the homogeneous pottery that these particular graves all belonged
to one epoch, but the diverse groupings of the graves
suggest that they span at least fifty years. They were
poorly furnished, usually with nothing but an oil flask,
a pitcher, and a cup. But the interesting thing is the style
of the pottery and what can be deduced from it. One group
resembles the Close Style at Mycenae, so-called because
of its close-packed, complicated patterns. In the Ceramicus
ware (Fig. 3.5) this is reduced to freehand concentric
semicircles on the shoulder, and broad and narrow bands,
or wavy lines between bands, on the belly of the jar. The
Germans named this pottery Sub-Mycenaean. With it were
found long bronze shoulder pins, and *fibulae* (safety pins)
used to fasten a kind of dress new to the Greek world, the
Doric peplos, a square of woollen cloth folded around the
body and pinned at the shoulder. There were also a few
rings of iron, which in this use and at this date (*ca.* 1125-
1075 B.C.) must still be a precious metal. No weapons at
all were found in association with this pottery, but in three
cases the pottery was found not in inhumation graves but
in cremation burials. Other such mixed burials, found on
Salamis with Sub-Mycenaean pottery, and in a cemetery
at Perati in Attica in association with Egyptian scarabs of
the XIXth Dynasty, prove that cremation was beginning
to be introduced into Attica, and carry it back perhaps as
early as 1237 B.C. The inference is that the Ceramicus
graves belonged to a people with unbroken Mycenaean
connections (on the evidence of the pottery), under some
Dorian influence (on the evidence of the pins), in an age
of transition (on the evidence of the new fashion of cre-
mating the dead). The excavators see in the pottery the
last echo of courtly Mycenaean art; in the potters, refugees
from the Dorian terror that ran rampant in the Peloponnese

FIG. 3.5 Athens, Ceramicus, Sub-Mycenaean pottery. Note crude freehand design. Ceramicus, Museum. (Karo, *An Attic Cemetery*, Pl. 5)

after the middle of the twelfth century B.C. Surely not the potters alone came; there must have been some survivors among farmers, ex-landed proprietors, and leading members of noble clans; perhaps it is their graves that turn up in the Attic countryside, where many Mycenaean and Sub-Mycenaean sites are known (Fig. 3.6). Special mention should be made of (a) a newly discovered Early Helladic town, Askitario, at Raphina, where twenty-eight rooms on an acropolis, and a cemetery have been excavated; (b) a tholos tomb at Marathon, with the skeletons of a pair of sacrificed horses at the entrance. Cremation does not necessarily indicate an intrusive race of invaders: the Achaeans, who buried their dead at home, cremated them before the walls of Troy; cremation is a logical way to dispose of the bodies of persons dying in far places.

But Sub-Mycenaean is not the only new style of pottery the Germans discovered in the Ceramicus. Seven of the graves contained a severe abstract ware (Fig. 3.7), decorated with compass-drawn circles and semicircles, crosshatching, and lozenges between bands—a throwback to the old-fashioned designs, Middle Helladic and earlier, which we saw at Orchomenos, Eutresis, and Dimini. All these pots—the Germans named them Protogeometric— came from cremation burials, all were associated with iron *fibulae* and iron weapons, the latter perhaps an index not so much to change of race as to troubled times. Protogeometric ware ushers in the Iron Age in Athens, the age when, as the old Boeotian poet Hesiod was to write 200 years later, "never will men cease from toil and misery by day and night as they plunge to their ruin. . . . No reverence for the man who keeps his oath. . . . Right shall rest in the power of the hand; there will be no sense of honor." Grim enough the beginning of the Iron Age was in the rest of Greece: almost no buildings survive from the period, and the grave-gifts are pathetically poor. But Athens, bypassed by the Dorians, did not suffer complete

Iron Age depression: the pottery actually shows a technique improved over Sub-Mycenaean. And there was no violent transition from bronze to iron: Sub-Mycenaean and Proto-

Fig. 3.6 Attica, prehistoric sites. Over 100 are known. (Travlos, 1960, p. 17, by permission)

geometric pottery are occasionally found in the same Ceramicus grave.

The distinguishing mark of Protogeometric pottery is the compass-drawn circle. Freehand skill was a Cretan talent, imitated in Mycenae; with the fall of Mycenae, invention

FIG. 3.7   Athens, Ceramicus, Protogeometric vases. Note characteristic compass-drawn circles. Ceramicus, Museum. Karo, *op. cit.*, Pl. 6)

faltered, and mainland potters went back to the age-old geometric tradition, which had been kept alive by farm families in home weaving, leatherwork, wood carving, and basketry. This old tradition probably revived when the centers of courtly life and art were destroyed. With the battles, raids, and displacement of persons that followed their fall, pottery deteriorated sharply. But the improved techniques of Protogeometric ware, about 1075 B.C., mark the gradual return of peace and prosperity. This is especially marked in a strong, fortified, urban community such as Athens, where the genealogies of the kings are unbroken. But the new pottery probably symbolizes some profound inner change in Athens. The traditional date of the shift from kings to aristocratic archons matches the date of the shift from Sub-Mycenaean to Protogeometric pottery in the Ceramicus cemetery. Later Protogeometric—late tenth century—is reported from Nea Ionia, some four miles northwest of Athens. According to tradition, the father of Codrus, the last king of Athens, came from Pylos. The father's name, Neleus, appears in the genealogy of Nestor of Pylos, which also includes such famous mythological characters as Ion, Amphiaraos, Alcmaeon, Jason, Codrus, Minyas, and Orchomenos. Blegen's date for the sack of the Pylos palace makes the synchronism possible, but does not quite prove the connection. Codrus allegedly sacrificed himself to save Athens from the Dorian invasion. His younger sons supposedly led a migration to Ionian Asia Minor. Ionian Protogeometric pottery is enough like Athenian to prove a cultural connection, but scholars disagree as to which way it ran. From King Codrus' eldest son, Medon, some famous Athenian philosopher-statesmen traced their descent: Solon, the tyrant Pisistratus—whose name also occurs in the genealogy of Pylos—and Plato.

The earliest wells in the Agora yielded so much Protogeometric pottery that it may be used as evidence for a marked increase in population. But this was not predominantly a new race. The Germans measured the skulls from the Ceramicus, and in 1939 reported their findings objectively. The skulls of Mediterranean type outnumbered the Nordic in a proportion of three to two. Though cremation skews the evidence, a 1945 American study of over 100 skulls, from the Ceramicus, the Athenian Agora, and elsewhere in Attica, concludes that it is a process of biological blending, rather than dominance by any single racial type, which produced the greatness of Athenian civilization. Athens, like America, was a melting pot, and this may have been one of the sources of her strength, as it is of ours.

When the Dorians finally overthrew Mycenae, they destroyed, if not a great empire, at least prosperous commercial connections with the Near East. Late Mycenaean pottery has been found at over fifty sites on the Asia Minor coast; on the island of Kea, fifteen miles off the east coast of Attica; on Rhodes and Cyprus, in Syria and Egypt, and in a dozen more sites in South Italy and Sicily. On the island of Kea, in August, 1961, the first life-size Mycenaean (fifteenth to twelfth centuries B.C.) terracotta statuary was found. It represents priestesses of the Mother Goddess. American excavation here since, at Hagia Irini, has proved that Kea was a Minoan colony, with a frescoed Great House of thirty rooms, with stairs to a second story; a circuit wall, a stair to a well, and a kiln containing over 1,000 conical cups. Destroyed by an earthquake in the 1400s, the town was rebuilt, under Mycenaean auspices.

The latest phase of Phylakopi on Melos is entirely Mycenaean, and at Miletus, on the Asia Minor coast, evidence for Mycenaean settlements, superseding a Minoan colony, goes back to 1500 B.C.: there are three settlement strata, separated by destruction layers; the fourteenth-century settlement had a circuit wall with gates and tower. At Iasos, farther south, a Mycenaean (Milesian) settlement also succeeded a Minoan colony. At Ialysos on Rhodes the Italians excavated a settlement whose lowest levels (sixteenth century B.C.) show exclusively Minoan pottery. With the fall of Knossos Minoan pottery at Ialysos ceases, to be superseded by Mycenaean (the cemetery shows mixed cremation and inhumation, as at Kos, and Perati in Attica, where the latest Mycenaean phase is dated 1190-1075), but Ialysos was suddenly and inexplicably deserted before the end of the fifteenth century, leaving pottery scattered on the floors. Another example is Enkomi on Cyprus, an island whose copper made it a center of trade and an object of cupidity throughout the Aegean world. At the earliest settlement level (*ca.* 1600 B.C.) the pottery, unearthed by French excavations, is entirely Cypriote; after 1450 (while the Mycenaeans were ruling in Knossos) Mycenaean pottery begins; this is the date of the House of Bronzes, so richly furnished that it must have belonged to a ruler, perhaps the Mycenaean governor; its riches were protected by a massive towered circuit wall. This phase was destroyed by an earthquake (1375-65 B.C.), then rebuilt, to prosper to the end of the Mycenaean period. The evidence of prosperity comes from rich tombs, one of which contained gold-leaf diadems, toe-rings, and forty-five large gold Mycenaean necklaces. Another yielded two gold pectorals (cf. *Mute Stones Speak,* Fig. 2.20) and a gold cup decorated with bulls—like the one from Dendra, p. 74, in the technique called niello, which involves engraving, lining with black, and granulating with gold. Then, in the late thirteenth century, Enkomi was again destroyed, rebuilt by Achaean colonists, and then laid waste once more, perhaps by the "Peoples of the Sea" who are a part of the same phenomenon as the Dorian invasion; but it rose again, this time with a towered wall and streets in a grid pattern. In this phase its weapons are iron and its pottery is Sub-Mycenaean. This might suggest that the invaders passed on, and that its new settlers were Mycenaean refugees from the mainland, but the contents of Mycenaean tombs were impiously * tossed out when

---

* Perhaps not so impiously or cavalierly: once the deceased had reached the underworld, his skeleton could be pushed aside without hardheartedness.

the tombs were reused, and the pottery is clumsy imitation. The excavator sees here an example of the contamination of a Bronze Age culture by a foreign element, or, to put it another way, an early example of captive Greece taking captive her fierce conqueror, but the evidence is equivocal, and, on balance, the hypothesis of a Mycenaean refugee settlement has a slight edge, especially if we take into account legends that Cypriote Salamis, Paphos, and Lapithos were founded by heroes returning from the Trojan War. From Tomba tou Skirou, at Morphou, near the coast west of Nicosia, the excavator reports only one Mycenaean sherd. Minoan influence is strong enough to justify the generalization that Mycenaean links with the eastern Mediterranean were pioneered by Minoans. At Kition, underlying Larnaca on the southeast coast, are sacred areas with five large temples and sacred gardens. Adjoining copper smelting workshops show how religion controlled metallurgy. (In the tomb under the Temple of Ares at Athens, later burials treat earlier ones cavalierly* without any change of race, while poor pottery is just as likely to imply poor Mycenaean potters as imitative foreign ones.) The best argument for the Mycenaean refugee hypothesis is that here, as perhaps nowhere else in the Aegean, literacy survived: two clay tablets in a Cypriote linear script have been found here, in a disturbed level that is dated *ca.* 1225, but the tablets might be later. One of them has allegedly been deciphered as Cypriote Greek, referring to a boundary dispute, but since another attempt makes it into poetry about Jason and Medea, we may safely say that the Cypro-Mycenaean script is still a mystery; it shows signs of "suffixation," and is possibly related to Hurrian, whose speakers lived in northern Syria. The conservative Cypriotes, always mercifully spared any catastrophic change, continued to use a Bronze Age syllabary, different from their linear script, and decipherable as Greek, until

* See footnote, p. 144.

after the rest of the Greek world had adopted the Phoenician alphabet. The Cypriote dialect is related to Arcadian; mountainous, landlocked Arcadia in the central Peloponnesus must have been one of the places where the Mycenaeans took refuge from the Dorians, and some Mycenaeans almost certainly migrated to Cyprus. A horned god or worshiper twenty inches high, from a twelfth-century shrine in Énkomi, is held by some to be related to a horned Apollo worshiped in Arcadia, by others to have been locally made under Aegean influence.

Greek historical tradition recorded that refugees from Pylos became kings of Athens, and that in the sixth generation after the fall of Troy one of the princes of the royal house led a band of settlers to Asia Minor, the so-called "Ionian migration." Taking Blegen's date for the fall of Troy VIIA, and figuring three generations to a century, we may place the date of the migration somewhat before 1000 B.C. What can archaeology do to confirm or deny the tradition? Very little deep-level excavation has been done along the Asia Minor coast, but excavations on the island of Kos in 1940-41 revealed Protogeometric tombs in unbroken association with a Mycenaean settlement; tombs at Assarlik in Caria as long ago as 1887 yielded pottery with the telltale compass-drawn semicircle of Attic Protogeometric, in association with iron weapons. That more excavation would yield more evidence of this kind is indicated by a joint British-Turkish dig (1948-51) at Old Smyrna, northeast of the modern city. The excavators found that some of the pottery in deep levels on the site resembled that of Troy I-II, and thus showed that habitation there went back a very long way. But, at a level dated by them about 1000 B.C., a pottery begins to appear that is in décor very like the Protogeometric found by the Germans in the Ceramicus in Athens, though the shapes are local. This is the kind of evidence that may be used to justify the hypothesis of *émigrés* from Athens teaching local potters to make the ware they had been used to at home. If the hypothesis is sound, archaeology has at last confirmed the historical tradition of the Ionian migration.

The excavators were extraordinarily lucky. In the midst of the time of trouble following the Dorian invasion, its victims were too impoverished to build buildings that would last, and very little of the architecture of this dark age survives, not even ground plans. But in Old Smyrna the archaeologists found, under the platform of a seventh-century B.C. temple of Athena, the remains of apsidal buildings. An oval, one-roomed mud-brick house contained Protogeometric pottery, dated about 900 B.C. Architecturally it is unimpressive, but as illustrating from what humble beginnings the brilliant culture of later Ionia arose, the house is of the highest importance, not least because one of the inhabitants of Old Smyrna may have been Homer himself. We have seen such ground plans before, at Orchomenos and elsewhere; apparently the Dorian invasion forced its survivors back to the past for the inspiration, such as it was, of their architecture as well as their pottery.

The new settlement developed. By 850 Old Smyrna had a circuit wall of mud brick, with bottom courses of stone to prevent enemy undermining (Fig. 3.8). The wall enclosed a densely populated town, which by now had houses

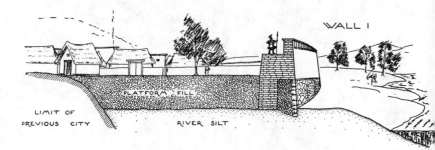

FIG. 3.8   Old Smyrna, earliest wall, reconstruction sketch. (Cook, 1958, p. 51, by permission of British School, Athens)

rectangular in plan, some of them resembling mainland megara; their north-south orientation suggests an axial town plan. By the late eighth century the wall had been strengthened until it was over fifty feet thick. In the late seventh century Old Smyrna fell before King Alyattes of Lydia, at a date well beyond the lower limit of this chapter. Just before its fall it may have looked like the imaginary reconstruction shown here (Fig. 3.9) to illustrate what developed out of the humble beginnings of the Ionian migration.

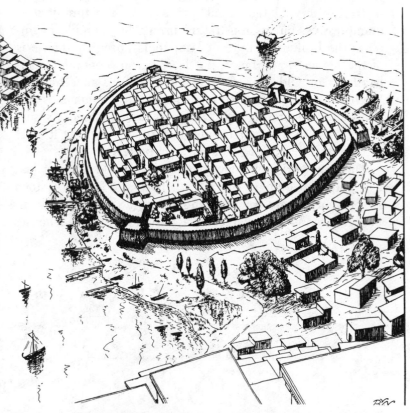

FIG. 3.9   Old Smyrna in the late seventh century B.C., reconstruction drawing. (Cook, 1958, p. 15)

At Emborió on Chios, British excavation since 1952 has revealed occupation since 2075 B.C. (carbon-14 date), plus a settlement of Mycenaean refugees, destroyed by fire about 1100, then abandoned until about 750, when we find an embryo Homeric city with fifty houses of megaron type, a temple of Athena, and another temple, archaic, remodeled in the fifth century. Underwater archaeologists have found numbers of amphoras, which testify to the importance of the wine trade in ancient Chios.

Did Crete, too, feel the impact of the Dorian invasion? Two sites, Karphí and Vrókastro, supply the clearest answer. Karphi, over 4000 feet above the sea in the mountain range of Dikte, but only twenty miles east-southeast of Knossos, was identified as a prehistoric site by Evans as long ago as 1896, but was not excavated until 1938-39. The workmen included two Albanian murderers, a lame sheepstealer, and a (possible) leper from Cyprus. Donkeys, and girls to wash sherds, were hired at the same rate: thirty-five drachmas (then about thirty cents) a day. The dig aroused great local interest: schoolmasters brought small boys up 1200 feet from the plateau to be shown the finds. What was unearthed was a city and a cemetery. It must have been a city of refuge, for its most inaccessible part was settled first. There was (Fig. 3.10) a Great House, large, sheltered, elaborate, with a megaron in the main-land style; a temple, with an altar, and a ledge for cult statues (one, put together out of 500 pieces, derives from Minoan prototypes); a Priest's House (nearly as large as the Great House), so named because it had direct access to the temple; a bazaar quarter; opening on the main square a room found full of pottery, which may have been a tavern, like the *kaphenion* of a Greek village today; paved streets, *terrazzo* courtyards, limestone walls, wooden columns, flat roofs. The tombs are the beehive type, showing, like the megaron of the Great House, mainland influence.

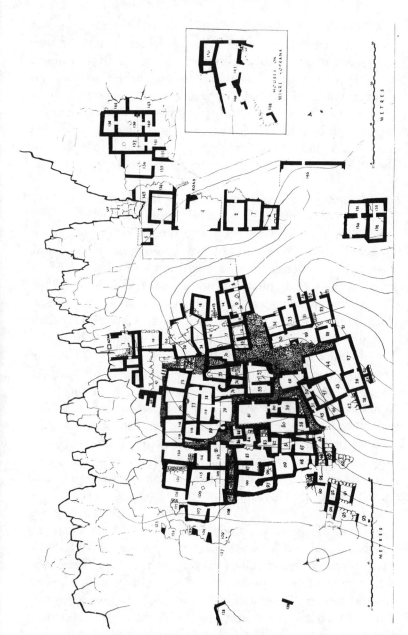

Fig. 3.10   Karphi, plan. 1, temple; 8, 9, 11-18, Great House; 58-61, 80, Priest's House; 49, tavern. (Pendlebury, 1937), Pl. IX, by permission of British School, Athens)

Safety pins show that the inhabitants dressed in Doric fashion; the pins occur in iron as well as in bronze, and therefore belong to a period of transition. There were no cremation burials, and no gold: nothing of intrinsic value was found either in the town or in the tombs; but no trace of conflagration either: the inference is that the site was peacefully abandoned; the inhabitants took all their valuables with them. The pottery is either the debased and spiritless imitation of Late Minoan III called Sub-Minoan, or the designs show the compass-drawn circles of Protogeometric. Such pottery, in Crete as on the mainland, is usually dated 1100-900 B.C. How may we read these stones and sherds? Their date is that of the Dorian invasion; the city is inaccessibly perched: the citizens must have been refugees. The megaron is Mycenaean, the cult-statue is Minoan. This suggests a Mycenaean minority ruling over a native Cretan population, both alike the victims of a scourge that had overwhelmed Knossos. In the 300 years since the late fifteenth-century sack of the palace, a good deal of race mixture must have taken place; lords and vassals alike, like true Cretans, armed themselves and took to the hills. Since Karphi is the largest and richest of the cities of refuge, it was probably the seat of the old regime. Intensely conservative, and probably poor, it imported nothing for 200 years. The pottery, in which Minoan motifs persist beside the Protogeometric; and *fibulae* and iron, which are rare, suggest knowledge but distrust of Dorian fashions. For 200 years the rulers of Karphi must have lived in their eyrie like robber barons; then, the invaders having been at last absorbed, they deserted their mountain fastness and moved down into the plain.

Vrokastro ("Jew's Castle"; its ancient name is unknown) lies three miles east of Gournia, on a steep limestone spur 1000 feet above the sea. It was excavated by an American woman, E. H. Hall, in 1910 and 1912. The likeness of its situation and its finds to those of Karphi is striking. Here too is a settlement and a cemetery, on an inaccessible crag sheer on two faces, affording a good seaward lookout. Its houses are humbler, but its abundant pottery (the site yielded thirty baskets of sherds a day) is better stratified than Karphi. The top layer was a mixture of Late Minoan III ware (showing a strong Mycenaean influence in its slip [clay coating], polishing, and lustrous paint) with compass-drawn Protogeometric. Miss Hall compared it with the Mycenaean pottery from Phylakopi III. In one house hundreds of scraps of bronze indicated a smithy. The tombs were of two kinds: chamber tombs, rubble-lined and pebble-floored, containing inhumation burials in which Protogeometric pottery was found in association with bronze *fibulae* and iron blades. One spearhead of cast bronze was found fastened to a shaft made of iron, than which nothing could be more transitional. Matching finds (iron blades, seals of glass paste, peplos pins) from Salamis, Mycenae, Enkomi, Assarlik, and the Argive Heraion place the chamber tombs in a familiar context. The most significant find was a bronze tripod with volute-topped legs; one like it from Enkomi is dated about 1000. Some of the seals can be matched in Egypt from the XX-XXIst Dynasties (1075-850 B.C.). The other type of burial consisted of cremations in bone-enclosures or ossuaries. Among the finds iron preponderates, and the pottery is Geometric, identified especially by hatched meander patterns (cf. Fig. 3.11). Similar examples come from Dodona in west Greece, one of the points of departure for the Dorian invasion; the island of Thera, seventy miles north of Crete, according to tradition invaded by Dorians in the late twelfth century; and the later Ceramicus tombs in Athens. At Vrokastro the top level of the town is Sub-Minoan, ending about 1050 B.C.; the chamber tombs range in date between 1000 and 850; the ossuaries, 850-700. The town and the chamber tombs reflect the same history of invasion and resistance as Karphi; but Vrokastro was not abandoned; it endured, and its last

FIG. 3.11 Athens, Ceramicus, Geometric vases. Note typical hatched meanders, upper right. Ceramicus, Museum. (Karo, *op. cit.*, Pl. 10)

phase, reflected in the ossuaries, tells us a little about how Crete at long last made its peace with the Dorians.

Before we leave Crete let us descend still further in time

to describe one of the few examples of architecture from the dark age. In 1935 a farmer leveling his land at Dreros, a dozen miles northwest of Vrokastro, came upon a stone foundation forming a twenty- by thirty-foot rectangle; subsequent excavation, sponsored by the local tourist club, revealed early Geometric pottery, an altar filled with the horns of sacrificed animals, a bench supporting bronze statuettes and a bronze Gorgon's head, a table of offerings, and iron sacrificial knives: enough to prove that the building was a temple, the only one of its period found up to then in Crete where the cult objects were still in place. In the center of the rectangular floor plan were traces of a hearth, with column bases north and south of it (Fig. 3.12) which might have supported a pitched roof with open gable ends to let the smoke escape. The published restoration, with its combination of pitched and flat roof, is bizarre; more probably the pitched roof covered the whole temple, as in the clay model from the mainland (Fig. 3.13). The importance of the Dreros temple is not in this detail, but in the fact that it is dated by its associated pottery—Geometric but not yet orientalizing*—to the early eighth century B.C., and is thus one of the four earliest known temples in Greek lands. It faced an agora, one of the earliest known. From here came also two bilingual inscriptions, in Greek and Eteo-Cretan, the pre-Hellenic language of East Crete.

About sixteen miles south of Heraklion, on the Phaistos road, lies Prinias, from whose temple comes the archaic limestone frieze of horsemen (Fig. 3.12a) of about 640 B.C., the earliest stone frieze known from any Greek temple. It is now in the Heraklion Museum. The long-legged thoroughbred horses are shown in profile, the undersized armed riders full face, warding off evil spirits.

* The term refers to motifs or materials originating in Syria (floral or animal motifs), Phoenicia and Palestine (ivories, faïence), or Egypt (lotus-flower handles on vases).

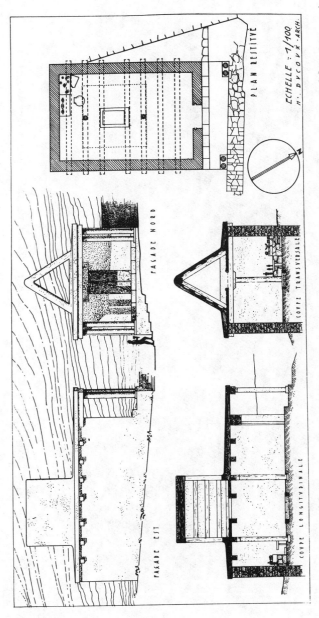

FIG. 3.12 Dreros, temple of Apollo Delphinios, side elevation, front elevation, and plan (showing votive offerings on bench, right rear). The pitched roof probably continued the whole length of the temple. (Marinatos, 1936, Pl XXXI, by permission of École Française, Athens)

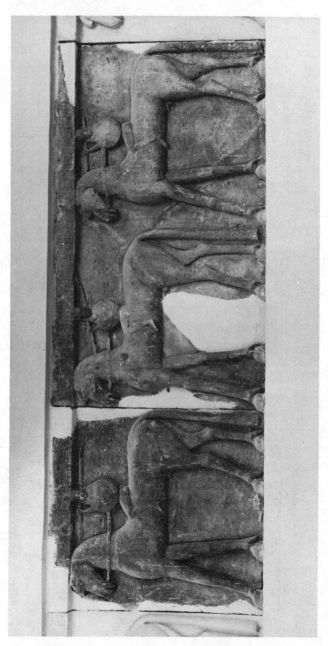

FIG. 3.12a   Prinias, temple, horsemen frieze, *ca.* 640. (Alison Frantz, by permission)

FIG. 3.13 Perachora, temple model (right). Note apsidal end, thatched roof, and painted wattle-and-daub walls. The rectangular model (left) was found in excavating the Argive Heraion. (After Payne, 1940, Pl. 9b, by permission of Clarendon Press, Oxford)

Another early temple was excavated by the British (1930-33) under Humfry Payne, on the still deserted promontory of Perachóra, north across the bay from Corinth, where the blue-gray of the limestone blends with the soft-shaded foliage of the pines and the incredible deep aquamarine of the sea, and the view embraces the heights of Acrocorinth, Helicon, and Parnassus. Here, some twenty yards north of the minuscule harbor, the British unearthed the plan, perhaps inspired by Middle Helladic buildings, of an apsidal structure that must have looked very like one of the several clay models (Fig. 3.13) found on the site. It must have had rubble walls (brick makes poor apses), smeared over the clay and painted; a thatched roof, an open gable, and a porch. Egyptian scarabs and early Geometric pottery date the temple in the early ninth century, earlier than Dreros, and earlier than any temple plan thus far discovered in Greece, unless the possibly apsidal plan of the temple of Apollo Ismenius at Thebes be of the same date.

Thebes, forty-six road-miles northwest of Athens, is another Mycenaean palace site, imperfectly known because overlaid by the graceless modern town. In mythology, which almost no ancient Greek except Thucydides distinguished from history, Thebes bulks so large that it must have been important in the Bronze Age. The legend of King Cadmus coming from Phoenicia with knowledge of writing is in part borne out by the discovery of thirty-odd Babylonian seals, datable to 1375-1347 B.C. (Late Mycenaean IIIA) in a context with Linear B tablets. Some amphoras with Linear B graffiti come from Crete. Other tablets may refer to the cow-eyed Hera, and to the disbursement of wool to a temple of Artemis in Euboea. The first palace, on the 725-by-425-yard height called the Kadmeia, was destroyed by fire about 1300; its successor, differently oriented, went up in flames about a generation later (*ca.* 1270). It is tempting to see in these destructions archaeological confirmation of the myth of the Seven against Thebes, led by the rebel Polynices, son of Oedipus, and of the Epigonoi, who allegedly destroyed the city a generation later. Thebes' legendary seven gates have all been identified. The chief finds are a goldsmith's workshop, which contained scraps of lapis lazuli, rock crystal, semiprecious stones, amber, and gold granules; and a processional frieze forty feet long portraying nine to twelve women with elaborate coiffures, bearing gifts in bronze, gold, silver, and ivory or alabaster. Mycenaean Thebes had a circuit wall, but it proved of no avail; the second palace was not rebuilt, and Thebes proper does not even figure in the Homeric catalogue of the ships which sailed against Troy.

Under the Perachora temple was a thick stratum of votive offerings; the whole site is richer in these than any other in Greece except Olympia, Delphi, and the Athenian acropolis itself. A similar temple model from Argos and bronzes from Corinth very like the Perachora votives may serve to symbolize the sites with which Perachora shows closest connections. Corinth's archaic temple, with seven monolithic columns of about 550 B.C., had a hip roof, tiled in yellow and black. Stuccoed panels, painted red and black, decorated the interior. The stylobate had horizontal curvature, like the Parthenon later; put-holes for votive shields, guilloche antefixes, ridge palmettes, and perhaps a terracotta sphinx as acroterion. The Romans removed the original interior columns for reuse in the Southwest Stoa. In 1801 the Turkish governor used gunpowder to blast four columns into fragments for building himself a house.

Very early Perachora inscriptions with dedications to "white-armed Hera," the marriage-goddess, consort of Zeus, with the cult titles Akraia (of the Promontory) and Limenia (of the Harbor) tell us to whom the sanctuary was dedicated. One inscription dedicates a fistful (*drachma*) of iron spits (*oboloi*) to the goddess, and dates from a time of transition (about 650 B.C.) from this primitive currency to coined money; this, and still later temple on the site, take us down into the archaic period. Close relations to finds from the temples of Hera at Argos, Samos, and the mouth of the Sele near Paestum in south Italy suggest intimate connections in the early Greek world between one Hera cult and another.

A hundred yards east of the apsidal temple the British found the footings of the temple of Hera Limenia (identified by a votive inscription), with a hearth in the center, and a votive deposit of thousands of small objects, including hundreds of scarabs, pottery dating the temple about 750 B.C., nearly 1500 terracotta figurines, fragments of amber and ivory, over 5000 complete rings; mirrors, strigils (for scraping after exercise), sickles, a mask, diadems, mint-fresh bronze nails (which the excavator suggests may have been dedicated by carpenters), a lovely bronze dove which from the curve of its feet may have been held in the hand of the cult statue of Hera; arrowheads, horse trappings, 200 bronze saucers (many found in a sacred pool between the two temples). All in all the deposits totaled between ten and twenty tons. Clearly by 750 B.C. Greece had emerged from her time of troubles.

The Argive Heraeum, where the temple-model (Fig. 3.13, left) was found, lies, like the Samian one, at a distance from its city. It was the first dig (1892-95) of the American School in Athens. Its Neolithic and Bronze Age predecessor was Prosymna; a Mycenaean tomb 350 meters north contained figurines and Late Helladic II to IIIc pottery; its archaic temple dated from the end of the eighth century B.C. Fire in 423 B.C. destroyed it; its successor contained a colossal chryselephantine statue of the goddess by the famous Poly-clitus; in the precinct were stoas and a banqueting hall.

Argos town, to the south, dates back to Middle Helladic times; the Dutch and French have excavated it. It had two citadels: the Aspis ("Shield," from its shape) with chamber tombs, shaft graves, and a precinct, archaic and later, of Apollo and Athena; and the Larissa, whose cone dominates the landscape; its concentric circuit walls are of the sixth and fifth centuries; its striking visible remains are Byzantine, Frankish, Venetian, and Turkish. Its agora had stoas (500-450 B.C.) on three sides, a prytaneum in the southwest corner, and a temple of Apollo the Wolf-God on the north. The bouleuterion, on its west side, was remodeled as a Roman Odeum. The most conspicuous remains are the theater (fourth century B.C.; eighty-one rows, seating 20,000) and the Roman baths.

When the British discovered the apsidal temple plan at Perachora, they were at once reminded of a parallel from Thermon, in Aetolia, above the Corinthian Gulf between sixty and seventy airline miles northwest of Perachora (overland it is much farther). Here the Greeks (Soteriades, Kawerau, Rhomaios) had excavated (1911-14) a complex of buildings ranging in date over nearly 2000 years, from Helladic to late Hellenistic times. The one that interests us lies under the long, narrow archaic temple (Fig. 3.14), and is called Megaron B. Its north wall has a slight curve, and around three sides of it lie eighteen stone footings for the columns of an elliptical peristyle, ancestor of the classical Greek temple colonnade. Nothing dates the megaron itself before the eighth century, and the peristyle may have supported a curved thatched roof. The building (parallels at Perachora and Dreros) was probably a house metamorphosed into a temple: it has a pavement in front for an altar. The successor to Megaron B was an archaic temple (620-550 B.C.) with terracotta revetments; there was another similar temple of the late seventh century. In Hellenistic times Thermon became the center of the Aetolian League, with bouleuterion and agora. After Philip V of Macedon sacked it (218 B.C.), a strong towered precinct wall (368 by 216 yards) was built. The earlier pottery belonged to the village of thatched-roofed apsidal and rectangular wattle-and-daub huts that surrounded the temple; there were enough sherds to reconstruct fifty whole pots.

At Eretria, on Euboea, an apsidal building of about 800 B.C., made of laurel wood, looked very much like the Perachora temple. Its successor, dedicated to Apollo Daphnephoros (Laurel-Bearer), dated 670-50, was also apsidal, but much longer, comparable to the first Heraion at Samos. Like the archaic temple at Thermon, it had a single row of internal columns. In front of it was a square altar with a sacrificial pit. From the successor to this temple came the late sixth-century pedimental relief of Theseus smilingly carrying off on his shoulder the Amazon Antiope, now in the Chalcis Museum. Houses have yielded a remarkable series of pebble mosaics, like those from Macedonia described in chapter 7.

Of the storied cities of Greece, only Sparta remains to be mentioned. Archaeologists never expected its ruins to be spectacular, for they knew Thucydides had said that if it suddenly became an archaeological site instead of a living

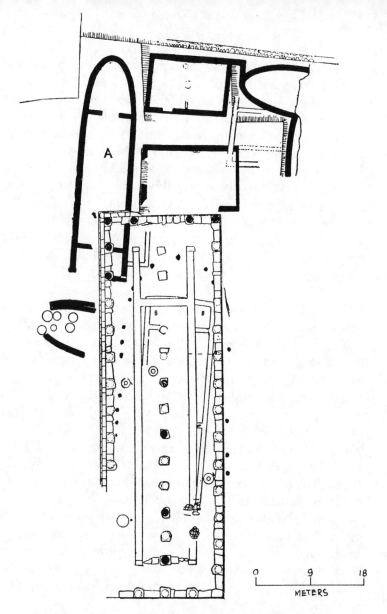

0   9   18
METERS

FIG. 3.14 Thermon, site plan. Megaron B is under the long, narrow
archaic temple. Note the slight bowing of the north wall, and
the eighteen column-bases (black dots) in an ellipse around it.
(Rhomaios, 1915, p. 231, by permission of Archaiologikê
Hetaireia, Athens)

city, no one could gauge its actual power by the remains of its temples and public buildings, for it remained a collection of villages, "giving an impression of inadequacy." And indeed British excavations there (1906-1910) found nothing as spectacular as Athens and Mycenae: no Mycenaean remains at all on the site of classical Sparta; the city of Menelaus and Helen, several miles south, at Therapnae, shows a change of pottery style and a break in continuity, owing no doubt to the Dorian invasion. Their shrine, post-Bronze Age, rises on three platforms, with imposing masonry and a fine view. A house with two pre-Mycenaean phases has been excavated. Amyclae, south of this, had a late Mycenaean shrine of Hyacinthus, in whose honor Spartans later celebrated a festival. Architectural fragments from a sixth-century altar from here, miscalled "the throne of Apollo," are in the Sparta Museum. The celebrated pair of Vaphió gold cups (*ca.* 1500 B.C.) were found not far south of here. They are Minoan work, showing bulls being netted and mated. Digging in 1906 north of modern Sparta by the Eurotas River, the British hit upon a temple identified by inscriptions built into neighboring Roman walls as that of Artemis Orthia, the huntress goddess of the mountain. The accompanying pottery at the lowest levels was Protogeometric; the metal finds were iron; there was Baltic amber; the excavators concluded that they had found a village of the Dorian invaders, but their eleventh-century date was two hundred years too early. The earliest temple was long and narrow, built of adobe brick with a timber frame, divided by a single row of wooden columns into two naves. Between 570 and 560 sand was laid over the cobbles of the precinct pavement, and the temple rebuilt. A Roman theater beside the temple afforded spectators comfortable views of the ritual flogging of Spartan boys, a sadistic tradition that lived long. On the acropolis to the northwest (Fig. 3.15) the scanty remains, identified by a stamped roof tile, of the temple of Athena of the Brazen House date not before the

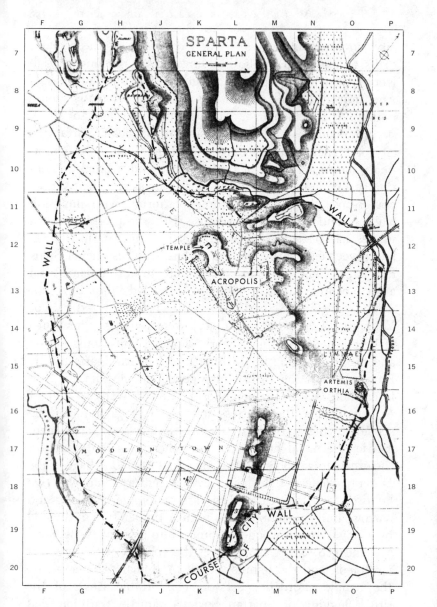

Fɪɢ. 3.15 Sparta, site plan. O 15, temple of Artemis Orthia, under
  Roman theater; K 12, temple of Athena of the Brazen House,
  on the Acropolis. (Dawkins, 1906, Pl. I, by permission of Society
  for the Promotion of Hellenic Studies)

eighth century; it has a large late Hellenistic theater; five hundred yards to the east, outside the Byzantine acropolis wall, are traces of the agora. Stamped roof tiles located four of the five villages of which classical Sparta was made up. Below the sanded level of the Artemis Orthia precinct was found a series of grotesque terracotta masks (Fig. 3.16), models of those used in ritual dances; and over 100,000

FIG. 3.16   Sparta, grotesque terracotta mask from temple of Artemis Orthia, now in Sparta Museum. (Émile Séraf)

cheap lead figurines, now on view in the town museum, which were perhaps dedicated by Spartan helots (serfs).

Lycurgus, quasi-mythical, sometime in the seventh century metamorphosed Sparta into a totalitarian military state, notoriously austere—revolting soup, cold baths, iron money (Sparta had no coined silver until 280 B.C.)—but austerity seems, until 550 to 525, not to have affected art or culture; e.g., the lively Laconian pottery (Fig. 4.18), the fine early figured ivories, Alcman's lovely maiden song. Discipline steeled Leonidas' Spartiates to die at their posts at Thermopylae (480). But by the time Sparta conquered Athens (404) Spartan culture was a contradiction in terms. So Sparta in archaeology looks like Sparta in literature: regimented and dull. Byzantine (fourteenth-fifteenth century A.D.) ruins— palace, houses, monasteries, churches—at Mistra, five miles west, are actually more exciting. They resemble Les Baux in Provence.

Other sites, Geometric or with Geometric levels, include Asine, Didyma, Gortyn on Crete, Iasos, Iolkos, Lefkandí on Euboea, Miletus, Argos, Phaistos, Thorikos, Xómbourgo on Tenos, and Zagora on Andros.

A final example of a Dark Age temples, the predecessor of a glorious one of the mid-sixth century, was excavated by the Germans in 1911 and after (Wiegand, Buschor, Walter) on the island of Samos. Dedicated to Hera, it was 100 feet long, had a double row of interior columns, was built of coarse limestone, and is dated in the eighth century B.C.

This somewhat thankless survey of the age of the nadir of Greek fortunes can end, at least, on an optimistic note, with a return to Athens, where the seeds of the vitality of the subsequent Archaic Age were quickening to a new birth. There, in 1933, Dorothy Burr (whom we have met as the discoverer of the rich tholos tomb at Dendra) discovered evidence for a remote age of Athens in an area ten yards square on the north slope of the Areopagus. What she found were the traces of a sixteen- by thirty-six-foot elliptical house (which she compared with the village houses at Thermon) with a hard red floor covered in places with sea sand. There was a central hearth, and platforms for beds. Under the house was the pathetic grave of a child four to six years old (archaeologists determine age by the teeth). It had been buried with two small seashells, a clay piglet, and a few miniature vases to friend it on its lonely journey to the house of Hades. The grave was earlier than the house: the miniature vases were Protogeometric of the ninth century. The house itself was in use, to judge by the pottery, from the late eighth century to about 640 B.C. The sherds ranged from late Geometric through orientalizing to a new exuberant style called Proto-Attic. Geometric pottery is Pan-Hellenic, but Proto-Attic is unique to Athens; it is the first city-state ware; it symbolizes a new era, and its emergence marks the end of the Greek Dark Ages and the beginning of the Archaic Age, when Greece comes forward into the full light of history and the more familiar treasures of early Greek art and architecture begin to reward the archaeologist's spade.

The archaeological discoveries recorded in this chapter cover over 500 years. On the face of it they are depressing, until one stops to reflect on the heartening evidence they provide for the indestructibility of the Greek spirit in the face of invasion, poverty, oppression, and hard times. The efforts expended by the defenders of the acropolis of Mycenaean Athens were crowned with success. The walls and bastions held, the emergency stairs to the water supply could safely be left to rot, for the attackers failed. Life could go on, more austerely, but undaunted, as Protogeometric pottery shows, with its spirited revival of a sense of design. There was peace at last: there are no weapons in the Ceramicus graves. And Athens could be proud to receive the refugees from less fortunate cities, who, encouraged by their welcome into Athenian civic life, contributed their share to the revival. They helped eventually to develop the new exuberant Proto-Attic pottery. If they died in their new homes, they were buried side by side with the Athenians in the city cemetery, in the fairest quarter of the city. But some of the refugees energetically carried the new amalgamated culture overseas. Some new settlers came direct to Miletus, Rhodes, or Enkomi in Cyprus from their devastated Peloponnesian homes. They did not always prosper, but at Enkomi at least they survived. And the rise of Smyrna, which was to become Homer's city, can pretty safely be attributed to *émigrés* from Pylos whose stay in Athens gave them encouragement and new energy for the enterprise that lay ahead.

In Crete, Karphi, the city of refuge, shows how age-old is the indomitable Cretan valiance in the face of the foreign invader. Cretans showed it again in World War II, to the unbounded admiration of the whole free world. The men of the resistance endured, too, at Vrokastro; and the remarkable temple at Dreros, together with the ambitious one on another island, Samos, show how spiritual life survived, and even had the vigor to innovate, through troubled times.

Out of the ruins wrought by the Dorian invasion a new spirit, which we can identify as related to that of classical Greece, was beginning to arise, and even to prosper. The evidence for it is the succession of temples at Perachora, with their rich votive offerings. The temple and village at Thermon show that West Greece, too, had the vitality to rise from the blow of the invader, and nourish the outer and the inner man.

Mycenaean Sparta fell, but the temple of Artemis Orthia and the splendid Laconian pottery show to what heights the new Sparta proved capable of rising, even in this Dark Age, before militarism stifled her sense of beauty forever.

Over the "Dark Ages," then, like the light of the strong Greek sun, plays the heartening warmth of the eternally gallant Greek spirit. Thanks to it, by the end of the eighth century Greece is back on her feet again, and the wonders of the Lyric Age are about to begin.

4

The Lyric Age:
Greece and the West

(700-480 B.C.)

Within the 220 years of the Lyric Age, history comes firmly to archaeology's aid: Olympic victor lists go back to 776 B.C.; Athenian archon lists begin in 683. It is an age of poets, lyric and elegiac: Sappho of Lesbos, Solon of Athens, Theognis of Megara, Pindar of Thebes; and lyric grace and elegiac solemnity are to be seen in its architecture and its art. It is an age that sees the beginnings—on the barren island of Delos, at Olympia in its sandy river valley, at Delphi, on its lovely mountainside—of the great international festivals that were to be the glory of the succeeding classical age. We shall begin with some of the archaic monuments from these places. It is an age of tyrants, strong-minded men who left great public works behind them: Pheidon in Argos, Polycrates in Samos.

Polycrates (reigned 538-522), pirate, fratricide, prideful patron of arts and letters, beautified the city with ill-gotten gains. The Megarian engineer Eupalinus built him an aqueduct with a rock-cut tunnel a mile long, still visitable; a mole with footings forty feet deep protected his hundred privateers in harbor; he surrounded his city with a four-and-a-half-mile polygonal and adobe brick wall with thirty-five towers; he embellished and enlarged Hera's temple to colossal dimensions: 520 by 160 feet, and filled her precinct— a veritable open-air museum—with stoas, treasuries, an odeon, and a temple to Aphrodite and Hermes. He subsidized the lyric poets Anacreon of Teos and Ibycus of Rhegium; the philosopher Pythagoras, a native son, could not stand the tyranny and emigrated to Croton in south Italy. Polycrates came to a bad end—crucified by a Persian satrap he had insulted. Samos was never so brilliant again, falling successively under the rule of Athens, Hellenistic kings (who added atop the fortifications a screen-wall with shuttered windows), and Romans. The rapacious Verres pillaged the Heraion; the precinct held statues of Marcus Cicero the orator and his brother Quintus, once governor of Asia; Antony and Cleopatra stole *objets d'art* from here for Alexandria; the future emperor Augustus stopped here after his victory over the larcenous pair.

Other tyrants were Periander in Corinth* and her colonies, and especially Pisistratus in Athens. It is an age when colonies flourished: it is no accident that its most impressive buildings are in the golden West † or on the way to it: on Corcyra off the Greek west coast, at Selinus in southwest Sicily, at and near Paestum south of Naples (see map, Fig. 4.3). The age ends with the Persian Wars: the great East-West conflict affected many monuments, even, perhaps, those masterpieces,

---

* An interesting work of engineering, possibly from Periander's reign (627-505), but with later additions, came to light in 1956 near the Corinth Canal. It is the *diolkos,* or road by which boats were hauled across the Isthmus. Paved with limestone, it averages fourteen feet in width, and has two parallel ruts, five feet apart, in which the wagons ran. On curves, a pair of low walls, to keep the wagons from slipping, replaces the tracks (Fig. 4.1). In 1961 was reported the discovery of a device for lifting vessels out of the water and onto a sort of tram.

† Except the archaic temple at Ephesus of about 560 B.C. (see page 350), and the archaic Acropolis of Larisa-by-Hermos, between Smyrna and Pergamum, rich in pottery and in architectural terracottas, and boasting a fine archaic palace (Fig. 4.2) and circuit wall.

FIG. 4.1   Corinth, *diolkos,* for hauling boats across the isthmus. (After *AJA* 61 [1957], Pl. 83.3)

FIG. 4.2   Larisa-by-Hermos, archaic palace, reconstruction drawing. (Boehlau, *Larisa* I, Fig. 29)

FIG. 4.3   Map to illustrate the Lyric Age,

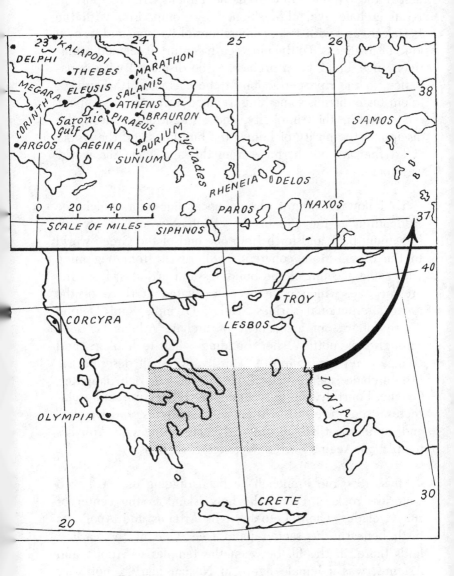

Greece and the West, 700-480 B.C.

the pediments from the Aphaia temple on Aegina, six miles across the Saronic Gulf from the Piraeus, Athens' port. It is an archaic age, old-fashioned by comparison with the Periclean, and with strict conventions of its own, and its own kind of liveliness. To the nineteenth century it seemed primitive, naïve, childlike, a preface, to be dismissed with impatience, to the ripe perfection of the classical fifth century; to our taste there is something tremendously attractive about the strength, the simplicity, the straightforwardness, the discipline, the purity of line of the buildings and the works of art that are our heritage from this age when the world was young.

To follow a straight chronological line (for which see Addendum at the end of the chapter) would involve us in leaping back and forth from one end of the Greek world to the other. More coherence will result from beginning with some account of the buildings and artifacts, from the archaic age, which have been excavated at three of the great international shrines: Delos, Olympia, and Delphi. There follows an assessment of archaic Athens, as seen through her pottery, her buildings, her technology and coinage, and her sculpture. Thirdly, we shall describe the little archaic island town of Thera, and her rich daughter, Cyrene. Fourthly, the burgeoning of architecture and architectural sculpture in the West will occupy us, and we shall end, upon the threshold of early classicism, with Aphaia's temple on Aegina, within eyeshot of Athens.

Since 1879 the French have been digging on the naked waterless rock of Delos, the holy island in the center of the Cyclades where Leto brought Artemis and Apollo to birth beneath the sacred palm tree. One of the earliest finds there, in the fill between the temples of Apollo and Artemis, was a female figure in Naxian marble, not very far in technique from primitive statues in wood, yet the first large-size marble statue known to us from the Greek world.* An inscription on it reveals that it is a dedication (mid-seventh century) to Artemis by one Nicandre of Naxos. Of Naxian marble too is a row of splendid colossal seventh-century lions (Fig. 4.4), first scientifically described in 1907, which bordered as majestically as a file of Egyptian statues the approach to the sacred palm tree where every spring all Greece celebrated in festival the birth of Apollo and Artemis. The lions, of various sizes, may just possibly have been dedicated in rivalry by various Naxian "tribes" (political subdivisions) or noble families. Their lean bodies, after 2500 years of weathering, still make their effect upon the visitor, the effect of majesty that was intended by the Naxians when they were lords of Delos. To house their Delian offerings they built a treasury (identified by an inscription), and a portico beside it to shelter pilgrims from

* For earlier life-size terracottas, see page 143.

FIG. 4.4   Delos, Lion Terrace, leading to temple of Leto, *ca.* 625-600 (Author)

the hot Aegean sun. Besides the treasury the French found a colossal statue of Apollo, and nearby, again used as fill, numerous statues of Naxian youths and maidens, dedications to the god or goddess.

On the island of Naxos itself, only twenty-five sea miles away, another colossus, bearded and therefore not Apollo (perhaps Dionysus?), thirty-four feet long, lies flat on its back in a quarry. Intended for Delos, it was never sent: the marble being of poor grade, the face developed cracks. The statue lies in its bed with the rock gouged out around it wide enough for a man to work. The intent was to pry it loose underneath with wooden wedges, which, wetted in the night, would swell and split the statue loose by morning. It would then have been taken on rollers down to the shore of Apollona Bay and rafted to Delos.

All this ingenuity cost money (derived from the quarries and from mines of emery, an abrasive used for polishing statues, of which Naxos is still the chief source of the world's supply). That the Naxians were willing to be lavish is an index of the value to them of controlling the tiny island where religion and trade, reviving after the Dark Ages, went so profitably, as so often, hand in hand.

The colossal Apollo symbolizes how the god took over the primacy from his sister. But the earliest temple on Delos was dedicated to Artemis, herself no doubt the descendant of the fertility goddess who in prehistoric times held sway over the minds of men in all the Cyclades and in Crete. In the fall of 1946 a trial trench was dug beneath the floor of the previously identified Hellenistic Artemision. The first stroke of the pick revealed fragments of gold, ivory, bronze, and pottery. The latter, both Mycenaean and Geometric, dated the deposit. It must have been put there deliberately, as we would place objects in a cornerstone. The earliest artifacts prove that Artemis had a cult on Delos from Mycenaean times; the latest date the archaic temple. The finds included an ivory plaque of a proud Mycenaean warrior with a magnificent Cyrano de Bergerac nose, a boar's-tusk helmet, and a figure-eight shield; another with a frieze of animals fighting; fragments of two gold diadems; ducks and bees in gold *repoussé*; statuettes and a miniature double ax and arrowheads in bronze.

The identified buildings of archaic Delos are not many; even the site of the famous altar made of horns is uncertain. More important than buildings was the open meadow south of the Sacred Lake (now dry), the goal of the processions of pilgrims that passed along the Lion Terrace. Here, on this meadow, there was room for sacrifice, cult banquets, choral dance and song, and competitions in athletics and music; here selections from Homer were recited for a prize; here Homer himself was said to have competed. Pindar, too, is associated with the island: he composed a processional ode for the Delian festival.

The archaeologists excavated, on the edge of the festival meadow, a small temple whose foundations are in local granite, its walls of *poros* (limestone) from Attica. This temple symbolizes the decline of the Naxians (who, the archaeologists think, built the foundations) and the rise on Delos of Athenian influence. Athens dominated Delos in the last half of the sixth century under the tyrant Pisistratus, who no doubt favored Apollo of Delos because his enemies, the noble clan of Alcmaeonidae, were enjoying in exile the hospitality of Apollo of Delphi. Pisistratus' estates in Attica were at Brauron: from a port near here, and not from the Piraeus, the Athenians regularly sent their sacred galley to the Delian festival. From Pisistratus' time too, probably, date various secular buildings. a senate-house southeast of the temple, a meeting place for the assembly to the northwest. Pottery dates some houses, in the district round the later theater, to Pisistratus' age. He was famous for his public works and for his patronage of the arts, in Athens as well as on Delos. He "purified" the island (543 B.C.; the Athenians did it again in 426) by removing all the dead, with the contents of their tombs, to the neighboring island of Rheneia: the pits where the bodies and the pottery were deposited have been excavated, and give mute if grisly evidence of centuries of Delian cultural and trade relations. Pisistratus' connections with Delos provided a precedent and a pretext for Athens' making the island the ostensible center of her maritime league in the next century.

Olympia, in the northwest Peloponnese, was an even more famous international shrine than Delos; its archives went back, as we saw, to 776 B.C., the first fixed date in Greek history. Here, in this beautiful and historic spot, made still more beautiful by the pines they planted long ago, the Germans have been digging since 1875; here, we remember, Dörpfeld learned his trade. He returned to the site in old age to work on the sanctuary of Hera, and published his results over fifty years after his first excavations there. In 1880 a foundation deposit had been found under Hera's temple, and Dörpfeld tried to prove how early it was. He dated its oldest phase in the early eleventh century, directly after the Dorian invasion. Most archaeologists, with a careful eye on the pottery whose importance they learned from Dörpfeld, would now date the earliest Heraion in the seventh century. The building was divided by cross-walls into side chapels which in later ages were filled with offerings of *objets d'art*: it was in one of these that in the spring of 1877 was discovered the Hermes of Praxiteles (Fig. 6.4), *perhaps* one of the few originals of Greek sculpture independent of architecture that we possess, and now the pride of the museum next to the site. Here too was found the limestone head, double life size, of the cult statue of Hera herself: its almond eyes and fixed smile date it in the archaic period, perhaps mid-seventh century. Dörpfeld noticed that the columns of the temple (Fig. 4.5) were of various dimensions, with different numbers of flutings and different capitals, showing progressive changes. He deduced that the original columns had been of wood, replaced with stone one by one as they rotted.

When the Olympics were held in Berlin in 1936, Hitler, to propagandize the event, gave a large sum of money to reopen excavation at the site of the first Olympics. The results of this excavation were remarkable. One project was to excavate the whole stadium (a job completed in 1960). In a trench fifty yards north of the stadium starting-blocks, the excavators hit upon a spot under the stadium wall where in the sixth century B.C., to judge by the pottery, there had been bronze-casters' workshops. The level had been artificially raised in the fifth century: the fill yielded

FIG. 4.5 Olympia, Heraion, *ca.* 645-640. (Émile Séraf)

an almost inexhaustible series of finds of the archaic period (mostly sixth century), including twenty-two bronze helmets, greaves (leg-protectors), bronze shield-straps in relief, unique bronze protectors for the upper arm, shield devices in thin bronze plate for nailing on wood, tripods, architectural moldings, victors' dedications, unique local pottery—all of which had been thrown away in antiquity as old-fashioned. The thin bronze plates had to be heated with blowtorches and strengthened with beeswax, gauze, and wooden slats before they could be removed for study. The devices included a winged Gorgon, centaurs, a cock, a bronze she-griffin suckling her young, a goat bitten by a huge snake, and the goddess called the Mistress of Animals, flanked by heraldic beasts. A foot in thin bronze plate came from a statue with a bronze-plated wooden core, like those already known from Dreros, but here life size. One of the dedications was of a jumping weight (used to add momentum, and therefore distance, to the jump) by a Spartan who won "without dust"; i.e., by default: the Spartan record, in athletics as in war (though no longer in the arts) inspired a healthy respect.

Adjoining the spot where these finds were made, and running westward, is a series of eleven "treasuries," where, as at Delos, Delphi, and elsewhere the archives and dedications of wealthy cities were kept. Of the eleven treasuries, six belong to cities of the West or en route to it—an index of the prosperity of these colonies in Magna Graecia (Great Greece, as the Greeks called south Italy and Sicily)—which, founded from the motherland from the eighth century onward, prospered in the sixth, when the treasuries were built. The pediment of the Megarian treasury (second from right in model, Fig. 5.1) portrays the battle of gods and giants.

Olympia did not reach its full blossoming until the great temple of Zeus was dedicated in 457. Its rich cult-statue by Phidias in ivory and gold (the Germans have found the terracotta molds for the gold plating) is twenty years later.

Here the center of cult interest shifted from the goddess Hera to the god Zeus, as at Delos it had shifted from Artemis to Apollo, but it was for victories at the archaic site that Pindar's famous *Olympian Odes* were written, and the archaic Heraion is still Olympia's most impressive building, for some of its columns are standing, or have been re-erected, while the gigantic column-drums of the temple of Zeus have been left where an earthquake toppled them, centuries ago.

Of natural beauty rocky Delos has none; sandy Olympia is redeemed by its pine trees; but Delphi in its natural amphitheater under the rosy outcrop of Mt. Parnassus, above the gray-green olive-clad Pleistos Valley, is one of the most beautiful spots in Greece, if not in the world. The French have been digging here off and on since 1892; they won the excavation rights from the Americans by admitting Greek currants duty-free. They found the villagers of Delphi less complaisant than the government. The modern village lay directly on top of the sanctuary, and the Delphians of the '90s bitterly and even violently opposed being moved to a new site farther west, even though the reconstruction, which cost $150,000, was entirely at the French government's expense. Nowadays, reconciled, they proudly regard the unearthing of the sacred precinct as the work of their own hands.

Delphi is one of archaeology's most complicated sites. An incomplete description lists 235 buildings and monuments, and the museum inventory (incomplete), catalogues over 7,000 objects, some of them, like the bronze Charioteer, world famous. Inscriptions were so numerous that the excavation director sometimes found himself obliged to transcribe 100 a day.

Before the work began, or the village was moved, ancient landmarks—the dip in the ground that marked the stadium, the Castalian spring, the retaining wall of the Gymnasium, the lower sanctuary, long used as a stone quarry—could be recognized, with the aid of the ancient Baedeker, Pausanias,

whose meticulous guidebook, written about A.D. 174, with
a contagious affection for religion, history, and art, is often
the Greek archaeologist's best friend. But for detailed study,
tons of stone, earth, and silt had to be removed, over more
than a mile of light railway.

One of the earliest finds connected archaeology with history. Herodotus tells how Cleobis and Biton, two young
men, sons of a priestess of Argos, finding that the draft
animals to draw their mother's car had not arrived on time,
themselves drew it the five miles and more to the temple,
and in response to their proud mother's prayer to Hera to
grant them the greatest possible blessing, were vouchsafed,
as they slept in the temple, the gift of death. Their fellow
citizens dedicated statues of them at Delphi. When in
May of 1893 the excavators found, propped against an
ancient retaining-wall, an archaic statue of a muscular
young man, perhaps represented in the very act of drawing
a car (Fig. 4.6; the twin turned up the next spring), they
hardly needed the inscription on the base to connect the
find with Herodotus' story. These, dated on stylistic
grounds 615-590, are the oldest large works in Parian marble
yet found on the Greek mainland. The low brow, strong
chin, square shoulders, and powerful chest at first suggest
mere brawn, but the slim waist, slightly bent-forward stance,
and straight look give a subtler impression, of eager, dedicated tension. Three generations after these statues were
carved, Pindar would sing, in lyric as stylized and as tense
as this sculpture, the victories of athletes like these at the
Pythian Games at Delphi.

Since 1903 work at Delphi has involved mostly preparing excavation notes for publication, which involves re-
checking, which involves new discoveries. The original dig
(1892-1903) aimed to get down only to the classical level,
and in many places reached only the phase that Pausanias
saw; new trenches occasionally reach archaic levels, as when
a deposit of archaic carved ivory plaques and gold orna-

Fig. 4.6 Delphi, the dis-
covery of the archaic
(615-590 B.C.) statue
of Cleobis, now in the
Delphi Museum, 1893.
(de La Coste-Messe-
lière & de Miré, 1943,
Fig. 36)

ments was found in 1939 under the Byzantine paving of
the Sacred Way. They represent Apollo and Artemis, and
have gold hair and headdresses. There is also a life-size silver
bull, with gold-plated hooves, horns, and genitals. No attempt
has been made to reconstruct Delphi for tourists, as Evans
reconstructed Knossos, but some walls and columns have
been re-erected to give scale, and steps have been restored
on the steep Sacred Way (1959). Using as clues the order

of over 150 inscriptions (including two hymns to Apollo with the ancient musical notation intact) on the outer faces of the wall-blocks, the gradual taper of the courses from top to bottom, and in some cases the keying letters placed on the blocks by the original masons, and knowing that in a good Greek building there are no interchangeable parts, J. Replat, with the financial help of the city of Athens, rebuilt the Treasury of the Athenians (1903-06), and it has been given a new column, fluted since World War II. In 1938 three columns of the tholos in the lower sanctuary were reset, and in 1939-41 eight columns of the major Temple of Apollo were re-erected. During the war the museum's major treasures were hidden (the Charioteer in Athens), and in the civil strife of 1945-46 work on Delphi, always slow, became even slower, but over twenty volumes of the final publication are out, and more are expected.

From the archaic period the most important Delphic finds are the fragments, totaling more than half, of the frieze from the Siphnian Treasury. Siphnos had been rich in gold and silver until its mines were flooded (served them right, said the Delphic oracle sagely, for cheating Apollo of his tithe), and it fell before the Samians in 525. Its treasury reflects its ripe prosperity, and, with its lovely maidens (Caryatids) holding up its porch, is a jewel box of Ionian art, the earliest marble building on the Greek mainland. Its site can be identified from Pausanias, and its footings are to be seen on the Sacred Way just before it curves up to pass the Athenian Treasury (see model, Fig. 6.6). The order of the frieze has been reconstructed from careful notes taken in 1894 of the findspots of the various frieze blocks as they lay where they had fallen on the four sides of the footings mentioned above. Careful study reveals that the friezes were originally richly painted, and are by two different hands, so different that when they meet at a corner it is a shock. One, whose interest, like a lyric poet's, is in décor, did the Judgment of Paris on the west (front) face, and Castor and Pollux' rape of the daughters of Leucippus on the south (the side farthest from the Sacred Way). His Aphrodite, adjusting her necklace as she leaves her chariot, might serve to illustrate an ode of Sappho. The other, whose interest like an epic poet's is in narrative, carved the scenes from the Trojan War, and the battle of the gods and giants, labeled with their names, on the north (Fig. 4.7). The latter subject, symbolizing as it does the victory of intelligence over brute force, of order over disorder, of reason over emotion, was a favorite with Greek sculptors. Its treatment here is the major success of the archaic school in the narrative as opposed to the more typical lyric style; the sculptor has reduced to order the violent movement of over fifty figures. The giants outnumber the gods, but they fight with crude weapons, and they lose.

Just above the Siphnian Treasury, round a bend in the Sacred Way, is the sanctuary's most perfect surviving monument, the Athenian Treasury (Fig. 6.6). The metopes (Doric frieze-panels, separated by triple grooves called triglyphs) feature the exploits of the Athenian hero Theseus.

The Treasury's date is disputed: some scholars, finding its architectural detail matched in late sixth-century vase painting, see the building as commemorating Athens' liberation from tyranny by Cleisthenes in 509, while to others it celebrates her victory at Marathon (490).

Fifty yards farther up the Sacred Way is another Athenian building, a Stoa or portico set against the great polygonal wall that supports the terrace of the Temple of Apollo. Along the face of the upper step of this portico is an inscription, in letters about a foot high, which reads, "The Athenians dedicated the portico and the arms and the figureheads which they took from their enemies." Who were these enemies, what were the trophies displayed, and what was the occasion commemorated? Learned speculation ranged from the Athenian victory over the Boeotians and Chalcidians in 506 B.C. to Phormio's victory over the Peloponnesian

FIG. 4.7 Delphi, Siphnian Treasury; north frieze, battle of gods and giants (*ca.* 530 B.C.). L. to r., two giants, Dionysus in panther-skin; Cybele in her chariot drawn by lions, who are attacking a giant; Apollo and Artemis, as archers; a giant, labeled Kantharos, with a *kantharos* (drinking-cup) in his helmet-crest; a fallen warrior; and three more giants, with inscribed shields. (Delphi, Museum)

fleet in 429 B.C. Pierre Amandry of the French School found the right answer in 1948. By an analysis of the style of the architecture and the forms of the letters of the inscription he narrowed the date down to the time of the Persian Wars, the years around 480 B.C. He then noticed that the word *hopla*, which ordinarily means arms, was used by Herodotus for the cables of the bridge of boats built by Xerxes across the Hellespont at the time of his invasion of Greece in 480 B.C. After Xerxes' defeat at Salamis, the Athenians sailed to the Hellespont. When they returned, "they brought with them the cables of the bridge to be dedicated in the sanctuaries." Here then at Delphi, festooned against the great polygonal wall and protected by a narrow portico, the Athenians displayed the captured cables of Xerxes' bridge, a proud and distinctive trophy.

This brilliant interpretation by Amandry, so clear, so simple, so surely right once it has been proposed, shows that progress is to be made not only by excavation but by a correct understanding of ancient texts.

If we consider that the Siphnian and the Athenian Treasuries were but two of twenty-three such buildings known to have graced the precinct in its prime, we can get some idea of the dazzling effect of the total display. The treasuries were thank-offerings, and they were designed to dazzle—this too is the Greek way—to affirm success, to display wealth, to defy rivals, and to insult the vanquished. When, as often, the victors of one monument were the vanquished of another, the moral could not have escaped so quickwitted a people as the Greeks: perhaps it is in this context that we should interpret the famous mottoes, "Know thyself" and "Nothing in excess," allegedly inscribed in or near the Delphic Temple of Apollo. Perhaps it would break our stereotype of Greek restraint—which was really controlled excitement—if we could see one Athenian monument at Delphi of which we are told: a bronze palm tree with gold dates, surmounted by a golden statue of Athena.

The old Temple of Apollo (seat of the famous Delphic oracle and of the stone *omphalos* [belly-button], the navel-stone of the world), which crowned the site, was traditionally the fourth on the same spot. It was accidentally burned in 548, and the rebuilding was undertaken (513-505) by that great Athenian noble clan, traditional enemies of the Pisistratid tryanny, the clan to which both Cleisthenes and Pericles belonged, the Alcmaeonidae. The contract, Herodotus says, called for limestone construction, but the Alcmaeonids gained great fame by finishing off the front in Parian marble, as Pindar also mentions in his *Seventh Pythian Ode*, written in 486 to celebrate the victory of one of the clan, Megacles, in a Delphic chariot race. The French excavations have confirmed the accuracy of Herodotus' account of the Alcmaeonids' noble gesture: the steps, orthostates (lowest wall slabs), ornaments of the main door, inner pavement, inner columns, cornice, and roof tiles proved to be indeed of marble. The new temple, much larger than the old, required a longer, wider terrace, which wiped out a number of old shrines. Four generations later an earthquake destroyed the Alcmaeonid temple; the ruins the visitor sees today are of the fourth century. The motifs in the Alcmaeonid pediments glorified Apollo not as purifier, singer, or prophet, but as warrior. The subject of one was his epiphany, of the other (as on the Siphnian Treasury) the victory of the gods over the giants. In the nearby precinct of the goddess Earth, Apollo was portrayed again as a warrior, but this time as a baby vanquishing the serpent—the Python—to found his shrine.

The Alcmaeonids building their great temple, like the Siphnians building their treasury, felt their prestige at stake, as dedicators always did in the palmy days of this great international shrine. And so the offerings of the archaic period are always of high quality, using the purest of the styles and materials peculiar to each city, the finest of its craftsmen, or, failing them, the finest that could be hired elsewhere. Doric force, Ionic grace, Attic measure, all are here. They are the three legs of the Delphic tripod; lacking any one, it would fall. Delphi was a microcosm which, with the oracle's advice about the planting of colonies, influenced the whole Greek world. Here met east and west, mother cities and colonies, mainlander and islander. Here great events were commemorated in a living museum of history and of art. The treasures of the Delphi Museum do not represent a hundredth part of the sanctuary's ancient wealth: barbarians and emperors, villagers and connoisseurs have seen to that. We do not possess a single *objet d'art* of the many praised by Pausanias, with the exception of a bronze snake base of a golden tripod in Istanbul. What we have is but the small change from a great fortune, the pale reflection of a radiance that once illumined the whole ancient world.

Near Akraiphnion, twelve miles north of Thebes, the French have excavated at Ptoion a seventh-century triple-terraced sanctuary and oracle of Apollo, famous for its splendid archaic kouroi and korai, the choicest of which are on display in the National Museum in Athens. The upper terrace contained the temple, convenient to the oracular cave and salt spring, approached by a ramp. On the middle terrace was an archaic poros building and facing stoas of the third century B.C.; on the lower terrace an elaborate cistern with seven compartments. West of this sanctuary was another, also of seventh-century date, to the hero Ptoios, son of the earth goddess Gaia. Her temple was on an upper terrace, his on a lower, distinguished by twenty-eight tripod bases, dated 550-450 B.C. A quadrennial music festival held here in honor of Apollo flourished in Hellenistic times. A fine small site museum houses a remarkable number of animal figurines (some choice ones also in Athens): stags, horses, bulls, of a fine austere archaic grace.

At Kalapódi, in ancient Locris, some twenty kilometers

north of Orchomenos, Germans since 1975 have been excavating a sanctuary whose pottery, some of it with graffiti,
bridges the usual gap between Late Helladic III and Sub-
Mycenaean. The Geometric shrine (end of the eighth century) preserved a chronological series of votive offerings: a
lion, a bird, a tripod, jewelry, and armor in bronze, a mask
of Artemis, fibulae, iron spits and weapons, a kouros statuette of about 500 B.C. The excavators distinguish three phases
of a temple, which was burned about 550, rebuilt, and sacked
by the Persians in 480. It yielded a terracotta cornice, roof
tiles, and an acroterion (sphinx). To the latest phase (late
fifth century) belong an internal colonnade and the cult
statue, perhaps of Artemis Elaphebolia (Deer-Shooter).

No small part of Delphi's glory and of Boeotia's provincial
art was due to Athens. Archaic Athens could make dedications because she was prosperous. The cause of her prosperity was her increased commerce, and part of the evidence
for it is her splendid pottery, the study and sensitive classifi-
cation of which is one of the great triumphs of Greek archaeology in the last fifty years.

The ware that succeeded Geometric in Athens is called
Proto-Attic. It goes back to the very beginning of the
seventh century or even a little earlier, and shows a delight
in curves, a vitality, a robust individuality, massive, powerful, sometimes crude, in revolt against the discipline of the
Geometric. The style develops into one of broad contrasts,
turbulent and impatient. One of the finest examples, (Fig.
4.8) an amphora fifty-six inches high, containing a child
burial, was discovered by George Mylonas in 1954 in his
excavations of the cemetery at Eleusis, and is now in the
Eleusis Museum. He dates it about 675. On the neck is the
earliest known illustration of the famous scene from the
Odyssey, of Odysseus blinding the drunken Cyclops (note
the wine cup) by boring into his eye with a huge sharpened
stake. On the shoulder a lion enthusiastically attacks a slink-

FIG. 4.8 Eleusis, Proto-Attic amphora, over four feet high (*ca.* 675).
Subjects: Odysseus blinding Polyphemus, Gorgons (with meshed
teeth) fleeing. (Eleusis, Museum)

ing boar; on the body a pair of Gorgons in split skirts flee
in dismay from Perseus (his winged boots just visible at the
right) who has just beheaded their sister Medusa. Perseus is
under the protection of Athena, respondent in a long white
robe. This is the earliest known rendition of Gorgons, and
the painter is clearly experimenting, not without humor: the
Gorgons are more bewildered than fearsome. For a Gorgon
to make the flesh creep, Greek art has to wait nearly 100
years (see Fig. 4.19).

This riotous indiscipline reduces itself in a couple of
generations to the order and delicacy of Attic black-figure,
so called because the design was painted in black silhouette
against the handsome light red background of the clay.
The most famous and elaborate example of black-figure
ware has been known since 1844. It comes, like much of the
best Attic pottery, from Etruria, near Chiusi, and is called
from its discoverer the François Vase. The style dates it
about 570. It is now in the Archaeological Museum in Florence. Its six bands with their over 200 figures, labeled as
on the Siphnian Treasury, make up a meticulously detailed
anthology of archaic myth, relieved by touches of humor,
as when objects as well as figures are labeled: "Water-pot,"
"Stool," "Fountain." In Fig. 4.9, for example, the top band
shows Theseus and the young Athenian hostages, disem-
barking, probably on Delos, where they will dance their
crane-dance, after their escape from the Cretan Minotaur.
One young man (*under* the ship) is so eager that he swims
ashore. In the upper left corner is something new in Greek
art: individual pride in artistic creation, symbolized by the
signatures of the potter, Ergotimos, and the painter, Kleitias.
Next below, Lapiths, led by Theseus, fight centaurs. In the
central band, gods and goddesses magnificently mounted in
chariots and richly dressed take the curse off the nymph
Thetis' marriage to the mortal Peleus by bringing gifts to
the wedding. Their son was Achilles, doomed to die at
Troy. On the handle adjoining, Ajax carries Achilles' limp,

FIG. 4.9 The François Vase, a masterpiece of Attic black-figure (*ca.* 570). Florence, Museo Archeologico, by permission.

dead body from the field. Kleitias' mood could change from rollicking humor to deeply tragic irony. Next below, burlesque again: Hephaestus, drunk, mounted on a jackass and escorted by Silens, returns triumphantly to Olympus to release Hera from the diabolical chair he invented as revenge on her for ejecting him from heaven. Kleitias has drawn Zeus's fearsome consort stuck fast in a chair she cannot get out of. Below, stylized animals; on the foot, pygmies and cranes fight it out in a burlesque battle, which would remind the spectator of Theseus' crane-dance on Delos, thus harking back to the scene on the top band and binding the whole composition subtly together. For elegance of drawing and coherence of plan this vase has no equal in archaic painting. And the artist's chaffing, intimate treatment of his myths should teach us not to be too stuffy about our Greeks, while the stark pathos of the Ajax-Achilles scene should remind us that for them, sophistication was neither shallow, brittle, nor unfeeling.

About 530, Attic red-figure was invented to give the artist a freer medium for line drawing, making it possible for him to exalt the human figure and pay closer attention to anatomy, and set the figures in much more complicated positions. Recent experiments have so convincingly reproduced the ancient techniques that their publication will be very useful to forgers. The artist made a preliminary sketch with a pointed charcoal stick, then outlined his figure with a broad band of heavy glaze. Next, he filled in the background with a dark brown, glistening, heavy, creamy slip, made by mixing clay with water in the presence of a colloidal agent such as wood ash, whose function was to remove the heavier particles from the clay. After the slip was applied, the pot was placed in the kiln and heated to 800° centigrade. (A skilled potter can judge the temperature in the kiln by observing the incandescent color, and ancient potters experimented with temperature on test pieces.) This first stage of firing took place under oxidizing conditions; i.e., by admitting air through vents. At 800° C. the potter cut down the oxygen by closing the air vents and throwing in green wood. He now raised the temperature to 945° C., then lowered it to 875° C., by which time the green wood was all consumed. Then he opened the air vents, and oxidizing conditions again prevailed. The reducing process had changed the red ferric oxide in the clay to ferrous oxide: at this stage the whole vase was black. The reoxidizing affected only the unslipped, porous parts of the vase, the parts that contained the drawing. These turned back to red, while the background, covered with slip, was nonporous and remained black. Some black lines in finished red-figure ware stand out in relief. The recent experiments prove that this effect was produced with a still heavier slip, thickened with honey, which the potter or painter applied with a syringe like a pastry tube. Egg white brushed on to the relief line could be used as an adhesive for applying gold leaf if desired; the gold would not melt in the kiln because the melting point of gold is higher than the highest kiln temperature the potter wanted to achieve. Burnishing with a polishing stone and polishing further with a soft cloth helped to bring out the metallic luster of the slip when it was fired.

The handsome pots, in varied and graceful shapes, that resulted from this ingenious and practical technique took over the whole Greek market. Since many of the pots are signed, many artists' techniques have long been recognizable. The discriminating eye and retentive memory of J. D. (later Sir John) Beazley, at work on these pots over the last fifty years, have associated hundreds of unsigned pots and fragments with known painters, and reduced the history of the red-figure style to an admirably convincing classical order.

One distinguishing mark of the new style is the frequent abandonment of myth in favor of scenes of everyday life. An example is the shallow drinking cup in Würzburg (Fig. 4.10) by the Brygos Painter (at work about 500-470; this cup perhaps of 490). (What may well be his workshop—at any rate a room filled with sherds of his pottery—was found recently in Marathon St., between the Ceramicus and Plato's

FIG. 4.10 Würzburg, cup by the Brygos painter (*ca.* 490): revelry and aftermath. (Seltman, *Attic Vase-Painting*, Pl. 26, by permission of the Harvard University Press)

Academy, by the busy salvage team of the Greek Archaeological Service.) On the outside of the Würzburg cup a
bearded man, somewhat the worse for drink, in a cloak and
slippers, mishandles a girl and tries to snatch from her the
drinking cup she is balancing in her left hand. The delicate
finality of the gesture by which she brushes him off has been
described as "one of the finest impressions ever achieved by
an artist." Our cup was no doubt designed to hold trans-
parent white wine, which would have left visible the delightfully Attic cautionary tale painted on the inside, wherein
a young man is being sick, his head tenderly held by a flute-
girl, perhaps the same girl who repulsed the advances of the
older man on the cup's exterior. One is reminded of Aristotle's notion of temperance, which, he says, lies in a mean
between drunkenness and total abstention. The object-lesson,
plus the perfect composition, combine to make a work of
art that is Greek in the best sense, in which perfection of
form is wedded, with sophisticated humor, to subtlety of
content.

Typically Greek, too, is the conservatism with which red-
figure was adopted, from about 530. At the beginning, we
find transitional pots, black-figure on one side, red-figure on
the other. Another piece of conservatism: at the Panathenaic
festival (founded 566), the prizes were amphoras filled with
olive oil. At the time the competition was founded, black-
figure was the conventional style: Panathenaic prize amphoras continued to be painted in black-figure for centuries,
even after red-figure had become the vogue on all other
pottery; and the latest examples belong to a time when even
red-figure had died out. After 480, red-figure painters began
to split into more or less manneristic schools; by 450, vase-
painting had sunk to a minor art; by 320, the *genre* was
finished. But in its prime it supplied to Greek commerce the
handsomest containers the world has ever known.

Sixth-century Athens, in which the black-figure and red-
figure vases were painted, was dominated by two strong-

minded figures, Solon (archon 594/3: the split date means
that the Attic civil year began in July) and Pisistratus
(tyrant probably 560-556 and 546-527). They brought prosperity, reflected in an ambitious building program, a new
coinage, and a flowering of the arts. One pious duty was to
build on the Acropolis, in thanksgiving, a worthy temple to
Athena, the city's patron saint.

In modern times, hardly had Greece been freed from the
Turks when, in 1833, Greek archaeologists set to work to
clear the Acropolis of all vestiges of the hated Ottoman
domination, and to uncover the remains of the glorious
past. Four slabs of the Parthenon frieze were found in the
1833 campaign, the first guards of the Acropolis antiquities
were posted, and in September of 1834, in the presence of
the new King, a column of the Parthenon was re-erected,
and the temple decked with myrtle and olive boughs. The
great classical monuments were uncovered in rapid succession: the Nike Temple and the Propylaea steps in 1835,
the Erechtheum in 1837. In that same year the Greek
Archaeological Society was founded: it held its first meeting
in the Parthenon, then still disfigured with a Turkish minaret
that survived till 1905. The building of the Acropolis
Museum began in 1864; in 1875, with funds supplied by
Schliemann, the Frankish tower at the Acropolis entrance
was taken down. But not till 1885-90 was excavation in
depth attempted.

Among the incalculably rich finds, of which more will
be said later, the area south and southeast of the Parthenon
yielded in 1888 a remarkable three-bodied monster in *poros*
(limestone) now in the Acropolis Museum. It tapered away
in a coiling mass of tails in a way which revealed clearly
that it had been carved to fit into the acute angle of a
pediment. Most archaeologists assign the sculpture to the
early archaic predecessor of the Periclean Parthenon, the
Hekatompedon ("Hundred-Footer"), whose foundations
now lie concealed under the surviving building. The lime-

FIG. 4.11   Athens, triple-headed sea monster from pediment of a
poros temple (*ca.* 570), affectionately known as Athos, Porthos,
and Aramis. (Acropolis Museum)

stone had been brilliantly painted, and the colors were
still vivid when the piece was found, though they have
faded since. The right-hand head (Fig. 4.11) had a blue
moustache and beard, and hence, inevitably, was nicknamed
"Bluebeard." The eyes had a blue iris with a deeply incised
pupil, the eyelids were dark, the lips red. The flesh was
rose-colored, the tails blue and red. The hair is white, and
crimped in front into a high fringe. From the opposite angle
of the pediment comes another snaky-tailed group of Heracles wrestling with Triton, "the Old Man of the Sea." In

the center was a pair of lions. Other similar fragments belong to the opposite pediment.

Pisistratus built another temple, whose plan has been unearthed (see frontispiece), between the Parthenon and the Erechtheum. It lay over the old Mycenaean palace. It had marble figures in the pediments, of Athena battling the giants. After the battle of Marathon (490 B.C.) the Athenians demolished the "Hundred Footer" to make way for a new temple, the "Older Parthenon," built of marble from the newly opened Pentelic quarries. This temple remained unfinished when the Persians sacked Athens in 480. Some of its column drums, showing damage by fire, are still visible, built into the Acropolis wall.

Besides the temple on the Acropolis, Pisistratus the Younger (ca. 515) planned a temple to Olympian Zeus. It was abandoned at his death, taken up again in Hellenistic times, and not finished until Hadrian's reign (A.D. 131/2). It thus has one of the longest building records in the history of architecture. But not all Pisistratus' public works projects were doomed to frustration. To him or his sons are to be ascribed an ambitious drainage system; a shrine of Eleusinian Demeter under the north slope of the Acropolis; a new market place with temples and secular buildings, including housing for law court and council, with a room for the deposit of official weights and measures. South of the Olympieion about 500 B.C. was built another law court, the Delphinion, for certain murder cases.

American excavations in the Athenian agora (see Chapter 8) have added much to our knowledge of the city's appearance in Pisistratid and earlier times. The excavators found that early Athens clustered close round the Areopagus and Acropolis; down to the early sixth century the Agora, like the Roman Forum, was a cemetery. It was taken over for public purposes because it was the largest open and level area under the shelter of the Acropolis, and because it was on the direct route from the Acropolis to the Dipylon Gate.

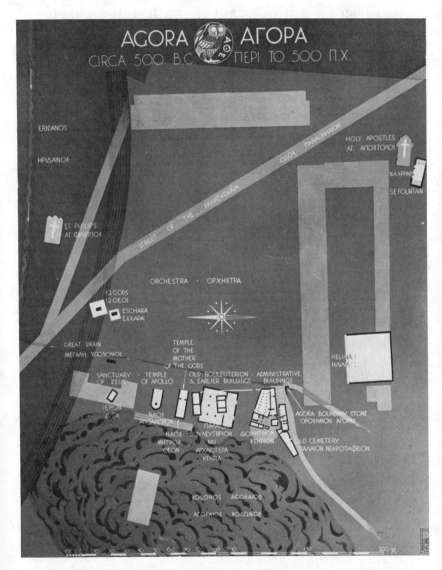

Fig. 4.12 Athens, Agora about 500 B.C., plan (Agora Excavations). North is to the left.

The earliest civic building, two rooms under the Metroön, on the west side of the Agora (see plan, Fig. 4.12), probably dates from the time of Solon (594/3). In 1931 a flood revealed the Cleisthenean Great Drain down the west side of the Agora, which fixed the line of later buildings west of it. Tiles in it stamped "Mother of the Gods" came from the nearby Metroön, in which the excavators distinguished sixteen complex levels. It began as a small archaic temple, was expanded to house the city's archives, and after 150 B.C. was remodeled into four rooms of various sizes sharing a 129-foot portico that faced the morning light; the slope of Kolonos Agoraios sheltered the buildings on this side of the Agora from the scorching afternoon sun. Between the Stoa of Zeus and the Panathenaic Way, excavation in 1970 revealed another Pisistratid building, the King Archon's Stoa, identified from inscriptions. It was used sometimes for meetings of the Areopagus, as law court, and perhaps as dining hall. Three more column drums from it turned up in an archaic context in the summer of 1980.

Also Pisistratid proved (1935) to be the Southeast Fountain House, a lobby with side compartments for water basins; its building produced a remarkable outburst of representations of fountain houses on black-figure vases. Pisistratid too is the Panathenaic Way, where passed the procession instituted by the tyrant and immortalized on the Parthenon frieze. On the flat, this road was metaled with layer after layer of firmly packed gravel; on the slopes, at least in Roman times, it was paved with large slabs. Rectangular sockets at the curb may have had something to do with snubbing or braking the ship-float that carried Athena's peplos (the ceremonial embroidered garment offered to the goddess at the Panathenaic festival), or with some means of spectator control, or with supports for spectators' stands. Pisistratus built the earliest (apsidal) temple of Apollo Patroös, where citizens were registered and the city fathers took their oaths of office. The mold for its bronze cult statue was found in a pit nearby. Like most of the Agora's Pisistratid buildings, it was destroyed in the Persian sack of 480/79, and not restored until the fourth century.

From Pisistratus' tyranny dates the predecessor of the Tholos, in this phase an irregular court surrounded by rooms. It was the headquarters of Athenian government, where the Committee of the Council in charge of Athens for the day took their meals, and where a number of them slept at night, so that responsible persons might be always on call. This practice continued long after Athens ceased to be politically important: a Hellenistic decree, found in 1938, authorizes the purchase for the Tholos of furniture, mattresses, and crockery.

Pisistratus' grandson (Thuc. 6.54), archon 522/1, built an Altar to the Twelve Gods. The excavators in 1934 found between the rail of the Athens-Piraeus electric railway the footings for the altar fence, and the pits for the plantings of olive and laurel that surrounded it. It became the zero milestone, the place from which distances from Athens were reckoned, like the Miliarium Aureum in the Forum at Rome. Its location, by the Panathenaic Way at the convergence of arterial highways, was appropriate for this purpose. The Athens-Piraeus electric railway covers its northeastern part. It was identified from a statue base inscribed, "Leagros, son of Glaucon, to the Twelve Gods." The dedicator was a popular young man in Athens between 510 and 500: five "love-vases" bear his name.

The Pisistratids left the Agora a loose series of small buildings in an arc along the west side of a graveled area crossed by the Panathenaic Way but eroded by freshets. The south edge is typical of how the Agora developed: at first a Bronze Age track serving a hamlet, then a cemetery path, finally (toward the end of the sixth century) a formal boundary. Cleisthenes, the founder of democracy, began in 509 to monumentalize the Agora and straighten its boundaries; some of his stone markers were discovered, one of them *in situ.* His chief building was the Old Bouleuterion (Council House) built to accommodate his new Council of 500. At this time the Assembly moved to the Pnyx, and dramatic contests were transferred to the south slope of the Acropolis. However, the Orchestra in the middle of the Agora, where they had been held, continued in use as the place where lots were drawn for jury duty and other public functions (for Athens carried the premise of democracy to its logical conclusion, and assumed that any citizen was capable of discharging any civic responsibility except the conduct of war). Near the site of the Orchestra a number of interesting machines for drawing and recording the lots was found; though Hellenistic, they almost certainly reflect earlier practice. The ingenious interpretation of these enigmatic objects is due to Professor Sterling Dow of Harvard. A hole is drilled vertically through the left side of the stele (Fig. 4.13), widening to a funnel at the top, opening on the face of the stele at the bottom. The slots at the right are for the tickets of those wanting jury duty. An official dropped into the funnel a number of white balls for jurors to be empaneled and black balls for jurors to be dismissed. Each ball, emerging at the bottom of the tube, determined the use or rejection of a whole horizontal row of would-be jurors. Once the chosen jurors were empaneled, they were assigned by lot to the court where they would sit. The last-minute allotment was obviously designed to prevent corruption of a jury sitting on a given case, and a check of the dicast tickets would prevent a juror's collecting for duty he had not performed. The assumption throughout is the realistic one that human nature is not proof against temptation.

The democratic Athens established by Cleisthenes had soon to face the Persian menace. Herodotus tells how the 192 Athenian heroes who fell at Marathon in 490 were buried on the battlefield under a mound. Greek archaeologists excavated it in 1890 and, nine feet below ground level, hit upon a floor of sea sand and marble chips, with one to

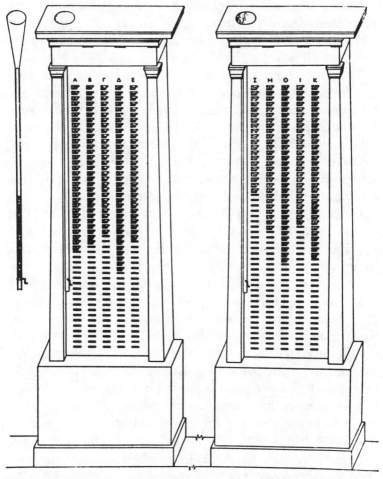

FIG. 4.13 Athens, Agora, allotment machine, reconstruction draw-
     ing (S. Dow)

four inches of ash, charcoal, human bones, and black-figure
lekythoi. The next year they found a sacrificial trench lined
with fired brick and containing the bones of animals, pottery
used in the funeral banquet, and quantities of arrowheads in
obsidian (used by Ethiopian archers) and bronze. One set
of bones in a special pot might be the remains of the Pole-

march or Minister of War, who gave up to Miltiades his turn to command and fell fighting. At Vrana, about two miles west-northwest of the Athenian mound, another covered the remains of Plataeans, loyal allies.

The funds for all these ambitions schemes came in part from exploiting newly discovered veins of silver in the mountainous Laurium district of Attica, near Sunium, not far from Pisistratus' Brauron estates. In 1860, examination of slag from the ancient workings proved that it was worth reprocessing for silver, lead, manganese, and zinc. The engineers coöperated with French archaeologists and made possible a fruitful study of the mining processes of Pisistratus' day and after.

Laurium's geological strata are limestone and schist. The Greeks early discovered, perhaps as early as Minoan and Mycenaean times, that the ore lay between these strata, and their tunnels for it, reused by the modern engineers, are like wormholes in wood. Red iron oxide on the surface, which usually accompanies lead crystals, supplied the clues for digging. Since the tunnels are seldom more than a meter high, the workmen—usually slaves and criminals—had to work on their knees or bellies, but this, with the tools at their disposal, was probably preferable to enlarging the tunnels to man's height. Since the ore was carried out in sacks, not cars, there was no need for the tunnels to run level. Archaeologists have found rings for chaining the slaves, driven into the tunnel walls, and lamps with a ten-hour capacity, but the shifts were probably only two hours long. Where the tunnels went deep into the mountainside horizontally, they were also connected with the surface by vertical shafts from 200 to 350 feet deep, up which the baskets of ore were run on pulleys. Parallel or inclined shafts with dampers supplied ventilation. The mines were underground cities, with streets, wells, squares, crossroads, and workshops. They were state property, but let to entrepreneurs on seven- to ten-year leases, at ridiculously low rates (twenty to 150 drachmae a year.) Since 1949 over seventy-five inscriptions (of the fourth century) recording such leases have been excavated in the Athenian Agora.

The ore was pulverized with mortar and pestle, then washed so that the heavy lead would settle. At Dhemaliaki, in the Laurium area, three miles inland from Thorikos, the Belgian excavators found a unique washing device: an inclined helix with rock-cut cups in it. Pulverized ore mixed with water ran down it, and, settling in the cups, classified itself according to density. On the acropolis of Thorikos has been excavated an early Mycenaean tholos, uniquely oval in shape, which looks like an overturned boat. Numbers of ancient washing basins survive. Methods of extraction were efficient: the surviving slag heaps never showed more than 12 per cent mineral deposit. The lead was extracted by melting it with iron, with a flux (to make slag) such as calcium carbonate; this yields ferrous sulphide and pure lead. The lead flowed out of the high-chimneyed furnaces down channels into forms for ingots. The Athenians extracted silver by filtering the lead ore through a porous material, bone ash or certain clays, and superheating the silver-bearing lead with an excess of oxygen. Archaeologists have identified the treasury where the precious metal was kept: a tower at Sunium, connected with the operations of a mint, where they found a bronze pinion wheel designed to engage a ratchet for lifting such heavy objects as bar silver, and also a weight (1,000 tetradrachms) inscribed with a mint magistrate's name. The silver kept there was .978 fine. The total production has been calculated at over 2,000,000 tons of silver-bearing lead. The richest veins were not exploited early; it was hardly worthwhile to work the Laurium mines intensively until rivals were eliminated, as after the Siphnian mines were flooded in 525, and after the mineral-rich island of Thasos in the north Aegean fell to Athens (463). In the years after Marathon the surplus silver from the Laurium mines was struck into handsome ten-drachma coins (Fig. 4.14) for distribution to the citizens as a bonus. But in 484

Fig. 4.14 Athens, silver decadrachm, Athena and owl, *ca.* 486.
(Seltman, *A Book of Greek Coins,* Pl. 47, a & b)

they voluntarily surrendered the bonus: Themistocles used it to build the triremes that beat the Persians at Salamis.

One of the finds from the Acropolis excavations of 1886 was a small hoard of silver coins hidden before the Persian sack and never recovered. Some of the coins bear the familiar Athenian device of the owl and Athena; others are stamped on the obverse with a four-spoke chariot wheel; the reverse is deeply cut with what numismatists call an "incuse square," intended to prove that the coin is silver all the way through, and not just base metal plated. Ancient coins were struck from blanks placed between two dies. The lower, let into an anvil, produced the obverse; the upper, let into the end of a punch, produced the reverse. When the silversmith struck the punch with a hammer, the blank received simultaneously the impression of both dies. Since punch-dies wore out faster than anvil dies, sequences of coins can be arranged by careful attention to the degree of wear on their anvil-dies.

Other obverse devices besides the wheel occur on early Athenian coins (Wappenmünzen) found elsewhere than in the Acropolis hoard. They include, among others, the triskeles (three bent legs radiating from a center), the forepart of a horse, the hindquarters of a horse, a bull's head, and a horseman. These same symbols occur as shield devices on vase paintings, and may be intended to identify persons, like the shield devices of King Arthur's knights. Greek literature suggests that they may be the badges of various noble clans: triskeles and chariot wheel perhaps associated with the Alcmaeonidae (Pindar wrote an ode on the chariot victory of the Alcmaeonid Megacles at Delphi); the bull's head with a priestly clan called the Eteobutadae, etc. The choice of the hindquarters of a horse may be ironic, mocking: this device shares the same anvil die with the Alcmaeonid chariot wheel: the most likely mocker of this clan would be its enemy, Pisistratus. The chariot-wheel types in the Acropolis hoard have been approximately dated, from the die sequences and from similar devices on datable vases, 589-561:* they fit the period between Solon's archonship and Pisistratus' first tyranny, when the nobility was in the ascendant. If Seltman's date for the owl-Athena series from the same hoard (555-527) is right, it falls within Pisistratus' period of exile and his second tyranny. Perhaps while he was jockeying for power he used his personal, mocking, horse's hindquarters type; when he won control, he chose a device symbolizing all Athens. Other scholars date the owl-Athena series 520/10, when Pisistratus' son Hippias was in power. Whoever initiated it, it remained Athens' symbol right down through Roman times. Some of the earlier owl-Athena types in the Acropolis hoard bear an unusual lettering, found also on Attic coins from Paeonia, far to the north, where Pisistratus was in exile (probably 555-546). This series used up no less than twenty-six anvil dies, an index to great mint activity. Perhaps it was Pisistratus' war-chest to pay the troops who were to secure his return. Some of the later Pisistratid coins are as handsome as medals: they may have been struck to commemorate Panathenaic festivals. After 546 the Attic mint produced no more individual badges, though the Alcmaeonids still used them on coins they struck in exile at Delphi.

The coin propaganda, therefore, marks Pisistratus as the precursor of Athenian democracy, since his choice of the owl-Athena type remained the democracy's symbol to the end. However little the progaganda may have fitted the facts, the change from aristocratic badges to the owl-Athena type is concrete evidence for what the historians tell us: that he broke the political power of the Athenian aristocracy.

---

* A 1962 analysis of copper impurities dates the Wappenmünzen 575-25, and the owls 525-479. Some scholars (not all) think this dating (Seltman's) is too high, and the coin devices religious, not personal. Yet Seltman's ingenuity is worth recording, and the numismatic evidence for the Pisistratids' breaking the nobility's power and preparing the way for democracy is not in doubt. The owl-Athena series is unquestionably Pisistratid, and the owl and Athena continued to symbolize Athenian democracy as long as it lasted.

Though Pisistratus might break the aristocrats' political power, he could not so easily undermine their social position. The outward and visible sign of their prestige was the dedication of statues of their sons (*kouroi*) and daughters (*korai*) on the Acropolis. When the Athenians returned to their blackened shrines after the Persian sack in 480 B.C., they determined to waste no time on repairs or patching, much less on antiquarian respect for archaic art (the Greeks were so modern!), but to make a clean sweep of the debris and start the beautification of the Acropolis afresh.* During the 1885-90 Acropolis excavations, on two fruitful days in February, 1886, fourteen of the finest sixth-century statues of maidens (now in the Acropolis Museum) were found packed together in a hole northwest of the Erechtheum. These serene, festal types of aristocratic Athenian young womanhood are known, rather unfeelingly, by their inventory numbers. One of the loveliest, No. 679 (Fig. 4.15), the small-scale Peplos Korê (only four feet high, in Parian marble), explains why one Greek word for "statue" is also the word for "delight." It is in as nearly perfect condition as an ancient statue can be (the lower left arm is missing; the dowel hole for it is visible in the photograph). It must have stood under cover from the time of its dedication, about 530, until the Persians overthrew it: it shows no signs of weathering, and its ancient painting is well preserved. The maiden wears a green necklace, her robe is green-bordered at the throat, her sleeve bears a pattern of green running spirals. Her hair, lips, and iris are dark red; pupils, brows, and lashes black. Her ears are pierced for earrings, and she originally wore a bronze coronet, of which the insertion holes and some of the nails survive. The sculptor has rendered to perfection her taut vitality, the independence of her body beneath her dress. This is archaic

---

* In the summer of 1980, a deposit from a similar clean-up was found beside the Panathenaic Way in the Agora.

Fig. 4.15   Athens, Acropolis Museum, Peplos Korè, *ca.* 530, detail.
(Lullies, *Greek Sculpture*, Pl. 43, by permission of Hirmer
Verlag, Munich)

art at its lyric best. It successfully reproduces the forms observed in nature, and yet conforms to the language of a convention (the archaic smile, the hair style) as precise and exacting as the rhythm of the most strictly metrical verse. The Peplos Korê, then, is a true product of the lyric age of Greece. It achieves the universal without falsifying the unique. One feels that it was from the loins of girls like these that sprang the heroes who commanded at Marathon and Salamis.

At Myrrhinous, in central Attica near Markópoulo, was found in 1972 a splendid pair, kore and kouros, in Parian marble, of about 540 B.C., carefully buried before Xerxes' invasion. An inscription tells us the kore's name: it was Phrasikleia, she was perhaps an Alcmaeonid, and she died a virgin—her breasts are immature. The painted decoration was almost intact: her dress bore rosettes in yellow and black, swastikas, stars, a meander; down the front, lotus flowers and buds; at the hem, a tongue pattern in red and black. She wears necklace, earrings, bracelet, and coronet. Her sandals have thick soles; she carries a flower. The kouros stands six feet two, wears his hair in a fringe and in a bandeau; his hair and irises are red. The sculptor was Aristion of Paros, active 550-525. The quiet pathos of Phrasikleia is related to that of a famous later series of Attic grave stelae from the Ceramicus (Hegeso, Ampharete), which embodies the noble simplicity and quiet grandeur so much admired in the eighteenth century by Winckelmann. The korai, kouroi, and stelae also symbolize family and clan solidarity.

The search for inscriptions for the massive Berlin *Corpus*, embracing all Greek inscriptions, led to the excavation (1896-1902) by Baron Hiller von Gaertringen of a charmingly sited little archaic Greek mountain town, Thera, on the picturesque volcanic island of Santorin, in the Aegean some twelve hours' steaming southeast of Piraeus; some, including the excavator of Akrotiri (see p. 125), have thought it is Plato's lost Atlantis. Hiller first went there to study some very old (seventh century) rock-cut inscriptions, recording boy-love of the Spartan sort. He soon decided that their meaning would not be clear without the excavation of the buildings adjoining (see plan, Fig. 4.16).

Hiller dug and published the site at his own expense: his four volumes on Thera are charmingly discursive, more a personal journal than a formal excavation report. He was on the friendliest terms with his forty-five workmen: they made him an honorary citizen of their village, and, led by their bearded Arcadian foreman, danced their age-old dances in front of the Thera museum at its dedication. At the start of the 1900 season the island band, the Phira Philharmonic, resplendent in uniform, played in the recently discovered Hellenistic theater. They were very proud: "we have a theater just like the Athenians." It had been covered by the excavation dump, and was accidentally discovered by the foreman working on his own in Hiller's absence, an incident typical of the informality of the whole dig. The workmen camped during the excavation season in neat stone huts like igloos, built from such nonsignificant ancient stones as the dig turned up. The site was virtually inaccessible; Hiller nearly killed his mules getting his gear up the mountain. He and his galaxy of volunteer assistants—a roster of the best-known archaeologists of the day—lived and worked in tents, and, with the full consent of the local abbot, in a chapel convenient to the site. Wind was a constant difficulty; the digging had to be shifted from one side of Thera hill to the other, depending on the quarter from which it blew. It ripped the excavation tent, and whisked a mule loaded with ancient pottery off the mountain path to his death. The finds had to be brought down on sledges 1140 feet over slithering volcanic pebbles, and then transported in home-made wagons over roads whose ruts and potholes only the seasoned traveler in out-of-the-way Greek places can visualize.

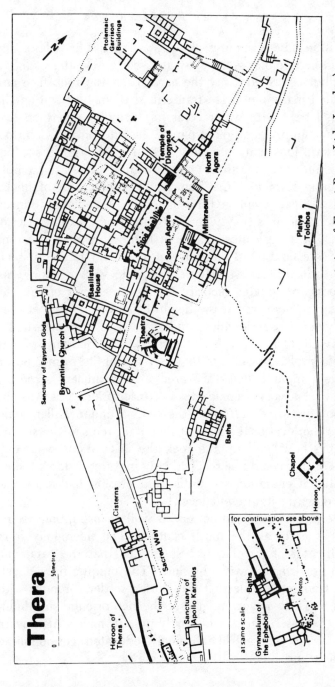

FIG. 4.16 Thera, site plan. (*Blue Guide, Greece*, p 631. By permission of Ernest Benn, Ltd., London)

Within ninety minutes of the start of the first day's dig, Hiller had found seven new rock-cut inscriptions, and a cloudburst washed away the earth from the rock face and revealed many more. He transcribed them by painting the rough letters with water color for legibility and then taking their imprints on oiled paper. The site proved rich, too, in inscriptions conventionally cut in *stelae*: Hiller's eventual grand total was 1070. One of them identified the temple of Apollo Karneios (the Ram Apollo), protector of flocks. At his festival at vintage time, handsome nude youths danced in his honor; it is they who occasioned the rock-cut inscriptions. The temple itself is set in bedrock, and in the rock of its threshold pious pilgrims scratched the outline of their feet. From its cella two entrances, one with a double set of doors for greater security, led to treasuries cut in the cliff face. Thera was at the height of its prosperity between 631, when it was founded, and 571, when it replenished a colony at Cyrene in North Africa. The building of the temple probably belongs to the years of its prime. South of the temple Hiller discovered a very ancient structure built over a very archaic rock-cut inscription: this was the Heroon or shrine of Theras, the city's founder. Hiller could gauge the level of the ancient mountain road to the site by noticing how high up the rock the inscriptions were cut. Some of them could be reached only by three ladders lashed together. Generations of traffic and erosion had worn the road down to its present level.

Thera proved rich in pottery as well as inscriptions, some of it as early as the ninth century. The necropolis from which most of it came was so prolific that the catalogue could not keep up with the finds. The unique, fully developed Geometric style that the Dorian settlers brought with them to Thera never underwent the rich orientalizing influence that, as Hiller picturesquely puts it, makes Attic ware look beside Theran like a finely educated cosmopolitan beside a bureaucrat of the better class.

Besides inscriptions and vases, Thera yielded a large coin hoard, 760 pieces, of the seventh and sixth centuries. Thera's trade relations with Aegina must have been close, for over 70 per cent of the coins found were minted on that island.

Thera's daughter-city, Cyrene, is an Italian excavation. Interest in it was first aroused when a cloudburst in 1913 flooded the temple area and uncovered the voluptuous Aphrodite now in Rome's Terme Museum, perhaps a copy, made for a bath, of a bronze original by Polyclitus. As in the mother city, the most important temple was Apollo's (see plan, Fig. 4.17), whose earliest phase is dated in the early sixth century, and Cyrene, like Thera, has huge necropoleis; its burials range from the sixth century B.C. to the fourth century A.D. Beside Apollo's temple was one to his sister Artemis. The Italians hit upon its foundation deposit, containing objects of gold, silver, bronze, hematite, ivory and amber; ostrich eggs, Corinthian and Attic vases, and lamps, dating from the seventh to the fifth century. It prospered from the export of silphium (asafoedita), which enjoyed wide currency in the ancient world, as condiment, panacea, and aphrodisiac. The plant appears on Cyrene's coins and on a famous archaic Laconian cup of about 560, now in Paris. Arkesilas, King of Cyrene, is portrayed (Fig. 4.18) supervising the loading of bags of silphium onto a ship. Some of the profits were used to support the arts: Cyrene has yielded three fine archaic *kouroi* and two *korai,* of the mid-sixth century B.C.; and Pindar was subsidized to write his longest and most splendid ode, the *Fourth Pythian,* for a king of Cyrene, "the city of noble horses . . . at the shining breast of the sea." Her prosperity lasted down to the end of the archaic period and beyond: the evidence is the temple of Zeus (480-450). Even in its fifth century phase, it was a giant; only the temple of Zeus at Agrigentum and Temple G at Selinus, both to be described later, exceed it in size. It is larger than either the Parthenon or the temple of Zeus at

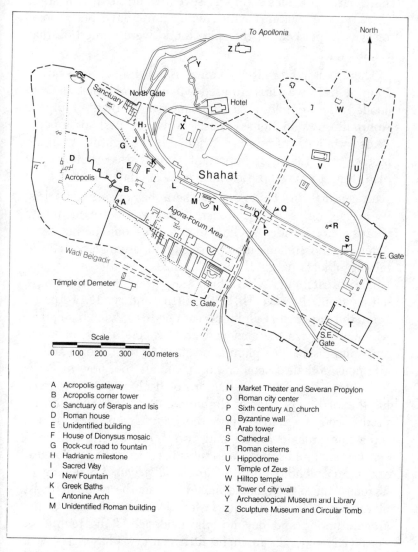

FIG. 4.17 Cyrene, plan. (From P. MacKendrick, *The North African Stones Speak*, Fig. 5.1. Courtesy of the University of North Carolina Press)

FIG. 4.18 Arkesilas cup, Laconian ware from Vulci, in Etruria
(about 550). The king of Cyrene, under canvas on the deck of
a ship, supervises the loading of silphium. (Paris, Bibl. Nat.,
Cabinet des médailles)

Olympia. In its present state (Antonine), with several massive
columns re-erected, it measures 104 by 225 feet. Cyrene's
Agora is mainly Roman, and will be described in the last
chapter, but the alleged tomb of the founder Battus was
venerated there; a copy of the original foundation decree

from Thera was set up in it; one of its porticoes is of the sixth century, and there was a Nike on a ship's prow, perhaps commemorating Pompey's victory over the pirates (67 B.C.).

Traditionally, the Sicilians beat the Carthaginians in the battle of Himera on the day the homeland Greeks beat the Persian off Salamis. Thus did the colonies pay their debt to the mother cities. The archaic age was, as we saw, an age of colonization, and some of the colonies rivaled or outstripped the homeland in wealth and in artistic sophisication. For example, Corcyra, modern Corfu, off the Greek west coast, early achieved prosperity as Corinth's staging point for voyages to Italy and Sicily: from Corcyra's highest mountain the Italian coast is visible on a clear day. In the fields south of the modern town farmers kept turning up ancient architectural blocks, and in December, 1910, they found, upside down where it had fallen, an extraordinary series of pieces of early archaic limestone sculpture, of which the most striking was a fearsome Gorgon (Fig. 4.19), obviously, from the shape of the block, belonging to a pediment. During further excavations the following spring, Kaiser Wilhelm II, vacationing on the island, took a personal interest, summoned Dörpfeld to the spot from Olympia, and won a concession for a German dig. Dörpfeld's pupils published the Gorgon pediment from the epigraphically attested Temple of Artemis. Greek architects and sculptors proved to have been capable of mathematical precision in the early sixth century. The pediment fell into five groups, rendered on three panels each, symmetrically related in width (the outer two not shown in the photograph): they measure 3.02, 3.10, 3.35, 3.10, 3.02 meters. Enough remained of the temple cella ground plan to prove that it was exactly as long as the pediment, and exactly a third as wide. Some of the original cornice was found. It is of terracotta, which ceased to be used for this purpose by 580 B.C.: therefore the sculptured pediment is usually dated 590-580. It was carved probably by a Corinthian sculptor, near the end of Periander's tyranny. The balance in the pediment

FIG. 4.19 Corcyra, pediment of temple of Artemis, *ca.* 580, with Medusa, her sons Pegasus and Chrysaor, and lion-panthers. (Lullies, *op. cit.*, Pl. 15)

is not lifeless. It shows double movement, toward the middle, and toward the corners. It foreshadows the ripe archaism of Aphaia's Temple on Aegina, and the classicism of Olympia and the Parthenon.

The central Gorgon figure is stupendous—over nine feet high—and terrible, with her frightful grin, bared teeth, protruding tongue, and scaly snakes for hair and belt. Her face is frontal, but her bent knees are in profile: the archaic convention for rapid running. Her chiton (shirt reaching to the knees) was originally painted red, her snakes blue, the feathers on her boots alternately red and blue. She was flanked heraldically by her sons; on her right was a rampant Pegasus (the symbol of Corinth). All that remains are his forefoot resting on her arm, his hindquarters, and part of his wings, which are feathered exactly like his mother's. On her left is Chrysaor of the golden sword (this to be restored under his mother's left arm); he has blue hair bound with a red fillet, and a rather bestial grin, obviously inherited. The gigantic felines, a cross-breed of lion and panther, are orientalizing in style, and subtly varied: the left one is angry, the right one placid. But all, Gorgon, brood, and beasts, are apotropaic; i.e., their function is to ward off wicked powers from Artemis' temple and its contents. With the myths of Artemis they have, of course, nothing to do: archaic architectural sculpture seldom bears any relation to the divinity of its temple. In the corners of the pediment (not shown) were unrelated mythological figures. Myth is just beginning to conquer the apotropaic. When it conquers, something solemn, awesome, and hieratic is lost from Greek religious art. But the tension between the apotropaic and the mythological led in the end to the classical pediment. The discovery of this sculpture opened a whole new chapter in Greek art history, a chapter concerned with one of the many early sculptural schools, a selection from which was to make the classical style. Excavation between 1962 and 1967 revealed in the grounds of the former royal summer palace (Mon Repos), a sanctuary, perhaps of Hera, founded in the eighth century, flourishing in the fifth (along with shrines of Apollo, Aphrodite, and Hermes), and surviving into the third. Finds from it, in the local museum, include bronze figures of men and animals, a Gorgoneion, and a lion's head downspout. At nearby Kardaki a small adobe Doric temple, perhaps of Apollo, of about 570, known since 1822, on reinvestigation yielded an acroterial Nike in terracotta, also an altar within a cave, perhaps sacred to Poseidon Hippios.

Selinus in southwest Sicily had, like Corcyra, close trade relations with Corinth. This is proved by Protocorinthian pottery in the Palermo Museum, at last examined scientifically in 1958. Selinus, however, was ultimately a colony not of Corinth but of neighboring Megara, home of the bitter Tory poet Theognis (flourished 548-40). On the acropolis of fever-ridden Selinus, two young English architects, Angell and Harris, excavating at their own expense in 1822-23, were rewarded by the discovery of some of the finest archaic metopes ever unearthed. (Metopes are squarish sculptured slabs that run above the columns of a temple.) The Bourbon government of the Kingdom of Naples interrupted the work, and Harris soon died of fever, but Angell lived to publish his finds. One of the finest (Fig. 4.20), in the Palermo Museum, from Apollo's temple, C, portrays Heracles carrying on his shoulders, trussed like game to a pole, two Cercopes, imps who had annoyed him by changing themselves into blue-bottle flies and troubling his sleep. This, unlike the Corcyra pediment, is real provincial work, with a charming primitive quality of robust realism, and a good instinctive feeling for geometric composition. Because of the time lag between art in the metropolis and on the periphery, provincial work is always difficult to date, especially when, as here, there is nothing but style to go by, but 550-530 seems a likely date.

The treasures of Selinus have neither been completely excavated nor definitively published. On the acropolis are at

FIG. 4.20   Selinus, temple C (550-530), metope of Heracles and
Cercopes. Palermo, Museum. (Villard, 1955, Pl. 96)

least three other temples and blocks of houses; there are silted-up ports on either side; metopes from a very early temple were found in the acropolis north wall (one shows Demeter, Persephone, and Hecate, the other probably Persephone and Pluto in a four-horse chariot); the city proper to the north has never been excavated. Local clandestine diggers consistently rob the seventh-century sanctuary of Demeter Malophoros (pomegranate-bearer) to the west, of its numerous early figurines. Only in the east, where there are three more temples, has there been recent work, limited to re-erecting columns to attract tourists. Of the eastern temples (called, with customary archaeological caution, E, F [Athena's], and G), E, perhaps Hera's, has yielded metopes also, now in the Palermo Museum, but, lovely as they are, they are fifth-century, and fall below the lower limits of this chapter (see Fig. 5.21). G, dedicated to Apollo, is colossal, begun as early as 540, and still unfinished when the Carthaginians sacked Selinus in 409. Selinus may stand as the type of provincial city of the archaic age, rich, but remote from the creative centers of art, which it imitates energetically but without understanding.

Paestum, Greek Posidonia, in south Italy below Salerno, is a different case. There in 1934, at the mouth of the river Sele, two devoted archaeologists, Paola Zancani-Montuoro and U. Zanotti-Bianco, working with private funds, and following clues in ancient literary sources, discovered to their intense joy the largest archaic find in the history of Greek archaeology: an almost complete series of sandstone metopes from a small building (at Olympia or Delphi it would be called a "treasury") in a sanctuary of Hera. Corinthian pottery in the fill dated the building after 575. The work was long drawn out. The excavators had no derricks, no roads, no vehicles but ox-carts. Malaria and pneumonia laid them low, and 1940 found them in a race against war. which finally claimed all their best workmen. Fortunately the finds, stored in a hut on the site, were ignored by both sides in

the war, and between 1948 and 1952 it was found possible
to toughen the friable metopes by sponging them with
sodium silicate, to repair them with brass pegs, and to
install them in a specially built museum near the more
famous temples of Paestum proper.

The metopes survive because they were carved in sandstone. If they had been in limestone or marble, they would
long ago have been reduced to useful whitewash in local
kilns. Even so, many of the metope blocks were found in
reuse in ancient buildings more or less remote from where
they belonged. Of the thirty-two more or less complete
metopes, eleven are unfinished. In them, the relief is blocked
out in angular fashion, but not rounded. Only a sudden
catastrophe could have halted the work thus in mid-course.
Since the frieze blocks had to be put in place before the
building could be roofed, and the sculptors naturally
worked more slowly than the carpenters, the metope blocks
were mounted anyhow, finished or no. The excavators believe the emergency was the threat to the sponsoring city,
Siris, from the coalition against her, sometime between 570
and 560, of the neighboring cities of Sybaris, Metapontum,
and Croton.

The excavators have been able to assign almost every
metope to its place on the treasury, by careful observation
of the subject of the relief, the cuttings on the back for
the ends of roof beams, masons' marks, or, where the
metope was not reused, the spot where it fell. Eighteen
metopes related to Hercules, eleven to the Trojan War; the
rest portray miscellaneous myths. For the sake of comparison and contrast with Selinus, I have chosen (Fig. 4.21)
the rendition of Heracles and the Cercopes, where the
treatment is much crisper, more mature and detailed; e.g.,
one of the Cercopes is bearded, one is not. Here the stiffness is not primitive but deliberate, to enhance the humor
of the situation: one may imagine that the culprits are stiff
with fear of the muscle-bound hero and his mighty club.

On the other metopes, archaic humor abounds, as on the
François Vase: Heracles tries to stuff the boar in on top
of Eurystheus, who set him his labors, and is hiding in a
large jar; Odysseus rides a tortoise; centaurs have human or
horse feet according as they are considered more human
or more beastly. The total effect is one of freshness, intelli-
gence, refinement, boldness, and skill, by more than one
sculptor. One feels this work was done by pioneers. The
excavators claim that the treatment of the myths was influenced by a pioneer lyric poet of the Far West, Stesichorus ("the Choirmaster") of Himera, but their argument

FIG. 4.21   Heraion at mouth of Sele, metope of Heracles and Cercopes, 570-560. Paestum, Museum. (Fototeca)

is more ingenious than cogent, since of Stesichorus' poems hardly more than titles survive.

There was a temple to Hera also on the site; some of its metopes, of graceful dancing maidens, survive. Their technique is riper, and they are dated 510-500. It is possible to argue, from religious buildings in Magna Graecia dated 575-475, of which Selinus and the sanctuary at the mouth of the Sele are only two of many examples, that the fervor, skill, and detail of their architectural sculpture was not matched again in Europe until the Middle Ages.

Five miles southeast of the mouth of the Sele lie the three handsome temples of Paestum proper, so rightly beloved of travelers—though in antiquity no one saw the golden-brown patina: the limestone was stuccoed over. Of the three temples the middle and most perfect is classical (Fig. 5.20) and does not concern us here. The other two are archaic. Excavations since World War II, which have yielded over 1,000,000 small finds, have produced *graffiti*, inscriptions, and foundation deposits like the one under the the archaic Artemision on Delos. These have proved that the three-mile circuit of the city wall is of sixth-century date, that the southern temple, called since the eighteenth century the "Basilica," was dedicated to Hera; the northern ("Ceres") to Athena. Paestum was little visited till the nineteenth century. The railroad did not come till 1884, and the area was infested with malaria and brigands.

The "Basilica," unusually wide in proportion to its length, was built about 550 of limestone with some sandstone details, visible in the photograph (Fig. 4.22) between the two courses of the architrave. The sandstone was used where it was desired to have a soft stone on which to carve moldings. The upper course reveals U-shaped lifting grooves, through which ropes were passed to raise the blocks. These were never intended to be seen; this course was originally two blocks thick; the front blocks, together with the pediment and the cella walls, were long ago carried away.

FIG. 4.22   Paestum, Basilica, *ca.* 550   (Author)

Some of the blocks are built into the eleventh-century churches of nearby Salerno and Amalfi. Different columns show different details under the sturdy, spreading Doric capitals; these may have been artisans' signatures. The columns show entasis, or swelling in their vertical profiles, an aesthetic refinement to be discussed in more detail when we treat the Parthenon. The details were picked out in color, always the same color for the same element. This is part of the formal lyricism of archaic architecture: red for the rings under the capital and the projecting band at the top of the architrave; blue or black for triglyphs, and red and blue for leaf ornaments.

The Temple "of Ceres" (Fig. 4.23) is of a greater delicacy, and a more comfortable size: like the temple under the Parthenon, it is a "Hundred-Footer," while the "Basilica" is over half again as long. Though it is Doric on the exterior, some Ionic capitals have been found that belonged to its cella. Its pediment, partly preserved, is too shallow ever to

Fig. 4.23   Paestum, temple of Ceres, *ca.* 510. (Author)

have contained statuary. The perfection of its technique suggests a date about 510. Paestum as a whole represents the sturdy perfection of the archaic Doric style. In the fifth century this is infused, in the so-called "Temple of Poseidon," with an Attic grace.

The new excavations revealed, 190 yards west of the site museum, an underground shrine (hypogaeum) of the late sixth century, to a fertility goddess, which yielded eight gilt-bronze vases and a splendid black-figure one showing a Bacchic scene and Hercules arriving on Olympus.

For our last example of archaic lyricism, abandoning for better or worse the sixth-century conventions and looking forward to the earliest classic phase, we return to the motherland and to the island of Aegina. Here, in 1811, on a rocky mountain in the northeast corner of the island, falling steeply to the sea, two friends of Lord Byron, the architect C. R. Cockerell (shown in a drawing carrying on his investigations in a tall hat), and the Bavarian Baron Haller von Hallerstein, discovered close to the surface some strikingly handsome pedimental sculpture. It was bought in 1812 by Prince Ludwig of Bavaria for 100,000 francs, drastically restored in Rome (1815-17), against Cockerell's will, by the fashionable classicizing Danish sculptor Thorwaldsen, and set up in 1828 in the Munich Glyptothek, where it now is, with the restorations removed; the result has all the excitement of a new excavation. In 1901 Adolph Furtwängler reopened investigations on Aegina. On his first day he discovered some further remains (now in the National Museum in Athens) of an east pediment older than Cockerell's and Haller's finds. This earlier sculpture had been destroyed before 487 by the Persians (or by Aeginetan democrats, or by lightning) and replaced by the version now in Munich. The metopes of the southeast side were set in place again by the Greeks in 1959. Furtwängler found an inscription establishing that the temple had been dedicated to Aphaia, an obscure Mycenaean goddess, related to Artemis, "Mistress of Animals." Furtwängler was able to reconstruct the temple floor from the masons' marks in series on the blocks. The corner columns tilt inward, another aesthetic refinement found later in the Parthenon.

The key to the interpretation of the pediments lies in the presence of Heracles in both the earlier and the later east pediments, which probably portrayed his expedition to Troy to punish Laomedon, who had cheated him of his fee for building the citadel walls. The other pediment, then, probably treated a related theme, Homer's Trojan War, including certain heroes from Aegina. From the later east pediment the most famous piece is the bowman Heracles (Fig. 4.24), himself as tense as a drawn bow. Thorwaldsen did him little essential harm, and centuries of bird droppings had protected his lower limbs from the weather. He is recognizable from the head of the Nemean lion, which he wears on his head like a helmet. Originally he held a bow of metal (restored in the photograph), had lead hair,

FIG. 4.24 Aegina, temple of Aphaia, later east pediment, *ca.* 485 (Prof. R. M. Cook would date it to 500). Heracles drawing the bow. Munich, Glyptothek. (Clarence Kennedy)

and was brightly painted. The figure is freer than earlier archaic work. We are in a different world from the Heracles of the Selinus or even the Sele metopes. It is no longer the world of archaic conventions, enormously attractive, but somehow remote. The world of the Aegina Heracles is suddenly *our* world. The figure is carved entirely in the round, and with true Greek perfectionism the back, which was never intended to be visible, is as carefully finished as the front. The tension of the arms drawing the bow, the sharp contours (derived from bronze technique), and the realistic modeling all bespeak a new spirit, transitional between the archaic and the classical: it synthesizes naturalistic form, geometric design, and refinement of detail. Aeginetan sculptors were briefly famous just before and after the Persian War; their cultural debt (like ours) was divided between Spartan solidity and Attic grace, as the Heracles shows. But Aegina's cultural primacy was brief. Aeginetans were better at piracy and athletics than at poetry: when one of their athletes needed a poet to celebrate a victory he borrowed Pindar.

Just west of the modern town a rather scruffy area, Cape Colonna, embraces a late-sixth-century temple to Apollo (one column standing), a shrine of Aeacus (one of the judges in Hades, and an Aeginetan hero), a bouleuterion, and buildings erected by Attalus II of Pergamum, including the remains of a stadium and theater. Aegina's impressive mountaintop (St. Elias, 1742 feet) had as early as the thirteenth century B.C. a cult of the Thessalian Zeus the Rain-bearer.

Between the Gorgon amphora from Eleusis and the Aegina Heracles, the lyric age of Greece spans a little less than 200 years. As we have described selected examples of its vase painting, its architecture, its sculpture, its coinage and technology, we have seen it develop from stark, sturdy simplicity (the Delian lions, the columns of the Heraion at Olympia, the Cleobis of Delphi, Theran pottery) through religious solemnity (the Corcyra Gorgon) and naïveté (the Selinus metopes), to humor (the François Vase, the Acropolis Bluebeard, the Cercopes metope from the Sele) and cosmopolitan sophistication (the Brygos and Arkesilas cups, the Peplos Korê, the Siphnian Treasury frieze, the temple of Zeus at Cyrene, the Aegina pediments). Here are great riches. It would be a mistake to see in this age, as some earlier critics did, a primitive forerunner of the perfection of classicism. This is the lyric age that produced Sappho and Pindar, as well as the masterpieces we have been surveying. Archaic Greek art, like early Greek lyric, is increasingly naturalistic in content, and precisely, exactingly conventional in form. The artists of such an age, with their zestful vitality and strong sense of geometric design, need to apologize to no one—not even to Phidias and Pericles.

ADDENDUM

The plan of the book, which draws inferences as to dating from archaeological observations in the field, makes it undesirable to begin a chapter with a chronological synopsis, but for convenience the monuments and artifacts discussed are listed below in a time sequence. All dates are approximate.

B.C.

675	Eleusis, Proto-Attic amphora
660-650	Delos, Nicandre statue
645-640	Olympia, Heraion
631-571	Thera, Temple of Apollo Karneios; Cyrene founded and refounded
627-585	Corinth, *diolkos*
625-600	Delos, Lion Terrace
620	Attic black-figure begins
615-590	Delphi, Cleobis and Biton
590-580	Corcyra, Gorgon pediment
570	François Vase
570	Athens, Acropolis Bluebeard

570-560	Sele, archaic metopes; Ptoion, Kouros
560	Arkesilas cup; Samos Heraion
550	Paestum, "Basilica"
550-530	Selinus, Temple C metopes
550-515	Athens, Pisistratid coinage and building activity
550	Larisa-by-Hermos, archaic palace
540	Selinus, Temple G begun
538-532	Polycratean Samos
530	Attic red-figure invented
530	Athens, Peplos Korê
525	Delphi, Siphnian Treasury
513-505	Delphi, Alcmaeonid temple
510	Paestum, Temple "of Ceres"
510	Sele, Heraion metopes
509	Delphi, Athenian treasury
490	Brygos Painter cup
485	Aegina, Temple of Aphaia, later east pediment
480 ff.	Cyrene, Temple of Zeus

5

The Classical Age:
Greece and the West
(480-400 B.C.)

International archaeology, especially in the last eighty or
ninety years, has thrown floods of light on the picture given
us in Greek literature of the fifth century before Christ as
the greatest, the most classical—a term which will need
defining—and the most tragic of ancient centuries. Germans have made plain to us the setting of the first Olympic
games; Americans, Greeks, and Danes have painstakingly
measured, interpreted, and even restored the architecture
and sculpture of the Periclean age and after; Italians and
Germans have studied the temples and the art of Magna
Graecia. The result is a clearer view than ever before of
the material, social, political, religious, and artistic life of
the classical age. Archaeology reveals that age as one in which
Ionian elegance was wedded to Dorian strength: in which
craftsmen put quality before quantity, and architects and
sculptors showed an intelligent, controlled passion for clear,
simple, generalized ideas. In Athens especially and in Athens
especially on the Acropolis, archaeology has shown us how
the unique blend of self-confidence, imperial wealth and

ascendancy, a noble artistic tradition, a great leader, and craftsmen who loved and understood their materials and their work combined to produce the tragically brief flowering of the classical age.

Treatment of so richly documented a period as the fifth century must be selective. We begin with Olympia. The first hint in modern times of the riches the site concealed came in 1829. In that year the French sent an expeditionary force to help the Greeks in their struggle against the Turks for independence. The French task force had a scholarly branch, the *Expédition scientifique de Morée*. Operating from a camp in the pines under the Hill of Kronos, the French were lucky enough to find almost at once fragments of metopes from the great temple of Zeus, depicting the labors of Heracles. These metopes are now in the Louvre; later excavators operated under an agreement with the Greek government that all the finds should be left in Greece, so that most of the justly famous sculpture from Olympia is now to be seen in its local museum; a few pieces are in the National Museum in Athens.

When the Germans opened their dig at Olympia in 1875, the site was a vineyard, there was no communication with the outside world, and when in the second season carts for hauling the excavated earth were imported from Corfu, they had to be brought over unfinished roads. Digging had to be done after the vintage, since the labor force was recruited from local field hands. (The ancient games themselves were held in August, a time of rest for farmers.)

Five campaigns enabled the Germans, with the help of Pausanias' invaluable ancient guidebook, to clarify the whole plan of the Altis, the sacred precinct of Olympia (Fig. 5.1). They found, built into the walls of postclassical huts, or lying where they fell, or scattered at random about the site, pieces of sculpture, of every degree of fragmentation.

FIG. 5.1 Olympia, model, by A. and E. Mallwitz, of Altis from southwest. Note how temple of Zeus stands out (right center). The windowed building, lower left, is Phidias' studio; behind it, the palaestra. Round building, r. of palaestra, is Philippeion; behind it, the Prytaneion. Along north side, below Hill of Kronos, the Heraion, exedra of Herodes Atticus, treasuries, with Metroon in front. The vault of the stadium entrance is just visible behind the Echo Stoa (upper r.). On right edge, Victory of Paeonius, on its column; below it, Bouleuterion apse. Center, Pelopion; bottom, a corner of the Leonidaion. Many of these buildings will be discussed in later chapters. (DAI, Athens)

One of these was Paeonius' famous Victory, represented as hovering near the earth, thrusting firmly into the wind and full of passionate movement, a *tour de force* in which marble is made to appear weightless. Messenians (pro-Athenian) dedicated her about 421 (Peace of Nicias). Most of the sculpture, however, the excavators could identify as coming from the metopes and pediments of the temple of Zeus.

The French had already established that the metopes portrayed the twelve labors of Heracles, presumably six at each end of the temple. Since the metopes would have had to be put in place before the temple roof went on, they had to be earlier than the pedimental sculpture, and indeed their severe style is appropriate to a date between 470 and 460. Seeking a more precise dating, the Germans noted in Pausanias that the Spartans hung a dedication (whose inscription they found) on the east pediment, to commemorate a victory which we know they won in 457; therefore the pedimental sculptures must have been finished by that year. It was the year before Aeschylus died, and the sculptures have the rugged power of his tragedies.

Six of the metopes were peaceful in tone, showing the hero at rest after his labors; six showed him in more or less violent action: cleansing the Augean stables; subduing Cerberus, the three-headed dog of Hell; holding up the world for Atlas, who gets for him the golden apples of the Hesperides; slaying the triple-bodied monster Geryon; taming the horses of Diomedes; threatening Eurystheus cowering in his jar (as on a Sele metope) with the Calydonian boar.

The two sets of metopes ought to offer either comparison or contrast with the mood of the pedimental sculptures above them. The Germans knew that the east pediments of classical temples usually bore calm, stately subjects. Pausanias describes the subject of the east pediment. It was Zeus presiding over the sacrifices that preceded the famous

chariot race of Pelops and Oenomaus for the hand of Hippodamia, which Pelops won by cheating. (He removed the
linchpins from the axletree of his rival's chariot.) On the
east side of the temple the Germans in fact found, lying
approximately where an earthquake had felled them, fragments of the Zeus, the chariots, and some of the figures
Pausanias mentions. At the southeast corner they found the
Eurystheus metope, one of the violent ones. Therefore the
effect intended was contrast, and the violent metopes go
with the stately pediment. Beyond the temple's other end
the excavators found the pedimental masterpiece, the majestic, serene Apollo (Fig. 5.2). With the help of Pausanias'
description, they restored him in the museum, holding firm
control over the fighting Lapiths and centaurs on either
side of him.

Besides using the evidence of findspots plus Pausanias,
the archaeologists could place the pedimental figures by
noting their dimensions and shapes (kneeling figures mid-
way between apex and corner, prone figures in the corners),
and they could infer which way the figures originally faced
by assuming that the unfinished side had faced in, while
the weathered side faced out. The over-all assumption, safe
for classical architectural sculpture, was that symmetry
(but without rigor) was the effect the sculptor aimed at,
with the figures balanced in number and attitude on either
side of the central figure, Zeus on the east, Apollo on the
west. These are the inferences that produced the reconstructed pediments in the new Olympia Museum.

The temple itself is one of the most impressive ruins of
the ancient world, with its massive column-drums lying
in gigantic slices where the earthquake toppled them. The
columns were thirty-two Doric feet high, the space between
them sixteen feet; the triglyphs were spaced eight feet
apart on centers, the lion's head waterspouts were four
feet apart, the marble roof tiles were two feet wide; lead
plates were set into the temple's upper step, to mark the

FIG. 5.2   Olympia, Museum, Apollo, from west pediment of temple of Zeus. (Alison Frantz)

space between columns accurately. This precision, this meticulously proportionate use of modules, is one of the things we mean by "classical."

Pausanias saw in the cella the gold and ivory statue of Zeus enthroned, forty feet high, a masterpiece of the Athenian Phidias, friend of Pericles, sculptor in charge of the Parthenon, and the most famous artist of his age. The Zeus is lost; the bedding for the pedestal remains, and in front of it a large sunken rectangle in the cella floor which once contained a pool of oil, its function to reflect the statue and perhaps to provide a source of lubrication for the wooden core, lest it swell and crack the ivory.

West of the temple is a Byzantine church built on the ruins of a classical building. The Germans noticed as long ago as 1876 that its dimensions matched those of the temple cella, and deduced that it might occupy the site of Phidias' workshop. This brilliant deduction was confirmed in 1955-56, when further excavation in the area of the church revealed a pit for bronze-casting, the slag from it, earth pigments, lumps of modeling plaster, bits of worked bone, ivory, lead, bronze, iron, and obsidian (our first evidence for the use of the latter for decoration in classical times), and such sculptors' tools as the spatula and burin. The pottery (a fragment by the Kleophon painter) confirms a late date —after 438—for Phidias' gold and ivory statue of Zeus. Most interesting and important of all was the discovery of a whole series of terracotta molds, over which thin sheets of gold could be hammered to make the statue's drapery. Some of these are marked with serial letters on the back to indicate their place in the pattern. South of the workshop another long, low building proved to have housed subsidiary workrooms, late fifth century in date. There the most interesting find was the core of an elephant tusk from which the ivory for repair of the statue had been cut.

Naturally the great interest of Olympia apart from the temple of Zeus is in the stadium where the footraces were run.

(The hippodrome, for chariot races, was long ago silted over and destroyed by the floods of the Alpheus River. Simply in the ten-year lapse imposed upon the new excavations by the war, the river deposited a layer of silt a meter thick on part of the site.) The vaulted passage that connected the stadium with the Altis was excavated as long ago as 1878, and thought to be Roman; not until the new excavations did its level and the bonding of its walls prove it to be a rare example of Hellenistic vaulting, of the third or second century B.C. In 1880-81 the excavators found the stadium starting blocks, of marble, with grooves a few inches apart. There were similar blocks at the far end, 192 meters or 640 feet away. Since the stade, the unit of distance for Olympic footraces, was 600 Greek feet, this implies a "foot" of just over thirteen inches, a unit of some importance for settling the modules and proportions of temples. Since the Greeks were an individualistic race, their foot unit varied from city to city, and Athens, for example, did not use the same unit as Olympia.

The nineteenth-century excavators did not have the funds for moving the 70,000 cubic meters of earth that would have been required to uncover the whole stadium, but the task has been undertaken since (1937-42, 1952-60) and proved well worth the trouble and expense for what it revealed about the stadium plan, and because of the intrinsic interest of the finds. The excavators found that the stadium evolved through five phases. In the first two (sixth and fifth centuries), it opened directly onto the Altis, so that the races were held in sight of the great temples, establishing the closest possible link between the games and the gods in whose honor the contestants vied for the crown of wild olive. In the fourth century, as athletics grew more and more professionalized, and Philip of Macedon built the Echo Portico on the east side of the Altis, the stadium was closed off from the sacred precinct forever. The seats were set in graded earth, taking advantage on the north of the slope of the Hill of Kronos, but artificial and expensive on the south. The ends were square, not curved as in Roman and modern stadia.

Even more interesting were the finds from the stadium. Apparently victors in battle hung trophies of armor on the embankments above the track. As the archaic ones grew to look more and more old-fashioned, they were discarded, and the embankments raised above them. The result is the finest collection of archaic armor known anywhere: helmets (including one dedicated by the great Miltiades, victor over the Persians at Marathon in 490), breastplates, greaves, and shields. The bronze strips on the backs of the shields were decorated in relief with scenes that add up to an anthology of Greek myth, a notable addition to the repertory of armorial devices of noble clans; they shed—because the shields were dedications for victory—some new light on Greek history. The armor is an interesting index to the progressive refinement of archaic Greek life, until the fine edging and delicate engraving prompt us to call this not armor but military millinery.

Both the earlier and the more recent excavations unearthed numerous inscriptions—over 500—that connect archaeology vitally with literature when, as in two cases, the persons named are the heroes of odes of Pindar; and with history, as when the Hellenistic diplomat-historian Polybius is mentioned. One, written on a rough 316-pound block of red sandstone, records that a certain Bybon threw the block over his head with one hand. Some bases belonging to statues of Zeus, at least a baker's dozen of them, were dedicated from the fines of athletes who had cheated. Time's irony has spared few of the statues, but there must have been a forest of them in the Altis in its fifth-century prime (see the model, Fig. 5.1). The new excavations did turn up parts of three fine groups in terracotta, which had been acroteria or ridgepole ornaments of smallish buildings, perhaps of treasuries. There are an archaic warrior; Zeus carrying off Ganymede to be his cupbearer in Heaven ("the finest boy's head in all Greek sculpture," says its proud excavator); an exquisite head of Athena; and, in solid bronze, the taut, fiery beauty of a small-scale chariot horse, all in the severe style of 490-460.

On the western side of the Altis, excavation revealed the gymnasium and palaestra, for the athletes to train in; they arrived a month before the games. The amenities included a practice track shaded by a portico from the hot July and August sun, storage rooms for oil, sand, and apparatus, and rooms with benches for the gossip of spectator-sportsmen. There was a hostel (the Leonidaion) for distinguished visitors, a council house with double apsidal ends reflecting the building techniques of an age far earlier than the fifth century, and hot baths with radiant heating, reflecting the decadence of an age far later, but still not Roman—about 250 B.C., the earliest such baths known in Greece.

Archaeology, by nearly ninety years of patient, intelligent work on temple and sculptures, stadium and palaestra, inscriptions and armor, has made extraordinarily real for us the setting of the ancient Olympic games, where champions from the whole Greek world contended in chariot and footrace, pentathlon and race in armor. The ancient Olympics were conducted under a Truce of God. War in our time has passed over the Altis, but spared its treasures—packed in sand in the museum—and even added to them, for excavation continued during the Nazi occupation. A site that had endured Nero proved impervious too to storm-troopers. And when German scholars took up the work again after the war, in amity with their Greek colleagues, the spade proved in the long run mightier than the sword. And thanks to the work of the spade, when one visits Olympia now in August at the time of the great fair, with the noise, the singing, the lamplight, the hucksters asleep in their stalls, the donkeys braying all night long tethered in the dry, pebbly bed of the Alpheus, the gap between the fifth century and now seems not so great after all.

The glory of Olympia and of the fifth century in general is its architectural sculpture. Free-standing statues are rare, and full-scale bronze sculpture rarer still: until the late 1920's the Delphic charioteer stood practically alone. Therefore it was thrilling when the announcement came that chance and the sea had yielded up another. In April, 1926, fishermen from the island of Skiathos sweeping the Bay of Artemisium north of Euboea got their nets inextricably fouled at twenty-five fathoms on an object which proved to be a bronze statue. Unable to dislodge it after repeated diving, they broke off an arm to prove their good faith and carried it triumphantly back to Skiathos. In September, 1928, sponge-divers, with no more equipment than a stone to weight them, contrived to dislodge the torso. Fortunately the authorities got wind of it in time, and the statue is now a treasure of the National Museum in Athens (Fig. 5.3). It is still known as the "Zeus" of Artemisium; however, as long ago as 1931 careful analysis of the right hand suggested that it was curved not to clutch a thunderbolt, the attribute of Zeus, but to balance a shaft, like Poseidon's trident. But the superb figure has no need of an attribute for us to know he is a god. The superb vitality, the perfect balance (the spread of the arms matches the superhuman height to within a centimeter), the amplification of the essential planes (as when the crook of the right arm matches the bend of the left knee), the refinement of detail (as in the treatment of the beard in flamelike locks) are all characteristic of a period of Greek sculpture that has neither the hieratic stiffness of the archaic nor the sunny realism of the ripe classical, but is a blend of both. Art historians call it the severe style, and careful comparison with similar figures on painted vases proves that it is at home in

FIG. 5.3 Athens, National Museum. Bronze god found in sea off Artemisium. (Alison Frantz)

the years between 460 and 447. No one knows, though
there are many guesses, where it came from nor where
it was going when its ship was wrecked; what matters
here is that it makes the perfect transition between the
Apollo of the Olympia west pediment and the festal procession on the Parthenon frieze.

Such works of art as the Parthenon are not created in
an economic vacuum. They cost money, and archaeology
can tell us where it came from. Excavation on the Acropolis, after the Greek War of Independence, turned up between the Parthenon and the Erechtheum a number of
fragments, eventually mounting to over 100, of lists of
place names with amounts attached. These proved to be
the audited accounts of the quota (one sixtieth) levied by
the treasurers of Athena, out of the total tribute, based
on cultivable land or commercial prosperity, annually paid
to Athens by the citizens of her Empire. Pericles used any
surplus to beautify the Acropolis. He was criticized for
it; the critics are dust, the beauty is still there—or in the
British Museum. The accounts cover the forty years 454-
414; thereafter the empire's expenses were defrayed by
a 5 per cent tax on seaborne commerce. The accounts,
originally inscribed on four sides of a series of marble
slabs (*stelae*), the first one nearly twelve feet high, were
reconstructed, wrongly, in the last century. In 1927-28
two American scholars took them apart in the Epigraphical Museum and built them up again correctly (Fig. 5.4).
They have written four stout volumes about them, a monument of epigraphical learning. Their labors produced an
accurate map of the Athenian empire, a gazetteer of 265
cities. The amount of a city's quota is a gauge of its relative importance: thus Aegina pays 600 times as much as
the barren Aegean island of Rheneia. (But Aegina was
an enemy, and Rheneia's temple lands may have been
tax-exempt, so the matter is complicated.) Only 50 per

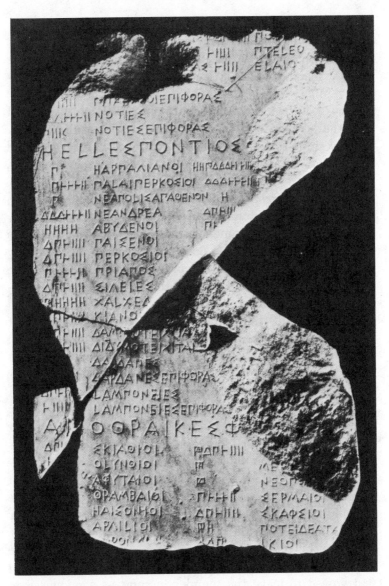

FIG. 5.4 Athens, Epigraphical Museum, tribute list of 440/39, as joined by Meritt. It includes the lists for Ionia, the Hellespont, and Thrace. (Kirchner, *Imagines*, No. 34, by permission of Gebrüder Mann, Berlin)

cent to 65 per cent of the tributary cities paid in any one year: the average annual revenue was under 400 talents—$500,000, with a purchasing power far greater. By the twelfth year bureaucrats had arranged the list geographically: Ionia, the Hellespont, Thrace, Caria, the Islands. In 425/4, after Pericles' death and under the stress of war, the assessment was doubled or tripled; unfortunately the inscription is fragmentary, experts still disagree, and the ordinarily accurate historian of the war, Thucydides, is silent.

However interesting these details may be in themselves, the important point is the use of the surplus to beautify the Acropolis. The nineteenth century stereotyped the Athenians into impractical dreamers. On the contrary, they kept meticulous building accounts, which survive, for the Parthenon, its cult statue, and the Erechtheum, and archaeologists have found, too, the specifications for the great west gate, the Propylaea. The accounts show that citizens, resident aliens, and slaves all worked side by side, and that all received equal pay for equal work. The achievements of Periclean Athens cannot be explained or dismissed by a scornful reference to "slave labor."

One other inscription bears on the great fifth-century Acropolis building program. In 1959 an American scholar recognized in a schoolhouse in Troizen, thirty miles east-southeast of Argos, where the Athenian women and children took refuge from the Persians in 480 B.C., a stone that purports to be in an early third-century copy the decree putting into execution Themistocles' evacuation plan for Athens and his battle plan for Artemisium and Salamis. The Persians sacked and burned the Acropolis. When the Athenians returned after the victory of Salamis, they at first vowed to leave the temples in ruins as a memorial to Persian *Schrecklichkeit*. It was only later, in 447, after the final peace with Persia was signed, that Pericles decided to use the tribute surplus for a public works program: Phidias as over-all designer, Ictinus as architect, and Callicrates as contractor began work on the most famous of all Greek buildings, the Parthenon, the temple of the maiden goddess, Athena, Athens' patron saint.

Since the emphasis of this book is on the history of archaeological discovery, not on art appreciation, discussion of the Parthenon here may best emphasize three matters: the work of Lord Elgin's agents, Penrose's analysis of the architectural refinements, and the careful scientific repairs of the 1930's, before turning briefly to the sculpture.

Lord Elgin, British ambassador to Turkey, had originally intended simply to have drawings and casts made, a task rendered difficult enough by Turkish objections to scaffolding, which, they said, would make visible to infidels the harem ensconced in the Erechtheum. Besides, "mercenary and insolent janissaries" stood perpetual guard over the draftsmen. At the time (1799) the Acropolis was covered with Turkish houses, the Parthenon boasted a minaret, and a small mosque encumbered the cella floor. It was not long since the Turkish officer in command had been the chief of the black eunuchs, a native of Borneo. However Greek patriots may fulminate at Elgin's "depredations," the fact was that under Turkish rule the marbles were deteriorating rapidly. For example, a drawing of 1674 shows twenty figures in the west pediment. The Venetian mortar that blew up the Turkish powder magazine in the Parthenon, on the evening of September 26, 1687, destroyed some of these, and knocked down a number of columns. Twelve pedimental figures were left in 1749, only four in 1800. When the Sultan, pleased at the British defeat of Napoleon in Egypt, gave Lord Elgin a free hand to remove "miscellaneous marbles" from the Acropolis, the ambassador could justify himself as a philanthropist interested in preserving priceless art, quite apart from his wanting Greek marbles to decorate a house he was building in Scotland, and quite independently of his later argument that to have the marbles in Britain would be "to the advantage of manufactures, whose progress depends upon progress in the arts." Lord Byron, a philhellene, disagreed, remarking, *"Quod non fecerunt Goti, fecerunt Scoti,"* which might be rendered "Scots rushed in where Goths did fear to tread." Metopes were lowered from the temple by a ship's carpenter, "with a windlass cordage, and twenty Greeks." When the Venetians had tried this with the pedimental sculpture in 1687, a priceless figure had fallen from the sling and been smashed to bits; the operation was then called off "for fear of loss of life." It took a gun-carriage and sixty men to get each metope down the Acropolis ramp; only the difficulty of transport caused Lord Elgin to satisfy himself with a single Caryatid from the Erechtheum porch; what he really wanted was to dismantle the whole porch and carry it off bodily. The precious, cumbersome marbles suffered every vicissitude en route from Athens to London. One consignment was shipwrecked; Lord Elgin himself suffered imprisonment in France for three years, and it was not till 1814 that the sculptures were finally displayed in London, in a special museum in Park Lane. Flaxman and Canova, to their eternal credit, refused to restore them. Sculptors and architects, used to nothing but Roman copies, were ecstatic; the drapery was imitated in a portrait of Macbeth, and milliners capitalized on the craze: the *Times* advertised a "Grecian volute headdress." Meanwhile Lord Elgin's finances suffered a reverse, and he offered to sell his marbles to the British government. After much Parliamentary debate they were bought in 1816 for £35,000, and installed in the British Museum.

Meanwhile, the architectural refinements of the Parthenon itself engaged attention. They were first noticed in 1814 by Allason and "Grecian" Cockerell (of Aegina fame); the first accurate measurements were taken by F. C. Penrose in 1845. What interested him was systematic deviation from ordinary rectilineal construction: curvature, inclination of columns, entasis (swelling) of columns, optical corrections. He found that the Parthenon architects were aware of the tendency of any curve in proximity to a straight line to distort that line into an apparent reverse curve. Therefore, Penrose found, the architects caused the Parthenon's stylobate, or upper step, to curve upward from the horizontal (like a slightly billowing handkerchief pinned at the corners) by precisely 228 millimeters, or 1/1,000th of its length, the curve of a circle with a radius of three and a half miles. On the long sides the curve was a little more pronounced. The columns were slightly cigar-shaped, attaining their maximum entasis (eleven sixteenths of an inch) two fifths of the way up. The door jambs showed entasis, too. The corner columns incline so slightly that their upward lines, projected, would converge a mile and a half in the air. The architraves curved to correspond to the stylobate. The curvature was achieved by countersinking the corners of the stylobate into the old foundations, which proves that the effect was not accidental, but designed. The same loving care was lavished throughout the building. The metopes were graded in size, the widest in the center of each side. The processional frieze was carved as carefully as though it were to be seen at eye level, and not from thirty-nine feet below by craning the neck. The back of the pedimental sculpture, unlike that at Olympia, was carefully finished, though it would never be seen. These refinements were worked out as the masons went along, not always with complete success: the pedimental space at the west end was miscalculated, and some figures had to be hacked to set them closer. And in the Parthenon the Athenians showed themselves, as Pericles called them, "lovers of beauty with economy," for the temple was planned to reuse as far as possible the valuable blocks from its predecessor destroyed by the Persians.

All this time, though the Turkish accretions were removed, the fabric of the Parthenon remained very much in the state in which the 1687 bombardment had left it, though all but six of the fallen column-drums of the north flank were extant. Finally, between 1922 and 1933, the Greek government entrusted N. Balanos with the re-erection of the columns and the discreet repair of the building. All the drums belonging to the same columns, Balanos found, had been marked in antiquity with an identical letter in red, and red strokes, I, II, III, etc., indicated the order of the drums. Complicated and ingenious scaffolding held up the architraves while the columns beneath were repaired. Where drums were missing, cement proved to provide a better match than new marble, which would not weather like the old, while all artificial patinas were washed off by the rain. New drums were therefore built up with cement on iron reinforcing rods, and ancient marble flutes readjusted on the cement core. New architrave blocks were slid into place on oil. New sections of capitals were fitted in with mortise and tenon joints. Capitals were turned 180° to put the handsomer unweathered sides facing out. Following what he found to be the ancient example, Balanos reinforced some front architrave blocks with iron bars, discreetly cut into the back of the block and hidden by the architrave backers. Where marble was used, it was cut as far as possible from the same quarries as those used in antiquity. The lintel and jambs of the great west door (its twin on the east would have admitted 440 square feet of light into the cella with its cult statue) were replaced, the east pediment was braced, and some fragments discovered in the nineteenth century were restored to it. By 1930, the centenary of Greek independence, the north flank was ready, and by 1933 all had been done that could be to the worse-damaged south flank. Short of actual restoration, which would have been a mistake, the Parthenon was then as complete as it can ever be, and handsomer than it has been since 1687. For this the world owes Balanos a great debt.

The glory of the Parthenon is not only its architecture

but its sculpture, which it is not the business of this book to describe or evaluate in detail. Thanks to Lord Elgin, most of it, including 247 of the surviving 420 feet of the frieze, is not in Athens but in London. It was hidden in a subway during World War II, remained there until 1948, and was then replaced in the British Museum at eye level, where we can appreciate its detail better than anyone since its sculptors carved it *in situ* 2400 years ago, especially as it is regularly (but meticulously) cleaned, while what remains in Athens is subject to pollution.

Archaeologists have fixed the date of the sculpture within narrow limits. We have ancient evidence that the work began in 447. The metopes must have been carved first, since they had to be slipped into their slots before the roof went on. The frieze must also have preceded the roof. We have building accounts for the pediments in 438/7 and in 434/3. The metopes, then, are early, the pediments late; the frieze falls between, overlapping both; the whole was finished in fifteen years. Phidias could not possibly have done all the carving himself, and indeed between seventy-five and eighty different hands have been distinguished in the frieze, but the over-all design bears the mark of one distinctive hand, and that must have been Phidias'.

The metopes, now in ruinous condition, were in high relief. Working round the compass to describe their subjects, we may note that they were canonical examples of impiety, violence, pride, and folly: the sack of Troy, gods against giants, Lapiths against centaurs, Greeks versus Amazons.

The frieze begins in the southwest corner. It contains the figures of over 400 people and 200 animals, and represents the Panathenaic procession bringing, as it did every four years, the new sacred robe or peplos to Athena. In the new Royal Ontario Museum model (Fig. 5.5) the frieze figures have been made three-dimensional and the actual procession reproduced. Parallel lines of horsemen, chariots,

FIG. 5.5   Athens, Acropolis, model, from northwest. Panathenaic procession winds its way up ramp, through Propylaea, and approaches Parthenon. (Royal Ontario Museum, Toronto)

FIG. 5.6 Athens, Acropolis Museum, four boys carrying water pots, from Parthenon north frieze. (Alison Frantz)

elders, musicians, tray- and pitcher-bearers (Fig. 5.6), and sacrificial animals converge upon the east front, where, in the presence of the gods—Hephaestus has a thick ankle and a stick; Eros holds a parasol over Aphrodite—of citizens, of magistrates, and of the ten heroes who gave their names to the Athenian "tribes" (voting districts), the maidens who wove the peplos present it to the goddess. What is possibly the room where they did their weaving has recently been discovered in the Ceramicus area.

The center of the east pediment was ruined, probably in the fifth century A.D., to make a Christian apse, but Pausanias describes its subject: the birth of Athena, full-armed from the forehead of Zeus. The bizarre subject is reproduced in vase-painting: Hephaestus stands with the ax with which he has just cloven the skull of the father of gods and men, in the presence of gods and goddesses (showing various degrees of surprise), and the chariots of the sun and moon. A recent analysis of the evidence places the figures in the following order: Helios, Heracles, Kore, Demeter, Artemis, Apollo, Leto, Dionysus, Hera, Hephaestus, Zeus, Athena, Poseidon, Amphitrite, Hebe, Ares, Hermes, Hestia, Dione, Aphrodite, Selene. The Dionysus or Theseus of this pediment is strikingly paralleled in Michelangelo's Creation of Adam on the Sistine Chapel ceiling.

The west pediment was badly damaged by the 1687 explosion, but its details have been ingeniously conjectured from reliefs on a wellhead in Madrid. The subject was the contest of Athena and Poseidon for Attica. The sacred olive was the focal point; the contestants' partisans look on: there are Iris, the gods' rainbow-messenger, the river-god Ilissus, chariots and horses. The whole scene vibrates with excitement; the art of placing and interrelating figures organically in a pediment has come a long way since Corcyra and Aegina.

The cult statue, in gold (the peplos) and ivory (limbs and face), is known only from copies. It was a colossus, standing nearly forty feet high, holding a spear, and adorned with gold earrings, necklace, bracelet, and armlets. The helmet, downright military millinery, had a sphinx and Pegasoi on its triple crest, griffins on the cheek-pieces, animal heads fringing the forehead. On the sandal edges (as on the metopes) was a Centauromachy; on the shield, an Amazonomachy outside, gods and giants battling inside (also on the metopes). Between the shield and the goddess's left leg was coiled the sacred snake, Erichthonius. The right hand, supported by a Corinthian column, held a life-sized winged Victory. All this seems garish to modern taste; to Periclean Athenians, it symbolized their imperial power.

On the Parthenon the relevance of sculpture to the temple and of pediment, frieze, and metopes to each other is closer than elsewhere. The Acropolis itself is the scene of the contest on the west pediment; the anniversary of Athena's birth on the east pediment is the occasion for the procession in the frieze; the peplos represented in the frieze bore, woven upon it, the battle of gods and giants of the east metopes and the shield. Gods in the round occupy the pediments, heroes in high relief the metopes, men and women (the human world on a sacred building, a bold innovation) the frieze. The frieze is perhaps our best surviving example of ripe classicism in Greek art. In it, the gods are benevolent and cheerfully served, the subject is treated with sunny realism, the style shows linear economy and a pattern symmetrical without being stiff. Content and style reflect men: Pericles' statesmanship, Phidias' taste. We may take the dramatist Sophocles, who was the contemporary of both, as symbolizing the spirit of the frieze. One feels that the frieze figures were, like him, active citizens, men about town, lovers of food, wine, and company, both sophisticated and devout. The frieze depicts men who were both human and humane. It is the tragedy of Western history that the cultures that produce such people and such art have always had so brief a time of flowering: the age of Pericles lasted little more than twenty years.

Not the Parthenon but the "Theseum," overlooking the Agora, is the most perfectly preserved temple of the age. American archaeologists, especially since 1939, have added much to our knowledge of it. Excavation south of the temple has uncovered so many pits for bronze-casting that an inference is clear: this was a bronze-caster's quarter: their patron was the smith-god Hephaestus, and this temple must have been his, a Hephaisteion, not a Theseum. This identification has recently been doubted, and the conjecture made that the Hellenistic arsenal just north of the "Theseum" overlies an original Hephaisteion. Not many archaeologists will find this convincing, and recent excavation of the arsenal found no earlier levels. One of the finds from this quarter was a bronze shield, a dedication of the Athenians after their victory over the Spartans at Sphacteria.

Excavating the temple footings revealed ancient graves and other pottery deposits ranging in date from Sub-Mycenaean to about 450, but none later, and also more modern graves, for the Turks allowed Protestants to be buried here, among them von Hallerstein, the excavator of Aegina. (Catholics were buried by the Capuchin convent near the Tower of the Winds.) The excavators also found that the stucco on the inner cella walls had been prepared to receive paintings: they were sealed behind with lead, against damp. But it was decided instead to equip the cella, in the newer fashion, with an interior colonnade that would block frescoes from view. American archaeologists and Greek technicians (summer, 1953) carefully cleaned the east frieze, revealing a battle of Greeks and barbarians of high artistic quality. Fourteen years earlier, the American excavators in the Agora had turned up fragments of sculpture, now in the Agora Museum, of a size and style to fit the temple's east pediment, which faced the Agora. Acrobatic work high up in the pediment itself, examining the cuttings, made conjecture about subject and arrangement possible. It was a peaceful subject, appropriate to an east pediment; probably Heracles, in the presence of his patroness Athena, ending one of his labors by bringing the golden apples of the Hesperides to Zeus. To the roof ornament or acroterion above has been plausibly assigned a pair of figures, one woman (a Hesperid?) carrying another on her back, the earliest life-size marble acroterion in the history of Greek art. Much later, in the third century B.C., the Hephaisteion area was landscaped, perhaps to represent the Garden of the Hesperides: the Americans found the rectangular holes for planting, some with flower-pots still in them, in formal rows on three sides of the temple. Modern landscaping (Fig. 5.7) attempts to reproduce the original.

Fig. 5.7 Athens, Hephaisteion, from southwest, with pomegranate and myrtle shrubs set in the ancient planting holes (ASCS, Athens)

The metopes, too, portrayed the labors of Heracles, including that favorite theme, which we saw also in the Sele and Olympia metopes, the unloading of the boar upon Eurystheus cowering in his jar. As on the Athenian Treasury at Delphi, Heracles receives in the pediment the reward of apotheosis for completing the labors portrayed in the metopes below.

The pottery dates the temple after 450; the sculptural style suggests dates interlocking with the Parthenon, with influences working both ways; the cella colonnade is experimental. All this points to a date between 449 and 444, after the peace with Persia and revenue from the empire made temple-building feasible. The American archaeologists have noted similarities of dimension, materials, and technique that would assign three other temples to the Hephaisteion architect: (1) the strikingly placed temple of Poseidon overlooking the sea atop the rocky promontory of Sunium, 44 miles southeast of Athens, where another column was reerected in 1959. The temple, built of blindingly white local marble, which will never weather, portrayed on its frieze Lapiths versus Centaurs, gods versus giants, and the labors of Theseus. Its predecessor was destroyed by the Persians in 480; the Athenians reverently buried seventeen kouroi from this phase in a pit east of the temple; one, now in the National Museum, is nearly ten feet tall. A precinct wall, with propylaea and stoas within, surrounded the temple; in the face of the Spartan invasion of Attica in 413, the whole top of the promontory (380 by 238 yards) was fortified by a wall thirteen feet thick, with towers every sixty-five feet. In Hellenistic times this wall was repaired and expanded, and on the north beach was built a roofed shipshed with a pair of slipways. On the hill north of Poseidon's temple lie the faint remains of an Ionic shrine of Athena Sounias, unique in having its colonnade on only two sides. An attempt was made in Roman times to dismantle this temple and re-erect it in the Athenian agora. In the environs at least five farmsteads have been identified, protected from pirates by a defensive tower. The coastline between Phaleron Bay and Sunium was dotted in antiquity with country houses (as it is today with villas): clustered together are a working farm at Vari, a possible priest's house at Vouliagmeni, and a villa at Voula.

Other relatives of the Hephaisteion are (2) the temple of Ares in the Agora (see page 438), whose cornice-blocks are interchangeable with those of the Hephaisteion; and (3) the temple of Nemesis at Rhamnus in north Attica, left unfinished at the outbreak of the Peloponnesian War in 432.* Of the four,

---

* Rhamnous ("whitethorn"), remote and unspoiled in romantic isolation, has yielded other remains of archaeological interest. Beside the Temple to

modern archaeology has been able to tell us most about the Hephaisteion, because it is the best preserved. It owes its preservation to its having been made over, perhaps in the fourth century A.D., into a Christian church. Archaeologists debit the Christians with the disfigurement of the Parthenon east, pediment, but they credit them with the present state of the Hephaisteion; for example, they built a wall across the cella to keep the Turks from riding through a Christian church on horseback. The church was dedicated to St. George the Untiring, himself, like the Heracles of his predecessor's temple, a slayer of monsters.

The Hephaisteion belongs to an early stage of a great building program that later produced the Propylaea, or entrance gate to the Acropolis. The Propylaea was begun in 437, to employ such masons as were no longer needed on the nearly finished Parthenon. Recent work upon it by a Danish architect, published in 1956, emphasizes two things: it was conditioned by previous buildings on the same site, and its virtues and defects are due, it is claimed, not so much to its architect, Mnesicles, as to the craftsmen who worked out its problems empirically as they built. The entrance was oriented on the colossal statue of Athena Promachos, which stood northwest of the Parthenon (the point of Athena's spear could be seen by ships approaching from Sunium). But a cutting in the rock shows that an earlier entrance, differently oriented, determined the location of

---

Nemesis (goddess of retribution), on the same broad man-made terrace, is a temple to Themis, goddess of Equity. There is also a citadel, picturesque but overgrown, dating in its first phase from the Spartan occupation of Attica in 413. There are similar forts in Attica at Phyle, Aegosthena, Eleutherae, and Panakton. The Rhamnousian citadel was strengthened by another circuit wall during the Chremonidean War (266-262); in places it is still twelve feet high. Within are a small temple, gymnasium, private houses, and a small theater, with four reserved seats inscribed for the priests. Rhamnous has proved rich in inscriptions: they bear the names of over five hundred Rhamnousians, but the list does not include the town's most famous son, the orator Antiphon (ca. 480-411). A stone now at Harvard mentions a torch race, and on another to Nemesis, the millionaire but unpopular Herodes Atticus (ca. A.D. 101-177) calls down curses upon his enemies.

Mnesicles' passageway. He was not a free creator: his job was to reproduce, with additions. Both for Mnesicles and for his craftsmen convention was the blueprint. From the west (Fig. 5.8) the building looks as though it had external unity, a central passageway between symmetrical wings. But the wings are not in fact symmetrical. The dimensions of the northwest wing, the so-called Pinacotheca, or picture gallery, may be predetermined by an archaic apsidal building (like the Bouleuterion at Olympia) underneath it, while the southwest wing is a mere façade only four meters deep; its southward extension was blocked by a Mycenaean wall forty-four feet high, and by the bastion on which was to stand a new temple of the Wingless Victory. The decision to build the Nike temple must have been made after the Propylaea was started, for the communicating stairs are makeshift, and have a gate post on one side only.

The central block, which has interior Ionic columns, is deeper on the west than on the east, because Mnesicles was bound by the dimensions of an earlier building, but he made a virtue of the necessity by providing benches in the western room where pilgrims might rest while waiting for the Acropolis gates to be opened.

To judge from the analogy of later building-inscriptions, Mnesicles probably provided his masons not with detailed plans, but with general descriptions of the work to be done. The exact measurements of the superstructure were perhaps not determined until after the euthynteria or leveling course had been laid. In fact, once the ground plan was marked out on a site, a Greek building more or less built itself. That the west front of the Propylaea is related in scale and appearance to the Parthenon may be due less to Mnesicles' planning than to the fact that his masons had worked on the Parthenon. Again, the west porch and the central building are on different levels, and the join between them at the roof line is totally without artifice, as though Mnesicles had never faced the problem, but left

FIG. 5.8 Athens, Propylaea, model, with end of Panathenaic procession. Left, picture gallery; r., Nike temple, with sculptured balustrade. Behind Nike temple, Mycenaean wall reduces south wing of Propylaea to shallow façade. (Royal Ontario Museum)

it to his masons to work out when they came to it. Some of the blocks have complicated cuttings. This looks extravagant, but a mason knows that it is really cheaper than splitting the block. The masons were careful workmen: they might spend from 50 to 110 working days on a single column, cutting the taper in the masons' yard, the inclination and the entasis during erection, last of all the fluting. To produce the entasis, they probably used an immensely long ruler (thirty feet or more) of pliant wood marked with red lead. Their only other instruments were the cord, plumb bob, level, and square. They had to work with column-drums not of uniform thickness, since this would be determined by the strata of marble in the quarry. Work under these conditions is much more creative than following a mechanical drawing, and a successful result depended on the traditional training in his craft of the artisan, who had a much freer hand than now (though good craftsmen today show a fine scorn of architects' blueprints). Greek architectural refinements, this late research suggests, come not as much from architects' drawings as from accurate execution by skilled craftsmen of principles that applied to every building. The architects were the organizers, and they deserve great credit for that, but the real artists were the masons: perhaps this is why not many ancient architects' names survive.

If it was the new Nike temple that blocked the symmetrical southward expansion of the Propylaea wing, that diminutive Ionic building must be dated 427-24, rather in the hope than in the possession of victory, for the Athenians were then locked in a death struggle with Sparta, with victory assured to neither side. But archaeologists have found remains of Mycenaean and archaic sanctuaries below the temple: it may have been the sanctity of these that limited Mnesicles. In that case the Nike temple need not be dated so early. Whatever its date, it suffered strange vicissitudes: the Turks dismantled it completely in 1685 and re-used its blocks in fortification walls. The liberated Greeks rebuilt it in 1835 with more enthusiasm than accuracy; Balanos, and, on his retirement, Orlandos dismantled and rebuilt it between 1935 and 1940. Its chief interest for us lies in what modern American archaeologists have been able to tell us about its sculptured balustrade, the slabs of which were found in and after 1835, and are now in the Acropolis Museum. Considerations of subject, style, the spacing of dowel holes, the angles at which slabs were mitered to meet, and cuttings for water channels have made it possible to reconstruct the order of the parapet sculptures. They began in the northeast corner, where, as a pilgrim ascended the little stair from the Propylaea, he found a Nike in relief ascending the stair beside him. As on the Parthenon frieze, the figures on two sides (north and south) move symmetrically toward a central point (here on the west) where a ritual act is performed in the presence of Athena. Each long face portrayed four trophies, decorated with armor by Victories, and each face had a central sacrificial altar in relief, flanked by attendants. Most interesting of all, each long side was apparently assigned to two sculptors, some of them masterly, whose hands can be distinguished. The masterpiece is the Sandal-binder from the south face (Fig. 5.9), poised marvelously on one foot, her drapery, as a poetic German writes, "in whispering harmony with the melody of a beautiful body," the catenary folds radiating fanwise from the left shoulder and dipping lower and lower till they overlap the vertical folds of the chiton at the bottom, which serve as a foil, a plumb line to remind us of the vertical, and of the fact that the Nike's lovely stance is off balance. This art justly reminds its best critic, Rhys Carpenter, of a flower just in blossom, not yet full blown. Though it is timeless, archaeologists are sticklers for dates. History would suggest, for such emphasis on victory, a date between the Peace of Nicias in 421 and the resumption of hostilities in 415. But the style suggests rather

Fig. 5.9 Athens, Acropolis Museum. Sandal-binder from Nike temple
balustrade. The clinging drapery is imitated in some tired, hack
work from the Nereid monument at Xanthos in Lycia, now in the
British Museum. (Alison Frantz)

a date toward 407, when, under the arrogant Alcibiades, the Athenians were boundlessly but unreasonably optimistic.

Alcibiades may have been responsible for the continuation of the work on the jewel of the Acropolis, the temple called the Erechtheum, for inscriptions record the details (in up to 2650 lines for a single year) of work resumed on the temple in 409, when he was in power. The temple had been begun probably in 421 during a breathing space in the Peloponnesian War, and work abandoned when the tide turned against Athens in the years after 415. Some of the inscriptions are in Athens; one, now in the British Museum, was discovered by the English traveler Chandler in 1765, and carried down from the Acropolis "by the strongest horse in Athens, while the Turks were at their devotions."

The inscriptions are noteworthy for their meticulous detail, and for the evidence they give about division of labor. Expenses are recorded for such items as sacrifices, paper, whitened boards for recording the accounts, gold leaf, lead, struts, gutters, and oiling; wagons and mules. Among the artisans are woodworkers, gilders, masons, carriers-up of paint pots, workers of block-and-tackle, dismantlers of scaffolding, wax-modelers, painters, and sculptors (who were paid up to sixty drachmae per figure; a drachma was a day's wage for skilled labor).

This division of labor reflects the refinements of the building, which American archaeologists had an opportunity to study while Balanos was repairing it (1902-09). It was complicated to begin with by the requirements of piety. Built on the site of the Mycenaean palace, it occupied the holy spots where Poseidon struck his trident, and Athena caused the sacred olive to spring up (a spindly olive, planted in 1917, struggles to grow on the west side). (Recently [1979] an unconvincing attempt was made to identify the Erechtheum with the house of the arrephoroi (maiden acolytes of Athena) about 160 feet to the west and north, over Broneer's cleft [p. 132], and to call the traditional Erechtheum the temple of Athena Polias.) A difficulty was that these holy spots differed in level by over ten feet. The solution produced the most unusual building in Greek architectural history, on two levels (Fig. 5.10), with four porticoes, four entrances, and four rooms, of which the central two have different floor levels. Space was limited on the south by the footings of the ruined Old Parthenon. What would have been the west porch in a normal temple had to be shifted round to the north to avoid the sanctuary of Cecrops, the mythical first king of Athens, so holy that no rainwater was allowed to drip on it from the temple roof; then, to balance the North Porch, the architect conceived the extraordinarily innovative Caryatid Porch, perhaps marking the site of Cecrops' tomb, in which six maidens, sisters to the peplos-weavers in the Parthenon frieze, support the roof with the proud dignity with which Mediterranean women still carry burdens on their heads. All but one are in marble; the second from the west is a cast; the original has been missing since 1803, when Lord Elgin had it shipped to London. To arrest pollution, the originals have been moved to the Acropolis Museum. It is planned to place copies *in situ;* in the summer of 1980 the architrave was upheld by titanium rods. The Greeks under Turkish rule believed that the maidens had been turned to stone by enchantment, which would pass when Greece was free. No two maidens are alike—one, for example, has pierced ears—and they are irregularly spaced. Their hands are broken away; complete copies found in 1954 at Hadrian's Villa at Tivoli, near Rome, show that they held *paterae,* sacrificial saucers. Their hair style, thick at the back of the neck, is functional; without it, they could not support the weight of the architrave. The architrave is enriched with rosettes, but they are not all finished, mute evidence to Athens' financial crisis and the loss of the Peloponnesian War.

The differences in detail among the Caryatids are refine-ments, which American archaeologists have assiduously studied throughout the building. The columns, doors, and

Fig. 5.10 Athens, Erechtheum from west, showing levels. At left, North Porch; center, sacred olive replanted; right, Caryatids. At r. edge, northeast corner of Parthenon. (Alison Frantz)

windows are all inclined slightly inward; the columns of the North Porch show the subtlest entasis; there is beading round the top of each flute; the eye of the Ionic volutes (spiral scrolls) is countersunk to receive a flat bronze disk; the volutes are deep-cut for *chiaroscuro;* their outer face is set with forked bronze pins to hold garlands for holidays. The bottom column moldings, a guilloche or ropelike plaited pattern of interwoven fillets, were set with colored glass, blue, red, yellow, and purple. The moldings have

mitered corners; the *anthemia* (moldings under the architrave) show nine different lotus-and-palmette patterns. The
frieze, of dark Eleusis stone, had its figures doweled against
it in contrasting white marble, giving the effect of Wedg-
wood jasper ware. The sumptuous surround of the North
Porch door is enriched with bead-and-reel, rosettes, and
tongue-and-dart patterns, but the rich volutes under the
lintel are nonfunctional, since the lintel (coarser work, a
piece of Roman repair) is carved in a projecting wall-block.
Painted meanders framed each wooden ceiling-coffer; the
marble ones had egg-and-dart suroundings, and metal rosettes centered in each. The space between the egg-and-
dart moldings of the Porch of the Maidens was pierced
on the south to let water run off; the roof joints were
sealed with lead. The marble coffer-blocks were cut away
above to reduce the bearing weight, which was unusually
heavy, for the marble beams of the North Porch have the
remarkable span of nineteen feet. In the North Porch roof
a hole was piously left to admit sunlight onto some mysterious marks in the bedrock below, probably believed to be
the marks of a thunderbolt, for the "sea" miraculously
produced by Poseidon's trident was probably in the narrow
west portico. If the columns on the west side had been
built up from ground level, they would have been grotesquely
out of proportion; the wall was therefore carried up to the
appropriate height below. Three of the columns are Roman
work; when a hurricane struck in 1852, these were the only
parts of the building that did not withstand it.

The hand of man has been crueler than nature to the
Erechtheum. The Byzantines knocked out the inner cross-
walls to make a church, of which the Porch of the Maidens
was probably the baptistery. For nearly 400 years from 1458
the Erechtheum was a Turkish house, complete with harem;
from 1676 it was also a powder magazine. Used as Greek
headquarters in 1826-27, it suffered ruinous Turkish bomb-
ing; the North Porch collapsed, killing eleven people, whose

bodies were still in the rubble in 1832. It was not until 1837 that clearing began.

To discover the elegance of the building well repays the trouble spent upon it. It is a precious jewel box, a reliquary. Many of the refinements would never be noticed; they point up the fact that a Greek temple was built not to edify a congregation, but to honor a god. The Erechtheum especially, with its sumptuous decoration, breaks with the archaic tradition of austere restraint on which Pericles had insisted; it marks a transition toward the more baroque architecture of the fourth century and Hellenistic times.

Excavation in the Agora has revealed its fifth-century plan and produced significant fifth-century finds. For example, one set of objects casts light upon the peculiarly Athenian institution of ostracism, a kind of political safety valve. If any citizen proved unpopular enough to be blackballed by 6000 of his fellows, indicating their preference by scratching his name on a potsherd, he was forced into a ten-year exile, after which he might resume his full civic rights. The thousand-odd ostraka from the Agora include all the victims' names (some amusingly misspelled) recorded in literature, including Aristeides "the Just," Themistocles, Pericles, and Alcibiades, plus many more. Among them are some which give evidence of sharp practice, and help to remind us that the Athenians were more subject to human frailty than the nineteenth-century believed. On these the names were professionally *painted*, not spontaneously scratched; this suggests that people with a grudge were present with baskets of previously prepared sherds, ready to help the undecided make up their minds.

The fifth century saw the Persian sack of Athens. Besides the evidence of the destruction of buildings, the Agora dig turned up a Persian Daric, one of the rare gold coins to be found, and a number of Persian arrowheads.

The excavators date about 470 the definitive phase of the Tholos (see plan, Fig. 5.11), a round building with a kitchen

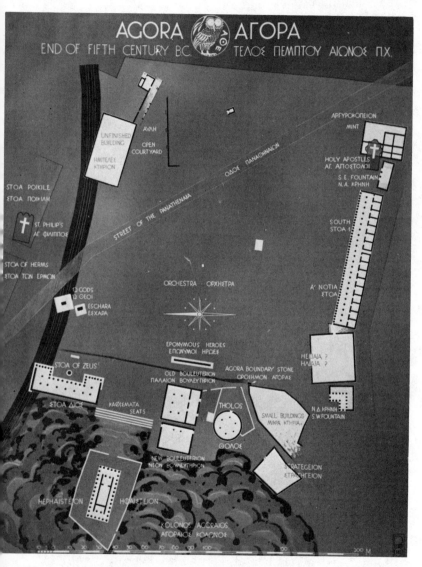

FIG. 5.11   Athens, fifth-century Agora, plan. Tholos, bottom center.
North is to the left (Agora Excavations)

attached. Socrates ate and slept in this building when he served as Committeeman for the day. The "Poros Building" in this part of the Agora has been identified as the prison where Socrates drank the hemlock. A fifth-century house, near the southwest corner of the Agora, was found to contain hobnails and bone rings—the eyelets for sandal laces. It was obviously the shop of a shoemaker. The excavators found his name incised on a pot. It was Simon; he has a modest place in intellectual history: Diogenes Laertius, a late (A.D. 250-300) biographer of philosophers, says he was a friend of Socrates. Socrates' contemporary, Sophocles the playwright, has his name recorded in an inscribed list, discovered in the Agora in 1937, as a competitor in the dramatic competition of 448/7. Socrates' pupil Alcibiades was involved in 415 in a drunken prank, which his enemies exaggerated into a profanation of the Eleusinian Mysteries; he was deprived of civil rights and his property confiscated. The excavators found near the southeast corner of the Agora numerous fragments of the inscribed sale list of his furniture. The items inventoried are so ordinary that we must suppose either that rich Athenians lived very simply, or that his friends abstracted the best pieces before the authorities arrived. The inscription belonged in a context appropriate to the Mysteries, and the excavators inferred, rightly, as it turned out, that its findspot marked the site of the long-sought-for Athenian Eleusinion, which goes back to Mycenaean times, and may have been Theseus' council house. From it the faithful used to set out on their long procession along the Sacred Way to the mother sanctuary in Eleusis. Another Agora inscription is a casualty list of the barbarian bowmen who fell for Athens early in the Peloponnesian War. And on a list of about 460 is carved the name of a casualty who over forty years before had been the toast of Athens for his good looks: the same name (Leagros; see p. 205) was found painted on a sixth-century Agora vase of the kind that middle-aged admirers used to present to handsome Athenian boys.

Among fifth-century buildings one of the most interesting, the Stoa Poikilê (Painted Porch) could not be excavated, since it lay north of the electric railway, outside the American zone. But west of the Stoa of Attalus the Americans found, in reuse in a wall, limestone architectural members which they dated about 460, and which very probably belonged to the Stoa Poikilê, for inserted in them were the iron pins that could have held the grid of scantlings on which the famous paintings, by Polygnotus and others, of battles mythical and historical that gave the Porch its name could have been hung. The Stoa became in Hellenistic times the haunt of philosophers, including Zeno the Stoic, whose philosophical school took its name from the Porch where he held forth.

Another fifth-century building was found in the southeast corner of the Agora in 1953, the last season of large-scale excavation. Since within it were found remains of two furnaces, and water-basins lined with hydraulic cement, and on its floor lay ten bronze disks struck by a chisel from a rod, suitable for use as the flans or blanks for coins, the excavators inferred that they had hit upon the Athenian Mint, a building of great historical interest, since the "owls" struck there were the standard coinage of the whole Levant for over 200 years. The inference was strengthened by an inscription found nearby bearing a decree having to do with coinage.

In 1954 an inscription turned up southwest of the Tholos, containing directions that it be set up "in front of the headquarters of the Generals." Thus another important civic building, the Strategeion, was identified: a large structure of fifth-century date, close to the findspot of the inscription, with a T-shaped courtyard for semipublic meetings, and several smaller rooms, including a dining room, opening off, which could be used for more private sessions. Here met the only Athenian officials not chosen by lot, the board of ten annually elected generals, the most famous of whom was Pericles, who directed the state in its palmiest days by virtue of repeatedly holding this office.

Late in the century (425-410) is dated the building the excavators call South Stoa I, a long double-aisled colonnade fronting a row of sixteen square rooms. Their doors were set off-center, perhaps to allow room for dining couches (Fig. 5.12); each room would thus have accommodated seven. The stoa may, then, have been a restaurant, serving over 100 at a sitting. It may have been used by the dikasts

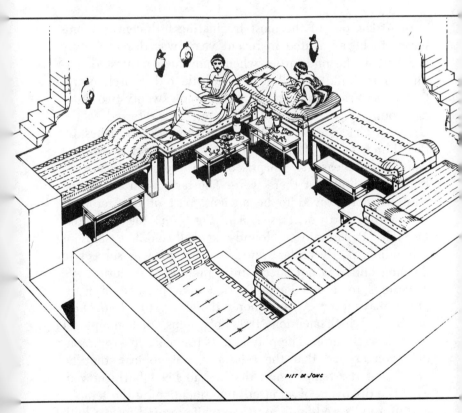

Fig. 5.12 Athens, Agora, South Stoa I, reconstruction drawing of a room arranged to hold seven dining couches. (Agora Excavations)

(jurymen) from the adjacent large building to the west, identified as the Heliaea, or People's Court.

The final fifth-century building worthy of mention lies on the Acropolis north slope, outside the Agora proper, but connected with it by a monumental stair. It is the Klepsydra, or fountain house. Over 2800 potsherds were found in it, bits of the pitchers broken by the women at the well. Since the latest of them are early first century, the inference is that the Klepsydra went out of use after Sulla sacked Athens in 86.

In Attica, one of the most fascinating fifth-century complexes to be excavated in recent years was discovered by accident in the mid-forties when some men requested permission to build a wall near the little old church of St. George at Vraona, ancient Brauron, some twenty-two miles east-southeast of Athens. The request was referred to the Greek Archaeological Service, who dug trial trenches by the church to see if there were any antiquities there, and were more pleasantly surprised than the would-be wall-builders to find that there were. The terrace on which the church stood proved to be ancient, part of the acropolis of Brauron; north of it (see plan, Fig. 5.13) the excavator, Dr. John Papadimitriou, found the wall and five steps of a building, partly under water, for the site was subject to flooding and was not successfully pumped out until 1958. The steps reminded Papadimitriou of a passage in Euripides' play about Agamemnon's daughter, the *Iphigeneia in Tauris*, which mentions the "holy steps" of a temple of Artemis at Brauron. The play had its première in 413; Papadimitriou argued that the reference was topical, that he had found the temple, and that it had been fairly new in 413. The discovery of an inscription, mentioning the temple, and of a kylix, red-figure outside, white-ground inside, both of appropriate date, soon proved him right. Brauron has turned out to be rich in inscriptions, mostly inventories of

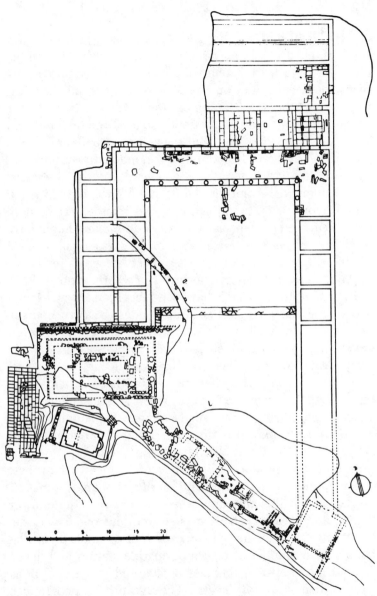

FIG. 5.13 Brauron (Vraona), sanctuary of Artemis, plan. Left center, the temple; upper right, "bears'" dining room. The columns of the peristyle have been re-erected. (*Ergon*, 1960, p. 27, Fig. 36, by permission)

objects dedicated to the goddess: archaic statues, rings, earrings, cloaks. One long inscription is dated 416/5, about the right date for the temple. Some of the inscriptions are twins to others found on the Athenian Acropolis, near the site of the Athenian Brauronion, the sister sanctuary to the one at Brauron; it lay on the south edge of the holy hill, just southeast of the Propylaea. But the cult of Artemis at Brauron proved to be older: Papadimitriou found sixth-century roof tiles from an earlier temple, and several *bothroi* (sacrificial pits) containing Geometric sherds and bronze and gilt rings. Furthermore, a cave southeast of the temple, explored in 1956, contained Mycenaean and later pottery, and might have been revered as Iphigeneia's tomb. She was to have been sacrificed (to obtain for her father's fleet fair winds for Troy) at Aulis, only forty miles northwest (where another fifth-century temple of Artemis has been recently excavated), and still another temple at Halae Araphenides (modern Loutsa), only an hour's walk northeast, was dedicated to Artemis Tauropolos, whom Iphigeneia served as priestess in the faraway Crimea, as described by Euripides in his play. Reliefs found at Brauron portray her and her brother Orestes, whose recognition of her in the Crimea, when he had believed her dead, is the moving climax of the drama. Papadimitriou believed that the play was first performed at Brauron, or at Halae, where the Rural Dionysia were staged.

Brauron has produced hundreds of terracotta figurines, of the goddess, her votaries, and sacrificial animals, some on display in the site museum; others fill drawer after drawer in the storehouse. Perhaps most interesting of all was the discovery, in 1950, in the hundred-foot stoa north of the temple, of a number of charming marble statues and heads of little girls between the ages of five and ten. Inscriptions refer to them as *arktoi*, "bears." The Byzantine lexicographer Suidas explains that they were the acolytes of Artemis Brauronia, the "Mistress of Animals," whose cult arose from her demand that the young girls of Attica serve her to atone for the killing of a bear. In 1958, in the northeast corner of the stoa, Papadimitriou found a room with low benches and diminutive tables, where the "bears" presumably ate. The stoa, whose north wing has been partially re-erected, was therefore probably their dormitory. In 1961 a join was made between the presumed head of a "bear" and the torso of what is unmistakably a small boy, so that the assumption now is that small brothers and sisters together served the goddess. Some of the columns—poros, with marble capitals—of their dormitory have been re-erected, and some of their enchanting likenesses are on display in the National Museum in Athens; others in the new site museum.

There are other fifth-century buildings in and near Athens on which recent archaeological activity has cast light; at Eleusis, the Periclean Telesterion had four predecessors: a late Geometric apsidal building succeeded the Mycenaean Megaron B; to this period also belong the Hiera Oikia, where sacrificial vessels suggest priests' quarters; Solon, in whose archonship (594/3) Eleusis fell under Athenian rule, enlarged it; Pisistratus (tyrant of Athens 561-55, 546-27) contributed a multicolumned building and massive walls, partly in adobe brick, enclosing both sanctuary and city. Cimon (fl. 478-50), son of the victor of Marathon, rebuilt the Telesterion and the circuit wall, which the Persians had destroyed or damaged. In the west cemetery, a set of six seventh-century graves, accidentally found, was attributed, in archaic Greek fashion, to six of the Seven against Thebes (the seventh, Polynices, was buried by his sister Antigone where he fell). Modern Greeks have perpetuated this pious fraud by making the graves a historical monument.

The Periclean Telesterion (Fig. 5.13a), designed by Ictinus, architect of the Parthenon, was nearly square (175 by 170 feet), and had a wooden roof supported by forty-two columns; rock-cut seats for 3000 surrounded the central area, where the secret rites of initiation were celebrated. Other Periclean buildings included a prytaneum (state dining

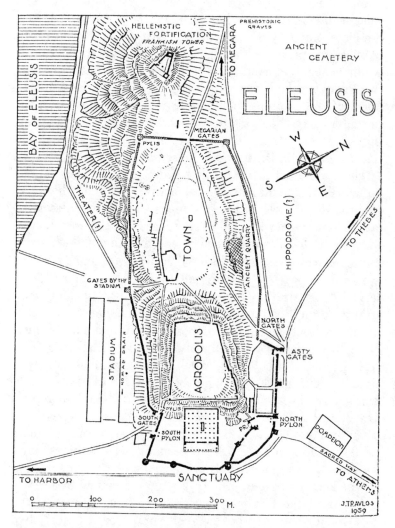

FIG. 5.13a   Eleusis, plan of the sanctuary and city. (From George
E. Mylonas, *Eleusis and the Eleusinian Mysteries*, © 1961 by
Princeton University Press. Reprinted by permission of Princeton
University Press)

room) and the House of Heralds (Kerykes: the Eleusinian clan which shared with the Athenian Eumolpids the official responsibility for the Mysteries: the Kerykes supplied the torchbearer and other functionaries, the Eumolpids the hierophant, and his consort).

In fifth-century Athens, the Pnyx or assembly place was reoriented in 404 to turn its back on the traitorous sea; on the south slope Acropolis are the shrine of the Nymphs; the fifth-century phase of the Theater of Dionysus and the covered Odeon of Pericles adjoining it; a new rectangular grid was evolved for the Piraeus by the famous city-planner, Hippodamus of Miletus. To theaters, city plans, and stoas we shall revert in later chapters; the rest of this chapter must be devoted to the archaeological evidence for fifth-century architecture and sculpture in the Peloponnesus and the West.*

The temple in the Peloponnese of which we know most because of modern archaeology is that of Apollo at Bassae (Fig. 5.15). It stands solitary in a heroic landscape, 4000 feet up in the stark Arcadian mountains, until 1959 inaccessible by road. Its first visitor in comparatively modern times was the French architect Bocher, who rediscovered it in 1765 while on a tour to relieve the tedium of designing villas on Zante. Returning to the spot a year later, he was murdered by brigands. Haller and Cockerell, fresh from Aegina, worked there in 1811; Cockerell discovered the first slab of the sculptured frieze, serving as the roof of a foxhole. The Turks were bribed, the twenty-three frieze slabs carried

---

* One remarkable structure from elsewhere demands mention: the palace at Vouni, near Soli in Cyprus, excavated by the Swedes in 1927-28. Its earlier phase (Fig. 5.14), dated 500-450, had forty-six rooms, its later (450-380) a hundred. Its excavators ingeniously reconstruct its history. The Persians let a Quisling build the palace to guard Soli after they took it. The Athenian Cimon expelled him in 449; the new occupant, a philhellene, rebuilt the palace in Greek style and ruled until the King of Soli overthrew him forever. The Swedes found the royal family treasure—gold bracelets and silver coins—hidden under the palace stairs.

FIG. 5.14 Vouni, Cyprus, fifth-century palace, ground plan, model.
(*Swedish Cyprus Expedition*, III, Fig. 121 by permission of
Professor Einar Gjerstad)

to Zante, and sold at auction to the British Museum for
60,000 Spanish dollars.

One of the recent valuable observations of American
archaeology is that the moldings of classical Greek buildings fall into datable sequences; this technique has been
used to date the Bassae temple about 420. (The frieze may be
twenty years later.) Pausanias, who never mentions the frieze,
attributes the temple to Ictinus, the architect of the Parthenon. New excavations in 1959 revealed the footings of an
archaic temple beneath the fifth-century one, together with
such copious deposits of worked iron that the temple area of
Bassae obviously attracted ironsmiths as that of the Hephaisteion on Athens attracted workers in bronze. The narrow
ridge on which the temple lies forced its orientation north
and south instead of east and west as usual. The cella has

Ionic interior buttresses; a freestanding column at the south end bore a Corinthian capital, one of the earliest known. Since the exterior columns are Doric, the temple uses all three orders. Since it was dedicated to Apollo the Healer in time of plague, it has been conjectured that the pious slept in the cella bays, hoping to be cured.

The architecture is limestone, the frieze marble. The sequence of the slabs has posed a fascinating problem, which the brilliant dean of American architectural historians, W. B. Dinsmoor, worked out entirely by objective structural evidence. His scheme has been much revised in Corbett's arrangement, now on display in the British Museum. I owe the following details (unpublished) to Peter Corbett. The new order is based on observation, unimpeded by modern backers or plaster, of ancient cuttings in the slabs. By a

FIG. 5.15   Bassae, temple of Apollo

painstaking process of long-distance elimination, Corbett matched holes bored vertically upward in the thickness of the slabs, one on each end, with sockets in the top bed of the architrave in Bassae. Overlaps in the sculpture proved the contiguity of three pairs of slabs. Two, whose left ends were left rough-dressed, must have been placed at corners, masked by the abutting slab. The slabs, completely finished before installation, had in some cases to be shortened, with some paring down of the sculpture to make them fit a new cella plan. Holes bored horizontally right through the slab from front to back may have been for stirrup-shaped lifting irons: rope slings would have damaged the sculpture. Vertical channels cut in the face of some slabs, sometimes right through the sculpture, must have been for repairs, to replace rusted dowels without having to take the temple roof off. The result is a sequence of eight slabs on each long side, three on the south, and four on the north. A 1975 analysis argues that Corbett's arrangement, while definitive for a fifth-century revision of the temple plan, does not reflect the sculptor's original intent, which was to begin each half of the frieze near the middle of the cella's long sides.

The frieze has two subjects, both canonical, and both Athenian: the battle of Athenians and Amazons, beginning with the first slab on the east and running round the south side to the first slab from the south on the west side; the battle of Lapiths and centaurs occupies the other eleven slabs. Nine hands have been distinguished; each of the three most important slabs is by a different master, all probably Peloponnesian, to judge by the rugged style. If the Parthenon frieze has Sophocles' sunny realism, the ninety-three figures here show daemonic passion combined with the pity, tenderness, humanity, and horror of war: this is Euripidean. The daemonic is *fortissimo*, emphasized with flying drapery and extravagant gestures against a background originally blue, with accessories in red, yellow, violet, and green, or added in metal. A centaur, stabbed in the belly, bites one adversary and kicks another. Victors seize the vanquished by the hair, rip their clothes from them, kick them in the groin, apply the hammer lock, knee them in the back, strangle them, drag them from sanctuary at altars. But tenderness is there, too, though muted: an Amazon pleads for her Athenian enemy's life. Apollo, with Artemis in a stag-drawn chariot, rescues Hippodamia, who has taken pitiful refuge at a cult-statue; the wounded are helped from the field. And these are not lay figures: the sculptors have distinguished them with minor details: a beard, crested helmet, horse, long dress, sandals, earrings; two Lapiths carry children in their arms. In the masterpiece (Fig. 5.16) midmost on the south side, an Amazon intervenes between Heracles, with lion skin and club, and the Amazon Queen Hippolyta, mounted to the left. The note of humanity is here: at the right, a Greek lifts a fatally wounded Amazon tenderly off her stricken horse. It was the note of pity that Goethe caught when he wrote that to look at this sculpture made one two thousand years younger and better. In the temple of Bassae, with its Attic myth and its Peloponnesian sculptors, we see the unifying effect of art triumphing over the divisive forces of politics and war.

Their victory over the Carthaginians at Himera in 480 brought the Western Greeks two long generations of prosperity, the archaeological evidence for which is a series of splendid temples and sculpture, a selection from which is presented here.

Among the most spectacular temples are those at Agrigento, Greek Akragas, on the southwest coast of Sicily, planned on the initiative of Theron, tyrant of the city, one of the victors of Himera, patron of Pindar. Theron in the west anticipated by a generation the kind of projects for beautifying a city that Pericles was to carry out in Athens. The most massive of these, still striking even in ruins, was

FIG. 5.16 Bassae, temple of Apollo, south frieze, Heracles and Amazons. (London, British Museum)

the temple of Zeus, whose gigantic Doric half-columns, beside the city's sea-gate, measured no less than thirteen feet
in diameter. The temple's area is one hundred times that of
the Athenian treasury in Delphi. Built by the labor of Cartha-
ginian war captives, this was one of the three largest temples
of the whole classical world, measuring over 150 by 350 feet,
and containing, by German archaeologists' calculations,
65,000 blocks of limestone; the half-columns were over fifty-
five feet high; its foundation courses went down twenty-nine
feet. When American amphibious forces occupied nearby
Porto Empedocle in July, 1943, few of them knew that the
harbor moles were built of limestone blocks robbed from the
temple of Zeus in the eighteenth century. Long before that
it had been in ruins; its last upright wall fell in 1401, so that
when the ubiquitous Cockerell visited it in 1812 he found
nothing standing. Not till 1894 was a successful reconstruction drawing made. In that year the German archaeologist
Robert Koldewey (who later excavated Babylon) studied,
with notable results, the gigantic figure, over twenty-five
feet long, its arms held palms up beside its head as though
to support a mighty weight, which lay reconstructed out of
twelve courses of limestone in the middle of the cella. The
figure has now been moved to the new site museum; what is
visible on the spot is a replica. Koldewey noticed other
blocks, parts of similar figures, in other places on the site;
one of them was a top course with the lower arm and hand
worked in the same block as a wall course. He noticed also
that the torso blocks lay as though they had fallen forward
from the temple's outer face. Thus a quick eye and a creative imagination enabled him to produce his now generally
accepted reconstruction (Fig. 5.17), in which the temple
walls are solid behind the engaged columns, and the colossal
figures, called Telamones, stand upon consoles between the
columns, and appear to support the architrave. The support
is only apparent, for Koldewey found architrave blocks
grooved on the underside to receive reinforcing iron bars,

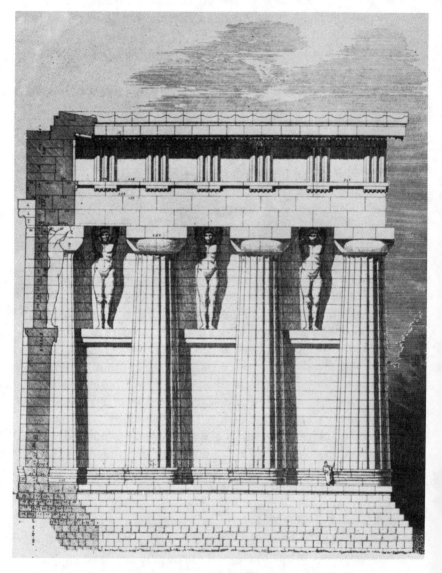

FIG. 5.17 Agrigento, temple of Zeus, telamones. (Koldewey-Puch-
stein, 1899. Fig. 143)

which ran from column to column: the architect did not trust his grandiose figures to be functional.

The temple was still unfinished when the vengeful Carthaginians overwhelmed the city in 405. Two other fifth-century temples, almost twins, traditionally called the temples of Juno Lacinia and of Concord, also lie near the south wall of the city, east of the temple of Zeus. Of these the temple of Concord is almost as perfectly preserved as the Hephaisteion in Athens, and for the same reason: it became a Christian church. The stairs that gave access to the attic still survive, and the mellow golden-brown patina of its weathered stone, set among olive trees overlooking the sea, makes it one of the most attractive buildings of the ancient world. West of the temple of Concord rise eight columns of the archaic temple of Heracles. It contained a famous statue of the demigod, which Verres, the rapacious Roman governor of Sicily (73-71 B.C.) tried in vain to carry off. West of the temple of Zeus, excavation has revealed a sanctuary of the underworld gods, with buildings ranging in date from archaic (sixth century) to Hellenistic times. Besides altars of various shapes and sizes, an L-shaped stoa, and a tholos, the area held at least four temples. The most prominent, to Castor and Pollux (dated 500-450) was put together in 1836 from heterogeneous pieces, and counts as landscape gardening. North of it are the foundations of two mid-sixth-century temples; south of it, the floor, column-drums, capital, and altar of a temple called L are Hellenistic. Still farther west, yet another sacred area contains small shrines and an altar. It is the seventh of a series which rose just within the city's circuit wall on the east and south. The others are to Demeter, Hera(?), Concord, Heracles, Zeus, and the underworld gods.

Over the whole area between temples and modern city ran a rectangular street grid, laid down in the sixth century, and surviving into Roman times. A number of houses within it had rooms with geometric and figured frescoes. In the middle of the area, the site museum incorporates the medieval church and monastery of San Nicola. Just to the west of it, a theatral area is probably the Roman comitium. Overlooking it on the northwest is the so-called oratory of Phalaris, named for a notorious sixth-century tyrant who allegedly roasted his enemies in a brazen bull; it is in its present state a shrine of the second century B.C. In the following century the comitium, its auditorium area filled in, became the shrine's forecourt.

Syracuse, founded from Corinth about 733 B.C., was Agrigentum's great rival. Its archaic monuments, on Ortygia Island, the heart of the city, include a temple (seventh-sixth century B.C.) to Apollo or Artemis; an Ionic temple of about 530, probably to Athena (included in the fabric of the city hall), and another Athena temple, of about 480, included in

Fig. 5.17a   Syracuse, silver tetradrachm. Arethusa. 480/78.

FIG. 5.17b Syracuse, temple of Athena built into Duomo. (Rome, Fototeca Unione)

the fabric of the cathedral (Fig. 5.17b). The temple and the
uniquely beautiful silver tetradrachms (Fig. 5.17a) symbolize the city's prosperity after her naval victory over Car-
thage off Himera (480), a prosperity which peaked under
Hiero I (478-67), whose court offered hospitality to Aeschylus, Simonides, Pindar, and Bacchylides. Shipsheds on the
Great Harbor remind us that Syracusan naval power deci-
mated a large Athenian expeditionary force (413) and imprisoned the survivors under intolerable conditions in the
forbidding stone quarries on the outskirts of the city. Syracuse in her prosperity now struck more handsome coins—
those by one Cimon are the most beautiful—and dedicated
a treasury at Delphi. Under Dionysius I (reigned 405-367),
the tyrant who suspended the sword over the head of Da-
mocles, were begun fortifications on the Epipolae plateau,
above and behind the city. Thirty stades (nearly four miles)
of its sixteen-mile circuit wall were built in twenty days. The
fort Euryalus, at its western tip, with its triple moats, its five
artillery-towers, casemates, drawbridge, pincer-gate, and tunnels for surprise sorties, was developed down into the third
century B.C.; the famous engineer Archimedes may have designed its later phases. Plato visited Syracuse twice, in 367
and 361, in an attempt, which failed, to set up an ideal state
there under his pupil Dion; the philosopher was actually
imprisoned.

Theron, tyrant of Akragas, had a son-in-law Gelon, who
was tyrant of Gela * and later of Syracuse. Gelon had a

---

* Gela's chief claim to our attention is its remarkable walls built about
338 B.C. by Timoleon, tyrant of Syracuse, and strengthened in 311/10 by
another Syracusan, Agathocles. Thanks to an elaborate modern shield of
special glass, and a plastic roof, a whole spur of the walls is preserved at
Capo Soprano, west of the town. Their lower courses are of sandstone, proof
against battering rams, the upper of adobe brick, preserved to our time by
sand dunes. Agathocles added stairs, parapet, and wall-walk; there are
barracks within. A stunning collection of finds from the site is on display in
the local museum.

brother, Polyzelus, whose fame rivals Gelon's own because he commissioned one of antiquity's most famous works of art, the bronze Charioteer in the Delphi Museum (Fig. 5.18). The French excavators found it in 1896, together with the inscription of Polyzelus, who dedicated it probably to celebrate a victory in the Pythians of 478 or 474. In World War II it was taken to Athens for safety; directly after the war it was for the first time expertly photographed and studied. It proved to have been cast, by the lost wax process, in seven parts: head, torso, lower half, and the four limbs. The lips were soldered on in copper, the eyes are in white paste, with iris in brown and pupils in black. The victor's band, with its meander pattern around the brows, made it possible to cast the head in two pieces, so that the eyes could be inserted from the inside. The hair is engraved, not modeled, as though it were plastered to the head in the sweat of victory. The garment falls in twenty-one folds, like the flutes of a column, except that no two folds are alike. The veins and tendons are brought out, so that the total effect combines geometry and naturalism, and the detail makes the figure alert, alive, and unique. The statue commemorates an athlete in the spirit of an ode of Pindar, with which it is contemporary, and, like it, it is hieratic, forceful, controlled, finished, intellectualized, a splendid example of the severe style.

Another masterpiece of sculpture from the West, this time a three-sided marble relief, is the Ludovisi Throne (Fig. 5.19) in Rome's Terme Museum; its style links it with Locri in south Italy. It was found in 1887, when Rome's expansion as capital of a united Italy decreed the breaking up into a grid of streets of the Ludovisi Gardens, east of the Via Veneto, in what is now the fashionable tourist quarter. It was probably not a throne, but the windbreak for an altar. The front portrays Aphrodite rising from the sea, which has brought out the wave in her hair and made

FIG. 5.18   Delphi, Museum. Bronze charioteer. (Émile Séraf)

Fig. 5.19 Rome, Terme Museum, Ludovisi throne. (Fototeca)

her garment cling gloriously to her breasts. On the sides are a young naked flute-girl on a cushion, her body all swelling, unbroken curves; and an older, slimmer woman, clothed, sacrificing with incense. Perhaps they symbolize profane and sacred love. Again the style shows the controlled excitement, here miscalled "severe," characteristic of Greek sculpture of the years around 460. Surrounded as it is in the Museum by pale, soulless copies of Greek originals, this masterpiece strikes the visitor as the finest piece of classical art in Rome, and its probable place of origin underlines the fact that Magna Graecia in the mid-fifth century rivaled Athens, Olympia, or any site in the motherland as a center of sophisticated art.

Paestum, too, flourished in the fifth century as in the sixth. The evidence is the sturdy classical Doric limestone temple "of Poseidon," now known from the votive deposit found in recent excavations to have been dedicated to Hera. The fever-ridden and brigand-infested site was, as we saw, little visited until the eighteenth century, and the temple was never scientifically studied until just before World War II. Friedrich Krauss, who knows it best, described it as the finest Doric temple in the world (Fig. 5.20). Its refinements rival the Parthenon. Krauss found that in precision of detail it marks a great advance over its neighbor, the sixth-century "Basilica." The corner columns are oval, not round, to correct optical illusion; the architrave curves imperceptibly upward to its center. The *antae* (corner pilasters) of the cella incline slightly inward. The errors in stone-cutting are limited to a thousandth of a meter; the proportions work out in multiples of nine. Such mature work belongs to the decade 460-450. All that architecture can express is said here, but it is architecture, not religion: the hieratic solemnity of the Gorgon pediment at Corcyra has vanished, and indeed the Paestan pediments are too shallow to have contained sculpture. Here architectural elegance is all; this

Fig. 5.20   Paestum, temple of Hera. (Author)

is a tribute not to the awesomeness of the gods but to the competence of men, which is another of the things that classical humanism means.

An important recent fifth-century find at Paestum is the Tomb of the Diver (Tuffatore) dated by an Attic oil flask to 480-70. One of its paintings, in the site museum, portrays a boy diving from a masonry pillar into the sea, perhaps an allegory of the soul leaving the body for the world beyond; another is a banqueting scene.

Our final example of fifth-century art in the West, as archaeology expounds it, comes from Selinus: the metopes of Temple E, dedicated, as an inscription found in 1865 reveals, to Hera. This is the southernmost of the temples to the east of the Acropolis. Two of the metopes, from the west, or back, façade, were found by Angell and Harris in

1823, but they were not extracted from the earthquake-caused debris until 1877; only in recent years has a start been made in re-erecting the columns. In 1877, too, three more metopes from the east front were found; all are now in the Palermo Museum. The subjects are miscellaneous: on the east, Athena and a giant; on the west, Actaeon attacked by dogs for having seen Artemis naked; Heracles battling with the Amazon Antiope; and the masterpiece (Fig. 5.21): Hera, a new bride, unveiling herself before her husband, Zeus. The style is earlier than the Parthenon; the material is local calcareous tufa (a chalky pumice), but Hera's head and limbs are done in white marble. In a ritual gesture of this divine marriage, the bride, grave and distant, lifts her veil to offer herself to the avid admiration of Zeus, who takes her possessively by the arm. The composition is simple but not awkward, the bodies sturdy but not heavy; Zeus' drapery falls stiffly from the waist, but the rigidity is redeemed by the swirling arabesque around his left wrist. His head is reminiscent of the god of Artemisium, and the metopes as a whole recall stylistically those of Olympia, re-minding us that however far apart geographically the exam-ples may be, Greek art of the fifth century is essentially one.

Selinus' greatest rival was Segesta, twenty-five miles to the north. Though the city itself has never been excavated, the great unfinished late fifth-century Doric temple is known and deservedly admired. It stands solitary in a lonely landscape, its unfluted columns weathered to a mellow gold (Fig. 5.22). Bernard Berenson said it affirmed reason, order, and intelli-gence amid the anarchy of nature. (Berenson felt about un-tamed landscapes the same as Oscar Wilde felt about sunsets.) Segesta also boasts a theater (third century B.C.), facing north, with a magnificent view of sea and mountains, and an archaic walled sanctuary with the remains of a sixth-century Doric temple.

FIG. 5.21 Palermo, Museo civico, metope of Hera unveiling herself to her bridegroom, Zeus, from Temple E, Selinus, *ca.* 466 B.C. (Fototeca)

FIG. 5.22 Segesta, temple. (Author)

Archaeology has underlined the unity of fifth-century classicism in both architecture and art. In architecture, the temple of Zeus at Olympia, the Parthenon, and the Hephaisteion and the temple "of Poseidon" at Paestum are demonstrably related by their adhesion to the canonical Doric plan, while their refinements of detail give them individuality. The Erechtheum, the Apollo temple at Bassae, and the Temple of Zeus at Agrigento show more idiosyncrasy, but no one could mistake them for archaic, Hellenistic, or Roman. All were built in a spirit that our age has lost, of self-confidence born of prosperity and empire, a self-confidence that seems all the more tragic when we contrast it with Athens' fall before totalitarian Sparta, and the humbling of Sicily before the Punic barbarian.

The unity and the tragedy are found as well in the art that the archaeologist's spade has uncovered and his pen interpreted. It is in the otherworldliness of the Apollo of Olympia, the bronze god of Artemisium, the Hera of the Selinus metope; in the calm self-confidence of the Delphi Charioteer, in the sunny realism of the Parthenon frieze, the sprightliness of the Nike balustrade, the pathos and the humanism of the frieze from Bassae, the delight in sheer beauty of the Ludovisi Throne. What binds these masterpieces together is the intoxication of man's discovery of himself—for the Nike and the Aphrodite are women first and goddesses afterward—and the artist's delight in the intellectual expression of what he has discovered. This is what classical humanism means. But the humanist has intellectual resources that help him to face tragedy, too: to realize how evanescent is the victory of the Nike balustrade, how constant the pathos of the frieze at Bassae. Strong in the realization of their cultural tradition, Greek architects and artists had more than fragments to shore against their ruins. This archaeology has proved by those of its discoveries that belong to the fourth century.

ADDENDUM
(most dates approximate. T.: Temple)

500-450	Agrigento, T. of Castor and Pollux
early 5th c.	Athens, Agora, Old Bouleuterion & Heliaia
490	Marathon, Soros
	Olympia, Miltiades' helmet
486	Athenian silver coinage
480	Syracuse, T. of Apollo
480-70	Paestum, Tomb of Diver
	Olympia, Zeus & Ganymede
479-45	Athens-Piraeus, Long Walls
474	Delphi, Charioteer (or possibly 478)
470	Agrigento, T. of Zeus
	Athens, Agora, Tholos
470-460	Rome (from Locri), Ludovisi throne
466	Selinus, Temple E
460	Piraeus, Hippodamian grid
	Athens, Stoa Poikile
	Olympia, bronze horse (statuette)
460-50	Paestum, T. "of Neptune"
460-447	Bronze god of Artemisium
457/6	Olympia, T. of Zeus
454-14	Athenian tribute lists
before 450	Sunium, T. of Athena
449-44	Athens, Hephaesteum
447-32	Athens, Parthenon
444	Acharnae (?), T. of Ares
	Sunium, T. of Poseidon
after 438	Olympia, Phidian Zeus
437-32	Athens, Propylaea
436-32	Rhamnous, T. of Nemesis
433-400	Athens, Mint
430	Eleusis, Periclean Telesterion
	Segesta, temple
425-10	Athens, Agora, South Stoa I
421	Olympia, Nike of Paeonius
421-07	Athens, Erechtheum
420	Bassae, T. of Apollo
416/5	Brauron, Stoa
413	Athens, sale list of Alcibiades' furniture
409-06	Athens, Nike T. parapet

6

The Fourth Century

From the overwhelming wealth of fourth-century material remains turned up by the archaeologist's spade, I have chosen seven major topics: the sanctuary at Epidaurus of the healing god Ascelepius; the shrine and oracle of Amphiaraus at Oropos; a set of theaters, especially the Theater of Dionysus in Athens; the continued expansion of the great international game sites; city planning; the Ionian Renaissance, which produced great temples and tombs, the wonders of the world, on the coast of Asia Minor; and the public-works projects in Athens of the only Greek rival of Pisistratus and Pericles, Lycurgus of Boutadae.

Nineteen miles east of Tiryns, in the lee of mountains rising from the Argive plain, lies the grove of Asclepius, his sanctuary at Epidaurus, where patients went to be healed. Its excavation was a by-product of the new Greek nation's pride in its past. In 1881 P. Kavvadias was commissioned to clear away the trees from the theater, which was known from Pausanias and had been cursorily excavated in 1829 by the *Expédition scientifique de Morée*. Kavvadias' discovery that its orchestra (dancing-place) was unique in being circular aroused enthusiasm, and modest funds were provided, which produced a major and highly successful excavation, documenting a fascinating chapter in Greek cultural history. Taking time out only to excavate the Acropolis korai (1886-87) Kavvadias excavated at Epidaurus twenty-six buildings or complexes, including the theater, Asclepius' temple, a handsome but puzzling circular building (tholos) adjoining; the patients' dormitory, a hostel, and a stadium (Fig. 6.1). He also found, and housed in the site museum, over 300 inscriptions, including the building accounts for

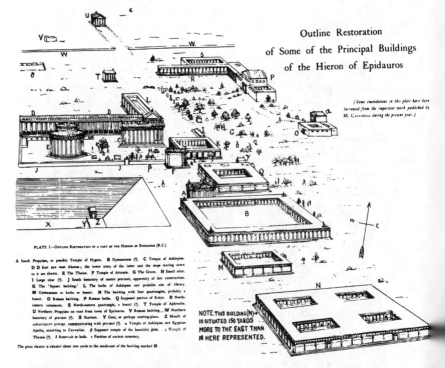

FIG. 6.1   Epidaurus, sanctuary of Asclepius, reconstruction drawing. Plan centers on temple (C), dormitory (D), and tholos (E). Theater is 350 yards off plan to east. (Caton, *Asklepios*, fac. p. 3)

temple and tholos, and an engrossing record of forty-three miraculous cures.

Of the temple only enough survived to reconstruct a ground plan, but the building accounts found nearby, inscribed in fourth-century letters, provide details of vanished glories. The temple cost 100 talents ($120,000 uninflated). It had ivory-inlaid boxwood doors studded with gold nails, and cypress and olive-wood ceiling inset with gold stars. Its pedimental sculpture (centaurs and Amazons; only fragments survive) cost eight talents. The accounts cover, with that meticulous detail more characteristically Greek than Romantics think, the quarrying, masonry, transport, timber, tile, stucco, glue, paint, whitewash, block and tackle, tools, letter-carving, awnings, wax, rope, sculpture, metalwork, ivory, and wages. Contractors had to give bond; a tenth of their fee was held out (as now) until their work was tested; and they were subject to fines for delays, skimping, or exceeding their estimates.

Building accounts, foundation courses, and epistyle blocks and ceiling coffers of almost unbelievably delicate workmanship also survive from the circular building or tholos southwest of the temple. Its footings are six concentric circles. The outer three supported its outer columns (Doric), wall, and inner colonnade (Corinthian). The inner three form a kind of miniature labyrinth, perhaps thought of as Asclepius' tomb. One Corinthian capital, now in the local museum, is so beautifully worked, and so unweathered, that Kavvadias thought it might have been the architect's model, never used on the building: on various segments of it, various numbers of acanthus leaves are tried out for effect.

North of the temple and tholos Kavvadias excavated a long porticoed building, two-storied on its west end, where the ground slopes down, and oriented on a sacred well, still full of water. It was in this building that the cure-inscriptions were found; this must have been the dormitory where ailing pilgrims slept, dreamed of Asclepius, and were licked by his sacred snakes or sacred dogs. The south face of the dormitory must have had openings high up, for the inscription records one Aeschinas, an ancient Peeping Tom, who climbed a tree to peer in, was blinded for his prying, repented, and was cured. The cures included every ill that flesh is heir to: barrenness,paralysis, dumbness, pockmarks, gallstones, pink-eye, blindness, lameness, baldness, dropsy, worms, tumors, ulcers, lice, migraine, gangrene, tuberculosis, gout, arthritis. Unbelievers were doubly stricken, or paid the offended god a heavy fine in silver. A mother-in-law administers leeches to drink, a boy nine days drowned miraculously revives, a man erstwhile lame climbs to the temple ridgepole, a worried slave (in a particularly touching entry) has a pot he has broken mended. The kick of a horse cured arthritis, the lick of a dog cured tumor, the nip of a goose cured gout. The credulity is remarkable, embracing high and low alike: a Molossian princess gratefully records how she was cured of barrenness. Thankful patients would dedicate to the god models, of which hundreds were found, often macabre, of the part of the body cured.

Between the theater and the sacred precinct Kavvadias in 1893 excavated the largest building in the sanctuary, with twenty rooms in each of four quadrants on the ground floor, and walls thick enough to presuppose a second story. Such a building, with 160 rooms, can only have been a hostel for pilgrims, a sort of Grand Hotel; the fourth-century Leonidaion at Olympia closely resembles it.

The sanctuary of Apollo Maleatas, fifteen minutes southeast of the theater, was much older than Asclepius'. Its altar dates from about 650, its temple from about 380, its stoa from 300; since Apollo was a healing god and Asclepius' father, a find of surgical instruments, including saws, is not surprising; a cistern and priest's houses are of Roman date. Older than all these is an Early Helladic settlement.

South of the temple complex the lay of the land led Kavvadias to the stadium (1894). It has square ends and starting blocks, as at Olympia: their distance apart suggests a foot-unit different from the Olympian. He found stone seats only at the center of the long sides. On the south long side was the umpire's platform, with a table for the crowns to be awarded as prizes. A passage under the northern tier of seats leads to tholos and temple; one may imagine the cheering crowds escorting the victor to give thanks to the god. The atmosphere must have been like that of Lourdes, Fatima, Ste. Anne de Beaupré, or the modern Greek summer pilgrimage to the miraculous island shrine of Our Lady of Tenos. One can picture the crowds, the piety, the gold that flowed into the priests' coffers, the different dialects and costumes, and the night scenes as the afflicted made their way by flickering torchlight through the silent grove to the dormitory, there to await the dream, the snakes, and the hoped-for glad awakening.

Another healing shrine to a hero-god is that of Amphiaraus at Oropos, thirty miles north of Athens. Since Amphiaraus had the second sight, his shrine was also oracular. He was an Argive, tricked by his wife Eriphyle into taking part in the expedition of the Seven against Thebes, though he foresaw his own death. Zeus saved him by swallowing him up, chariot and all, in a great chasm which a divine thunderbolt opened in the earth. Amphiaraus reappeared at a (henceforward) sacred spring at Oropos.

The site is charming: a deep wooded glen on either side of a ravine, carpeted with anemones in spring. The sanctuary buildings, in part restored since 1960, lie on both sides of the ravine. On the west (plan, Fig. 6.1a) lies the late fifth-century temple, with priest's house attached at the rear; in front, an altar to various gods: Pausanias mentions sixteen. West of the altar was an exedra with seats for spectators; east of it the sacred spring, where patients drank therapeutic water from shells, and into which they threw gold and silver coins.

The shrine's most interesting building is the long stoa of

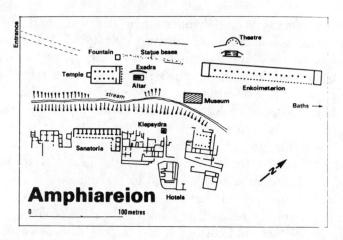

FIG. 6.1a   Oropos, Amphiareion, plan. (*Blue Guide: Greece*, London, 1977, p. 218. By permission of the publishers, Messrs. E. Benn, Ltd.)

about 350 B.C., northeast of the temple, where patients, having sacrificed a ram and slept in its skin, awaited dreams or the ministrations of a sacred snake. The uncomfortable-looking claw feet of the benches on which they slept have been interpreted by some as pillows. Women slept in separate rooms at either end. West of the stoa is a small theater (Hellenistic and Roman) for three hundred, with five marble thrones for the priests, and a stone proscenium whose eight Doric columns have been re-erected. Southeast of the stoa, by the site museum, was once a stadium for the quadrennial games revived by the Roman general Sulla. He exempted Oropos from taxes: the Roman tax collectors, feeling defrauded, objected on the ground that a god who had once been a man did not deserve exemption. A series of thirty inscribed pedestals southwest of the stoa bears the names of Roman worthies, including Sulla and Marcus Brutus the tyrant-slayer.

The buildings on the ravine's east side are a jumble, but the customs house (with notoriously grasping collectors) was there, a processional road, and two guest houses, smaller versions of those at Epidaurus and Olympia, one turned to catch the summer breezes. There are also the remains of a water clock with a bronze plug.

The theater at Epidaurus is only one of many built in Greece in the fourth century: in Greece, as in our culture, the stately playhouse seems to come after the craft of the playwright has passed its prime. The Epidaurus theater is the finest and best preserved in the ancient world; recent repairs show it to particular advantage (Fig. 6.2). It is still used for summer outdoor performances of Greek tragedy and comedy, when the sanctuary comes to life again, furnished with lawns, flowerbeds, patios flagged with imitation marble, and an ugly cyclone fence around the ruins. Much of this is disliked by old Greek hands who remember a simpler era, but it probably faithfully reflects the atmosphere of Epidaurus in its prime. Filled, the theater now holds over 12,000 spectators; when it was new, it probably held 2000 more. Its acoustics are perfect, and remarkable: they may have been achieved by imbedding hollow jars, neck toward the orchestra, under the seats to create a system of infinite baffles. The bottom seats have risers six inches lower than those of the upper tier: this implies that the front rows were cushioned. The front and the two middle rows (above and below the transverse aisle) have higher backs, and arms at the ends of the rows. All the seats were hollowed out below so that spectators could draw back their feet and let others pass. The front-row seats had footstools, and a wide aisle behind. The orchestra, perfectly circular, still shows the footings for an altar in the middle, to remind us that Greek drama was a religious rite, sacred to Dionysus.

The buildings behind the orchestra have given rise to a great and, on the whole, pointless controversy over whether

Fig. 6.2 Epidaurus, theater, showing (right center) recently reconstructed retaining wall and entrance. (Alison Frantz)

classical Greek theaters had a high stage. Appeal in this argument is often made to classical drama, but here the problem is that for the fifth century we have plenty of texts but almost no theaters, for the fourth century plenty of theaters but almost no texts. Those we have, however, show that the chorus has become less important, the actors more so; this should mean, in a building, less attention to the orchestra and more to the stage. The stage at Epidaurus is twelve feet high, and is not a Roman addition. It seems sensible, practical, and nonconfusing to raise the actors above the level of the chorus in front of them in the orchestra. The raised stage of the theater on Thasos is early third century, which is comparatively early for a raised stage.

One of the largest ancient theaters in Greece was excavated by the British in 1890-91 at Megalopolis in Arcadia, thirty-six mountainous miles southwest of Argos. The site had always been known: it was a made city, a spite-city built at one go by the Thebans to keep an eye on Sparta after her defeat at Leuctra in 371. Its most distinguished citizen was the historian and statesman Polybius (*ca.* 200-118 B.C.). When the British came there, the site of the Agora was green with young grain, the mayor was using the official standard of measure from it as a pig-trough, and the Thersilion (assembly hall) was a plowed field; to this state it has largely reverted, though the theater was tidied up in 1959. Though the five miles of the ancient town walls have been traced (in 318 they held 65,000; in 1973, 5161), and major buildings excavated, the town plan is quite unknown, and would repay excavation if the difficulties could be overcome that always arise, in a country as land-poor as Greece, over compensation for crops.

The Thersilion, a roofed and pillared building modeled on the Hall of the Mysteries at Eleusis, had a south porch that was ingeniously and economically used as the stage building of the theater immediately south of it. Whether the theater was actually used as such from the beginning is doubtful, for blocks of seats are inscribed with the names of various Arcadian tribes, which suggests that the structure doubled at least as the assembly place for the Arcadian League. The excavators, after consulting London theater managers, calculated the seating capacity as 19,700. They argued that in its fourth-century phase the theater had at least a temporary raised stage in wood; their evidence was some oblong sinkings, which they interpreted as slots for the wooden posts of such a stage. These they found on the under side of the reused foundation blocks of the later proscenium building of about 150 B.C. Grooves in the green-room floor were apparently used to slide scenery in for storage.

The most famous and most discussed of ancient theaters is of course that of Dionysus, on the south slope of the Athenian Acropolis (Fig. 6.3). Excavation and study since 1862 by Greek, English, and German scholars (including Dörpfeld, who had also helped Kavvadias at Epidaurus) have established that the stone-built auditorium that the visitor sees today belongs to the last third of the fourth century, having been commissioned by the puritanical orator, patriot, aristocrat, and financial genius Lycurgus, who administered the city after her defeat by Philip of Macedon at the battle of Chaeronea in 338. In seventy-eight rows it seated 14,000 to 17,000 spectators. The first two rows are Pentelic marble thrones, with footstools for officials and priests. Put-holes around the central throne, for the priest of Dionysus, suggest that it had a canopy. A drainage channel borders the orchestra, with bridges at the aisles; letters on the edge of the open spaces between the bridges probably refer to corresponding letters on slatted wooden covers designed to keep the chorus from falling in. In this phase the scene building may have had a temporary stage between its projecting wings, as Dörpfeld claimed in 1924. The statues of the Tragic Three, which Lycurgus set up, would in any case have been placed so as not to interfere with the spec-

Fig. 6.3 Athens, theater of Dionysus, from above. (Alison Frantz)

tators' view of the action. A stage may be said to mark the moment when drama becomes more entertainment than ritual. The late fourth century is such a moment, when Menander's bourgeois family comedy of manners held the stage. (The papyrus of *Dyskolos, The Bad-tempered Man*, was discovered in a Swiss antiquary's shop in 1957. Mosaics of scenes from his plays, dated about A.D. 250, were discovered in 1961-62 at Mytilene, Lesbos.)

Beneath the fourth-century building are scanty traces of earlier phases: of the theater of the great days of Aeschylus, Sophocles, Euripides, and Aristophanes nothing remains but ashes, nails, and a few stones. Yet these are enough to suggest that the original orchestra was circular, as at Epidaurus, that it had a long hall behind it, with a central platform perhaps used as a base for the *mêchanê*, the crane that permitted the apparition of gods, flying chariots, or (in Aristophanes) enormous dung-beetles. East of the theater are traces of a covered building, the Odeum of Pericles.

Post-fourth-century phases can also be distinguished. The Hellenistic theater certainly had a permanent raised stage. In Roman times a marble barrier was erected around the orchestra, to protect the spectators of beast fights or gladiatorial combats, and late in the Empire provision was made to convert the orchestra into a watertight basin for aquatic ballets.

Often in archaeology a find raises a problem, the pursuit of which leads to new finds. Research into theaters is a case in point; over a dozen have been investigated in Greek lands since the theater of Dionysus was first scientifically excavated. The late fourth-century theater at Eretria, on the island of Euboea, is unique in having a tunnel which runs from the back of the stage building to the center of the orchestra, for the convenient emergence of ghosts. One of the best-preserved theaters is at Priene, twenty-five miles south of Ephesus in Asia Minor. This was a planned city, to be discussed in some detail later, founded by Alexander the Great in 334. The technique of the theater is Hellenistic, the date about 300, with later additions. The presence of a water clock in the west corner of the orchestra suggests the use of the building at some stage for pleading cases at law. Since Priene is a small town, its theater is smaller than the others described; nevertheless it seated 5000. Its excavator, writing in 1921 under the influence of the then prevailing view that Greek theaters did not have high stages, argued that the Priene theater had no raised stage until 160, when statues were set up that would have been in the way if the stage had not been raised. The architectural remains demand restoration as belonging to a Hellenistic flat-roofed colonnade, called a *proskenion,* between the orchestra and the scene-building. (A famous Greek prostitute was nicknamed *proskenion;* hence one scholar, not otherwise noted for facetiousness, defined it as "a decorative exterior concealing something plain.") The point at Priene is the flat roof: why should it be flat if it was not to be used, along with the three-doored stage building behind it, and what better use for it than as a stage, with one or more of the openings behind used for interior scenes? The fact that there are seats of honor at Priene in the fifth row as well as the first is an argument in favor of the use, perhaps from the early second century B.C., of the *proskenion* roof as a stage. But in the end what matters is not this detail, but the proof offered by Priene and many another small city that a Greek community did not consider itself culturally complete without a theater. Thus the intellectual heritage of Athens, where Greek drama began, lived on after she became politically negligible.

Archaeology shows that throughout all the jockeying for power in the fourth century of individual cities and states, first Sparta, then Thebes, then Macedon under Philip II and Alexander, the great international game sites flourished.

At Olympia, (see Fig. 5.1) the evidence is in four buildings and one great statue. The earliest fourth-century building is the smallest and worst preserved of the three temples in the Altis. Miniature cymbals found in a level of ash west of it give a clue to the divinity worshiped in it: the clashing of cymbals (to drown out Zeus's birth-cry from the ears of his jealous father) was a part of the worship of the Great Mother, Rhea or Cybele. It seems appropriate that the mother should be worshiped in the son's precinct, so the temple has been identified as a Metroön. Appropriateness and piety yielded in Roman times to considerations of policy, when the temple was rededicated to Augustus. (Ruler cult is of course not an index to religiosity, but to how irreligious the worshiper is.)

An inscription identifies another fourth-century building, the second largest secular structure on the site, as the Leonidaion, donated by one Leonidas of Naxos, who may thus have shown his gratitude for being enriched in the marble trade. It is almost square, like the hostel at Epidaurus, and contains such a combination of large rooms, for formal occasions, and small ones, for bedrooms, as would be appropriate to a guesthouse. The rooms are arranged around a courtyard with a fountain in the middle, and were presumably luxurious, for distinguished visitors, since they were made over, centuries later, into the headquarters of the Roman governors of Achaea. Wheel ruts leading up to the building suggest that its guests were considered too distinguished to be allowed to arrive on foot.

Pausanias identifies the other two buildings: a tholos, called the Philippeion, and the Echo Stoa on the east side of the Altis, so named because of the sevenfold echo that reverberated from the buildings it faced. The Philippeion is a finely worked imitation of the Tholos at Epidaurus; the Stoa is in the same style. Less important than their architectural detail is what their existence implies. A pedestal found in the Philippeion once held statues of Philip, Alexander, and other members of the Macedonian royal family: here the form of a temple is used to house the statues of

mortal men, something new in Greek life, and destined to
bear bitter fruit, as the rededication of the Metroön to
Augustus and the later adulation of Nero show. The Echo
Stoa, from its style, is dated after the battle of Chaeronea,
where Philip humbled Greece: its fine-wrought marble
makes an ostentatious disply of victor's condescension to
vanquished.

Olympia's most famous fourth-century statue is the
Hermes of Praxiteles, found, as we saw, in the Heraion.
The work of Praxiteles, Lysippus, and Scopas, the three
great sculptors of this century, can all be plausibly illustrated from archaeological finds of the last century at Olympia, Delphi, Halicarnassus, and Tegea. Hermes' stance (Fig.
6.4) is the characteristic and beautiful Praxitelean S-curve,
though it is probably not a Praxitelean original. The baby
Dionysus in his left arm is of course his brother, whom he
was represented as teasing, probably with a bunch of grapes.
The god is rendered with fourth-century informality, with
his unruly hair (originally painted red-brown) and his debo-
nair handsome youthfulness. He is the glass of fashion, too;
his sandals were once gilded. It is hard to believe that this
concept of divinity is the product of the same culture that
made the Corcyra pediment, or even the superhuman Apollo
of this same precinct. The same emphasis on the human dimension, but much more modest and bourgeois, is to be seen
in the charming little terracotta figurines, made in Athens, to
judge from the molds found there, that archaeologists found
by the hundreds in late fourth-century graves at Tanagra in
Boeotia, which show women cloaked, baking, grinding grain,
nursing babies, or in traveling dress. The one shown (Fig.
6.5), acquired by the Metropolitan Museum in New York in
1930, has brown hair, wears a tunic, a rose mantle with a
bright blue border, and red peaked hat and shoes. She once
held a fan, and she wears a ring. The drapery is very delicately handled, and there is a fine swing to her fashionable
pose. She was a gift to the museum, and her precise findspot is

FIG. 6.4 Olympia, Museum. Hermes, with infant Dionysus. Found in Heraion (Alison Frantz)

unknown, as often, since collectors buy from art dealers who have clandestine sources, which they feel they must protect, but she is published as coming presumably from Tanagra. Many were exported to Alexandria, Myrina in Asia Minor, and south Italy.

At Delphi an earthquake destroyed the Alcmaeonid temple in 373. French archaeologists found the list of those who subscribed to rebuild it, from the king of Sparta to the humble contributions of women in Sicily, the Peloponnese, and the islands, whose pious obols hardly sufficed to pay the cost of carving their names on stone. From the subscription list and from the complicated accounts of the international commission in charge of rebuilding the temple, French epigraphists were able to learn precious details. Philip of Macedon's incursions into Greece interrupted the rebuilding, which consequently took thirty-five or forty years. Part of the expense was to have been defrayed from a 10,000-talent fine levied on the Phocians for robbing the shrine to pay mercenaries, but the culprits paid only 400. Another inscription records the per diem of Athenian and Corinthian experts who came to replace the sacred silver and gold vessels, the gift of Croesus, the millionaire sixth-century king of Lydia, which the rascally Phocians had melted down. As at Epidaurus, contractors were subject to fine for not meeting deadlines, but at Delphi they were also paid extra, because the temple was rebuilt larger than had been originally planned. As many blocks as possible of the Alcmaeonid temple were reused, the rest reverently buried, and the excavators found them. Some of the new stone (the poros) came from quarries west of Corinth; the inscriptions show prohibitively high freight rates: transporting the stone across the Corinthian Gulf and up the steep winding road to Delphi cost ten times as much as quarrying it. Hence local limestone was also used, from quarries two hours west of Delphi. Here, as on Naxos, one can still see where the wooden wedges were driven in and wetted to swell and split the stone. The build-

FIG. 6.5 Tanagra figurine, about 8½ inches high. (New York, Metropolitan Museum, gift of Mrs. Sadie Adler)

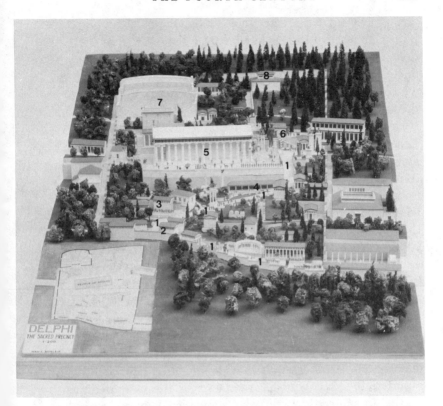

Fig. 6.6 Delphi, precinct of Apollo, model. 1, Sacred Way; 2, Siphnian Treasury; 3, Athenian Treasury; 4, Athenian Portico; 5,
Temple of Apollo; 6, Statue of Agias, findspot; 7, fourth-century
theater, for 5,000; 8, Cnidian clubhouse. (New York, Metropolitan
Museum, Dodge Fund)

ers' workshops lay beside the meeting place of the Amphictyonic Council (the delegates from neighboring states who
governed Delphi) at the spot where their descendants have
their threshing floors, beside the School of Fine Arts.

Nature and man have been hard on the fourth-century
temple. A landslip has twisted it all, toppling columns into
the ravine; Byzantines pried up the peristyle pavement, and

propped it up while they got at the metal clamps in the blocks beneath. Little is left but the plan, yet from the evidence of scattered architectural blocks conjecture has produced a model (Fig. 6.6) not only of the temple, but of the whole sanctuary. The temple plan is unusual. Separate from the four walls of the cella was a smallish room that once contained marvels: the golden cult-statue of Apollo, the tomb of Dionysus, the omphalos, or navel-stone of the world, of which Delphi, like Boston, considered itself the center; a bench for those waiting to consult the oracle, and a stair down to an underground room that may have been the holy of holies, where the prophetess allegedly sat over a crevice in the rock that emitted vapors. There was in fact no crevice, and no vapors. Nevertheless, the pious believed that under their influence the prophetess uttered sounds that the priests translated into hexameter verse (often ambiguous) and submitted to the pious awaiting the god's answer to their questions. Herms nearby bore the famous mottoes "Know thyself" and "Nothing in excess," the latter more honored by the Greeks in the breach than in the observance, which is what makes them so interesting as a people. In 1972 the French reported the discovery of fragments of the west pediment of the fourth-century temple, showing Dionysus and the Thyiades (local name for Bacchantes).

The Cnidian clubhouse, at the precinct's north edge, contained famous paintings by the fifth-century artist Polygnotus, depicting the fall of Troy and Odysseus' descent into Hades.

In the area northeast of the temple of Apollo were found the fragments of a graceful group of three dancers, fourth-century work, which originally supported a tripod atop a high column with baroque decoration of acanthus leaves (Fig. 6.7). The precise date and occasion of the dedicating is unknown, but the column rested on a base bearing the name of the entrepreneur Pancrates of Argos, who was active at Delphi shortly after 335. If the maidens' headdresses are

FIG. 6.7 Dancing girls from acanthus column, restored. (Delphi, Museum)

those of priestesses, then they are Thyiades, who buried the dismembered Dionysus, god of vegetation, and woke him by ritual incantations every spring. Less of a puzzle is the marble statue of an athlete (Fig. 6.8), which came from a base northeast of the temple with cuttings for nine figures. Verses inscribed on the base tell who they are: seven generations of a family prominent in Pharsalus. The dedicator was the Thessalian delegate, pro-Macedonian, to the Amphictyonic Council, (which administered the temple at Delphi) in the critical years between 338 and 334, after Athens' fall. The athlete, Agias by name, was a famous pancratiast (boxer and wrestler with no holds barred), who won once at Olympia, three times at Delphi, five times each at Nemea and the Isthmus, as the inscription records. The statue is of special interest because it is a contemporary copy of a lost bronze original from Pharsalus by one of the three great sculptors of the time, Lysippus. (A possible new Lysippan original is reported in the Getty collection, Malibu Beach, California.) The sculptor has succeeded in rendering the ideal athlete, indomitable and tense to win.

Less than a mile southeast of the main precinct lies another sacred area, Marmaria, whose most interesting building is the Tholos, of the early fourth century. Paul Bernard, using on its fragmentary metopes techniques like Dinsmoor's at Bassae, made a number of ingenious joins; the subject, as at Bassae, is the battle of Greeks and Amazons. Just east of Tholos, the Massiliote Treasury has exquisite masonry.

At Nemea, the third of the four great game sites, some thirteen miles southwest of Corinth (see map, Fig. 6.21), the three surviving upright columns of the temple of Zeus prompted Blegen to dig (1924-26). Here Heracles killed a local lion; the local red wine, called "Blood of Heracles," is famous. The temple (dated 330/20) was of special interest because its dimensions and style were so very close to those of a contemporary one (of about 340) at Tegea, forty miles farther southwest, that the two might well be by the same

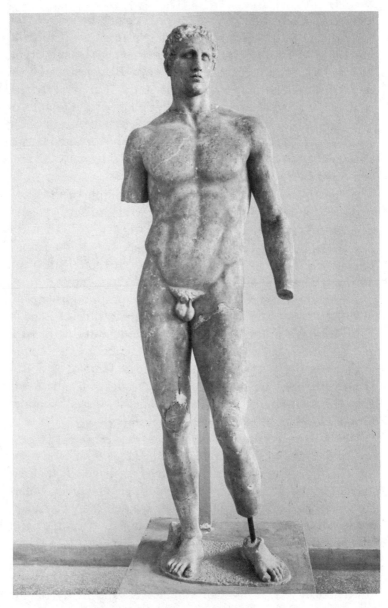

FIG. 6.8 Delphi, Museum. The athlete Agias, after an original by Lysippus. (Alison Frantz)

architect. That architect was Scopas, more famous as the third of the three great sculptors of this century. The striking thing about the Nemea temple is that it had a crypt, below the rear of its cella, described by Blegen as "an open depressed area with an impractible stair." It apparently represents the ground level of an earlier phase of the temple, or the grave of a local hero. Later excavation shows south of the temple nine "treasuries," including one Rhodian and one Epidaurian, of 500-475 B.C. At the east end of the excavated area is a bronzeworker's shop of 450-25.

While Nemea was the most rustic and simple of the game sites, its prize a simple crown of wild parsley, it must nevertheless have had, perhaps on a smaller scale than the others, the buildings appropriate and necessary to the games. Excavation here has proved fruitful, even though the land produces a profitable currant and grape crop, and is divided among eight or more owners, so that expropriation is complicated. Excavators have found the great altar of Zeus; a fourth-century porticoed gymnasium and hostel, with bath and bathtubs (but without outlets for draining!); a stadium (352-300 B.C.), 500 yards southeast of the temple, of sloped earth without stone seats; and a votive deposit and sherds going back through the archaic, Geometric, Corinthian, and Protocorinthian periods to early Neolithic.

The last great game site is Isthmia (see map, Fig. 6.21), near the southeast end of the Corinth Canal, where Broneer, for whom the local Greeks have named a village street, excavated for the University of Chicago. The biennial games here date from 582 B.C., and Pindar hymned the victors. Expertly surveying the terrain and noticing the roof tiles and column-drums reused in the wall of Justinian's fortress there, Broneer dug and immediately hit the footings of the fourth-century temple of Poseidon (plan, Fig. 6.9). It had been destroyed in 394, in the Corinthian War, and richly rebuilt in a rectangular, colonnaded precinct, but its archaic and classical phases were even richer, as a splendid archaic liba-

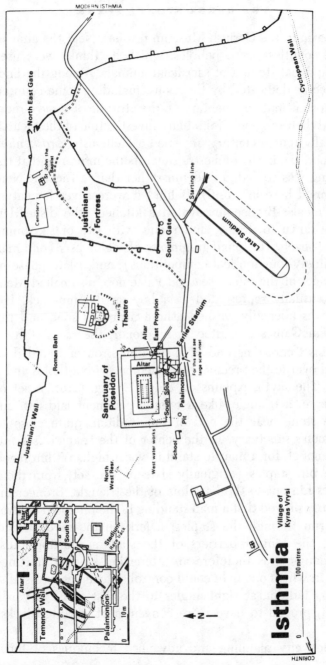

FIG. 6.9 Isthmia, sacred precinct and environs. Inset shows triangular plan of "enigma." (*Blue Guide: Greece*, p. 250, by permission of E. Benn, Ltd., publisher)

tion basin in the Corinth Museum testifies. Near the altar he found countless large pebbles, which he thinks were used for the ritual stoning of sacrificial animals. Among the finds were coins dedicated by the pious, including some counterfeits, a sufficient commentary on the attitude of some Greeks toward their religion. Preliminary investigation of the theater, originally fourth century, revealed a Hellenistic *proskenion;* the wood ash in the orchestra suggests the inference that the building was roofed, an odeum rather than a theater. Nero performed here in A.D. 67. Behind it were caves for eating ritual meals; Broneer excavated a kitchen (the dishes left upside down to drain), and rooms with five or six dining couches each. He found fragments of victor lists (one man won ninety-four musical competitions), and a late phase of a precinct of the minor sea god Palaemon, also called Melicertes, usually represented as a boy on dolphin-back. His body was allegedly washed ashore near this spot, and the Isthmian Games instituted in his honor, the races starting from his tomb. One end of a stadium Broneer found does indeed overlie the precinct of Palaemon, with a tholos and a crypt. The myth explains an enigma (Fig. 6.10): a set of grooves in a triangle, like a temple pediment laid flat, cut in the stone near the end of the stadium, quite close to Palaemon's sanctuary. In the center of the triangle is a pit, deep enough for a man to stand in waist-high. Within reach of the pit, staples (originally sixteen) are set; from them grooves fan out to the base-line of the triangle. Broneer ingeniously proved that a man standing in the pit could control cords run through the staples; a jerk on the cords would release the hinged barriers of the stadium starting-stalls. The triangle was therefore an interesting kind of starting-block, in which one man could control sixteen gates or stalls. A later stadium, at right angles to the first and 250 yards from it, proved to have more conventional starting blocks.

Skilled city planning and advanced techniques of forti-

FIG. 6.10   Isthmia, "enigma." Professor Broneer demonstrating the
working of the starting-gates. (Author)

fication were among the engineering accomplishments of
the fourth century. Two planned, fortified cities, Messene
and Mantinea (Fig. 6.21), both in the Peloponnese, were,
like Megalopolis, set up to help Thebes keep an eye on
Sparta.

Messene, modern Mavromati, twenty-five miles west of
Sparta, had long been a thorn in Sparta's flesh. To this
mountain fastness, in times gone by, Sparta's disaffected
helots (serfs) had fled, and her repressive measures against
them had rankled deeply. Thebes took advantage of this
ill-feeling to strengthen Messene's walls against her heredi-
tary enemy, and the result (Fig. 6.11) is one of the most
impressive pieces of fortification in the Greek world, remarkable for perfection of masonry and ingenuity of plan,
which was first drawn by the French in 1829; Greek

Fig. 6.11 Messene, circular court within Arcadian Gate, with stretch of circuit wall in background. Nineteenth-century photograph, taken on one of Dörpfeld's famous Peloponnesian tours. (DAI, Athens)

archaeologists excavated the walls in 1895, 1909, and since 1925. The Arcadian Gate (see plan, Fig. 6.12) has a mighty monolithic door post nearly nineteen feet long, and a circular courtyard walled without mortar, with almost invisible joins. The circuit wall itself, fifteen feet high to the battlements, and six and a half to eight feet thick, was built in two faces of squared blocks with a rubble fill between. To compensate for its lack of height, escarpments before its outer face prevented the bringing up of scaling apparatus. Two-storied square or semicircular towers, of which thirty-three are preserved or conjectured, with loopholes and posterns, strengthened the wall at irregular intervals. They average twenty-eight feet high and project thirteen feet, straddling the wall and sealing off its various sectors or curtains; even if an enemy occupied the wall-walk between a pair of towers, he could be blocked from the rest of the wall. (Another set of fourth-century fortifications, almost perfectly preserved, is the polygonal wall of Oeniadae, in southwest Acarnania. The docks here, built about 219 by Philip V of Macedon, are remarkable, with mooring rings, slipways, and a rock-cut basin surrounded by porticoes.)

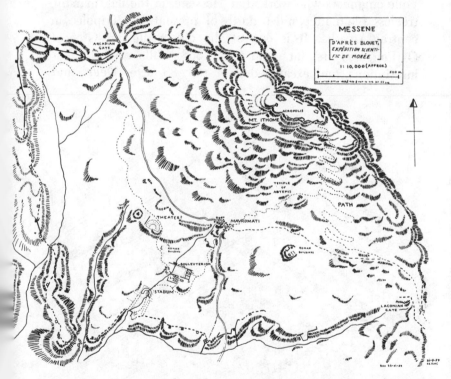

FIG. 6.12   Messene, plan. The area in Fig. 6.11 is to the north; area labeled "Bouleuterion" has been center of recent excavation. (ASCS, Athens) A fourth-century temple to Asclepius and Hygieia, restored in Hellenistic times, has now been discovered in the open area west of the bouleuterion.

In the town proper the theater and stadium had long been known; the Hellenistic Agora, more recently excavated (Fig. 6.12a), has on the east side a central Propylon leading into a vast peristyle, over 200 feet square, and contains a temple to Asclepius and Hygieia. On the right of the Propylon is a small theater, on the left the Synedrion, where the Messenian Assembly met, or perhaps it was a library. Cult rooms (one to Artemis Orthia), filled the west side, a (later) shrine to Rome and Augustus the north, a (possible) prytaneum the south.

Mantinea's walls were built around 370, probably by the same engineers who worked at Messene, in the flat, marshy, treeless plain nine miles north of present-day Tripolis, in central Arcadia. It is one of the oldest digs in Greece: G. Fougères first hit upon it in 1868, while exploring for inscriptions, and excavated it in 1887-88, after Delos, and

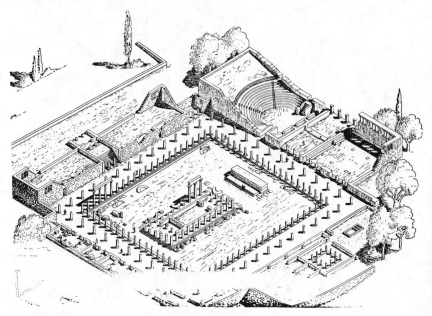

Fig. 6.12a Messene, agora, axonometric reconstruction. (École Française, Athens, by permission)

before Delphi. He found it a melancholy, desolate spot, fever-ridden and subject to extremes of temperature. His hands and legs grew gangrenous from working constantly in water, but he found uplift in the view of Mt. Maenalus to the west, dark blue, with purple shadows, like a tossing sea turned to stone. He kept doggedly at it, working from dawn to starlight. The workmen in their heavy goatskin capes dug trenches fanning out from the mound sown with wheat that marked the fourth-century theater (see plan, Fig. 6.13). Inscribed on its seats were names of local tribes, somewhat as at Megalopolis; there were five, and Fougères inferred that Mantinea had five quarters, like Sparta, each centering on a sanctuary, and walled when they united, in the fifth century B.C., but all this remains to be dug.

One of the radial trenches hit upon the Agora, mostly Roman, but with a fourth-century bouleuterion. It had been built over a swamp, like the Roman Forum. This was one of the first agoras to be excavated, and Fougères was quick to note its importance to the Greek city-state: as club, bourse, market, promenade, sanctuary, and museum, where the townspeople could talk, buy, and relax under the benign eye of their gods and heroes.

Face down in the pavement of the Byzantine church near postern gate H, Fougères found confirmation of Pausanias' accuracy: three reliefs, Apollo, Marsyas, and the Muses, of the school of Praxiteles, which that indefatigable traveler had singled out in his description of Mantinea.

The circuit wall, fourteen feet thick, was accurately mapped by noting the breaches that marked its gates. It was an oval two and a half miles around, with over one hundred towers (a bowshot apart) and ten gates, each with a different plan, as though the engineers were experimenting, but each gate forced those entering to present their shield-less side to the defenders. The structure in general is the same as at Messene, except that here the blocks were polygonal instead of squared, and the upper courses were of mud

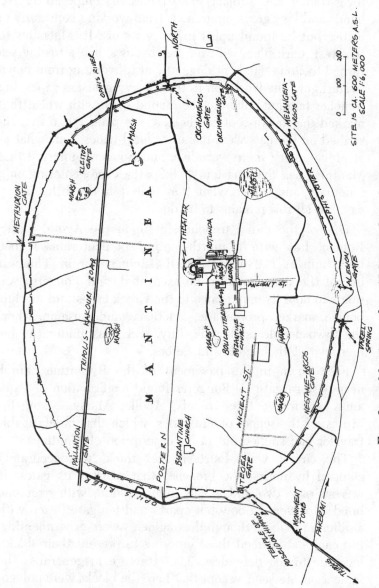

Fig. 6.13 Mantinea, plan. (*BCH* 14 [1890] Pl. I)

brick. The builders ingeniously diverted a river to fill their moat.

Mantinea covered too great an area to be dug entire: trial trenches were all Fougères could afford. He therefore had to be, and was, ingenious about where he dug them, though Schliemann (who later apologized, in Byzantine Greek) accused him of being "unsystematisch." Tiles or cut stones on the surface were a clue, and so were crop marks: the stunted growth of grain—or, at Mantinea, hashish—over buried ancient walls was already a useful indicator to Fougères in the field nearly sixty years before Bradford put it to use for air photography (see *The Mute Stones Speak*, Fig. 1.2).

Once the circuit of the wall was established, Fougères discovered that diagonals from gate to gate intersected in the Agora, whose off-center siting he thus explained. But the street plan was apparently not radial, but a rectangular grid (late third century B.C.), which he tentatively drew in on his map, cautioning that it is easy to mistake the lines of modern stone walls for ancient streets.

The excavation of Mantinea, though incomplete, was seminal. It showed that Arcadia was rather virgin than sterile soil, and led to the exploration of Megalopolis and Bassae; it was also the forerunner of the study of other fourth-century city plans elsewhere in the Greek world.

Over many of the archaeological sites dated in the fourth century looms the sinister shadow of Philip of Macedon. His destructive hand, paradoxically, preserved for us one of the finest examples of Greek city planning on a rectangular grid, for when in 348 he leveled to the ground Olynthus, on the peninsula of Chalcidice, thirty-eight miles southeast of Salonika (Fig. 6.21), it was only sporadically resettled, and its ground plan (Fig. 6.14) therefore preserved to us intact, under the earth of its crumbled adobe house-walls. An American expedition under D. M. Robin-

Fig. 6.14 Olynthus, North Hill, air photograph, showing grid, house
blocks, wall, and main north-south street. The South Hill is south
of the lower left quadrant of the photograph. (*Die Antike* 11
[1935] p. 281, by permission of the University of Mississippi)

son excavated here (1928-38); what was found made possible a reconstruction, from the ground plans and gear of
over a hundred houses, of the life of a fourth-century
Greek city ranking for interest with Priene and Delos in
Greek lands, and with Pompeii, Herculaneum, and Ostia
in Italy. Besides the house plans themselves, the evidence

is drawn from kitchenware, vases, lamps, baths, *chaises percées*, mosaics, murals, querns, grain mills, mortars, olive-crushers, and over 3500 coins, of which very few are later than 348. The city plan was probably first laid out in 432, when the Chalcidice revolted from Athens and united to form one strong city at Olynthus. The city seems to have expanded from the south, where indeed there had been a settlement in Neolithic times. Between the South Hill and the northern grid is an open area, probably the agora, but at first thought by Robinson to be a common for military maneuvers, since he found no public buildings in or around it. The northern grid is one of the most complete ever excavated. Robinson found that the city blocks were planned on a module of 120 × 300 Euboean feet. (The Chalcidice was colonized from Chalcis in Euboea.) The houses, five on each side of each east-west street, had each a sixty-foot frontage. Each block was all of one build, since the houses in it have their walls bonded into one another. Only the sloping streets were cobbled. The drains run in alleys behind the houses, not in the streets: the Olynthians thought inhabitable houses more important than passable streets. A towered wall of mud brick, surprisingly unpretentious, surrounded the city. By estimating the number of houses and multiplying by eight (philoprogenitive parents, children, and slaves), Robinson calculated the population at 9,000 to 12,000; variations in tribute paid to Athens suggest fluctuations in population, even up to 15,000 to 30,000.

A chance find in the fields on the East Spur of an inscribed deed of sale for a villa led to the excavation of Olynthus' best-known building, the Villa of Good Fortune, so called from an inscription in the pebble-mosaic floor of its reception room. It had two stories, as did most Olynthian houses: the evidence is surviving staircases or stairwells. On the ground floor its eight rooms were asymmetrically grouped around a wooden-pillared courtyard facing south, with a long corridor, called a *pastas*, typical of Olynthian domestic architecture, running behind it. At a corner, so as to have windows on two sides, was a dining-room with space for couches (for three to nine, not fewer than the Graces nor more than the Muses, the ideal size for a dinner party) around a central pebble-mosaic (again typical of Olynthus) representing Dionysus on a panther. In a mosaic in the anteroom, Thetis brings the armor forged by Hephaestus to Achilles. The unit of measure in the Villa is longer than in the houses to the west: it is the Attic foot. This should prove the Villa later than the town houses; one may reasonably suppose Olynthus to have shifted from the usages of the mother city to those of Athens, with whom, as imported Attic pottery, figurines, and lamps prove, she forged ever closer commercial relations. It was the alliance with Athens against Philip of Macedon's growing power that proved her undoing.

But Macedonians could build as well as destroy. In 334 Alexander fostered in Asia Minor, thirty miles south of Ephesus, the model planned city of Priene (see map, Fig. 6.21), whose excavation (1895-98) by Germans under Theodor Wiegand was an early exemplar of precise, thorough, Prussian scientific method. The English had excavated the temple of Athena (on the far side of the model, Fig. 6.15) in 1869, and found in a specially cut niche in the base of the cult-statue a hoard of silver coins. Forthwith the Turkish villagers came in streams and virtually took the temple apart block by block. Excavation was imperative, for dilapidation was proceeding apace. But there were delays: in getting permission to dig, in mending the road from Söke; in building an excavation house. Malaria, hurricanes, and earthquakes plagued excavators and excavation. Priene suffered six earthquakes in the four years the Germans were digging there; nearly 13,000 have occurred in the district since 500 B.C. For all that, Priene has its compensations: it is beautifully sited, on its four terraces in the lee of its acropolis, which looms

FIG. 6.15 Priene, model. Agora in center; above it to r., the North Stoa, with Ekklesiasterion (hipped-roofed building behind Stoa) Far edge, temple of Athena; r. center, theater. (Berlin, Staatliche Museen)

twelve hundred feet above sea-level, reached by a dizzying flight of steps cut in the cliff. From the top and from the town, the view is south across the rich Meander valley, green with crops in the early spring when the storks come in February, and anemones, asphodel, iris, and almond trees are in blossom.

The excavated area of Priene is about the size of Pompeii, one sixth the area of Alexander's major foundation, Alexandria in Egypt. Behind its towered marble wall lived some 4000 inhabitants. Six streets running east and west, sixteen running north and south, make up its neat grid; about 1000 cubic yards of cliff had to be cut away to accommodate it. The plan centers on the Agora, two blocks wide, which takes up about a fifth of the total area, with buildings grouped around it like Greek house-rooms round a peristyle. In its center was an altar; east of it the Germans found twelve lettered blocks with put-holes in them; these must have been for the supports of a canopy or awning that shaded the town fathers upon state occasions. Shady porticoes, with shops or offices behind, surrounded the Agora on three sides; on the east was the sanctuary of Priene's second most important god, Zeus (the small temple in the center of the model). The north stoa, 377 feet long (it was extended eastward later) is the grandest. Its columns have holes for the pegs where once hung painted portraits. The Agora of Priene is full of monuments of personal or municipal vanity, a number of which show in the model. They survive to us as the inscribed bases—sometimes comfortable curved seats or exedrae—of statues in gilt bronze or marble. The inscriptions often specify that the likeness shall stand in the most conspicuous possible place. Honorific decrees authorizing the statues adorn all available wall space. But the architectural remains are scanty; the German model of this rich Agora is a triumph of archaeological inference from the most unlikely looking evidence.

Behind the Agora, and entered from the east end of the

north stoa, is the Bouleuterion, or council house. Paradoxically, a fire preserved it: the roof fell in and covered everything, so that Christians never got at it. Its seats, for 640, are grouped around three sides of a square, with an altar in the middle. North of it was the theater, already described. The theater-quarter was the fashionable one: elegant private houses, with patterned stuccoed walls, furniture with lathe-turned bronze legs; hip-baths; and pleasant terracotta figurines like the ones from Tanagra. A closer source is Myrina, eight and a half miles north, where over 1,000 such figurines have been found. One large dwelling, not in the theater quarter but by the west gate, the Germans called the Holy House, because in it was found a private chapel with offerings (including a marble statuette of Alexander), and an inscription bidding none to enter unless dressed in white. Perhaps Alexander stayed here, and the house was later made a shrine.

The Ionic temple of Athena is noteworthy for having no figured frieze, and because on the pronaos was found the inscription, now in the British Museum, stating that Alexander dedicated this temple to Athena. The cult statue was a half-size copy of Phidias' in the Parthenon in Athens. The masonry is careful, beautifully finished, restrained work; the proportions are harmoniously, even mathematically worked out: the cella door was sixteen by twenty-two Ionic feet; the statue base was eight feet high; column bases and inter-spaces each six feet, the pronaos thirty feet, the cella proper fifty, and the opisthodomos (room behind the cella, usually the temple treasury) twelve. Several columns have now been re-erected. About 150 B.C., when piety had given way to ostentation, the view of the temple from the south was obstructed by a stoa.

In the Hellenistic lower gymnasium (Fig. 6.15, lower left) there survive lavatories and a lecture room, its walls covered with students' names as graffiti. The adjoining stadium has both Hellenistic and Roman starting blocks.

Altogether Priene makes a very pleasant impression, of an airy, sunny, clean little city surpassing all others of this century in the careful simplicity of its buildings in solid marble. As one approaches the Agora up the steep slope from the West Gate, noticing the fountain houses on the corners and the ⊏⊐ panels that once contained painted street signs, one can imagine the stuccoed houses with their red tile roofs, the Agora rich with bronze and marble, and buzzing with the inimitable noise of Greeks doing business. Priene, like Pompeii, is an ancient city that comes alive.

In 1899, following immediately upon his excavations at Priene, Wiegand transferred his activities ten miles south, to Miletus (map, Fig. 6.21), the birthplace of the fifth-century father of Greek city planning, Hippodamus; and the metropolis, and once, in the days of the philosopher Thales (fl. 585 B.C.), intellectual center of Ionian Asia Minor. Despite difficulties of climate (malarial), terrain (nowadays the main part of the ancient city is mostly under water), and land expropriation, Wiegand continued methodically season after season, laying bare block after block of the Hippodamian plan of Hippodamus' city. Hippodamus first laid down his grid probably in 479, when the city was rebuilt after the Persians destroyed it, but most of the public buildings Wiegand excavated are fourth century, Hellenistic, or Roman. The Mycenaean remains (Chapter 3) were found in the southwest quadrant of the city, near what was until late antiquity one of Miletus' four harbors: silting has left the site over five miles from the sea. A Mycenaean necropolis has been partially excavated; also traces of Sub-Mycenaean houses here, perhaps to be associated with Neleus (son of an eleventh-century king of Athens, and descendant of Nestor of Pylos), who, the Milesians believed, led a group of colonists here. Terracotta revetments of the late sixth century, found on Kalabaktepe, six hundred yards south of the Sub-Mycenaean houses, give evidence of a temple there. The archaic period was Miletus' Golden Age: in the seventh and sixth centuries she was, perhaps to relieve overpopulation, a vigorous colonizer, especially around the Black Sea and at Naucratis on the Canopic (westernmost) branch of the Nile. Her main harbor could be closed by chains whose ends were held in the mouths of stone lions, which the excavators found.

Figure 6.16 illustrates, from a model, buildings of various dates in Miletus' civic center. An early phase of the Delphinium (lower right corner, a sanctuary of Apollo where the sacred procession to Didyma assembled) is dated to the sixth century by an inscription and a rounded altar with archaic architectural details. Later, it housed the Milesian archives. It yielded over two hundred inscriptions, including lists of magistrates reused face down in the pavement by the

FIG. 6.16 Miletus, civic center, model (Berlin, Staatliche Museen)

Romans. Across the Processional Street is the North Agora, which fits into the Hippodamian grid, and received additions, in the form of (a) statues of the third- and second-century kings of Syria, and (b) a second story, dating from the early Roman Empire. The South Agora (upper left), perhaps the gift of the Seleucid Antiochus I (reigned 281-61), could vie with any in the ancient world for size: it covered over 33,000 square yards, embracing sixteen city blocks, whereas Priene's occupied only two. The profits from its seventy-eight shops were used to build the gigantic temple of Apollo at Didyma. Next in date is the gymnasium (left of Delphinium in the model), gift of Eumenes II of Pergamum (reigned 197-160/59), who also gave a stadium. North of it across the Processional Street is the bouleuterion, of 170 B.C., in its forecourt the tomb of a distinguished but unidentified Milesian. The baroque building in the left center is a nymphaeum or fountain house, masking the end of an aqueduct. The Emperor Trajan (reigned A.D. 98-117) built it, as an inscription tells us, to honor his father, who was proconsul of Asia in 79/80. It had three stories of aediculae (small columned or pilastered tabernacles) containing statues. Above it in the model is the equally overdecorated Great Gate of the South Agora, dated stylistically in the Antonine period, perhaps commemorating the Parthian campaign (162-65) of M. Aurelius' colleague Lucius Verus. The Germans reconstructed it stone by stone in what is now East Berlin's Pergamon-Museum. It has two stories, again with aediculae. They have Composite capitals (involving both Ionic volutes and Corinthian acanthus leaves). There are statue niches: in one, a trousered barbarian kneels before the emperor; a broken pediment crowns all. Also Antonine is the vast theater (off the model, 380 yards west of the North Agora). The largest in Asia Minor, it held 15,000, and had a two-story stage embellished with primitive reliefs of Cupids hunting boars and bears.

The importance of this city plan, like those of Priene and Olynthus, is that it expresses not regimentation but individuality; these cities were democracies; crooked, cramped streets suggest feudal conditions.

Fourth-century Ionia prospered, unafraid of the weak Persian kings; it used some of its profits to build sumptuous temples to the gods, or tombs for the rulers given credit for the prosperity. Two monuments, the Artemision at Ephesus and the Mausoleum at Halicarnassus, were reckoned (the criterion is chiefly size) among the Seven Wonders of the ancient world. (The others were the Pyramids of Gizeh, the Hanging Gardens of Babylon, the statue of Zeus at Olympia, the Colossus of Rhodes, and the Pharos [lighthouse] at Alexandria. All the classical wonders are described in this book.)

Ephesus, thirty miles north of Priene (map, Fig. 6.21), was first excavated (1869-74), for the British Museum, at a cost of £16,000, by a British architect, John Turtle Wood. His account of his adventures is more picturesque than informative; and his methods, since continued funds depended on tangible results, more ruthless than scholarly; they included the use of gunpowder to blow apart a Byzantine church that stood in his way. His catalogue of woes is longer than Job's. At first he commuted to the dig from Smyrna, fifty miles away; when he moved to a chalet nearer his work, he was in constant danger of brigands. He broke his collarbone, was almost assassinated, a vessel laden with his loot was wrecked, his men went on strike, his deep excavations struck springs and left the temple pavement under standing water, mice ate the paper squeeze-impressions of his inscriptions, the saws he used to cut the marble (to reduce the weight of architectural blocks for transport) froze in the blocks. But he loved the picturesqueness; when officers of the British man-of-war detailed to carry his finds to London stayed with him, they hunted boar, played whist, and admired the black camel's-hair tents of the Arab workmen.

And he got his tangible results. He dug seventy-five trial pits the first year in his search for the temple, finally hitting upon its precinct wall by following up a road leading eastward from the Hellenistic city. He moved 132,221 cubic yards of earth, digging down twenty-five feet to uncover an area of 300 × 500 feet. His most rewarding find was a series of sculptured column-drums, from a double row at each end of the temple. It took fifteen men fifteen days to extract one. Several of these columns, the gift of kings (one is inscribed "dedicated by Croesus") were loaded onto a man-of-war to the sound of fifes. At the London end, it took twenty dray-horses to transport them to the British Museum.

In 1904-05 D. G. Hogarth, who had worked with Evans at Knossos, and had dug at Kato Zakro, reopened Wood's dig, now overgrown with an impenetrable jungle, its reeds ten feet high. Though he pumped out 100,000 cubic meters of water, the site constantly refilled. Mornings had to be spent pumping; archaeological work could be done only in the afternoons, the men thigh-deep in slime. Nevertheless Hogarth was able to distinguish five phases of the temple, of which the last, which he called E, is late fourth-century and Hellenistic. It was of the same colossal dimensions (180 × 377 feet, with a veritable forest of sixty-foot columns) as its predecessor, D, which Hogarth called the "Croesus temple." A figured column base from Temple E, portraying Hermes, Thanatos (Death), and Eurydice or Alcestis, is in the British Museum. The interior of the base of the cult-statue was filled with archaic objects: electrum (gold and silver alloy) coins, scarabs, earrings, *fibulae*, and the bones of innumerable small animals and birds. Other archaic finds came from around the base: bits of ivory inlay, a miniature ivory sphinx, studs and beads in crystal and onyx, figurines of hawks in glazed terracotta and electrum, a large statuette of Artemis (not, as later, many-breasted*), beads of tawny Baltic and (in greater

---

* The Austrian F. Miltner wrote (1958) that the protuberances on the

quantity) red Sicilian amber, and a jar of nineteen electrum coins. They date the earliest temple, A, not earlier than 600-590, since one of them seems to bear the name of King Alyattes of Lydia, who reigned about 600. Hogarth catalogued 3000 objects, all much earlier than the fourth century, but piously preserved by the fourth-century rebuilders. His most significant find was a silver plate inscribed with a record of the origin of Temple C, only one fourth the size of its successor. Recent excavation has revealed the U-shaped altar (anticipating the one at Pergamum) in front of the later Artemision, and, under the pavement, figured column drums from the archaic temple. In Christian times the temple fell on evil days, and the silversmiths who had once profited from it rioted, crying nostalgically, "Great is Diana of the Ephesians!" (*Acts* 19:24).

Beginning in 1898, before Hogarth, and continuing at intervals to the present day, the site of the monumental city of Ephesus, as opposed to the Artemision, has been an Austrian dig. Most of what they have excavated is of Roman date (the Romans exalted Ephesus above Miletus), but the theater, with a capacity of 23,000, was probably begun at the very end of the fourth century, and the south gate of the Agora is contemporary with it.

Eleven miles south of Miletus, and connected with it by a Sacred Way, lined at the Didyma end with statues, lies the temple of Apollo at Didyma (Fig. 6.21), which for size (163 × 341 feet, with sixty-foot columns), delicacy of detail, and the contribution it makes to 350 years of architectural history deserves to be (though it is not) ranked as one of the Seven Wonders of the World. It, like Miletus, is a German dig, begun in 1906. Though all the expedition's film negatives were burned and all the small finds destroyed or stolen during the Turkish-Greek troubles of 1916-22, the

---

breast of the standard statues of Diana of the Ephesians represent not breasts but eggs! Either way, we have to do with a fertility symbol.

results, including over 600 inscriptions, have been exhaustively published. The work was rather one of clearing than of digging, since the blocks thrown down by an earthquake in 1493 encumbered the temple stylobate. One of them weighed over 100 tons. Many were built back into the walls by the excavators, to get them out of the way and to give some approximation of the grandeur of the temple when it was new (Fig. 6.17), in Alexander's time or slightly later. The older temple had a deeper forecourt, with figures of maidens on the column drums, and gorgons on, and couchant lions next to, the architrave corners; the lateral vaulted passages mentioned below belong to the later phase. It replaced a temple destroyed about 479 in the Persian Wars: Alexander ostentatiously built up what the Persians had knocked down. The bases of the front columns are varied—palmettes, serpentines, meanders, panels with vegetable motifs, on twelve-sided plinths. Pairs of these match, on either side of the temple's central axis. The great central door, over eighteen

FIG. 6.17 Didyma, temple of Apollo, reconstruction drawing. (Knackfuss, 1941, Fig. Z.511)

feet wide, has a sill over five feet above the pavement. Obviously no one entered by it: it was a stage for pageants or announcements of oracles. The entrances were lateral, through a pair of passages with barrel vaults, the earliest known in Greek lands; above these, stairs led to the temple roof. The striking feature of the temple was a sunken, probably unroofed, central court or adyton, a third as wide as it is long, approached by a monumental flight of steps. The central court was probably left unroofed for cult reasons; it could have been roofed if Greek architects had not been so timid about using timber trusses. At its back, a small shrine or *naiskos* is oriented on a spring within its walls, which served some oracular purpose. The south exterior steps served as seats for the stadium adjoining; there was in the archaic period a stoa facing the temple on the southwest. The labor involved was colossal; the temple was still unfinished when the great earthquake of A.D. 17 struck it. In the environs must have been a complex of buildings like those at Olympia or Epidaurus; only stoas have so far been excavated.

A final example of monumental Ionic temple architecture of the fourth century is the Temple of Artemis at Sardis, the capital of Croesus' Lydia, forty-five miles up the Hermus valley east of Smyrna (Fig. 6.21). It was explored (1910-14) by the American H. C. Butler; later excavation by a joint Harvard-Cornell expedition has found monumental Lydian buildings and city walls of 600-545 B.C., and has restored a Caracallan marble hall and a synagogue of about A.D. 200, richly veneered in polychrome marble. A Lydian industrial area (of 600-527 B.C.) contained workshops for refining gold. Butler's expedition was the most lavishly equipped of any up to his time: he used a locomotive to haul around the site a twenty-ton crane for raising large blocks. Various parts of the site were interconnected by telephone, and the excavation house, Villa Omphale, was palatial, though it had been built in the record time of nine weeks. It had a tennis court, and a butler to serve cocktails; the excavators dressed for dinner.

The temple proved to be one of the largest in the Greek world. It measured 160 × 200 feet, and covered over 5000 square yards. Begun in Alexander's time (as mint-fresh tetradrachms of his testify, found in the base of the cult-statue), it, like Didyma, was never finished, for most of its sixty-five-foot Ionic columns (there were once seventy-eight) are unfluted. Some of the columns are raised on pedestals left rough, but obviously intended to be carved like those of Ephesus. Three phases have now been distinguished; in the latest, Artemis shared divine honors with Faustina (died A.D. 141), wife of the Roman emperor Antoninus Pius. A capital from the Sardis temple is in New York's Metropolitan Museum.

It was not only the temples of fourth-century Asia Minor that were colossal. When Mausolus, satrap of Caria, died in 353, his widow Artemisia decided to build for his body, on the heights behind his capital, Halicarnassus (Fig. 6.21), a huge tomb, which has given his name to all mausolea since. This Wonder of the World was explored in 1857 by C. T. Newton. Using clues from Vitruvius and Pliny the Elder, he narrowed down the possible location and then dug, using tunnels rather than trenches, for the ground belonged to different owners, all recalcitrant and rapacious. He knew that he had had predecessors. Robbers in 1522, finding a cellarlike opening, had entered by candlelight to find themselves in a fine, large, square room, with marble half-columns and a frieze, which they first admired and then pulled to pieces to rebuild into a fort. A second chamber held a tomb. Postponing entry into it until next day, they were anticipated by other robbers (pirates, they called them). The first robbers on their return found nothing but strewn earth, fragments of cloth-of-gold, and spangles. Newton, in dismantling a wall made of column-drums, came upon a north-south cutting in the rock, with a pavement beyond it. Tunneling, he came to stairs, and a ten-ton block of green stone, which no doubt closed the tomb. Using Pliny's dimensions, he now found three of the four corners of the foundation, and at last knew which land to buy. He found, and sent to the British Museum, masses of architectural and sculptural fragments and, along the east side, four slabs of a frieze of Greeks and Amazons, by Scopas: dramatic and pathetic, in his manner; vibrant with the antithesis of oblique parallel lines. The figures lunge or draw back, with one leg stretched out full length. The relief is deeply undercut, for it had to be seen from ninety feet below. Though there is some controversy about details of the restoration (Fig. 6.18), it is clear from

FIG. 6.18 Halicarnassus, Mausoleum, reconstruction drawing. (Krischen, *Die griechische Stadt*, Pl. 37, by permission of Gebrüder Mann, Berlin)

ancient descriptions and from architectural fragments discovered by Newton, including pyramid steps hollowed out
underneath and grooved to fit into each other, that the architect's aim was to persuade the viewer that a vast pyramid
(80 × 100 feet) was supported by slim Ionic columns resting on a massive podium. (The pyramid was in fact supported by the cella walls.) Newton found a fragment of a
colossal chariot wheel, seven feet seven inches in diameter,
part of a quadriga or four-horse chariot group that crowned
the pyramid. He found, too, what are arguably the figures of
Mausolus and Artemisia themselves, who were probably represented as riding in the chariot; they too are in the British
Museum. Recent excavation, by Danes, has uncovered the
Mausoleum's precinct wall (288 × 114 yards) and an Amazon frieze slab. The local museum contains the bronze ingots
of *ca.* 1200 B.C., previously mentioned as discovered by scuba
divers in the wreck off nearby Cape Gelidonya.

The place in Greece where unquestioned examples of
Scopas' sculpture, albeit badly battered, have been found is
Tegea, about ten miles south of Mantinea. Dating from about
340, they filled the pediment and constituted the metopes of
the temple of Athena Alea, a place of asylum for, among
others, kings of Sparta. The east pediment concerns the Calydonian boar hunt, which involved the huntress Atalanta (allegedly born here), her suitor Meleager, and the Athenian
hero Theseus. The actual tusks of the monster were preserved
here till Augustus stole them and took them to Rome. The
west pediment, like the interior frieze of the Pergamum Great
Altar, told the story of Telephus, born of the rape here of
the princess Augê by Heracles: he fought against Achilles in
a battle by the Caicus River, in Mysia, Asia Minor. Casts of
the fragments are in the site museum, the originals in the
National Museum in Athens.

After the rather vulgar ostentation of Halicarnassus, it is

a relief to return to the comparative sanity of Lycurgan Athens. Though Lycurgus came to office in 338, the very year of Athens' crushing defeat by Philip of Macedon at Chaeronea, his faith in his city never wavered. But he backed his faith by legal precautions. During the period of his predominance, in 336 (the same year in which his fellow-citizens voted a gold crown to Demosthenes, despite the failure of his policy), was passed a decree against tyranny, found in the Agora in 1952, and now in the Agora Museum. The decree is in Lycurgus' doctrinaire spirit, and reflects the hysteria of the time by, in effect, abolishing due process and allowing each citizen to take the law into his own hands, for it empowers any Athenian to kill without fear of reprisal anyone whom he suspects of plotting against the democracy. The intent was apparently to prevent reactionaries in the high court of the Areopagus from supporting a pro-Macedonian dictatorship. The text is surmounted by a relief of Democracy crowning the Athenian People—as Athens had crowned Demosthenes. Some attempt was made in antiquity, whether by liberals, reactionaries, or connoisseurs of art is uncertain, to sever the relief from the text. The marks of the chisel are still visible. The mover of the decree, one Eukrates, died a martyr to the very tyranny he tried to circumvent: the pro-Macedonians executed him in 322, the year Demosthenes committed suicide, the year in which Athens' ancient political primacy ended forever.

But in Lycurgus' time Athens had not yet finally succumbed, and he proclaimed his belief in her future by his program of public works. Of his rebuilding the theater of Dionysus in stone we have already spoken. He also built, in a hollow by the Ilissus, 500 yards east of the Pisistratid Olympieium, a Panathenaic stadium that will be more appropriately discussed in the last chapter, in connection with its being restored in the second century A.D. by the millionaire Herodes Atticus. Lycurgus strengthened the city walls, and in a splendid if pathetic gesture built two stoas, promenades with shops in back, behind the assembly place on the Pnyx. His piety prompted him to build an altar between the stoas; the same piety moved him to add a portico to the Hall of the Mysteries at Eleusis, and probably to rebuild the temple of Apollo Patroos in the Athenian Agora, which had been purposely left in ruins after the sack of Athens in 479 as a reminder of Persian *Schrecklichkeit*. He also built the courtroom in the level beneath the north end of the Stoa of Attalus in the Agora, where the decree against tyranny was found. He was responsible, too, for the gymnasium in the Lyceum where Aristotle taught. His best-known building was the naval storehouse called the Arsenal, in Piraeus,* which is so clearly described in a building inscription that it can be reconstructed (there is a model of it in the basement of the Piraeus Naval Museum at Pasha Limani), though not a single block of it survives. Used to store sails and tackle, it was 400 Attic feet long and 100 wide, divided into a long central hall and two side aisles supported by thirty-five Ionic columns. This divided the aisles into thirty-six rooms, closed off by wickets, on each side, each with a window, and each with an upper floor. The sails were stored in 134 cupboards below, the tackle above. Thus did Lycurgus, by the building of this impressive

---

* In July, 1959, workmen digging a sewer in Piraeus hit upon the arm of a bronze statue. This led to intensive exploration of the area, and more sensational finds: a whole set of bronze and marble statues, mostly of the fourth century, lying neatly together (Fig. 6.19) as though awaiting shipment, presumably to Rome. The warehouse was burnt, perhaps in the Sullan sack of 86 B.C., and the statues forgotten. They include an Artemis, a crested Athena, a Muse, and a large tragic mask, all in bronze, some with their marble-inset eyes in place. One of them, an Apollo over six feet tall, who originally held a bowl and a bow, is not fourth century but archaic (*ca.* 530/20), the earliest-known large hollow-cast bronze, its iron armature still within it. The finds are in the National Museum in Athens. They make an impressive addition to the inventory of bronze statues of the archaic and classical ages. Two others, of warriors, larger than life, of the fifth century B.C., with inset copper lips and silver teeth, found in the sea off Riace in south Italy, are now (1981) on display in the Reggio Calabria museum.

FIG. 6.19   Piraeus, bronze statues of Artemis and Athena, as found,
1959. Piraeus, Museum. (Vanderpool, 1960, Pl. 65.2)

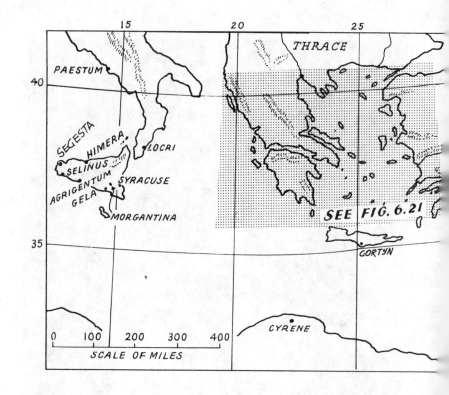

Fig. 6.20   Classical and post-classical sites

naval storehouse in a time of Athens' nadir, affirm her ancient
supremacy on the sea.

Sanctuaries where the afflicted are healed by faith, theaters that are also assembly places, game sites where tyrants
proclaim their might and magnanimity, city plans that
reaffirm democratic individualism, colossal temples too expensive to finish, patriotism displayed after the tradition

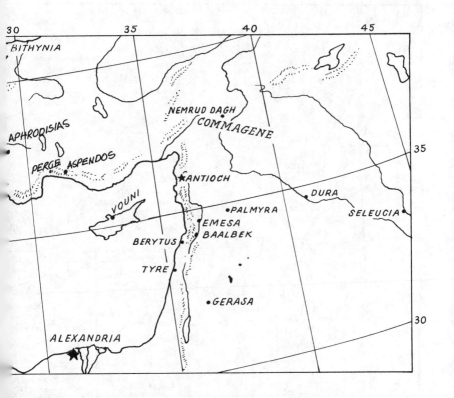

in Greek lands, to illustrate Chs. 5-8, map.

has faded—all this is a part of the kaleidoscopic picture presented by archaeology of the Greek world in the fourth century. It is customary to take 322, the date of the death of Aristotle the philosopher and of Demosthenes the orator, as the dividing line between the classical and the Hellenistic Age, an age of monarchy and cosmopolitanism about which archaeology has much to tell.

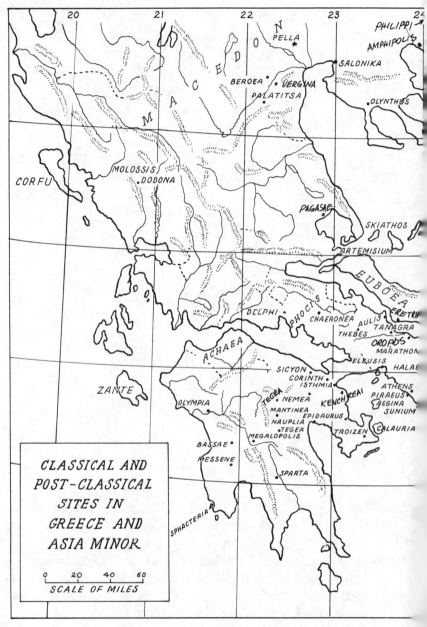

FIG. 6.21 Classical and post-classical sites in Greece

and Asia Minor, to illustrate Chs. 5-8, map.

ADDENDUM
(all dates approximate)

B.C.

380	Epidaurus, Temple of Asclepius
	Olympia, Metroön
370	Mantinea; Messene earlier
368	Megalopolis, Thersilion & theater
360	Delphi, Temple of Apollo; Tholos earlier
356	Ephesus, Artemision E
353	Halicarnassus, Mausoleum (Scopas)
350	Oropos, long stoa
	Miletus, theater, first phase
348	Olynthus destroyed
	Thasos, theater
340	Tegea, Temple of Athena Alea
338	Olympia, Leonidaion
	Athens, Theater of Dionysus; Stadium
334	Priene
	Olympia, Philippeion & Echo Stoa
	Hermes of Praxiteles
	Agias of Lysippus
330	Didyma, Temple of Apollo; Miletus, North Agora
	Eleusis, Prostoon
330/20	Nemea, Temple of Zeus
326	Athens, Stoas behind Pnyx; city walls
	Eleusis, Hall of Mysteries, Lycurgan phase
	Sardis, Temple of Artemis
300	Priene, theater

7

The Hellenistic Age

(322-146 B.C.)

For the years between the fall of Athens in 322 and Rome's destruction of Corinth in 146 B.C., excavation confirms the historical record: during these years Greece proper was in the doldrums. The wealth of building—palaces, new cities, grandiose works of engineering, splendid sanctuaries and stoas—was in the hands of the Hellenistic princes who succeeded Alexander: the Antigonids in Macedonia, the Ptolemies in Egypt, and the Attalids in Pergamum. (The Seleucids in Syria were great builders, colonizers, and city planners, too, but so far most of the archaeological evidence in Syria comes from Roman times.) At the sanctuaries—Ionian Claros, Lindos on Rhodes, Kos, Delos, the island of Thasos in the north Aegean—the gods competed with Mammon, and grandiosity was the hallmark of the age. Two of the Seven Wonders of the ancient world, the Pharos (lighthouse) at Alexandria and the Colossus of Rhodes, were built in Hellenistic times.

The year 1961 marked the centennial of excavation in Macedonia. In 1861 the Frenchman Leon Heuzey excavated an axially planned building set in the wonderfully rich vale

of Pieria, at Palatitsa, three hours south of Beroea, and forty
airline miles west of Salonika (Fig. 6.21). On a plateau
within the ancient city wall, known to him since 1855, Heuzey noticed Doric and Ionic capitals built into the walls of a
ruined church. Here his workmen, fifteen French sailors and
forty Greeks and Bulgars, dug a trial trench. Almost at once
they struck footings. In the forty days before the sailors fell
ill and the dig had to be abandoned, Heuzey uncovered half
the building, enough to reveal its plan. A paved area led to a
propylon between porticoes; on the left of the propylon was
a circular room with the footings of a dais or statue base;
beyond the propylon was a peristyle 150 Macedonian feet or
100 cubits wide. Within the peristyle were traces of flowerbeds or shrubs; around it were rooms, in at least two stories,
for Heuzey found stairwells in the rooms, one on each side
of the peristyle. The site was within eyeshot of Pella, the
Macedonian capital. Heuzey decided he had found a summer
palace, a Macedonian Fontainebleau, dated by its architectural technique in the Periclean age. A Greek expedition
under K. A. Rhomaios, in 1953, finished excavating the peristyle; it was square, with an epistyle furnished with triglyphs and metopes. Rhomaios discovered mosaic floors in
the rooms at the back, or west side of the peristyle. The back
wall was stuccoed to represent courses of stone. Rhomaios,
comparing the circular room with the Philippeion at Olympia,
and the architectural technique with the temple of Athena
Alea at Tegea, dated the building in the fourth century, in
the reign of Philip II or Alexander. Archaeologists are a per-
sistently unromantic breed: many, remembering the plan of
the Leonidaion at Olympia and the pilgrims' hostel at Epidaurus, suppose the structure to have been a hotel. More
recently, it has been dated to the reign of the Macedonian
philosopher-king Antigonus Gonatas (274-239).

At Vergina, a little more than a mile east of Palatitsa, excavators in November, 1977, hit upon a burial so rich they
thought it must be royal. Two larnakes (chests) of solid gold

contained bones. One set (Fig. 7.1), of a man of about fifty (Philip was forty-six when he was assassinated in 336), was wrapped in gold and purple cloth. There were small ivory heads of Philip and Alexander; also a pair of greaves (shin

FIG. 7.1 Vergina, gold larnax and diadem (by permission of the Smithsonian Institution, Washington, D.C.)

guards), one shorter than the other. Since Philip was lame, the excavator deduced that this was his tomb. Another possibility is that the tomb is that of Philip III Arrhidaeus, Alexander's epileptic half brother, and his redoubtable wife Eurydice. This deduction is based on the style of the tomb's construction and décor, and the presence of (a) a diadem, not in use until the 330s, and (b) of female armor: Eurydice had been trained for war, and actually led the Macedonian army. A second unrobbed tomb, northwest of the first, was excavated in 1978. It contained a single cremation burial, with weapons. The partly consumed bones were swathed in purple and placed on a table in a silver hydria (three-handled vase, used for carrying water), surmounted by a gold crown. There were also two silver-plated bronze containers, silver vessels, gilt bronze greaves, a silver-plated iron lampstand, a gilt bronze strigil, another with gold appliqué, a gilt spear point, and fragments of ceremonial dress in leather and cloth, with gold décor. A band painted round the antechamber portrayed a chariot race. This tomb, also royal, is dated 375-50.

Excavation has been going on since 1958 at Pella, the ancient capital of Macedonia, the birthplace of Alexander the Great. Finds in the lower town include roof tiles stamped "Royal" or "Philip." Some of the streets are ten meters wide; the area is an impressive three and a half square kilometers; the private houses are large, with rich bronze furnishings. But the most impressive finds are the pebble mosaic pavements of the late fourth century B.C. One of the four courts and several of the west rooms of a palatial structure, "Building 1," were floored with mosaics made of natural pebbles, not man-made tesserae, carefully matched and set, laid to bring out the modeling of the figures. Profiles, eyes, ears, and toes are outlined with thin strips of lead. One of the panels *may* portray Alexander's trusted second-in-command, Craterus, rescuing his young sovereign from the attack of a ferocious lion. Other panels show Dionysus on a panther

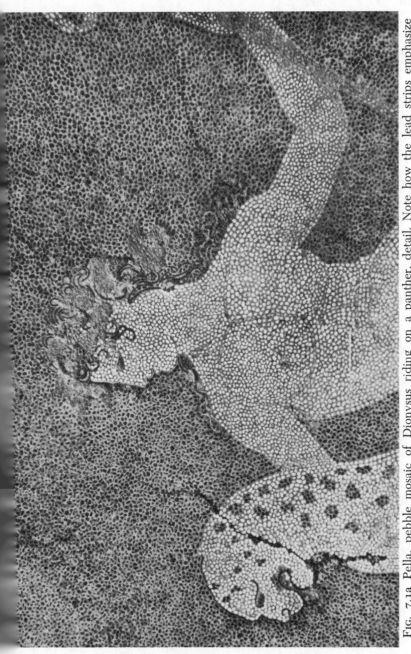

FIG. 7.1a Pella, pebble mosaic of Dionysus riding on a panther, detail. Note how the lead strips emphasize the profile, eyebrow, and hair. (AJA 62 [1958] Pl. 84)

(detail, Fig. 7.1a), a griffin bringing down a stag, and a pair of centaurs. These and more mosaics, found in adjoining houses, are on display in the site museum. All are masterpieces, ranking among the major discoveries in Greece in recent years. Other examples are now known from Alexandria and Corinth. Their effect must approximate very closely that of monumental painting.

At Leucadia in Macedonia, 27 miles southwest of Pella, excavation of a tumulus in the early 1960s revealed a temple-tomb of the early third century B.C., the largest yet found in mainland Greece. Its painted façade, 28 feet wide and ex-

FIG. 7.1b   Lefkadia, temple-tomb façade, reconstruction. (Photios Petsas)

traordinarily well preserved (Fig. 7.1b), showed, in intercolumnar panels, the dead warrior, Hermes Conductor of
Souls, and Aeacus and Rhadamanthus, judges of the dead.
(Rhadamanthus bears a striking resemblance to a figure identified as a philosopher from a villa at Boscoreale, near Pompeii.) Above the panels are eleven metopes of centauro-
machies, delicately painted in earth colors and chiaroscuro to
imitate the Parthenon reliefs. Above the metopes is a con-
tinuous frieze in colored stucco on a blue ground, showing
Greeks fighting Orientals, probably Persians. Above the
frieze, also in stucco, are seven intercolumnar doors, or shuttered windows.

In 1962 roadbuilders at Dherveni, seven miles north of
Salonika, hit upon six unrifled late fourth-century tombs of
extraordinary richness. Their contents included vessels in
bronze, silver, alabaster, clay, and glass; implements, arms,
jewelry, coins of Philip II and Alexander, and a gold-plated
head of Heracles, alleged founder of the Macedonian royal
house. The most remarkable finds, now in the Salonika museum, but slated to form part of a traveling exhibition in
1981, were a gilt bronze crater weighing forty kilograms and
nearly three feet high (Fig. 7.1c); also a papyrus roll, the
oldest known and the only one ever found in Greece. The
crater, more distinguished for technique than for taste, was
found shrouded, as befits a funerary urn, and crowned with a
gold wreath. Its decoration, in high relief, in the style of
Lysippus, includes bearded masks and snakes on the volute
handles, an animal frieze, four statuettes of seated sleepers,
and a central band portraying Dionysus, Ariadne, Maenads,
an ithyphallic satyr, and an uncouth figure carrying two
spears and wearing but one sandal: he may be Pentheus,
victim of Dionysus and the Maenads, but also an allegory
for the lame and assassinated Philip II. The papyrus contains roughly the top third of a commentary on an Orphic
poem, recording mystical equations between Zeus and air,
Being, Becoming, and Passing Away, with fragmentary refer-

FIG. 7.1c   Dherveni, gilt bronze krater. (Smithsonian Institution)

ences to the heavenly Aphrodite, Hera, Demeter, and the demigoddesses Persuasion and Harmony.

Since Philip of Macedon is chiefly famous for his victory over the Greeks in 338 at Chaeronea, thirty-six miles west-northwest of Thebes, it is appropriate to describe the site here. The most conspicuous monument is the Lion, now re-erected (Fig. 7.1d), twenty-eight feet high with its plinth.

FIG. 7.1d   Chaeronea, lion. (Alison Frantz)

It commemorates the Theban dead of the Sacred Band, vowed to fight to the death; their skeletons, 254 of them in seven layers, found buried within the precinct wall of the monument, were taken to the National Museum in Athens. Near Chaeronea's Kephissos River a mound, the Polyandrion, 222 feet wide and 23 feet high, containing a pyre, charred bones, and fragments of weapons, covered the Macedonian dead. Chaeronea, always an insignificant town, owes its later fame to the biographer Plutarch (ca. 46-127), who lived, held religious and civic office, and died here.

Southwest of Pella, 120 tortuous miles into remote Epirus, lies Dodona, seat of an oracle of Zeus, outranked in prestige only by Apollo's at Delphi. Its pottery goes back to Mycenaean times; Homer mentions its priests, who slept on the ground and never washed their feet. Various manifestations of the oracle are recorded: the rustling leaves of a talking oak, the cooing of doves, the murmur of a spring, the echoes of a brazen gong. In historical times questions to the oracle, pathetically banal, were submitted on strips of lead, some now in the Carapanos Room of the National Museum in Athens.

The oracle first achieved international fame under King Pyrrhus of Epirus (reigned 297-272): he built the theater (Fig. 7.1e; metamorphosed into an amphitheater under Augustus), larger than Epidaurus'; monumentalized Zeus' precinct, dedicated a small temple to Zeus' consort Dione and another to Heracles and Aphrodite; was probably responsible for the bouleuterion, a columned hall like the Thersilion at Megalopolis. The Aetolians sacked Dodona in 219, the Romans in 168/7, and though it never regained the prosperity it had enjoyed under Pyrrhus, it had a stadium, and still under the Roman Empire celebrated to Zeus a festival, revived in modern times with the restoration of the theater (1959). The talking oak allegedly survived to A.D. 391. If Alexander had endowed it with the 1,500 talents he promised, its glory would have been still greater.

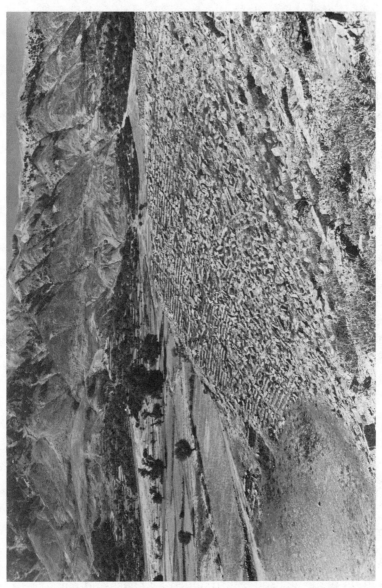

Fig. 7.1e   Dodona, theater. (Alison Frantz)

Another oracle, often paired with Dodona, and also in Epirus, is at Ephyra, above the junction of the rivers Cocytus and Acheron, reputed entrances to the underworld. It was an oracle of the dead, and sanctuary of Persephone and her husband Hades. Three concentric circuit walls, the outer and inner polygonal, the latter ten feet thick, enclose the extraordinary central building, with mazelike passageways, windowless rooms, arches (rare in Greek architecture), and a vaulted crypt. Fragments of a bronze windlass suggest some sort of hocus-pocus, no doubt assisted by the hallucinatory drugs mentioned in the ancient sources.

Alexander's most competent general was Ptolemy, who took Egypt as his inheritance and made his capital at Alexandria (Fig. 7.2), that new foundation in a wasteland by the Canopic mouth of the Nile, between Lake Mareotis and the sea, which was to become under the first three Ptolemies the intellectual capital of the ancient world. From literature we know much about the city, from archaeology tantalizingly less, for Alexandria has been continuously inhabited since its foundation, and the populous modern city of 2,000,000 lies over the ancient one. Since Nasser expelled the Greeks in the 1960s, even its Greek veneer is gone. As late as 1866, when a plan of the ancient city was made to the order of Napoleon III, one could still detect a part of the ancient grid of streets, and of the circuit of towered Ptolemaic walls (over nine miles), but now the Hellenistic city is almost entirely built over. The remains of a temple under the modern bourse suggest that the present civic center overlies the ancient one.

The geographer Strabo describes the palace compound in 24 B.C. It lay southeast of the eastern harbor, occupying from a fourth to a third of the city's total area. It took shape in Ptolemy II's reign (285-246), and included the mausoleum of Alexander, where the world conqueror lay, according to legend, in diademed state, surrounded by books and papyri, in a golden sarcophagus, replaced in the first century B.C. by

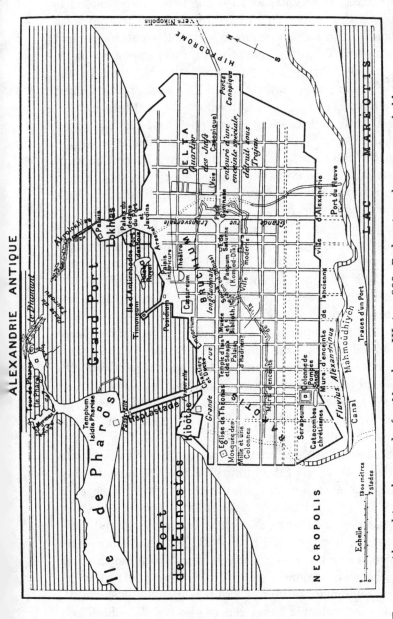

FIG. 7.2 Alexandria, plan, made for Napoleon III in 1866. Ptolemaic palace was probably at east corner of Great Harbor (Grand Port); Library and Museum in Bruchium quarter. Pharos (lighthouse) at top of map. (Guide Bleu, *Egypte*, p. 41, by permission of Librairie Hachette, Paris)

one of glass. As recently as 1850 one Schilizzi pretended to have seen this marvel in its cage of glass in the crypt of a mosque by the railway station. Within the palace precinct was a botanical garden and zoo and, most important of all, the famous Library and Museum, "the birdcoop of the Muses," as an ancient satirist called it. It was a philanthropic foundation, like All Souls, Oxford, or the Institute for Advanced Study at Princeton, where poets and scholars subsidized by Ptolemy II lived, strolled in the shady peristyles, ate in the refectory, and read and wrote. Its collection of 700,000 scrolls, the cream of classical literature, was burned in the rioting between Egyptian troops and Julius Caesar's occupation force in 47 B.C.

The palace was built of alabaster and polychrome marble (or marble veneer over brick); its furniture was inlaid with ivory, gold, and silver; its mosaics and rich rugs were famous. Of all this elegance all that archaeologists have been able to recover is a block of serpentine marble, a few syenite (Egyptian granite) columns, and Ionic and Corinthian column capitals of Hellenistic workmanship. These were found in the area indicated by Strabo as the palace site, on the waterfront under Alexander the Great St. Of the Library the only trace remaining is a block found in 1848, hollowed to contain three rolls of the works of Dioscorides, probably the epigrammatist; the botanist of the same name, author of a *materia medica* of which a number of handsome illustrated manuscripts exist, lived and wrote after the destruction of the Library. Of the Museum, nothing remains but a statue base inscribed with the name of a rhetorician, which probably once stood in its peristyle.

Of the city itself, too, literature has more to tell than archaeology, but the 1866 plan distinguishes, on uncertain evidence, eleven east-west streets and seven north-south ones. The main avenues, we are told, were 100 feet wide, and (as seldom in antiquity) lighted at night. From wall-paintings in tombs we know that the houses were high and towerlike. The city had a hippodrome, theaters, stadia, baths, gymnasia, temples of Greek and Egyptian gods, and a synagogue, for, in ancient as in modern times, Alexandria was a melting pot. It was famous for its multilevel vaulted reservoirs, 700 of which were still in use in 1866.

Alexandria's landscape, ancient temples, and public buildings reek of history and romance. On its beach were built the huts of the seventy rabbis who first translated the Old Testament from Hebrew into Greek, thus, as E. M. Forster drily remarks, enriching Greek literature with its earliest example of a book of revealed religion. West of Lake Hadra were found some granite columns of the Thesmophorion, where Antony and Cleopatra appeared as Osiris and Isis. An inscription bearing the name of Mark Antony was found in the area of the Caesareum, near the Ramleh railway station. In its precinct Cleopatra set up her obelisks in honor of Antony, the famous "Needles," one of which was set up on Victoria Embankment in London in 1877, the other in Central Park in New York in 1879. Near the east end of the main east-west street to Canopus was the gymnasium where Antony proclaimed Cleopatra Queen of Kings. When Pompey was murdered and decapitated by an Egyptian intriguer, on the beach at Alexandria in 48, the place where Caesar buried his head became a shrine or Heroön; its location is known, an alabaster tomb in the Chatby quarter. Another alleged memorial of Pompey, "Pompey's Pillar," near the Serapeum in the southwest quarter, is actually Diocletianic (A.D. 284-305). Its eighty-eight-foot height was tempting to nineteenth-century travelers. In 1832 twenty-two people lunched on its top, "in a circle," and in 1843 an ascent was ingeniously made by flying over the Pillar a kite carrying a line and a hawser, which was then made fast on both sides, and people pulled up in a loop of rope to the top, where they drank Queen Victoria's health, eight at a time. More important archaeologically is the Temple of Sarapis, and the discovery, reported in 1942, of a mausoleum south of the Pillar so large as to be royal, probably the last resting place of the Ptolemies.

In the picturesque native village of Rosetta, east of Alexandria, a French officer discovered in 1799 the trilingual Rosetta Stone, now in the British Museum. When in 1822 Champollion guessed that the hieroglyphics enclosed in oval "'cartouches'" spelled a royal name, that of Ptolemy V Epiphanes (as he knew already from the Greek version of the honorific decree of 196/5 on the stone), Egyptian hieroglyphics had been deciphered, a landmark in the history of archaeology as important as Ventris' cracking of Linear B.

As often in archaeology, we know most about Alexandrians living from Alexandrians dead. A number of necropoleis has been excavated, a Greek one in the eastern quarter, Egyptain ones in the western and on the Pharos Island. At Kom-el-Shugafa, near Pompey's Pillar, a three-level catacomb, discovered in 1900, filled with water; the results of pumping it out and excavating it to the bottom were not finally published till 1942. The striking thing about the décor is the curious mixture of classical Greek and Egyptian motifs. Hellenistic Greeks in Alexandria were far from purebred, and a far cry from the nineteenth-century ideal, which never actually existed, of classical Greeks, cool and detached, seeing life steadily and seeing it whole. These were Levantine types, clever at trade, intermarried with natives. To the Matthew Arnold sort of classicist, they gave Hellenistic Greek a bad name, from which it has hardly recovered until our own Hellenistic Age, in which E. M. Forster and Lawrence Durrell have felt and expressed the exotic fascination of Alexandria.

Alexandria's most famous monument was of course its lighthouse, the Pharos, the Wonder of the World, whose name in Arabic, Manara, became the name of minarets on mosques. Its white stone footings were discovered in 1898 in Fort Kait Bey, which guards the western arm of the eastern harbor. To reconstruct its appearance in antiquity, récourse must be had to Arabic descriptions made before an earthquake felled it in A.D. 796, or before its complete demolition in the thirteenth century. It rose over 400 feet in the air from a terrace on the island cliffs. It was built in three levels, the bottom one square and containing a reservoir and 300 stalls for beasts of burden, the middle one octagonal, the top one round (Fig. 7.3). A ramp and circular stair mounted to the light; they wound about a central shaft in which fuel could be raised, probably by a hydraulic lift. The light itself was reflected from a curved metal mirror, which made it visible from twenty miles at sea. Apparently the mirror could also be used as a burning glass to set enemy ships on fire. It took twenty years to build, and was probably finished under Ptolemy II Philadelphus, about 280. Its towering height and ingenious mechanisms made it a symbol of the might of the Ptolemies and the engineering skill of the Hellenistic Age.

Ptolemaic influence at its height extended widely over the Aegean basin.* Part of the archaeological evidence for it has been found on the remote, lovely, and inaccessible island of Samothrace in the north Aegean, where since 1863 French, Austrian, Swedish, and American investigators have worked on the sanctuary of the Samothracian gods, which profited richly from Ptolemy II's benefactions. The sanctuary was the Delos of the north Aegean, second only to Eleusis as a center for initiation into mysteries. Its soil has yielded a bilingual inscription in Greek and Latin reading, "Let no

---

* An interesting out-of-the-way example of it turned up at Thera, which became a main Ptolemaic base for control of the Aegean. Here Hiller found dozens of inscriptions set up by a pious Hellenistic soldier who had fought for Philadelphus in the Arabian desert, and then served as admiral on the Thera station. His name was Artemidorus of Perge, and he enriched the island with a rock-cut Altar of Harmony, an eagle for Zeus, a lion for Apollo, a dolphin for Poseidon, and a splendid medallion of himself. He gives an excellent idea of the half-educated upper crust of the great world that now centered on Alexandria.

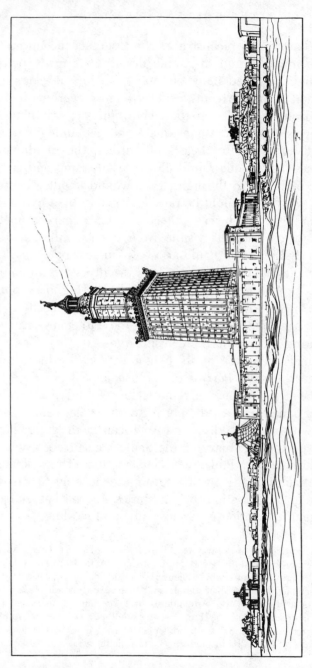

FIG. 7.3 Alexandria, Pharos, reconstruction drawing. (Thiersch, *Pharos*, front, by permission of B. G. Teubner Verlag, Leipzig)

uninitiate enter here." The cult buildings stand picturesquely in a ravine shaded by plane trees. Interest in them was first aroused by the French discovery there (1863), in over 100 fragments, of the famous Victory of Samothrace (Fig. 7.4) now in the Louvre. Austrian excavations in 1873, 1875, and 1891 barely scratched the surface. Definitive results were first obtained by a series of New York University campaigns begun before World War II under Karl Lehmann († 1960). Among other things, he investigated the findspot of the Victory, a fountain house where the statue had stood on a prow above and behind a water basin amid rocks in an architectural frame. He found more fragments of the statue: the right ring finger, and parts of the prow. Lehmann identified still more fragments in the storeroom of the Vienna Museum: all are now on display beside the statue in the Louvre. More important, he found pottery in the fountain house which at last firmly dates the statue to the early second century B.C. The statue, its drapery windswept and swirling like storm-tossed waves, was a Rhodian dedication (as a fragmentary inscription reveals) for a victory of about 190 over Antiochus III of Syria.

Excavation revealed that the site had been occupied since the sixth century B.C. Though the ancient town southeast of the sacred precinct remains unexcavated, the builders of the government tourist pavilion in 1957 hit upon the town cemetery, which had been in uninterrupted use for 700 years from the sixth century B.C. The excavators noted that the Samothracians were generally short in stature and had bad teeth. One of the finds, from a third-century-B.C. grave, was a terracotta model of an air-inflated ball, with polygonal sections and lacing, very like a modern basketball.

From the sixth century, too, date the earliest Hieron, or shrine of the Samothracian gods (see plan, Fig. 7.5), and a stoa east of it where votive gifts were displayed. In the seventh century the Anaktoron or Hall of Mysteries was built, with later phases down into the early Roman Empire; the excavators found in it put-holes for seats as in a theater,

FIG. 7.4 Nike of Samothrace. (Paris, Louvre)

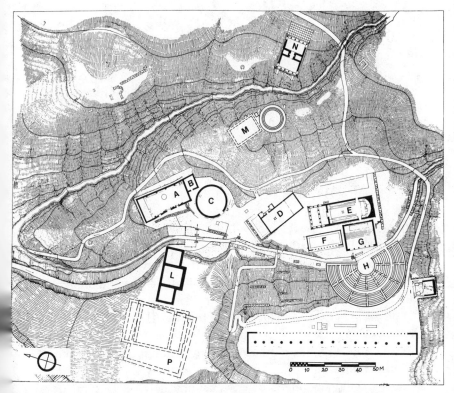

FIG. 7.5 Samothrace, plan. A, Anaktoron; B, Sacristy; C, Arsinoeion;
D, Temenos; E, Hieron; F, Hall of Votive Gifts; G, Altar Court;
H, Theater; J, fountain with Nike; K, Stoa; L, treasuries; M, dedi-
cation by Philip III and Alexander IV; N, Propylon; P, Milesian
building. (Lehmann, 1960, back, revised, by permission of J. J.
Augustin, Inc., Locust Valley, N.Y.)

for viewing the initiation ceremonies. Initiation involved a
confession of sins and a religious trial, which very few passed.
The challenge made successful candidacy all the more
attractive, especially, in later times, to the Roman aristocracy.
Yet slaves, too, were eligible, and the symbol of initiation
was a simple iron finger-ring.

In the fourth century Philip and Olympias, the parents

of Alexander the Great, met here and fell in love. To this century belong an archaistic frieze of dancing-girls from the temenos-propylon (fragments on display in the site museum), and an altar east of the Hieron. On the ridge between the Arsinoeion and Ptolemy II's Propylon (plan, N) lay a paved circular area and a Doric structure (M), the gifts of the feeble-minded Philip III and Alexander's posthumous son Alexander IV (reigned 323-*ca.* 310).

In the third century the sanctuary was in its prime: Arsinoe, wife of King Lysimachus of Thrace (she later married Ptolemy II), dedicated (289-281 B.C.) to the Great Gods the Arsinoeion (see plan), over twenty meters in diameter, the largest round building known in classical architecture till Hadrian's Pantheon in Rome, built over 400 years later. Ptolemy built, too, the impressive western propylon. Evidence for the ruler-cult that the Ptolemies took over as a political expedient from the Pharaohs of Egypt was a colossal statue of Ptolemy II as Dionysus-Osiris, which once stood just east of the Hieron. The Hieron itself in its Hellenistic phase is dated about 250, late in Ptolemy II's reign; to excavate it, Lehmann's workmen had to move over 500 fallen blocks. Its uniquely early domed apse exerted its influence later on Roman buildings. The two hearths in the nave are an archaic feature; the *bothros* (sacrificial pit) in the apse reminds us that the Samothracian gods were deities of the underworld. The ceremonies were witnessed by the community of initiates seated behind parapets on marble benches in the lateral aisles. Lamps prove that there were night services; finds of crockery, that the service included a cult meal. Building P, a Byzantine structure made of reused blocks, covers a three-roomed marble building (third century B.C.) with a central Ionic porch, dedicated by a Milesian woman. East of it (north is to the left of the plan) were three Hellenistic buildings (L) that look like treasuries. When the theater was built (*ca.* 200 B.C.),

Samothrace had all the buildings it needed to make it one of the great Panhellenic shrines.

After two seasons, World War II interrupted the American excavations at Samothrace. When Lehmann returned in 1948, he found that the Bulgarians who had occupied the island had wantonly destroyed and damaged the ruins, the finds, and his equipment. They had pulled down what was left of the Arsinoeion, scrambled the carefully sorted pottery, and stolen his tents, the building material for the projected museum, and the rails of his light railway. The latter were subsequently recovered in Alexandroupolis, the nearest mainland town, and a Greek collaborator who had robbed stone from the Anaktoron was caught and tried. Samothrace had suffered what was neither its first nor probably its last destruction. Carefully kept excavation notebooks made it possible to re-sort the pottery; the museum has been built; and despite Bulgarian wantonness, the final reports have begun to appear. It is poor consolation for the delay that Samothrace was not the only archaeological site to suffer war damage.

Important inscriptional evidence for Ptolemaic influence has turned up also in Louis Robert's excavations at Claros, between Colophon and Ephesus. He was attracted there on a search for inscriptions. He found many, mostly lists of visiting delegations from the Crimea, all over Asia Minor, and Crete. But the search led to the discovery of something even more important and interesting: an early Hellenistic oracular shrine of Apollo, nearly as extensive as the temple at Delphi, with complicated and fascinating underground arrangements. Its general location had been known since 1907, but only Robert's discovery, under four meters of silt, of some fallen Doric columns from the temple made possible a more precise idea of how the oracle worked.

Robert found that from the temple porch a steep and

initially winding stair gave access to a labyrinthine corridor, which changed direction at right angles seven times in thirty meters, to arrive at the first of two underground rooms with vaults too low to permit standing erect. The rooms were below water level, and full of fallen marble. They had to be pumped out and cleared before investigation could proceed.

One of the encumbrances was the colossal arm of Apollo's statue, of Roman imperial date. The arm was over eleven feet long: the statue must have been over five times life size. Later the sandaled foot was found, bearing on the buckle the figure of a sphinx, the symbol of the oracle. Other colossal fragments, of female statues, showed that Apollo had been flanked by his mother Leto and his sister Artemis. The trio appears on Roman imperial coins of nearby Colophon.

The cleared front room of the underground oracular shrine had benches where privileged consultants might await the oracle's response. The wait might be long, for the priests, as we know from inscriptions, retained the services of a *thespiode*, to put the god's answer into verse. At the back of the waiting room was a postern, through which Apollo's prophet used to go alone, at night, into the mystery of the dark, low, stifling inner chamber, where he drew his inspiration from a secret well. Robert found the well. It still held water, and, undeterred by the ancient report (of Pliny the Elder) that it was dangerous to drink, he tried it. It proved perfectly potable. Included also in the sanctuary were a Sacred Way, lined with statues of early Roman governors, including Q. Cicero, the orator's brother; an omphalos (navel stone), associated with Apollo also at Delphi; an altar fifty-eight feet long, shared with Dionysus; a small sixth-century temple to Artemis; a stoa with shops; and some late Roman houses.

The colossal size of the cult statue, the long lists of visitors, who must have paid handsomely for the responses they sought, symbolize the tastelessness, the credulity, the commercializing of religion that archaeology has found to be increasingly characteristic of Greek culture in Hellenistic and Roman times. For monumentality not quite so tasteless we must travel north from Claros to Pergamum, capital of the Attalid dynasty.

Among the greatest rivals of the Ptolemies in politics and in philanthropic support of scholarship and the arts were the Attalids of Pergamum, a small kingdom in northwest Asia Minor (Fig. 6.21). Their dynasty had risen to power through the defeat by its founder, Eumenes I (263-241 B.C.), of a wave of Gauls who swept over mainland Greece and northern Asia Minor in the mid-third century. (Aetolians, also part of the resistance movement, dedicated in 279 Galatian arms in a new stoa at Delphi, west of the Apollo temple.) Defeated, they settled down on the central Anatolian plateau; their descendants were St. Paul's Galatians. Pergamum's power and prestige were greatest in the first half of the second century B.C.; in 133 the last Attalid bequeathed his kingdom to Rome.

The modern rediscoverer of Pergamum was the German architect Carl Humann. He came in 1861 for his health to the dry climate of Samos, where he helped to dig the Heraion. As a traveling surveyor, he first visited Pergamum in 1864, and prevented the Turks from breaking up for the limekiln the marble sculpture of the Attalid kings. He became chief road-engineer for the western Ottoman Empire, and in 1868 set up headquarters in Pergamum, where he ruled like a Pasha over 2000 workmen, 1000 oxen and 500 camels, horses, and mules. He began a collection of antiquities, which he showed in 1871 to Curtius and Adler, the future excavators of Olympia. They encouraged him to send some of his finds to Berlin. Thus began, as a museum dig to recover *objets d'art,* an excavation that was to develop over a span of ninety years into a scientific exploration of a whole city, and to be responsible for making the whole of Asiatic Turkey into a German archaeological domain.

On a chilly day in December, 1871, Humann extracted from the tough mortar of a Byzantine wall on ancient Pergamum's Acropolis a marble slab with the figure of a giant, which he recognized as a masterpiece, and sketched with frost-stiffened fingers. He got the slab down from the Acropolis on a sledge and shipped it to Berlin, where it evoked wide comment. Humann thought it came from the frieze of the nearby temple of Athena. However, in 1872 a scholar in Berlin happened upon a passage in Ampelius, obscure late-Roman author of a book *On the Wonders of the World,* mentioning an Altar of Giants at Pergamum. A slab from this frieze was what Humann had found. It proved to be the first of ninety-four, plus some 2000 fragments, which archaeological ingenuity pieced together and set in order in a frieze 400 feet long, second in length only to that of the Parthenon. Around it were built in 1901 the collections of Berlin's Pergamon-Museum. During World War II the slabs were first hidden in a bunker under the Reichsbank, then in an anti-aircraft tower in the Tiergarten, but the Russians discovered them and carried them off. They became a ponderous plaything in the propaganda war over Berlin. Since the Pergamon Museum was in the Russian zone, the Russians sent the frieze back (1958); it is now reinstalled in East Berlin, available once more for admiration and study as the most extensive and characteristic example of Hellenistic art, massive, bursting, explosive, a far cry from the repose which for Winckelmann (1768) had been the hallmark of classical art.

Humann knew that heavy slabs built into the Byzantine wall could not have come from far away: one ten-ton piece took twenty men half a day to get down from the Acropolis. Exploring near the wall, he soon exposed the ground plan of the altar, a rectangular grid, like a waffle iron, of foundation blocks. But it was not until cleaning the altar was almost finished that its first architectural member was found in place: a step on the west side. Here architecture and sculpture interlock: one of the frieze-slabs had a stepped bottom profile, along which a giant's serpent leg wound its way. Another giant supports his knee and hand on a step, so that it is clear that the altar had, enclosing the stair, two projecting sculptured wings. All three outer walls of the altar were sculptured. Twenty-eight steps led through a double Ionic colonnade to a rectangular court enclosing the altar proper. Round this court ran a smaller frieze illustrating—an innovation—the story of Telephus, mythical ancestor of the Attalid dynasty. The tale is like that of Moses in the bulrushes, or Romulus and Remus. The subjects on the thirty-five slabs found include Telephus' parents, Heracles and Augê (Heracles, who appears also on the Great Frieze, links the two compositions); the child Telephus being exposed on a hillside to die, in accordance with an oracle; mother and child being put into a sort of ark; and the landing in Mysia, whose king, Teuthras, rescues them.

It remained to determine the order of the slabs of the Great Frieze. Its cornice blocks bore key letters in three series, to help the ancient workmen assemble the slabs in proper order on each of the altar's three outer faces. Besides, the figures on some of the slabs were labeled, their names inscribed on the stone. The arrangement thus determined could be double-checked by observing mason's marks, and the put-holes for clamps and dowels, as Dinsmoor was to do later at Bassae. Besides, there were joins between slabs, which were cut in varying widths, the principle being not to cut through torsos. (This means that the frieze must have been carved from an over-all cartoon, though over a dozen hands worked at it.) A sophisticated, even humorous touch established the juxtaposition at one corner: Ares and Aphrodite, who were once caught in adultery by Aphrodite's husband Hephaestus, are portrayed fighting, rather shamefacedly, back to back. This detail has been used to argue that the altar was conceived not as a religious dedication but as a courtly monument, too learned for ordinary mortals. But the allusion would not have escaped any reader of Homer, who tells the story, and Homer was everybody's poet.

The key letters begin on a slab that portrays Zeus impaling with his thunderbolt the giant Porphyrion, who here had bright inlaid eyes. This strikes the leitmotif of the whole composition: as Zeus, symbol of civilization, defeats the giant, symbol of barbarism, so the civilized Eumenes defeated the barbaric Gauls. But the altar belongs not to the time of the third-century Gallic invasion, but to the embellishment of the whole Acropolis after Eumenes II's victory over Prusias of Bithynia at Magnesia in 190 B.C. So the symbolism is plural, and the frieze projects, Greek fashion, historical events into a mythological world.

The Porphyrion slab had adorned the altar's east face. As one entered the precinct through a gate on the southeast, the eye was attracted to Zeus and Athena on this same face, which is therefore established as the main one in the composition. Athena has the giant Alcyoneus by the hair to pull him off the ground, but his outstretched left foot still touches the strength-giving breast of his mother, Earth. From this face, too, come the "Biter Group" illustrated here (Fig. 7.6) as typical of the violence of the whole composition. Chariots and teams frame Zeus and Athena, as on the Parthenon west pediment. This is not the Pergamene sculptor's only tribute to Phidias. On the altar's south face are the gods of light; on the north face, the gods of darkness; just so, the Parthenon east pediment is framed by the horses of the sun in one corner of the gable and of the moon in the other. Sea-gods line the altar's left stair wall (the side nearest the Aegean), Dionysus and his mountain band the right. Thus the great central battle on the east face is enclosed between day and night, mountain and sea.

Humann, besides being a skilled engineer, was something of a pirate, combining energy and ingenuity with ruthlessness. He spent 1300 working days dismantling the Byzantine wall, 700 on tracing the plan of the altar, 600 on transporting and loading the slabs. For this purpose he built a serpentine

FIG. 7.6   Pergamum, Great Altar, Biter Group from east face. The
contorted features, writhing snakes, weapon raised to strike in
upper right corner typify violence of this sculpture. (Berlin,
Staatliche Museen)

road that wound round the Acropolis; when the excavation was finished he cut away a stretch of the road to discourage dilapidators. He had made the Turks build their bridges of wood to teach them the necessity for maintenance, but he found himself hoist with his own petard when the camel-drivers used the wood from the bridges for their campfires, thus cutting his precious slabs off from the port. But despite difficulties, he loaded his treasure on a German gunboat, and quickly transshiped it to a Lloyd Triestino freighter before the Turks should realize he was violating his firman. He had little use for either Greeks or Turks, referring to the former as "half-educated sons of Hellas," or "Bulgarian lumps who want only to dicker," and remarking on the latter that the frieze fragments in the Constantinople Museum could be extracted by the judicious use of backsheesh. Lest the Turks should discover the beauty of the slabs, he left the Byzantine mortar on them, or left them lying face down (thus postponing his own discovery of the key slab with Zeus and the thunderbolt). His compatriots appreciated all this more than the Greeks and Turks: when he visited Berlin in 1880 he was received like a victorious general. In 1884 the Turks forbade all further export of antiquities.

Aesthetic judgments on the frieze vary, but we must grant that the sculptor's powers of invention are well nigh inexhaustible; the drama he unfolds is immense and cosmic. He is a master at representing violent movement; his rendering of drapery, with its pronounced ridges and valleys, has been well described as "loud." Perhaps we can best epitomize the equivocal position of the Pergamum frieze in art criticism by noting that it appealed strongly to Roman taste, and that the notorious Laocoön in the Vatican, and Augustus' Altar of Peace are deeply influenced by it.

The frieze is by no means the only thing that Pergamum has yielded up to the archaeologist's spade. The excavation of the altar precinct was only the beginning; it led to the exploration of the whole city; first, in the nineteenth cen-

Fig. 7.7 Pergamum, Acropolis, model. From top to bottom, arsenal, palace, temple and precinct of Trajan, Library (the two-storied building), with temple of Athena in front and theater below, left; Great Altar (left of center), and Upper Agora. (Berlin, Staatliche Museen)

tury, the Upper Agora (see model, Fig. 7.7) and temple of Athena. The latter's orientation, together with that of the precinct entrance, determined that of the Great Altar, which was so placed that the line of the temple's northwest side, prolonged, would just touch its northwest corner. From a round building near the temple came the famous sculpture of the dying Gaul, and the Gaul and his wife in Rome's Capitoline and Terme Museums. Enclosing the temple was a two-

storied stoa, containing, appropriately enough in the precinct
of the goddess of wisdom, a library of 200,000 volumes, the
second largest in the Hellenistic world. (The word "parchment" is derived from the name "Pergamum.") Antony made
a present of this library to Cleopatra.

Also on the Acropolis were excavated the Trajaneum, of
Hadrianic date (A.D. 117-138), on the topmost point. Here,
too, is the spectacular theater, of about 170 B.C., one of
Pergamum's five, with steeply sloping tiers of seats. The
theater terrace has five floors of rooms below it, and on top
a temple of Dionysus transformed in the early third century
A.D. into a temple of the Roman Emperor Caracalla. The
Acropolis boasts no less than five palaces, with mosaic floors
in black-and-white triangles with green and red banded or
floral surrounds, and walls painted in yellow, blue, rose, and
red, with dados imitating marble; meanders and egg-and-
dart moldings painted to look three-dimensional; and wall
paintings of swags of fruit and flowers, and birds, as in the
Villa of Livia at Prima Porta near Rome. Some think the
bronze original of Augustus' statue, found in that villa and
now in the Vatican, came from here. In an area once known
as the "Queen's Garden" excavation in 1927 unearthed a
complex whose thick walls and heavy floors proclaimed it
an arsenal, built probably about 200 B.C. against the threat
of Philip V of Macedon. Its warehouses could hold a year's
supply of grain for 1000 men. Most interesting of all was the
discovery here of 894 stone catapult-balls, in seven calibers,
ranging in weight from a mina (14.3 lbs.) to three talents
(167.2 lbs.). They are now in the lower agora.

Between 1900 and 1914, the Germans excavated the
middle and lower cities, and found a massive triple-terraced
gymnasium, dated by an ephebe list to 147/6, whose amenities included an odeum, or covered theater, seating 1000, and
a covered stadium; sanctuaries of Demeter and Hera, the
former with impressive buttressed walls (and seats as in the
Telesterion at Eleusis). East of the latter they excavated two-

storied private houses of Roman times, with frescoes and mosaics. Since World War II the building of a new road to the Acropolis, to replace the one deliberately cut away by Humann, disclosed a residential quarter of Hellenistic and Roman date, the houses crowded together on a forty-five-degree slope. Unfortunately no archaeologist was present when the road was built, so that the pottery found has no context. But the molded ware called *terra sigillata*, which used to be considered of Roman date, has had to be pushed back into Hellenistic times as a result of discoveries at Pergamum, and so has the encrusted stucco interior decoration called Pompeian First Style, found also at Pella.

Since 1927 activity has concentrated on the lower town. Modern Bergama, a city of 25,000 (about the size of ancient Pergamum) overlies the Roman city; its streets and alleys follow the ancient ones, as digging of trenches for water mains has proved. The lower town contains ancient Pergamum's largest building, a triple temple, to the Egyptian gods Isis, Sarapis, and Harpocrates, built of red brick and called the Red Courtyard. Its total area is 280 × 108 yards; it had a crypt for a mystery cult and a pool for ritual bathing. The most interesting recent excavation (since 1951) has centered in the Asklepieion, approached from the east by a Sacred Way. It was founded in Hellenistic times (with Sub-Mycenaean or Protogeometric sherds from lower habitation levels) but at its height in the second century A.D., when Galen the physician taught and practiced here, and the hypochondriac rhetorician Aelius Aristides lectured in its theater. The theater, for 3,500, has been reconstructed, and is used for performances of ancient Greek plays and modern Turkish folk dances. It lies on the northwest side of a large peristyle (see model, Fig. 7.8). Bordering the east side are a library, Asclepius' temple, modeled on the Pantheon in Rome and therefore to be dated after A.D. 125; and a round building with six apses, perhaps a hospital, and, in the court-yard, the dormitory where, as at Epidaurus, the faithful

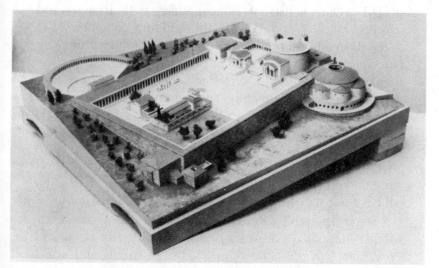

Fig. 7.8 Pergamum, Asklepieion, model, from southwest. Across back, from left to right, library, propylon, temple of Asclepius, and Pump Room, where patients slept. (*SPHS Arch. Rpts*, 1960, p. 33)

were healed in their sleep. (The sanctuary was founded, as an inscription records, by a Pergamene who had been cured at Epidaurus.) Mud baths assisted faith in the healing, and neither, apparently, was always entirely successful, for the body of a woman with arthritis, found in the sanctuary, bears evidence of having been buried in a hurry, before the other patients should discover that the god was fallible. From the apsidal building an underground passage leads to a well near the middle of the enclosure, and a vaulted corridor leads westward to an elegant latrine, with thirty-five marble seats and handsome Corinthian columns. There are plainer and smaller facilities for women.

During World War II Pergamum suffered vandalism, though not to the same extent as Samothrace: 525 heaps of ancient architectural members, piled in the peristyled enclosure, were stolen and put to some practical use; they might have been used in further reconstruction of the sanctuary.

Despite the wealth of finds, which makes Pergamum the best-documented of Hellenistic sites as well as one of the most interesting, much work remains to be done, for example, in the area of the largest of Pergamum's five theaters (for 50,000), with a Hellenistic level dated by stamped amphora handles to 180-100 B.C. Here were also an amphitheater (rare in Greek lands) and a stadium.

The Attalids were not content to adorn only their own city. Attalus II (159-138) had been educated in Athens, and in gratitude he built on the east side of the Athenian Agora the stoa that bears his name. Attalus' brother, Eumenes II (197-159) had already set the example by building a stoa on the south slope of the Athenian Acropolis, between the theater of Dionysus and the spot where later the Odeum of Herodes Atticus was to stand. (It had two stories and used Doric, Ionic, and Pergamene capitals.) Both served practical purposes: promenade, shopping center, grandstand—the Panathenaic procession passed the Stoa of Attalus on its way to the Parthenon. The Middle Stoa, at right angles to the Stoa of Attalus (see plan, Fig. 7.9), half promenade, half market, like the Stoa of Philip V at Delos (to be described later) was probably the gift of Attalus' brother-in-law and fellow-student in Athens, King Ariarathes V of Cappadocia (162-130). What the excavators call South Stoa II belongs to the same period. It served, with the Middle and East Stoas, to separate off a smaller area from the main square, possibly for the use of the law courts: the excavators found no shops, booths, stalls, weights, or measures in it.

The Stoa of Attalus has been completely rebuilt, and now houses the Agora Museum, storerooms, workrooms, and offices. A description of the Agora excavations as a whole is best postponed to the chapter on the Greek world under

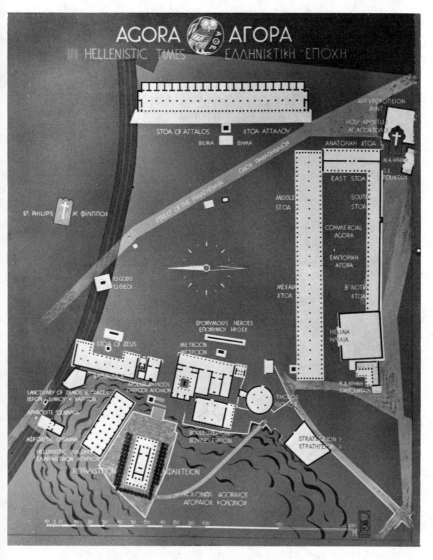

FIG. 7.9 Athens, Hellenistic Agora, plan. North is to the left. (Agora Excavations)

Roman sway, since the Agora reached its peak of development under Augustus, but this is the place to describe the Stoa and its reconstruction.

Its dimensions (382 feet long, 64 feet broad) and plan (two-storied double colonnade, with twenty-one shops behind on each floor) had been known since Greek excavations of 1859-62. It was then that the discovery of epistyle fragments bearing King Attalus' name put the identification of the building beyond doubt. Much of the remains had been shielded by the so-called "Valerian Wall" which was built right through the ruins of the building after its woodwork had been burned in the Herulian sack of A.D. 267. Under the north end were found several Mycenaean chamber tombs, and a room in use in the fifth and fourth centuries was part of a law court, an inference from some jurors' ballots found in it. These are bronze disks with an axle through the middle, pierced for conviction, solid for acquittal. If the juror held the disk by the axle between thumb and forefinger, he could drop his ballot into the urn without anyone's knowing how he had voted. These ballots had apparently fallen by accident at the time the room was abandoned. A gutter-block that had settled out of position proved to conceal a well that yielded enough sherds (dated 520-480 B.C.) to fill sixty-five five-gallon containers. They must have come from a retail potter's shop, since many of the vases were of the same type or even by the same hand. Several of the Hellenistic shops have been restored for museum exhibits, with shelving modeled on the ancient, whose position was revealed by cuttings in the walls. One shop yielded surgical instruments. At the north end the oldest visible arch in the history of Greek architecture masks the end of a barrel-vault supporting the stairs.

The story of the reconstruction of the Stoa provides one of the most interesting examples in the history of archaeology of scientific inference at work. The guiding spirit was Homer A. Thompson, Director of the Agora Excavations, acutely and ingeniously assisted by John Travlos, the Agora architect. From surviving ancient blocks they knew the materials needed: blue Hymettus marble for the steps, gray Piraeus limestone for the walls, white Pentelic marble for the façade, columns, and interior trim, clay from the clay-pits of Attica for the roof tiles. Material from the same places was used when the reconstruction began in 1953. The drums for the columns were delivered from the quarry roughly squared; the corners were then chamfered, and with careful hand work, by sixty marble-workers, using toothed and straight-edged chisels little changed since antiquity, the marble began slowly to assume cylindrical shape. The restorers knew from surviving capitals that the outer columns were Doric on the ground floor, double Ionic above, with a balustrade for safety closing the intercolumniations. Only the outer row of columns was fluted, since fluting depends for its effect on being struck by the sun. The inner row was Ionic on the ground floor, palmleaf above, the latter capital being one much favored by Pergamene architects. The columns of the bottom outer row, since each consisted of three drums, were best fluted *in situ,* the bottom drum being left unfluted to avoid damage from foot traffic. Teams of four men worked seventy-six man-days to flute the first column, at a cost of $300. (The Erechtheum building-accounts show that in 407/6 teams of five to seven men worked 350 man-days per column, at 350 drachmas per man, but those were taller columns, fully fluted, and of harder stone.) The original floors had been a rough mosaic of marble chips (*lithostroton*); the reconstruction uses the same material which, polished, is called *terrazzo*. The ancient beams were restored, for protection against fire, in reinforced concrete, reveted with laminated wood (imported, but so must the wood have been to deforested Attica in Hellenistic times.) The position and size of the beams were determined from sockets in the ancient stonework. Reinforced concrete piers were inserted in the heart of the ancient walls, but enough ancient blocks were bonded with the modern to show the evidence on which the reconstruction was based.

In September, 1956, the finished Stoa (Fig. 7.10) was dedicated by the Patriarch of Athens and All Greece, in the presence of King Paul and Queen Frederica, and 1500 invited guests, for all of whom the building successfully discharged its original function of keeping crowds of people cool on a hot day. Again as in Attalus' time it serves as a screen between market and city. Since it sits low, it does not compete with the buildings on the Acropolis or the Hephaisteion, and, as the loving hand-work weathers, it offers a still better opportunity to appreciate the spatial effect of a splendid piece of Hellenistic civic architecture. And ten shops thrown together on the ground floor house the Agora Museum, whose displayed finds, from Neolithic to Turkish, span 5000 years of Athenian history. In the lower portico, statues and inscriptions are set up near their find-spots, showing to advantage in a raking light. In the basement and upper story material (over 68,000 inventoried items, plus over 94,000 coins), unsuitable for public display, is made accessible to scholars, and a model of the Agora enables visitors (the numbers growing annually) to orient themselves from a point of vantage. Thus a philhellenic gesture of a Hellenistic philanthropist from the east has been repeated in our time by philanthropists from the west: the new world redressing the balance of the old.

At Eleusis, there are a Hellenistic bouleuterion and a treasury whose gable reproduces at one-third scale the Parthenon west pediment.

The remaining Hellenistic monuments to be described in this chapter all happen to be on islands, five in the Aegean and one on Sicily (see maps, Figs. 6.20 and 6.21). This is more coincidental than important, except insofar as it

FIG. 7.10   Athens, Stoa of Attalus, reconstructed, photo taken before dedication, 1956. (Agora Excavations)

illustrates once more the comparative poverty and obscurity of mainland Greece in the Hellenistic Age. The more significant common feature of all six is that though they all have something to do with religion, they have, in one way or another, more to do with commerce: the Hellenistic Age is an age of God and Mammon.

Delos, holy city and mart of trade, vastly expanded in extent and scale since archaic days, reached the height of its prosperity in the Hellenistic Age. The French excavators, who, it may be remembered, have been working here since 1872, subsidized by a rain of gold from the philanthropic Duc de Loubat, found that Hellenistic Delos "masked and stifled" the rest. To the Hellenistic Age, when pilgrimages— or tourism—were especially fostered, belonged "a Marble Stair-cafe, moſt of whoſe steps have been taken away, and carry'd to Mycone to make Window-cafes of" which a French traveler saw on Mt. Cynthus in 1729 (English translation of 1741). Delos remained, during the first three quarters of the nineteenth century, a vast ruin-covered expanse with a few courses of wall rising here and there above the rest. Now, thanks to the French excavators, it is, with its Hellenistic temples, theater, stoas, gymnasia, stadium, palaestra, houses, port, quays, moles, warehouses, and dockside taverns, the most varied—as well as the most ravaged—site in Greek lands, the Pompeii and the Ostia of the Aegean world. The staff of the American School of Classical Studies in Athens regards it, and rightly, as the ideal site on which to introduce students to the fascination and complexity of archaeology. The French used it as a training ground for the young Fellows of their School in Athens, who were to become their most distinguished archaeologists. Oblivious to boredom, an austere and Spartan standard of living, and bouts of fever, they would stay on the island for five and a half months at a time, supervising gangs of 160 to 200 workmen, measuring, drawing plans and reconstructions, restoring, cataloging, deciphering inscriptions. These last they found especially valuable. During the period of Delian "independence" (314-166), and even more in the following years, when Delos was an Athenian colony, the dated temple-accounts are detailed enough to make possible an architectural history of the Hellenistic city. Expenditures recorded for varnishing wood or replacing roof tiles tell us when a temple was restored; lists of over thirty buildings, arranged by regions, make the epigraphic evidence as useful as Pausanias. The records of nineteen sacred houses and estates survive, including those of farms on the island of Rheneia, westward across a narrow channel: the farmhouses were provided with towers for lookouts and defense against pirates. All combine to show how rich and powerful the temple bureaucracy was.

Delos, nominally independent, came successively under the influence of the Ptolemies, the Antigonids of Macedon, and the Attalids, who vied with each other to adorn the temples, monumentalize their setting, and provide amenities. Thus Ptolemy I built about 308 a sanctuary of Asclepius at the south end of the island, and beautified the temple of Apollo; Ptolemies and Antigonids both contributed, over a period of sixty years from about 300, to the building of a theater (see plan, Fig. 7.11) modeled on the one in Athens. Sheltered from the prevailing north wind, it has seats for 4000 to 5000, a stage eleven feet high; the proscenium had slots for inserting painted scenery. The "Monument of the Bulls" (plan, H3), extraordinarily long and narrow, probably housed a war galley, perhaps dedicated by Demetrius I Sacker-of-Cities (king of Macedon 294-287) to celebrate a naval victory of 306. An inscription records that King Antigonus Conatas of Macedon (283-239), to celebrate a victory over the Egyptian fleet off the island of Kos (ca. 260), built north of the temple of Apollo a vast double stoa, some 400 feet long, with projecting wings, modeled on Philip II's at Megalopolis and the Stoa of Zeus in the Agora in Athens. Philip V of Macedon (211-179) built early in his reign another stoa southwest of the temple, also identified by its dedicatory inscription. It is the largest roofed building in the sanctuary; it was intended to compete in grandeur with a rival building of Attalus I of Pergamum (241-197). The Attalids finished, though the Ptolemies or the Antigonids began, a south stoa that combined in a typically Delian way the customs house and a chapel to Hera of the Harbor.

Foreign trade attracted foreign gods, whose sanctuaries clustered on the slopes of Mt. Cynthus, above the theater. The Samothracian gods were there, and from Egypt came Sarapis, Isis, and Anubis, who cured the sick and saved sailors; from Syria Hadad and Atargatis. From their temple come lead figurines, bringing down curses on the person of the dedicant's choice. The heads are hammered away and iron nails are driven through the bodies. Thence, too, comes a pair of bronze ears, to help Atargatis listen to the prayers of the faithful. Among the foreign interlopers old Greek heroes still had a place, like Castor and Pollux, before whose shrine torch bearers ran races under the stars.

The whole island, marsh, plain, hill, and shore, was crammed with sanctuaries; the sacred precincts swarmed with pilgrims, tourists, and souvenir-sellers. The pilgrims would disembark, singing, traverse the processional way and the Lion Terrace to Apollo's temple, and whip themselves around the venerable Altar of Horns. The air was full of chanting, the smoke of sacrifice, the smell of incense, the beat of the sacred choral dance, in which the daughters of Delian and Athenian first families took part. Apollo's temple was full of dedications and relics: crowns high on the walls, cups on shelves below, more dedications on tripods and tables, minor or discarded offerings in chests. Among relics* the credulous

* The cult of relics in antiquity is a fascinating subject. The temple of Apollo in Sicyon, west of Corinth, boasted Agamemnon's sword and shield, Odysseus' cloak and breastplate, a sample of Penelope's weaving, the kettle Pelias was boiled in, the Argonauts' oars, the hide of Marsyas (the satyr who was flayed alive for daring to compete with Apollo in a musical contest), and Athena's ballot cast to acquit Orestes on the charge of matricide.

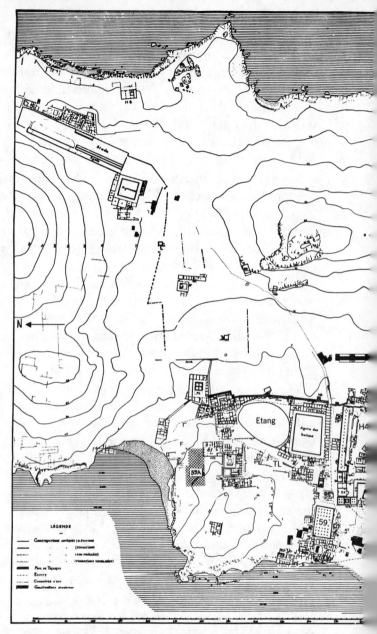

FIG. 7.11 Delos, plan. The Lion Terrace (TL) lies below Sacred Lake
(Etang); H2, temple of Apollo; left of H4, Stoa of Antigonus;
51-55-56, Stoa of Philip; 59, Hypostyle Hall; 59a, House of Comedians; 89, House of Hermes; 111, House of Dolphin; 112, House
of Masks; 120, House of the Dionysus. Theater and theater qua

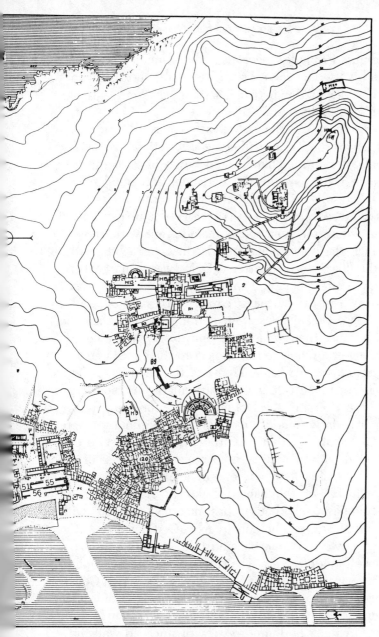

er in lower right quadrant; sanctuaries of foreign gods to r. of
center (Syrians at 15); Mt. Cynthus in upper r. quadrant. (Vallois,
Documents [1953], folding plan at back, by permission of École
Française, Athens)

could admire Eriphyle's necklace, Agamemnon's tiller, the jewels and ivory daggers of Darius' generals, and the helmet of Leonidas, the Spartan hero of Thermopylae (for Delos, like Delphi, played both sides).

Delos the holy city flourished as a mart of trade. An index of its prosperity, provided by inscriptions, is soaring house-rents. A rich merchant would buy a block of houses, knock down walls, enlarge the peristyle, and build colonnades. One result is the palatial second-century House of the Masks (discovered in 1939), perhaps a luxury hostel for actors, whose nineteen rooms include four with mosaics (from which the house is named), latrines, terracotta baths sunk in the floors, slave quarters (Delos was a mart where 10,000 slaves might change hands in a day; there are traces of a slave pen in the northeast corner of the island), and a porter's lodge. Delian houses are better preserved than the temples, because their walls were built of less valuable and tempting materials, and so less subject to stone-robbing. The mosaics are famous, as in the House of the Dionysus, where the god is portrayed riding on a particularly ferocious panther; and the House of the Dolphin, where the French have done a particularly fine job of restoration. The houses were sometimes oriental in their ostentation, their peristyle columns reveted with plaques of gilt bronze. The House of the Comedians, of after 125 B.C., one of a block of three 100 yards northwest of the Sacred Lake, at right angles to the Poseidoniasts' clubhouse, has metopes painted with scenes from New Comedy, and tragedy (Oedipus and Antigone), and a two-story marble peristyle. It yielded a hoard of gold jewelry dated 88 B.C. The House of the Hermes (plan, 89, 170 yards west of H15, the Sanctuary of the Syrian Gods), of the second or first century, is on three levels, conforming to a steep slope. It had a sanctuary of a water nymph, a statue by Praxiteles, a dining room with stuccoed walls imitating marble, and a room with a marble crazy-pavement.

Delian streets were winding and steep, often with steps,

but paved, and lighted at night by lamps in niches on each side of the doors of the principal houses. These were often owned by South Italians, who began to come to Delos as early as 250 B.C., to engage in marine insurance, or the profitable grain trade. They and other foreigners founded gilds and cult associations, often splendidly housed, like the Poseidoniasts of Beirut. The Italians built toward the end of the second century an Agora of their own, north of the Stoa of Antigonus. It is the most spacious on the island, covering nearly 7800 square yards; it is surrounded by offices, like the Piazzale delle Corporazioni at Ostia. There is no physical connection between the warehouses where the grain was stored and the city proper, for goods reaching Delos were usually in transit, not intended for home consumption. The commodities stored in the warehouses were bought, sold, and speculated in in the Delian Stock Market, the Hypostyle Hall, northwest of the temple of Apollo, a huge building—only Philip's Stoa is bigger—covering some 2000 square yards, with a roof supported, a little shakily, by a forest of columns. The excavators date it about 208.

Visitors to Delos, businessmen or pilgrims, were housed in a hostel on the slopes of Mt. Cynthus, and fed in the quayside restaurants. They and the permanent residents formed a motley crowd, speaking every language of the Near East, and of every profession: inscriptions and shop signs mention grain-, oil-, and wine-dealers, fullers, millers, flute-makers, sculptors, contractors, architects, stonemasons, potters, jewelers, blacksmiths, workers in bronze and lead, carpenters, mosaic-makers, and painters. All worshiped the gods and made money. Some time not long before 166 the Athenians expelled the Delians to Achaea and replaced them with their own colonists. Of these, 20,000 out of 35,000 were massacred by King Mithridates of Bithynia in 88, and the survivors became victims of the pirate Athenodorus in 69. By Pausanias' time the only inhabitants of

Delos were the guards of the ruins; when the Athenians tried to put the island up for sale, they could not find a single bidder, not even for one drachma. It was left for Christian writers to rejoice in the death-throes of Apollo in the solitude of his deserted island. A traveler in 1710 notes a "great store of Rabbits magnificently lodged in Marble."

When the Athenians made Delos a free port in 166, they ruined one of the most prosperous Hellenistic centers, the Dorian city of Rhodes. Rhodes, isle of butterflies, roses, oleander, bougainvillea, and hibiscus, "the sea's child, bride of Helios" (Pindar), is inevitably associated with that wonder of the world, the bronze Colossus, which guarded but did not span the harbor. If it had, it would have had to straddle 400 yards! Literary evidence states that it was built between 304 and 292, broken off at the knees by an earthquake in 227/6, and demolished by the Arabs in A.D. 653. But we may also have some three-dimensional evidence. The most likely location for it, though some think it was in the agora, is Fort St. Nicholas, at the end of the picturesque mole, dotted with windmills, between the Mandraki and the commercial harbor. The mole is ancient (there were shipsheds here), and much ancient material is built into the fort, notably a Hellenistic doorsill, whose curved profile would fit a base fifty-five feet wide, the right size to fit the Colossus, which was sixty cubits (about 90 feet) high. The Byzantine Philo gives construction details. For scaffolding, the contractor used a 135-foot tower built by Demetrius of Macedon, whose unsuccessful siege of Rhodes earned him the sarcastic epithet Poliorcetes, "Sacker-of-Cities." This tower the Rhodians had toppled and captured. The bronze was poured stage by stage (Fig. 7.12), the bronze skin held by dowels to an armature of iron, and the hollow core filled with limestone blocks, perhaps the very ones that now lie in the sea by the mole. The whole was braced with earth and scaffolding;

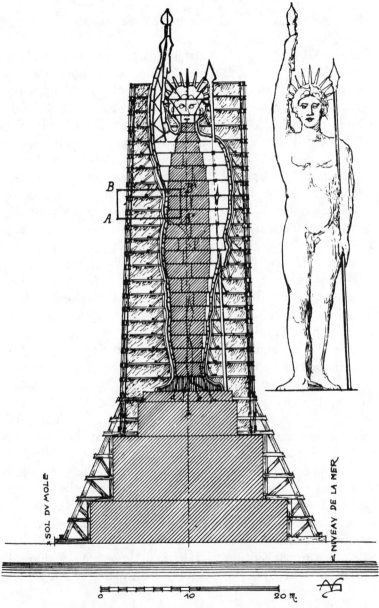

Fɪɢ. 7.12 Rhodes, Colossus, sketch showing method of construction:
armature, scaffolding, blocks within. (Gabriel, 1932, p. 337)

when the bronze had set, its surface was polished and the scaffolding removed.

Since World War II, archaeologists have learned more about the city plan of Hellenistic Rhodes. Air photography, the tragedy of air bombardment, and the need to build bomb-shelters have provided the evidence; J. D. Kondis, when Ephor of Antiquities for Rhodes, and John Bradford [*] interpreted it. The fifth-century city planner Hippodamus of Miletus allegedly laid down the grid, but the present evidence—pottery, amphora stamps, profiles of moldings, lamps, fragments of mosaic—is fourth century or later, and most of it is Hellenistic. It shows that Hellenistic Rhodes was five or six times the size of the medieval town of the Knights. But the medieval main thoroughfare, the Street of the Knights, overlies a Hellenistic predecessor, and the Grand Master's Palace is built over an important ancient building. Even in 1936, when the Italians controlled the Dodecanese, their archaeological plan of the city recorded thirty-four classical finds within the medieval walls. We now know Aphrodite's temple at the commercial harbor, the south necropolis, and a find of one hundred amphoras in the cellars of the Sun Hotel. But the westward suburbs, rising steeply to the acropolis, Mt. Smith (named for the English admiral who observed Napoleon's fleet from it in 1802), provide better evidence for the grid and for ancient buildings. On or near the acropolis are three temples, a stadium, and a gymnasium with a theater-like lecture hall, as at Pergamum. The stadium occupied two blocks of the grid; ancient drains underlie the modern street leading to it. The more northerly temple, Athena's, lay on a terrace as at Pergamum, and, as we shall see, at the Asklepieion at Kos.

Rhodes in Hellenistic and Roman times was a cultural center, with an epic poet, Apollonius (author of the *Argo-*

---

[*] For Bradford's work in air photography, see *The Mute Stones Speak,* pp. 1-7 and Index.

nautica), a sculptural school which produced the Laocoön, and philosophers like Panaetius and Poseidonius, who attracted the Romans here.

In the north Aegean, only a mere six sea-miles south of Thracian Keramoti, the French excavated the lush, beautiful, hilly, pine-scented island of Thasos, thickly wooded with conifers, ilex, gnarled old olives, and chestnuts. In the agora, they date the impressive northwest stoa (plan, Fig. 7.13), because of its proportions, to about 300. Remark-

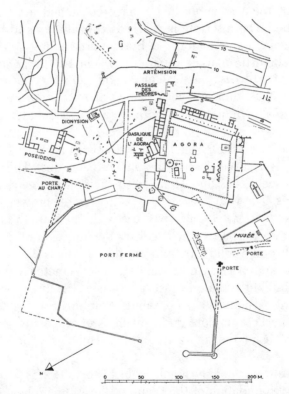

FIG. 7.13   Thasos, Agora, plan, actual state. Northwest Stoa at left. (*Guide de Thasos* [1968] by permission of École Française, Athens)

ably, it has no interior colonnade; huge beams from the Macedonian forests enabled the builders to span wide spaces without intermediate support. The northeast stoa (late fourth century), with projecting wings, illustrates Greek architecture's common language: parallels are Zeus' stoa (Athens), Philip's (Megalopolis), Artemis' at Attic Brauron, Antigonus' (Delos), Athena Lindia (Rhodes), and one (not previously mentioned) at Calauria near Epidaurus, where Demosthenes committed suicide. An inscribed shrine in the agora honored a Thasian, Theogenes, who won 1300 times at various games; i.e., once a week for thirty years. Plutarch says he regarded most of them as rubbish. He once consumed a whole bull for a bet! The inscription demands contributions to his cult. The agora, monumentalized by its surrounding stoas, typifies Hellenistic market square or precincts: the commercial agora at Miletus, the Delian Apollo sanctuary after Philip V's stoa was built, or the Athenian agora's Attalid phase.

Thasos town had a wall with twelve towers and nine gates, nearly two and a half miles around. Several gates bear archaic or classical reliefs: of Artemis in a chariot, Silenus, Heracles as archer (seen also on Thasian coins), Hermes and the Graces, Zeus and Hera, with their messengers, Hermes and Iris. The wall rises steeply to the temple-crowned acropolis, with its sweeping view eastward to Samothrace, fifty miles away. Thasos town had its theater, odeum, and temples. From Apollo's temple on the acropolis comes a fine archaic kouros carrying a ram; Heracles' sanctuary yielded a splendid late archaic Pegasus. A rather effeminate Dionysus, from his sanctuary; a charming Amphitrite on a dolphin, from the Poseidonion; and a likeness of Augustus' grandson Lucius, from the agora, exemplify Hellenistic and Roman taste.

Thasos was deeply involved in history. It was a seventh-century foundation of the island of Paros; an archaic inscription from the agora memorializes a friend of the Parian satiric poet Archilochus. Polygnotus the artist was a Thasian.

Thucydides the historian, as an Athenian admiral, operated in these waters in 425/4, and was exiled for defending Thasos (in whose mines his enemies said he had an interest) when his orders were to protect Amphipolis. Hippocrates the Coan physician spent three years here beginning about 410, and recorded weather observations. The body of Cassius, him of the lean and hungry look, was brought here in 42 B.C. after Philippi. Such are the associations that make the stones of Thasos speak.

Proceeding chronologically, we next travel far westward to Morgantina, in central Sicily near Piazza Armerina, where a Princeton expedition under Eric Sjöqvist and Richard Stilwell, beginning in 1955, excavated a major city unrecorded in literature. It proved to be Hellenistic and earlier, with a grid plan. Paolo Orsi, the great Sicilian archaeologist, discovered it in 1912. What he hit upon, the Princeton expedition excavated completely: two splendid monumental flights of steps meeting at an obtuse angle (Fig. 7.14), which was probably what the Romans called a *comitium*, or town-meeting place. A Princeton geological survey shows its builder's technical insight: steps and retaining wall carefully planned to stabilize insecure banks of clay in the subsoil. A house west of the lower agora, with a mosaic of Ganymede, cupbearer to the gods, is dated by coins somewhere between 260 and 211; the agora steps date perhaps from 450. The upper agora was bounded on the east by a long commercial stoa with central piers, left unfinished, probably when Rome overran Sicily (211). On the north, it had a gymnasium and bouleuterion; on the west, another portico, and a "factory" found crammed with lamps; in its open area, an early altar was overlaid—God and Mammon again—with a meat market. South of the monumental steps rose the small fourth-century theater, for 2000 to 3000, Sicel, not Greek, in its décor; 280 yards west of it, the House of the Official had separate quarters and separate peristyles for men and women.

FIG. 7.14   Morgantina, Agora steps. (Author)

The lower agora contained one of several sanctuaries to underworld gods, and, on the east, a long, narrow granary, resembling the Piraeus arsenal, and a brick kiln.

The acropolis, still called Citadella, lies, on this elongated site, a mile northeast of the agora. It has traces of archaic buildings and the circuit wall. This, of the late fourth century, was over four and a half miles around; its gates and posterns were sited in relations to springs. Extramural finds include houses, and burials, some rock-cut, going back to archaic and even Neolithic times (here, twelfth century B.C.), as determined by the latest techniques of pollen- and carbon-14 analysis.

Hellenistic Syracuse also prospered, under the reign (275-216: nearly as long as Victoria's) of Hiero II, who was patron of the poet Theocritus, and who built the spectacular theater, with inscriptions dedicating seats to Zeus, Demeter, Heracles, Hiero himself, and his family. He also built the stade-long altar, originally towering forty feet high, with ramps for sacrificial animals, hundreds of which could be slaughtered at once. Of Roman date is the large amphitheater, larger than Pompeii's, smaller than Verona's.

Of the sites selected for treatment in this chapter, perhaps the handsomest is the sanctuary of Athena Lindia on the Acropolis of Lindos, thirty-four miles southeast of the city of Rhodes. The temple rose on the edge of a sheer cliff high above the blue Aegean, and the golden patina of the limestone columns of its propylon and stoa makes a brave effect against the equally deep blue of the incomparable Greek sky. Danes (Kinch and Blinkenberg) excavated here (1902-14), and another Dane, Einar Dyggve, studying the architecture further in 1952, found that the temple's off-center position (see model, Fig. 7.15) was dictated by the presence directly beneath it in the face of the cliff of a sacred grotto, still venerated, though the Panagia—the Virgin Mary—has supplanted the maiden goddess Athena. The temple was finished about 330, its propylon (modeled on Athens' Propylaea) about 300, and the stoa with its projecting wings (now seen to be typical of Hellenistic architecture) about 200. Discreet restoration (by Italians, before 1938), has made the Stoa particularly effective. The terraced treatment, the monumental staircases, the axial symmetry, the supporting of the terrace in front of the stoa on transverse barrel vaults have parallels, as we shall see, in the Asklepieion on Kos, and both had their effect upon Roman architecture, especially the splendidly terraced Sanctuary of Fortune at Praeneste; * the barrel vaults reappear in the Colosseum. Distinguished Romans knew Rhodes well: Scipio the Younger studied here under the Stoic Panaetius, who came from Lindos and held religious office here in 149, as an inscription

* See *The Mute Stones Speak*, 117-132.

FIG. 7.15 Lindos, Acropolis from east, model. Note vaulted substructure, stoa with projecting wings, and temple on cliff edge. (Dyggve, 1960, XIV.1, by permission of Carlsbergfondets, Copenhagen)

found by the Danes records. Caesar, Brutus, Cassius, and Cicero all studied here, and Sulla (who probably sponsored the sanctuary at Praeneste) and Pompey were visitors.

One of the most interesting finds from Lindos is the Temple Chronicle of 99 B.C., discovered in 1904 in re-use, fortunately face down, in the pavement of an early Christian church, on the southwest slope of the Acropolis, northwest of the small cult theater. It is now in the Ny Carlsberg Museum, Copenhagen. It records gifts to the goddess by mythological and historical characters: Cadmus of Thebes; Minos of Crete; Telephus of Mysia (the mythical ancestor, it will be recalled, of the Pergamene kings); Heracles; Menelaus; Helen (a breast-shaped cup); Cleobulus of Lindos (flourished 500 B.C.), one of the Seven Wise Men of Greece (a large masonry tumulus fifteen minutes away to the east, allegedly his tomb, is in fact Hellenistic); Phalaris, the cruel Sicilian tyrant; Amasis of Egypt; Artaphernes of Persia; Alexander; Ptolemy I; Pyrrhus of Epirus; Hiero, tyrant of Syracuse; Philip V of Macedon. The chronicle also records miraculous apparitions of the goddess in time of Rhodian peril, as in the sieges by Darius and Demetrius Poliorcetes. At Lindos flourished a famous school of sculptors: Chares, who built the Colossus of Rhodes, was a native son; the name of Pythokritos, the sculptor of the Victory of Samothrace, is recorded here, and, cut in the rock beside the steep stair leading to the Acropolis, is a handsome ship (15 × 18 feet) that was a statue base, like the Victory's prow; the Danes date it about 170; it supported, appropriately, the figure of a priest of the sea god Poseidon. If the Danes are right in believing that they have also found the names of the sculptors of the Laocoön, they were born between 80 and 75, and that sculpture must be of the late first century B.C., but this is controversial.

Our last Hellenistic complex is close in spirit and plan to the Acropolis of Lindos: the triple-terraced Sanctuary of Asclepius, about two miles southwest of the island city of Kos. The first scientific visit to the site, then known locally

as "Hippocrates' Castle," was made in 1891 by the English-
man W. R. Paton, looking for inscriptions. He found and
published 450; Rudolf Herzog, a young instructor at Tübingen, soon found 575 more. They revealed that the site was
an Asklepieion. (That one existed in the suburbs of Kos was
known from a vignette in verse, one of the *Mimes* of Heron-
das, who flourished about 275; it described the crush of
visitors and the feeding of the sacred snake.) Herzog, envi-
sioning a rival to Epidaurus, determined to excavate it, at his
own expense. He hit almost at once upon the crowning
temple (Fig. 7.16); he soon turned up inscriptions to the
goddess Hygieia (Health) and to Asclepius. His finds roused
excitement in the town and greed among the local landowners, who asked exorbitant prices for the land on which the
sanctuary stood. But the Turkish government, which then
ruled Kos, expropriated the land, and gave Herzog official
status. His Greek and Turkish workmen dug in amity side
by side. The German Archaeological Institute finally gave
him a modest subsidy. He ran his dig on a shoestring, doing
his own cooking, and doing without a light railway. Working
under drenching rains and suffering bouts of malaria, he
nevertheless, by December, 1902, could report the excavation
of three temples, an altar, an exedra, and a monumental
stair. The dig lasted from 1898 to 1907. What finally emerged
shows in the reconstruction drawing: a sanctuary on three
terraces, set in a sacred grove of cypresses, with a Doric
temple at the top in white island marble, bounded on
three sides by a portico, with rooms for patients, all dated
about 160, and all commanding a splendid view of the sea
and the peninsula beyond, where Cnidus and Halicarnassus
lay. The middle terrace contained older buildings: an altar
like the Great Altar at Pergamum, once decorated with
statues by the sons of Praxiteles. It faced a temple dated
about 280, which contained a painting by Apelles of Aphrodite rising from the sea; behind the temple an Ionic building
of about 300 B.C., which perhaps housed priests; behind the

FIG. 7.16 Kos, Asklepieion, reconstruction drawing. (Kerenyi, *Der göttliche Arzt*, Fig. 30, by permission of CIBA, Basle)

altar a stoa or *lesch*ê, perhaps built about 205, for displaying votive offerings, as at Samothrace or Delphi. The lowest terrace, whose U-shaped stoa faced the one two terraces above, is the earliest (360-250), and also contained rooms where the patients slept. It is supported on vaults as at Lindos. Though the total effect is axially symmetrical, the terraces are not all on one axis but slightly skewed, as at Pergamum. Indeed, the monumentality, the sense of the theatrical, the central altar, all show strong Pergamene influence.

In 1933 an earthquake destroyed most of the city of Kos. The Italians, who then controlled the island, seized the opportunity to excavate the ancient city, where Hippocrates had lived and worked; credulous tourists may still admire the huge plane tree, its trunk forty-five feet around, under which he allegedly held his consultations. The caduceus (snake-twined staff) on Coan coins, now the symbol of physicians, goes back to Asclepius, not Hippocrates. What the Italians found was a planned city, dating from 366 B.C., with a circuit wall, agora (some of its stoa columns reerected, stadium, theater, odeon, baths, gymnasium, and temples: the one to Dionysus may have borne the frieze with masks now built into the medieval castle wall. The *cardo* was paved and the *decumanus* lined with porticoes. The houses are of the type familiar from Delos, and they, too, yielded mosaics, of Europa, Orpheus, the Judgment of Paris. Lower levels go back in unbroken sequence to Mycenaean times. The Italians also excavated at the sanctuary and did a great deal of restoration. They found Roman baths (where faith was aided by water containing salts of sulphur and iron) and an inscription honoring the Emperor Nero as the New Asclepius. It was set up by a Coan doctor, Xenophon, whose main claim to fame is having poisoned Claudius.

Out-island are Neolithic and Middle Bronze Age remains, two Hellenistic theaters (at Kardamaina and Kephalos), and villas. Here the pastoral countryside has changed little since

Theocritus described it over 2250 years ago: elms and pop-
lars in a pleached shade, goatherd pipers playing at a harvest
home.

Such, in selection, is the picture archaeology draws for
us of the Hellenistic Age, an age of cosmopolitanism in society, monarchy in politics, eclecticism and commercialism
in religion, monumentality in architecture, and strong the-
atricality in sculpture. Classical restraint, if it ever existed,
is in this age conspicuous by its absence. As periodically in
Greek cultural history, influence from the east is strong: it
is symbolized by the translation of the Hebrew Old Testament into Greek at Alexandria, and by the temples of exotic
foreign gods on Delos. In this age, too, the heavy hand of
Rome is first felt in Greece, with the influx of Italian businessmen into Delian countinghouses. In 196 the Roman
general Flamininus proclaimed the freedom of Greece in
the stadium at the Isthmian games near Corinth, but fifty
years later Corinth lay in ruins, wrought by Roman hands.
Hellenistic monumentality is the work of kings: the Pharos
at Alexandria, the Acropolis of Pergamum, the Stoa of
Attalus in Athens. Only the Colossus of Rhodes is a work of
a Greek city-state on the old model: the prosperous Rhodian
burghers proudly refused a subsidy for the purpose from
Ptolemy I. Of commercialism in religion we have presented
abundant evidence: its best symbol is perhaps the meat
market built over the altar at Morgantina. Axial symmetry
enters the picture at Lindos and Kos. The sculpture of the
Pergamene altar is unforgettably theatrical. All these ten-
dencies were intensified and extended in the next phase of
Greek archaeological history, the last to be treated in this
book, the era in which captive Greece took captive her
fierce conqueror, and Romans built Greek buildings in a
Greek world under Roman sway.

ADDENDUM
(all dates approximate)

B.C.

360-250	Kos, bottom terrace
after 338	Palatitsa, summer palace; Pella, mosaics; Vergina, royal tombs; Dherveni, papyrus grave; Chaeronea, lion
330	Thasos, Agora, N.E. Stoa; Lindos, Temple of Athena
308	Delos, Asklepieion
304-292	Rhodes, Colossus
300	Lindos, propylon; Thasos, Agora, N.W. Stoa
300 ff.	Delos, theater
297-272	Dodona, theater
289-81	Samothrace, Arsinoeion
Early Hellenistic	Claros, oracle of Apollo Eleusis, bouleuterion and treasury
280	Alexandria, Pharos; Kos, Temple B (on middle terrace)
270-263	Pergamum, Temple of Demeter
260	Morgantina, agora
250	Samothrace, Hellenistic Hieron
246	Delos, Stoa of Antigonus
238-215	Syracuse, theater; altar of Hiero II
225	Samothrace, theater
220	Delos, Stoa of Philip V
208	Delos, Hypostyle Hall
205	Kos, leschê
200	Lindos, stoa; Pergamum, arsenal
180	Pergamum, Great Altar
170	Pergamum, upper theater
160	Kos, Asklepieion; Pergamum, Library; Athens, Stoa of Attalus & Middle Stoa
150	Athens, South Stoa II
after 125	Delos, House of the Comedians

8

The Greek World under Roman Sway
(146 B.C—A.D. 267)

To read the archaeological record of the Greek world under
Roman sway we shall have to range far and wide, from Dura-
Europus on the Euphrates to the parts of Libya round about
Cyrene (see map, Fig. 6.20). We shall visit sites where we
have been before, such as Delos, Athens, Cyrene, and
Ephesus, and see to what extent the Romans, creatively
imitating Greek architecture and sculpture, overlaid Greek
glory with Roman grandeur, at the expense of a Roman
emperor or an Athenian millionaire. We shall visit new and
exotic places to see to what extent native architects and
sculptors understood, misinterpreted, or transformed the
Greek tradition: on a mountaintop metamorphosed into a
tomb at the very back of Turkey, in baroque temples in
Lebanon, in monumental cities on oases in the Syrian desert,
in Jordan, and in Mesopotamia. We shall see Corinth
and Ephesus as St. Paul saw them, and after. Everywhere
we shall see Greek forms monumentalized, exaggerated,
made massive; provincialized, orientalized, barbarized. To
those for whom everything after Pericles is decadence, all
this makes a picture from which to avert the eyes, but the

point is that this is the unvarnished archaeological record of what happened to Greek art and architecture in the Roman Empire: intentions were nearly always good, results sometimes striking and almost invariably stupendous. If classical Greek rationality and simplicity of line seem to be missing, that may mean not that the new forms are un-Greek, but that the sources of Greco-Roman flamboyance, latent in earlier Greek art forms, have been ignored or unnoticed by those espousing an untenable thesis: that Greeks were always cool, detached, and restrained, in their lives, in their art, and in their architecture. The archaeological excavations reported here should help to break the stereotype forever.

For the century following the Roman destruction of Corinth in 146 B.C., the Greek archaeological record is singularly sparse, sparser than for any period since the "Dark Ages." The inference is that Greece during these years was undergoing a depression. Only on Delos is any building activity noticeable. There an Athenian, Theophrastus, built in 126 northwest of Apollo's temple (see plan, Fig. 7.11) an Agora of ambitious proportions: it covered over 7000 square yards. North of it, on the seaward side of the Lion Terrace, the Posidoniasts, a guild of Syrian shipowners and traders from Beirut, built in 112 the previously mentioned large peristyle house as their headquarters; typically, it included four chapels, three to their native triad of gods, and one to the goddess Roma. After the pirate raid of 69 the Roman legate Triarius built out of secondhand architectural blocks an emergency wall—too little and too late—around the sacred precinct and the residential quarter near the theater.

Athens showed perverse genius in always choosing the wrong side in Rome's civil wars. Sulla sacked Athens in 86, and cut down the trees in Plato's Academy and Aristotle's Lyceum, outside the walls, to make his siege-engines. But

about the middle of the century there is evidence of revival.
Numerous buildings testify to the importance of Eleusis in
Roman times. Cicero's contemporary Appius Claudius Pul-
cher built the Lesser Propylaea in the 40s B.C. Basket-bearing
Caryatids formed its décor; one, carried off in 1801, is now in
the Fitzwilliam Museum in Cambridge. Emperors—Hadrian,
Marcus Aurelius—were initiates: Hadrian built a monumental
arch imitating the one in Athens; Marcus Aurelius the
Greater Propylaea, a replica of the Periclean entrance to the
Athenian acropolis. Hadrian's wife, Sabina, and Antoninus
Pius', Faustina the Elder, were deified and had temples close
to the Telesterion; there is also a Roman temple to Artemis
in the court outside the Greater Propylaea, and a Mithraeum
beside the archaic Hiera Oikia.

In Athens, perhaps as early as 50, was built the octagonal
Tower of the Winds (Fig. 8.1), which in Turkish Athens
travelers used to visit to watch the whirling dervishes. Each
face of the tower bears a sculptured allegorical representation of a wind, and a sundial. There was an interior water-
clock, perhaps worked by some sort of clockwork mechanism
like the modern ones in Munich and Venice. The building
was apparently accessible at all hours of the day and night;
at any rate there is no evidence that its doors were lockable
from the outside. It has been plausibly conjectured that in
late Roman times the building was in reuse as a baptistery.
It adjoined the Roman Agora, planned by Julius Caesar in
44, an area still partly encumbered by modern buildings
and a Turkish mosque. Its marble pavement survives in part,
and an inscription dates its west Propylaea, the Gate of
Athena Archegetis, to 10 B.C. By this time Augustus, in
power in Rome, was disposed, in view of the propaganda
value of exploiting Athens' glorious past, to forgive her for
siding with Antony. He allowed to be built on the Acropolis,
just east of the Parthenon, a small round temple of Rome and
Augustus, on the model of the shrine of Vesta in the Roman
Forum. Its ruins seem a puny effrontery beside the splendor
of the great temple.

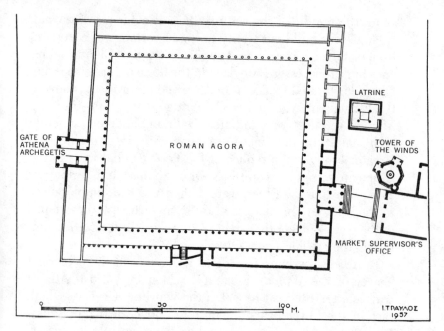

FIG. 8.1   Athens, Roman Market-place (left), and Tower of the
Winds (Horologion), plan. (Travlos, *op. cit.*, p. 99, Fig. 55,
lower half)

Augustus' lieutenant Agrippa built in the center of the
Greek Agora an Odeum, the last major building to grace the
area. The account of how it was excavated and identified
will provide at long last an opportunity to describe in some
detail the Agora excavations as a whole, which were for
over forty years (1931-40, 1946 to date) the major American archaeological enterprise in Greek lands. Here the
archaeologist's threefold duty, to dig, to preserve, and to
publish, has been carried out scientifically, efficiently, and
promptly, under three directors, T. Leslie Shear († 1945),
Homer A. Thompson, and T. Leslie Shear, Jr., with lavish
support from John D. Rockefeller, Jr., Ward Canaday, and
other American philanthropists. To have laid bare 5000 years

of the history of the working center of a major city-state of mainland Greece has been well worth the time, money, and energy expended. The statistics are impressive: 365 houses equitably expropriated, between 4000 and 5000 people resettled, sixteen acres excavated, over 246,000 tons of earth removed (to fill in malarial marshes along the Sacred Way to Eleusis); the 68,000 objects (exclusive of 94,000 coins) catalogued so efficiently, thanks to the inventory's late presiding genius, Miss Lucy Talcott, that any object can be made instantly available to scholars. The collection is so rich in pottery that when *Paris-Match* asked Miss Talcott for a

FIG. 8.2 Athens, Agora, excavation notebooks and catalog card, illustrating method. The black-figured amphora, center left, is completely recorded: pottery inventory number, findspot, date of finding, complete description, references to publications, and photograph. (Agora Excavations)

picture of how Themistocles' dinner-table might have looked, she was able to provide every item of crockery without difficulty. The catalogue derives from the contents of carefully kept excavation notebooks, transferred to cards (Fig. 8.2). There are different-colored cards, with photograph attached, for each category: sculpture, pottery, 16,000 stamped and datable amphora handles (much of this from over 1000 closed deposits from wells, especially valuable for dating); nearly 7000 new inscriptions; 5400 lamps, and over 1200 ostraka. Each card bears a tab indicating whether the catalogued object is Greek, Roman, or Byzantine.

The work of conservation included general tidying up, and landscaping. The plans of the stoa of Zeus and the temple of Apollo Patroös, on the west side (lower center to right center of the model, Fig. 8.3), for example, were outlined with ancient blocks and filled in with excavated field stone, while the original crumbly poros walls were buried. The Hephaistcion east pediment sculptures were cleaned by swathing them in wet burlap, and chipping away the softened deposit with a light steel chisel, judiciously used. The result was to reveal once more the lovely Parian marble, the delicate modeling, and even the color: blue background, red drapery, green rocks. Landscaping, planned by the landscape architect Ralph Griswold, defines areas, takes account of the dry climate (with the assistance of a special irrigation system), and is faithful to the ancient flora, so that the Agora and environs are now green and blooming with oak and laurel (the first trees planted by the King and Queen of Greece), pomegranate, myrtle, oleander, pine, cypress, and olive.

Hundreds of dedicated workers cooperated on the job. Each sector, meticulously divided into one-meter squares, was supervised by an archaeologist, seasoned or in training. Each kept a field notebook, assigning a serial number to each object found, recording its dimensions, and supplying a drawing or photograph. Each group of objects found in

Fig. 8.3 Athens, Agora in Roman times, model, from northwest. Odeum of Agrippa in center; to its left, Stoa of Attalus and Library of Pantainos; behind it, Middle Stoa; in front of it, temple of Ares and Altar of Pity. Near center of r. edge. Hephaisteion, below it, from north to south, Stoa of Zeus, temple of Apollo Patroös, Metroon, Bouleuterion, Tholos. The newly discovered Royal Stoa lay north of the Stoa of Zeus; the smaller plaque in the lower left quadrant represents the Stoa Poikile. (Agora Excavations)

a given square was given a wooden tag bearing date, number, and findspot. The tag remained with the group until each object was washed, catalogued, and painted with its own inventory number.

A chemical branch analyzed finds, identifying, for example, resin from the island of Chios in the bottom of a wine jar, tin plate on copper, the varying content of bronze in coins, for arranging them in sequences; and beeswax in marble ceiling coffers painted by the encaustic process, where wax is the binder for the pigment. This branch cleaned coins electrolytically, finishing the job, to avoid abrasion, with a dental polishing-machine and a felt brush. Bronze coins thinly plated with silver proved to come from a crisis-year, 339, the year before Philip II of Macedon defeated the Athenians at Chaeronea.

Miss Alison Frantz, some of whose exquisite pictures embellish this book, was in charge of photography, and John Travlos' alchemy of skill, feeling for architecture, and patience produced the plans. Foremen and workmen—up to 300 in a given season—who had learned their craft at Corinth, Delphi, or Mycenae, contributed their skills; the personalities of some of them, as Professor Thompson writes, "made Aristophanes credible." World War II interrupted the work for six seasons (1940-45). The staff carefully packed important finds and records for the duration; duplicate catalogue-cards, photographs, and microfilm of the field notebooks were sent to America for safekeeping. The excavated area reverted to use as a garden or pasture, and loyal foremen performed miracles of maintenance under conditions that did not allow them the use of a single board or nail.

It should not be thought that all this efficiency was in-human. The excavation reports often record the pathetic, the homely commonplace, or the amusing: the kitchen struck by catastrophe, containing the remains of a small donkey and a purse of thirty-four coins; the dog buried with a large beef bone close to his nose; the stillborn babies, between a hundred and two hundred of them, lovingly buried in the sanctuary of Aphrodite Urania under the north slope of the Acropolis; the two superimposed pots, the upper one with a large hole in the front and one in the bottom, which remained puzzling till the pot-mender set his baby in the upper one and made it plain that it was a child's "potty"; the ashes from ancient workmen's lunch-fires, the remains of broken jars for their drinking water, and the plain little dishes from which they ate their mid-day beans and olives.

Agora finds from earlier centuries have been recorded in earlier chapters. Of Roman buildings the most impressive is Agrippa's Odeum, which rose majestic in the Agora's very center (see plan, Fig. 8.4), over the old Orchestra. John Travlos and Homer Thompson, using the techniques of archaeological inference with consummate skill, have since 1934 succeeded in winning back the design of this great building from a few scattered blocks. Its corner emerged in 1934; the 1935 campaign produced the outline of an orchestra and some marble benches which proved that the building was a theater; the earth scooped out for the orchestra had been used to support the cavea seats. Tiles, some marble, some terracotta, showed that the structure had been roofed, and was therefore an Odeum. When the Herulians, a marauding Teutonic tribe, sacked Athens in A.D. 267 the building was set on fire, which sealed in some readable blocks; more were found in the Valerian Wall.

The core of the building was the auditorium, lobby, and dressing-rooms. The auditorium once had seats for 1000, in eighteen rows of seats with comfortable scooped tops, the foundation walls of the core are very heavy, suggesting (see model, Fig. 8.5) an upper story, for which three series of large columns are available. Surrounding the core on three sides was a balcony, once used, like the second story of the Stoa of Attalus, for viewing the Panathenaic procession. Its entrance was narrow, like a wicket-gate, which

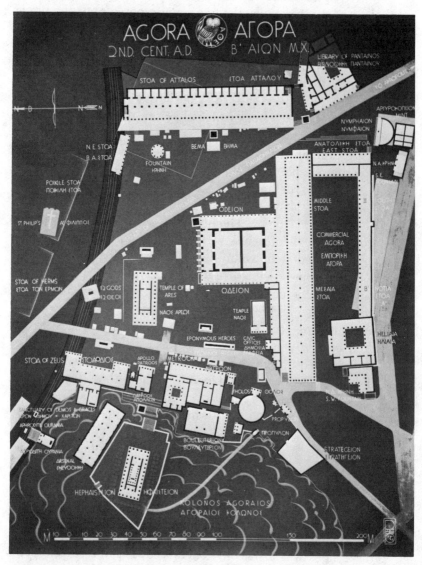

Fig. 8.4   Athens, Agora in Roman times, plan. North is to the left.
(Agora Excavations)

justifies the inference that admission was charged. The basement under the balcony could have stored theater properties, but it seems to have been very little used. The terracotta roof tiles are stamped; there are five series, the earliest from a factory which was in production in the time of Augustus. This confirms the attribution of the building to Agrippa, who is recorded in literary sources as having visited Athens about 15 B.C. and donated the Odeum about that date. The auditorium span is extraordinarily wide (over seventy-seven feet); therefore it must have been bridged by a self-supported timber truss, a method recommended by the architect Vitruvius, who was Agrippa's contemporary. The core proved to have been enclosed on three sides by a thin wall reinforced with Corinthian pilasters; on the south, not visible in the model, was an open colonnade of heavy Corinthian columns, the Romans' favorite order (because it was most ornate). The technique of the capitals re-

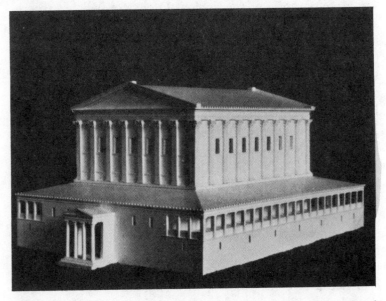

FIG. 8.5   Athens, Odeum of Agrippa, model. (Agora Excavations)

sembles that of the Tower of the Winds, which helps to
confirm the dating. The orchestra pavement was five layers
thick: a bottom course of fist-sized stones, then mortar,
more stones, more mortar, and finally slabs of different-
colored marble: white, gray-blue, green, purple, and pink.
This is the method of paving recommended by Vitruvius.
Pausanias mentions in the Odeum a statue of Dionysus
"worth seeing": Professor Thompson found fragments of
it. It must have been a colossus, for one "flake" of it was
a full burden for four workmen. More pieces were found
in the Valerian Wall in 1959. Since all were unweathered,
the statue must have stood under the shelter of the north
porch, where most of the fragments were found.

Agrippa's gift was timely, for the Periclean Odeum, on
the Acropolis south slope by the theater of Dionysus, was
sadly out of date. Too many of its seats were behind columns,
and it had been used for the grain dole, as a cavalry barracks, and as a haunt of lounging philosophers. The new
site was appropriate: the ancient Orchestra had been here,
and a large and lofty building axial at the back of a colonnaded square was a Hellenistic idea very much to Roman
taste: we may compare the temple of Zeus by the Agora at
Priene, the North Agora at Miletus, and, in Italy, the Fora
of Caesar and of Augustus in Rome and the temple of
Hercules Victor at Tivoli.

In 1937 the Americans excavated, at right angles to the
Odeum and northwest of it, a temple (in the center of the
model, Fig. 8.3), known from Pausanias to have been dedicated to Ares, god of war. Its technique was a puzzle: it
was fifth-century, by the same architect as the Hephaisteion,
but it stood on a podium in Roman fashion. The solution to
the problem was finally published in 1959, worked out
from three key Greek letters, in a style typical of the Augustan period, cut in each of 230 blocks. In the third place in
each set of three key letters, only four different symbols occurred: the monogram for AR, D, E, and O. Once these

were interpreted as meaning *Aristera* (left), *Dexia* (right), *Eisodos* (entrance), and *Opisteros* (back), it was clear that they represented the four sides of the temple, and that the Romans had dismantled it stone by stone, transported the blocks from their original site (at Acharnae?), and reconstructed the temple in the Agora, where its new location defined the west side of a more or less symmetrical square. The other key letters stood, one for the course in which the block fell, the other for its position in the course. The altar, too, was reassembled in front of the temple, on its axis, and on the axis of the Odeum north porch (see plan, Fig. 8.4). North of the altar a marble block with an iron ring inset with an eye-pin was the hitching-post for fastening animals to be sacrificed. The motive for all this reassembling, reminiscent of tales of American millionaires dismantling Scottish castles stone by stone for reconstruction in California, seems to have been propagandistic: Augustus' grandson Lucius Caesar was adulated as the New Ares; the fifth-century temple in its new location had the double advantage of high antiquity and a prominent site.

The years from Tiberius to Trajan (14-98*) were lean ones for building in the Agora. The first clue to a structure of note from just after this period turned up south of the Stoa of Attalus in 1933, in the form of a notice carved on stone, whose austerity would delight any librarian's heart: "NO BOOKS CIRCULATE. OPEN FROM SIX A.M. TO TWELVE NOON." Another inscription, of about 100, found in the Valerian Wall, records the donors of the library, one Ti. Flavius Pantainos, his son, and his daughter. The library rooms were grouped about a peristyle; there were porticoes facing the Panathenaic Way and the Stoa of Attalus. The rooms opening behind these porticoes were not connected with the library and could be rented separately as shops, thus providing endowment revenue for the library. Two of

---

* Henceforth all dates are A.D. unless otherwise indicated.

them served as a sculptor's studio, as was revealed by the discovery in them of marble chips, emery dust, and some sculptures "of mediocre quality." As long ago as 1869 the library's chief and very appropriate *objets d'art* had been found: two female figures in armor, personifying, as an inscribed base found in 1953 disclosed, the *Iliad* and the *Odyssey*.

Athens bet on the wrong horse again: Brutus, Caesar's murderer, who in 42 B.C. was beaten at Philippi, on the Via Egnatia, about nine miles northwest of Kavala, in Thrace, by Mark Antony and Octavian. Brutus committed suicide, and the poet Horace, notoriously, threw away his shield. The original name of the place was Krenides; in 356 Philip II of Macedon renamed it for himself—a sinister precedent. It prospered as a gold-rush town, and had (Fig. 8.5a) a theater-amphitheater, a forum with twin Corinthian temples, library, stoa, and civic buildings; a market, baths (of A.D. 250), a palaestra with a remarkable fifty-seat underground latrine, and rock-cut shrines to Silvanus, Bendis (the Thracian Artemis), Bacchus, and the Egyptian gods, embellished with 140 rock cut reliefs. St. Paul was here in A.D. 49, and wrote a letter to the Philippians: the crypt of a Byzantine church here used to be pointed out as his prison.

The Romans and their satellites built massively in the Greek style all over the world they now controlled. One of the most impressive and remote of these complexes, discovered by a German engineer in 1881, was not scientifically excavated until 1953-56, by a joint German-American expedition, in spite of severe extremes of climate, danger of landslides, and shortage of workmen. It all began when the German engineer noticed that the top of the 7000-foot eagle-haunted peak of Nemrud Dagh, in the inaccessible Antitaurus mountain range in southeast Turkey, was man-made, an enormous artificial tumulus 160 feet high and

480 feet in diameter. The next year Otto Puchstein (who later worked on the temple of Zeus at Agrigento) visited it from Alexandretta, a grueling nineteen-day journey on stub-

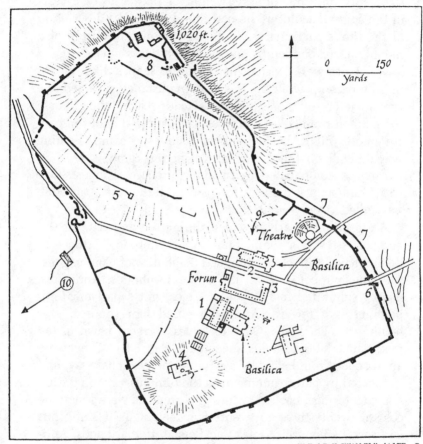

W. F. & R. K. SWAN (Hellenic) LTD. ©

1. Palaestra or Gymnasium
2. Speaker's Tribune on N. side (Centre) of Forum
3. Library
4. Baths
5. Aqueduct
6. Gateway

7. Byzantine outer-wall
8. Acropolis
9. Reliefs cut in rock in this area
10. Between two low hills, on the plain two miles away from Philippi, was the battlefield of 42 B.C.

FIG. 8.5a   Philippi, plan.

born horses wearing highly uncomfortable pack-saddles. The following year he revisited it with Carl Humann, the excavator of Pergamum, this time with a large caravan of horses and mules, to carry excavation gear, architects' instruments, and four hundredweight of plaster to take casts of the colossal sculpture he had found there. His description of the site is particularly vivid; like a mountain on top of a mountain, surrounded by snow-covered peaks whose rugged lower slopes were twisted into fantastic shapes, like the sea in a hurricane, while in the eastern distance gleamed the upper waters of the Euphrates. Heads, each taller than a man, fallen from colossal statues, lay scattered about in confusion. By night, bears prowled round the camp. Footing was difficult on the sliding gravel of the tumulus.

But the complicated cast-making proceeded apace. One cast, of a lion, was made in 170 pieces; all the casts, packed in hay, filled twenty-eight cases.

An inscription early revealed the nature and date of this complex: it was a tomb, built in his lifetime by the self-deified King Antiochus I (reigned 69-38 B.C.) of Commagene, a Roman puppet-state on the upper Euphrates. Antiochus, having submitted to Pompey (64 B.C.) got a part of Mesopotamia as a reward; Antony deposed him (38 B.C.) for helping the Parthians. On three sides, terraces hewn in the rock flanked his tumulus (see plan, Fig. 8.6). They were approached from below by a winding processional way, and connected by paths running atop the tumulus' retaining wall. On each terrace, backed against the tumulus, were limestone colossi, twenty-three to twenty-five feet high, of Antiochus enthroned among his Greek and Persian tutelary gods. Antiochus' tiara (Fig. 8.7) typifies the artistic style of this extraordinary place: on it is a striding lion against a background of pomegranate blossoms and fruits; his diadem shows a procession of lions, highly orientalized. The colossi of the east terrace face a court; lining its sides are life-sized relief portraits of Antiochus' ancestors, Greek and Persian,

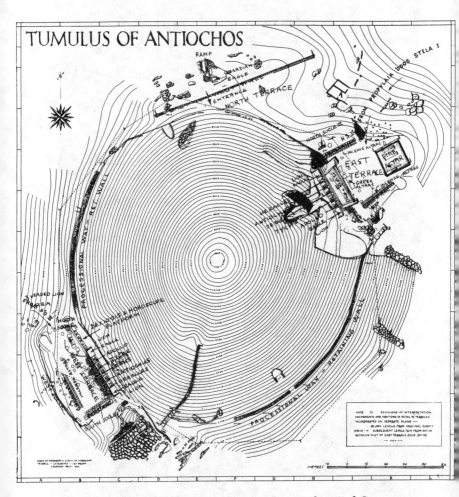

FIG. 8.6 Nemrud Dagh, Hierothesion of Antiochus I of Commagene, plan. Colossal statues of Antiochus and his gods are flanked on ends by lions and eagles. Along north side of East Terrace, Antiochus' Persian ancestors; on south, his Greek ancestors, and their deifications. On east, a stepped altar. The West Terrace (at left) has a related arrangement. (Courtesy Teresa Goell, 1962)

Fɪɢ. 8.7 Nemrud Dagh, Colossal head of Antiochus I of Commagene (NDA, p. 75, Fig. 2, by permission of the excavator, Miss Theresa Goell)

going back on his father's side to Darius I of Persia, and on his mother's to Alexander the Great, and portraits of himself greeted by his fellow gods; on the backs are genealogies and dedications, in Greek. Facing the colossi is a stepped altar; on their bases are inscriptions: they provide for the eternal celebration and maintenance of Antiochus' cult. One is a horoscope, supplying an exact date for the dedication of the complex: July 7, 62 B.C.

Tunneling to find the tomb proved unsuccessful, but did reveal the sloping stepped revetment of the tumulus, a ramp, and the tunnels of previous searchers. At Eski Kale, nearby, however, excavators found the burial-place, unfortunately already plundered, of Antiochus' father Mithridates Kallinikos. A vaulted entrance led to a stair hewn in the solid rock down to a chamber so far within the mountain—over 500 feet—that there must have been some artificial means of supplying air to the workmen.

At Nemrud Dagh, architecture, sculpture, and inscriptions all interlock, to symbolize the fusion of Persian, Hellenistic, and Anatolian traditions in this puppet kingdom under Roman sway.

Of the kingdoms founded by Alexander's generals, Seleucid Syria has left little archaeological evidence from Hellenistic times, but finds from the Roman period are abundant and impressive, especially at Baalbek and Palmyra.

Baalbek, ancient Heliopolis, the City of the Sun, lies 3850 feet above sea level, between the Lebanon and the Antilebanon, fifty-one miles east of Beirut, on the cavaran route between Damascus and Emesa. Its archaeological interest lies in the incredibly baroque massiveness of its complex of temples, to Jupiter, Bacchus, and Venus (Fig. 8.8), inspired by Greek forms, paid for with Roman money, built by Syrian architects for Syrians to worship in. The site first became known to the western world in 1508. Istanbul's Suleiman mosque (1550) incorporates some of its columns; earthquakes toppled more. Stuart and Revett were here in

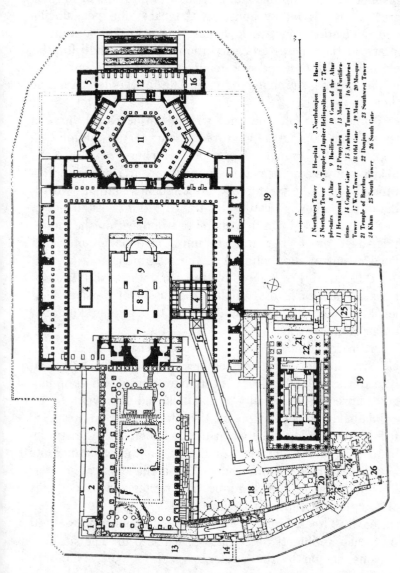

1 Northwest Tower   2 Hospital   3 Northodonjon   4 Basin
5 Northeast Tower   6 Temple of Jupiter Heliopolitanus   7 Temple-stairs   8 Altar   9 Basilica   10 Court of the Altar
11 Hexagonal Court   12 Propylaea   13 Moat and Fortification   14 Copper Gate   15 Arabian Tunnel   16 Southwest
Tower   17 West Tower   18 Old Gate   19 Moat   20 Mosque
21 Temple of Bacchus   22 Donjon   23 Southwest Tower
24 Khan   25 South Tower   26 South Gate

Fig. 8.8 Baalbek, plan. (Robinson, 1946, fac. p. 7, by permission of J. J. Augustin, Inc., Locust Valley, N. Y.)

FIG. 8.9 Baalbek, model, in Museo della civiltà romana, Rome. Lower left, temple of Venus; left center, temple of Bacchus; lower right, propylon, hexagonal court, altar court, and temple of Jupiter. (Fototeca)

1750; the French poet Lamartine shipped home a camel load of sculpture fragments in 1833: they were lost in transit. The historian Renan headed an archaeological mission hither (1860). The Arabist Richard Burton, as British consul-general in Damascus, studied the site for an *Encyclopaedia Britannica* article (1870). But the inspiration for modern scientific work there arose from a state visit by Kaiser Wilhelm II in 1898. Koldewey and Puchstein dug there (1899-1904); their architect spent five solid years on the site (escaping epidemics of cholera and plague but not dysentery). More recent excavation outside the temple area has revealed porticoed streets, a stoa, bouleuterion, theater, Roman gate, and houses and villas with mosaics of the third and fourth Christian centuries.

The temple of Jupiter (Syrian Baal) stands on a terrace 880 feet long and 400 feet wide, built up artificially with enormous blocks, one of which, sixty-three feet long, fourteen feet high, and eleven feet thick, weighs 1650 tons; its stone would build a house sixty feet square and forty feet high with foot-thick walls. One still larger, still in the quarry, would have taken 40,000 men to move. Baal was the chief god of the Syrians, as Jupiter was of the Romans. This colossal temple, its pediment rising 130 feet above the altar court, had a double propagandistic value. It symbolized Rome's might while it flattered Syrian self-importance. Its date is controversial, since so enormous a structure could never really be finished, and must have been worked on over several centuries. But the massiveness is Roman, and the earliest possible date for a Roman temple at Baalbek is about 16 B.C., when Augustus planted a colony there. But there was a Seleucid temple here, and one archaeologist dates the gigantic podium blocks late in that period. A safe if vague solution is that the whole complex dates, in its final form, from the times of Antonine and early Severan emperors (138-217).

The approach to Jupiter's temple is through tower-flanked Propylaea, 165 feet wide and thirty-eight feet deep. The towers (one restored by the French in 1933), thirty

feet square and 100 feet high (as tall as an eight-story building), are faced with two stories of engaged pilasters. They
provided the requisite "high place" for Semitic worship. Between them ran a row of twelve tall, polished, unfluted
columns with gilded Corinthian capitals; over the middle six
was a pediment with a raking cornice, over the middle two,
a relieving arch, the latter a hallmark of the second century
A.D. The portico had gilded bronze niches with a shell-
ornament in their half-domes. The Propylaea typifies the
mixture of influences in the whole plan: the towers are
Egyptian (compare the Egyptian temple on the Barberini
mosaic in Praeneste), the colonnade Greco-Roman, the décor
oriental. The 250-year building history represented here be-
speaks a powerful continuity.

Behind the Propylaea is a hexagonal court of about A.D.
250, with a double colonnade and exedrae (rectangular recesses for sitting). The plan allows for four triangular corner
rooms, where Baal's priests may have lived. From the hexagonal court a triple entrance leads into the enormous Altar
Court (120-200). It is 340 feet square. In the peristyle were
128 columns, polished and unfluted like those of the Propylaea. On either side of the central altar were ablution basins.
They were rectangular, with semicircular niches in their
outer faces. The altar itself rose fifty-eight feet in four
stepped stories, a third as tall as the Statue of Liberty. In the
courtyard walls are twelve niches (one for each of the
Olympian gods) alternately semicircular and rectangular, as
in the Pantheon in Rome; the total effect is like one of the
Imperial Fora there; perhaps the architect was the famous
Apollodorus of Damascus, who worked for Trajan, or one of
his school.

From the Altar Court sixteen steps led up to the temple,
which once had ten Corinthian columns across the front and
nineteen along the sides, counting corner columns twice.
They enclosed a 160 × 290-foot cella, over five times the size
of the Parthenon's. But the Artemision at Ephesus, the temple

of Zeus at Agrigentum, and Apollo's temple at Didyma are all larger. Six hundred-ton columns remain standing. Their golden patina makes a striking effect at sunset. Sixty-five feet high, they carry a sixteen-foot entablature, every inch of which is decorated: first fascia and frieze of fantastic fauna and flora, then dentils, egg-and-dart, corbels and rosettes, meander, and finally cornice, repeating the acanthus motif of the column-capitals.

The temple of Bacchus, Semitic Eshmoun, adjoining Jupiter's, is the best-preserved and most richly decorated Greco-Roman ruin in Lebanon or Syria. Ward Perkins' term for it, "disciplined opulence," is well chosen. It was standing in 130, for it bears an inscription in honor of Hadrian, who visited Baalbek in that year. The inscription is in Greek, whereas most Baalbek inscriptions are in Latin: another symbol of the combination of influences at work. It stands in Roman fashion, like its neighbor, on a high podium, with a crypt within. The podium steps are used for dramatic performances (in 1961 by the Comédie Française), opera, and ballet, and at night a tableau of sound and light, "The Wrath of the Gods," was played out with the temple as background. The taste of this widespread enterprise, which is bad on the Athenian Acropolis, dubious in the Roman Forum, perhaps appropriate at Versailles, is unquestionably suited to Baalbek's baroque extravagance (see model, Fig. 8.9). Nineteen of the temple's forty-six columns (of the Composite order, combining Corinthian acanthus with Ionic volutes) are standing. Though they are eight feet shorter than those of the temple of Jupiter, the temple itself, with its 75 × 87-foot cella, is bigger than the Parthenon. (Whether it is *better* is quite another question.) The cella portal is uniquely rich in its décor, though inspired by the quieter motifs of the door from the Erechtheum north porch in Athens. Like it, it has its lintel supported by consoles, but here the lintel's underside bears a great spread eagle in relief. The Germans in 1902 replaced the enormous central lintel block, in danger of falling, by ingeniously raising a tower of bricks under it. The jambs are carved with bacchantes and panthers (appropriate to a temple of Bacchus), satyrs, genii, birds, lizards, and other small animals, amidst clusters of grapes, nuts, and garlands, reminiscent of the Altar of Peace in Rome, though there again the taste is far quieter. The bacchante motif is repeated in a frieze just above eye level on the cella's outer front wall. The peripteros ceiling is coffered with six-pointed stars (Semitic influence?), with heads in relief in their centers. The stone entablature decoration is almost incredibly lavish: it has eighteen elements, Greek, Roman, and oriental in their various origins: strigils (parallel concave grooves, simulating the marks of the workman's thumbs in the days when temple décor was rendered in clay), egg-and-dart, bead-and-reel, palmettes, an alternation of projecting bull's and lion's heads, a Lesbian cyma (quarter-round molding), a console, a meander, and a crowning cornice in which, repeating motifs below, palmettes alternate with lions' heads. The outer face of the cella wall is theatrically enriched with pilasters partly concealed by fluted Corinthian half-columns; stairs in the pilasters lead to the roof. The pediment has doors and windows, which would have made possible some effects of religious pageantry, possibly even more spectacular than *Son et Lumière*. The inner cella wall has arches below, niches containing Victories above. In a deeply recessed, vaulted, coffered *aedicula* (shrine) with a shell half-dome, at the back of the cella, stood the cult-statue, flanked by sculptured animals, and wearing a curious oriental paneled garment, bearing representations of the planets. Pilasters framed the aedicula; they were framed in turn by pairs of polychrome marble columns, enclosing two stories of statues in their own subsidiary aediculas. Over all was a relieving arch and a pediment with acroteria (roof-ornaments). No briefer or less detailed description can possibly convey the bizarre profusion of the carved décor that the architect has lavished upon his temple. To compare it with the archaic temples of Dreros, Perachora, or Thermon is to revise radically one's views of what progress means.

Compared with this staggering magnificence, the neighboring temple of Venus (Semitic Atargatis), extravagant as it is, seems elegant and refined. In its final form it dates from about 245. It is a round building on an apsidal podium approached by steps, and with two rows of four columns. Four columns support the peristyle; their stylobate is scalloped out in niches, as is the outer cella wall, which supports a stone dome. Within the cella is a ring of twelve columns. The whole effect anticipates and in profuseness outdoes a garden-house of the Renaissance.

Halfway between the Mediterranean and the Euphrates (its very location a symbol), 150 miles northeast of Damascus, 1300 feet above sea level, is the oasis of Palmyra. It lies on an oil pipe line, as in antiquity on an age-old caravan route: ancient Chinese silks were found there, and the caravan road is the *decumanus,* one of the grandest avenues in all Syria, 1240 yards long, once bordered by 375 columns of pink limestone each as tall as a five-story building, of which about 150 are still standing (Fig. 8.10) clear-cut against the gray-gold background of the desert. Germans, Frenchmen, and Poles have dug it.

The approach to Palmyra is through a necropolis: exotic, thoroughly un-Greek tower-tombs, rising out of a smoking film of wind-blown sand. Sarcophagi serve as balconies, or are arranged in threes as at a banquet. Sealing slabs show busts of priests or bejeweled women. The dates range from 9 B.C. to the third Christian century. An inscription dates an early phase of its main temple (see plan, Fig. 8.11), to Bel, in 44 B.C., but later in the century its gigantic 650-foot peristyle court was built, and the temple was equipped with a curious off-center side entrance: in 174 a Propylaea and towers were added. Though the temple has been described as the grandest monument in all Syria, the total effect is

FIG. 8.10   Palmyra, monumental street. Note consoles on columns. (Author)

barbaric. It was the holy place of an Aramaic population with Roman names, who used Greek architectural forms without understanding them, perhaps as a tribute to the Macedonian origin of the old Seleucid kings. It has crow-stepped merlons and a flat roof reached by stairs, behind false pediments. Its Corinthian capitals were of gilt bronze. A relief shows a dromedary carrying a veiled image under a canopy. Within the temple, the cult image had a ramp in front of it for easy transfer to a processional litter. The temple of Bel alters, some would say debases, classical forms, as is inevitable when Levantine meets Greek.

The agora is of the early second century A.D. An exotic touch is provided by an inscriptional reference to caravans, so that this market square might better be called a cara-vanserai. A temple in the agora's west corner was used for

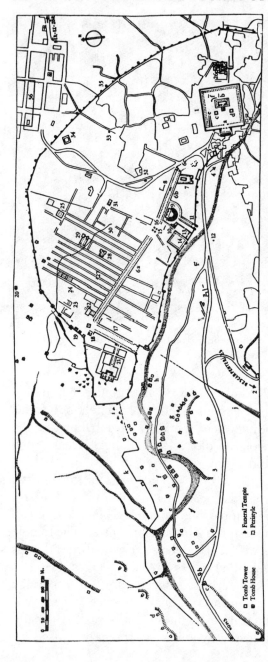

1 Temple of Bêl: *a* High portico and Propylaea   *b* Cella   *c* Sacrificial
altar   *d* Sacrificial basin   *e* Ramp   *f* Surrounding fortress wall
2 Southwest Necropolis   3 Valley of Tombs: *a* Tomb of Elahbêl   *b* Tomb
of Atenatan   *c* Tomb-house   *d* Archaic tombs   *e* Tomb of Yarhai
f Tomb-house   *g* Tomb of Jamblic   *h* Tomb of Aailami and Zebida
i Subterranean cellar   *j* Ancient surrounding fortress wall   *k* Aqueduct
4 Southeast Necropolis   5 Museum   6 *a b c* Great Colonnade   7 Temple
8 Baths of Diocletian   9 Theater   10 Senate   11 Transverse Colonnade

12 Column of Honor   13 Temple or Market   14 Agora   15 Tetrapyle
16 Inscription of Zenobia   17 Transverse Colonnade   18 Funeral Temple
19 Tomb-houses   20 Tomb-house   21 Camp of Diocletian   22 Public
or private building   23 Peristyle House   24 Peristyle House   25 Rhodian Peristyle House   26 House to the East of the Temple   27 Jewish
House   28 Christian Basilica   29 Christian Basilica   30 Omayyade wall
31 Temple of Bêlshamin   32 Spring of the Harem   33 Column of Honor
34 Building with great court   35 Bastion of Justinian   36 Modern village

▫ Tomb Tower   ▸ Funeral Temple
▪ Tomb House   ▫ Peristyle

Fig. 8.11   Palmyra, plan. (Robinson, *op. cit.*, fac. p. 41)

religious banquets; to these admission was charged: the excavators found some of the tickets. The Corinthian temple of Nabo (plan, 7) east of the agora, because it is differently oriented from neighboring complexes, is differently dated, in about 100. The neighboring complexes are the second-century theater, surrounded by a unique semicircular portico, and the monumental main street with its four-way gate, which the excavators date between 120 and 150. The theater was probably also used for town meetings; a separate building (plan, 10) housed the Senate. The temple of Baalshamin (plan, 31), of A.D. 130, is unusual in having windows, and in being set in a labyrinthine complex of courts. Over seven miles of circuit walls can be traced: they date from Diocletian (A.D. 284-306), with repairs by Justinian (527-65).

Palmyra was the financial capital of the eastern world in the mid-second century. An inscription of 137 reveals the nature of her trade. It mentions slaves, dates, pine-cones, purple (antiquity's most expensive luxury cloth), oil, salt fish, skins (camel-skins are duty-free), grain, and wine. The customs officials were not connoisseurs: bronze statues pay duty as bronze, not as works of art. Rich merchants advertised their own philanthropy by putting statues of themselves on consoles on the columns they donated for Palmyra's splendid main street, thus relieving the clutter caused by the usual statue bases. The city was laid out on a grid plan; arches mark the junction of the main with the principal cross-streets. The most impressive of these are the tetrapylon (a quadruple arch near the Agora and theater), and the tripylon near the Corinthian temple, the latter a marvel of illusionary architecture, its purpose being to mask the avenue's change in direction to approach the temple of Bel. Palmyrene houses were balconied, with ground plans like those of Olynthus. Their third-century mosaics are on Greek themes: Achilles among the women, evading the Trojan War; Asclepius; Cassiopeia, mother of Andromeda. The colonnaded street ends in a funerary temple (plan, 18) a transverse portico (17) leads past the "Camp of Diocletian," actually older than the emperor; it was in use as early as 148. It is a Palmyrene temple made over into a Roman *praetorium*, or governor's headquarters, in plan not unlike the Hadrianic firemen's barracks at Ostia, with its shrine, here apsidal, for the worship of Roman emperors centered at the back. Palmyra in her prime defied the Roman Empire, but Aurelian humbled her. In 272 her queen Zenobia walked in gold chains in Aurelian's triumph, and perhaps pined in elegant exile in Hadrian's Villa at Tivoli. Rome used Palmyra as a buffer against the Parthians. The unfortunate emperor Valerian (reigned 253-60) was killed and allegedly stuffed, the king of Palmyra using him as a cushion.

Another Seleucid foundation bearing the Greco-Roman stamp is the rectangular-gridded city of Gerasa, eighty-five miles northeast of Jerusalem and twenty-six miles north of the Jordanian capital, Amman. A Yale expedition dug it (1928-34), removing fallen columns from its streets, recovering the plan (Fig. 8.12) of its north and south theaters, choked with vegetable gardens. The south theater, built before 83, had a capacity of 5000, numbered seats, and an elaborate stage building; the north theater is third century. The Yale archaeologists drew plans of twenty temples, including one of Zeus that was 140 years a-building (A.D. 22-160s). The temple of Artemis covered, with its immense walled precinct, over 35,000 square yards, and was buried seven feet deep; a majestic stair provided access to its baroque magnificence. Its columns, restored to the light of day, were weathered to a rich bronze color. Its podium was designed hollow, to provide chambers or reservoirs. The excavators deciphered 150 inscriptions, besides inventorying thousands of coins and small finds. They traced Gerasa's two-mile circuit wall, with its 101 towers. The wall enclosed 237 acres, nearly three times the area of Roman Ostia, but the population never exceeded 10,000 to 15,000. An inscrip-

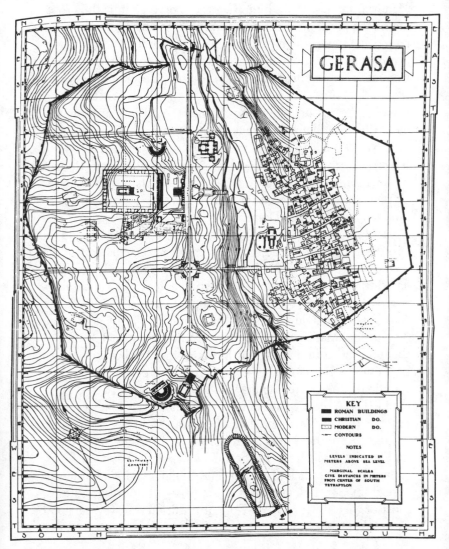

Fig. 8.12 Gerasa, plan. Note north and south theaters, and huge precinct (upper left quadrant) of Temple of Artemis. (Kraeling, 1938, Plan 1)

tion by the northwest gate reveals that the walls were finished before 75. South of them rose a five-bay monumental arch (Hadrianic) and a stadium. Gerasa's nerve center, the crossing of the *cardo* and the *decumanus,* was an elliptical colonnaded caravanserai measuring 214 × 321 feet. The whole presents yet another picture of the adaptation of Greco-Roman civic amenities to the needs of a desert culture.

At these Syrian sites, the Romans built on and monumentalized Hellenistic Greek foundations. They did so also in a North African city, Cyrene, whose lower levels, as we have seen, go back to archaic times. Cyrene became Roman under Ptolemy VII's will in 96 B.C. "The parts of Libya about Cyrene" became a Roman province in 74 B.C.; Augustus combined it with Crete. Domitian (81-96) monumentalized the Agora (see plan, Fig. 4.17). Italian archaeologists in 1956, in 1200 man-days, re-erected the Caryatids in the stoa east of the Agora: thirteen herms, alternately of Hermes and Heracles, flanking wide windows and supporting a heavy Doric entablature. They spent 1500 man-days on the north side of the Agora, and excavated part of the Julio-Claudian Caesareum. At the sanctuary of Apollo they studied the theater-amphitheater, and found the great baths in the Apollo precinct to be Trajanic. Romans, they discovered, re-erected the colossal temple of Zeus, after its destruction in a revolt (115). Here again the Greco-Roman décor is a thin veneer over a native culture, one curious evidence of which is a series of peculiar statues from the huge necropolis. They are of women or goddesses; some have no bottom half, some have no faces, some have the face half-veiled. The Italian catalogue of sculpture from Cyrene contains the impressive total of 483 items, most of them in the Greco-Roman tradition, but few as good as the Aphrodite.

The associations of Cyrene with the *Acts of the Apostles* make a convenient point of transition back to mainland

Greece: to Corinth, where in the Agora (Fig. 8.13) the Americans have excavated the very bema or rostrum from which in 51 St. Paul addressed the Corinthians. Christianity grew at Corinth: a basilica church of 450-520 at Lechaion,

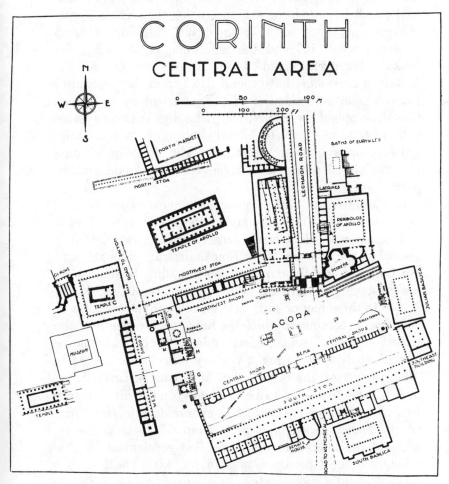

FIG. 8.13 Corinth, central area, plan. Three rectangular exedrae should be added at back of Julian Basilica. (Broneer, 1947, Plan 1)

the port, was nearly as long as St. Peter's in Rome. For many visitors Corinth's interest will center in its associations with St. Paul, who lived here for eighteen months (51-52), plying his trade of tentmaker, his preaching tolerated under the Roman governor, Gallio, who "cared for none of these things." Corinth's origins go back to Neolithic times, and it flourished in the archaic period, the evidence being the archaic temple of Apollo (550-525 B.C.), "a squat surly building with no nonsense about it," and the handsome pottery. But the Romans destroyed the old city in 146 B.C.; most of what the American excavators have found dates from the years after Julius Caesar refounded it as a Roman colony in 44 B.C. Corinth is one of the earliest American digs in Greece; excavation began in 1896, and is still continuing, as a training-ground for young archaeologists. The final publication (incomplete) has reached sixteen volumes, totaling thirty parts.

Of Corinth's pre-Roman remains the most impressive and best-known is of course the archaic temple. Just south of it the Americans discovered mute evidence, at Corinth's arsenal, of the savagery of the Roman destruction of 146 B.C.: ash, burned wood, fire-damaged rooftiles, sling-bullets, spear-heads, stone catapult-balls of five different calibers. Above it, two to three feet of earth and gravel, with a few coins of neighboring Sicyon (to which the Romans gave charge of the ruined city) and some orderly piles of debris summarize Corinthian history during a century of eclipse.

Northwest of the Agora the Americans excavated the theater, which proved to be originally of the fifth century B.C., with seats for 18,000, and Roman revisions. Nero had a special Imperial box built in it, from which in 67 he re-affirmed the liberation of Greece, first proclaimed by Fla-mininus at the Isthmian Games in 196 B.C. (The inscribed text of Nero's proclamation was discovered in 1888 in Acraephnium, Boeotia. It is now in the Thebes museum.) It was in 67 that Nero tried (and failed) to dig a canal through the Isthmus of Corinth, using 5000 captives sent to him by Vespasian from the war in Palestine. About 135 the theater was rebuilt in marble, and between 211 and 217 its orchestra was remodeled for water ballets (by ballerinas like those represented in the later mosaics from Piazza Armerina*), and gladiatorial contests. An inscription records the familiar story of the gladiator Androcles, spared in a beast-fight by a lion from whose paw he had once extracted a thorn. Connected with the theater by a peristyle court is the 3000-seat odeum, of about A.D. 175, of which only an unrecognizable piece of rubble masonry was above ground when excavation started. The court, if not the odeum itself, is one of the many benefactions of the Athenian millionaire Herodes Atticus, some of whose other gifts of buildings, in Athens and elsewhere, will be described later. To the southwest was the potters' quarter.

Corinth's Agora slopes upward from north to south. Just southwest of the main basilica (see plan) the Romans overlooked (because it had been built over before 146 B.C.) a Greek oracular shrine of the fourth century B.C., which presents interesting evidence of the manipulation of human credulity. It centers on a small circular altar with a retaining wall beside it, faced with triglyphs and metopes. The altar was served by an underground channel for pouring libations. Parallel to this channel runs a tunnel just big enough for a man, the entrance to which was through one of the metopes, cleverly pivoted as a secret door. Behind this was another door, with a lock, and beside the wall was an inscription forbidding trespass, on the pretext that the spot was sacred. Protected by all these precautions, a priest could slip through the secret doors into the tunnel and crawl to the altar end, where his sepulchral voice could utter oracles through a hole in the pavement to the assembled faithful.

---

* See *The Mute Stones Speak*, p. 340 and Fig. 13.1.

Early in the colonial period (about 44 B.C.) the Romans remodeled the South Stoa, the largest Corinthian secular building of classical times, a two-storied fourth-century building with thirty-three shops on the ground floor, most of them thoughtfully equipped with a well in the center for cooling wine. A vast quantity of drinking cups was found in the wells, together with fragments of marble bar-tops, and roof tiles and architectural terracottas thrown there at the time of the Roman sack; enough were found to make possible the reconstruction of the cornice, displayed, together with some Roman mosaic floors, under an adjoining shed roof. The upper story contained guest rooms, which may not have been exactly havens of rest, in view of the taverns below. The excavators think that these rooms were planned to house the delegates to sessions of the Panhellenic League convened at Corinth by Philip II of Macedon in 338. The stoa north of the archaic temple yielded a gold necklace and fifty-one gold coins (staters) of Philip II and Alexander. Some 200 yards north of the civic center, the Hadrianic baths covered over 10,000 square yards; 300 yards beyond was a sanctuary of Asclepius, of about 300 B.C., remodeled under Marcus Aurelius, with dormitory, dining-rooms, and a sacred fountain; a number of terracotta dedications from here, by grateful patients, are kept in the museum west of the Agora. West of the Asklepieion was an archaic sanctuary of Zeus, largest of its time. Corinth's walls (fourth century B.C.) are two and a half times as long as Athens'; they run to the sea from Acrocorinth, a steep climb of over an hour south of the city, with a temple of Aphrodite, where 1000 temple-prostitutes plied their trade: it was naturally a favorite haunt of sailors. But most of the ruins are seventeenth-century, and the classicist climbs Acrocorinth chiefly for the magnificent view, west to Mt. Cyllene, east to Cape Sunium. While the classical remains were being excavated, one archaeologist climbed Acrocorinth fifty-six times in one season. Between Acrocorinth and the agora is a sixth-century-B.C. shrine of Demeter and Kore, with rock-cut steps as at Eleusis, a theatral area, and provision for ritual banquets.

The Agora, larger than the Forum in Rome, was the glory of Roman Corinth. Beside its monumental approach, the colonnaded Lechaion Street, the Romans when they refounded Corinth as a colony built a basilica on the canonical plan, with a nave and two side aisles, not unlike the Basilica Julia in the Forum at Rome. It was the colony's legal and commercial center; in the second century it was enlarged and given a monumental two-storied false front, the Captives' Façade, adorned with colossal figures of barbarians, standing on bases carved with representations of Roman victories. Beside them is the monumental entrance to the Agora, through a triumphal arch built in Augustan times. Only its foundations remain, but Pausanias says it was surmounted by the chariots of Apollo and his son Phaethon, in gilt bronze.

The excavators date between 25 and 50, on the evidence of coins, the central shops axially arranged on either side of the Bema. They marked the dividing line between the upper and the lower Agora, which the Romans treated as two terraces.

At the west end of the row of central shops was a shrine of Dionysus, on the east a circular monument surmounted by a column; it may have belonged to a hero-cult. In front of it a curved retaining wall must have supported a tribunal for the judges of foot races, for beneath it, at an early Hellenistic level, the excavators found two sets of stadium starting-blocks, one fifth-century, the other—differently oriented—Hellenistic. Apparently here, as at the Isthmian sanctuary, a hero's burial place determined the starting-point of races in his honor.

The line of the Hellenistic starting-blocks runs under the steps of the Julian Basilica, bounding the Agora on the east. It is named from portraits of the Julian family found in its cryptoporticus. In 1948 the excavation of three rectangular exedras in its back wall proved that it was the exact

twin of the South Basilica, squeezed in behind the South
Stoa. On the evidence of coins, both were built in Claudius'
reign, about 40. A statue of Lucius Caesar, Augustus' grandson, from the South Basilica, bears the pointing-marks used
by sculptors making an exact copy; the original turned up in
the other basilica. Handsome inscriptions, treated as part of
the décor, adorned the interior walls.

The monumental entrance to the South Basilica was added
in Antonine times (mid-second century). The evidence is
from lamps, which at Corinth were first accurately classified
by Broneer (1930), to help archaeologists in dating. He
analyzed with the greatest precision the shapes, profiles,
spouts, and molded decoration of over 1400 Corinthian
lamps, some of which, having been found in dated contexts,
provided firm benchmarks. He distinguished thirty-four
types, best presented in a tabular view:

Type	No. of Examples	Date
I-III	58	sixth century B.C. or earlier
IV-VII	69	fifth and fourth centuries B.C.
VIII-XVIII	185	Hellenistic
XIX	60	early Roman
XX-XXIII	84	Augustan
XXIV-XXVI	76	A.D. 50-100
XXVII-XXX	903	second to fourth century A.D.
XXXI-XXXIV	66	Christian

The lamps found in the porch of the South Basilica belonged
to Type XXVII. Fifty-seven per cent of all the lamps studied
were in use between the years 100 and 400; this is evidence
that Corinth survived the Herulian sack of 267. The South
Basilica is across the road from the apsidal Council Chamber; the Julian Basilica adjoins the Southeast Building, which
housed the archives. This suggests that both buildings served
administrative purposes, but the possibility of commercial
use cannot be excluded, since they closely resemble in plan

the Eumachia in the Forum of Pompeii, which was a cloth-market.

In 79—the same year as the eruption of Vesuvius that destroyed Pompeii—Corinth suffered from an earthquake, after which the northwest shops were rebuilt. Thereafter the excavators have found little evidence of building activity, except in the theater, until 161, when the fountain Pirene, east of the Propylaea, underwent the grandest of its many transformations, this time at the expense of Herodes Atticus, in honor of his wife Regilla, as an inscribed statue-base discloses. Pirene always has water, even in the depths of summer, a rare thing in Greece; an underground reservoir with a 400-cubic-yard capacity feeds six draw-basins, one of which has on its side wall some Roman paintings of local fish. According to legend, Pirene first bubbled up where Bellerophon's winged horse Pegasus stamped his foot; in consequence, Pegasus appears as Corinth's device on her silver coins. Many generations of Corinthians delighted in adorning Pirene with various styles of marble façades, in nine phases. Herodes further enriched it by adding to the north, around an open pool, a cloverleaf of three semicircular covered exedras, each with three niches for statues of members of his family.

Two hundred yards west of Pirene is the Fountain of Glaukê, of similar plan. Its origins are very old, as old as Greek mythology: it is named for the princess Jason married, who is said to have flung herself into it, vainly seeking relief from the poisoned robe which was Medea's wedding present to her. The adjoining Roman temple (C on the plan) may have been dedicated to Hera Akraia, on the spot where Medea's children vainly sought refuge from the avenging fury of the citizens of Corinth.

The Romans defined the Agora's west end with six small temples, of which the central pair, Poseidon's (185) and Heracles' (191) belong to the reign of the Emperor Commodus, who fancied himself as the reincarnation of the hero of the twelve labors. These were Roman temples, on high podia. Corinth had become a Roman city, seat of the governor of the Roman province of Achaea. Of its major published inscriptions, 226 are in Latin. But 331 are Greek; the great archaic Greek temple looms over all, so that what the American archaeologists have excavated is a Roman provincial capital, whose main square combines the functional and the aesthetic in a balanced and orderly way, which is Roman, but not with rigid symmetry, which would have been very un-Greek.

At Kenchreai, two-and-a-half miles south of Isthmia, is an Isis sanctuary (Roman), on the harbor mole, containing one hundred cut-glass panels, of about A.D. 370, portraying seaside buildings, wild life, and human figures. Here Lucius, in Apuleius' novel, was changed back from ass to man. Around the harbor, and also Roman (after 44 B.C.), were warehouses, shops, a stoa, and a shrine of Aphrodite. The Isis precinct itself had an apsidal hall, a roofed dromos, colonnades, a fountain court, and a distyle temple.

Another historic Greek city that prospered under Roman sway was Ephesus, which the Romans elevated to be the capital of the province of Asia. Its excavators calculate that at its peak it reached a population of 500,000. Austrian archaeologists, in part subsidized with Rockefeller money, excavated its Roman phase, with up-to-date equipment and methods. A Latin inscription (with "IMPERATOR" misspelled "IMBERATOR") dated the Agora west gate (see plan, Fig. 8.14) in 4/3 B.C. The theater was remodeled under Claudius (41-54) and Trajan (98-117). About 54 the "Marble Street" was lined with monuments on both sides, giving a splendid idea of what Ephesus was like in its prime. Nero gave the city a stadium: the excavators found built into a later pavement its balustrade, with a crude representation of the prizes offered. Later the stadium was remodeled for

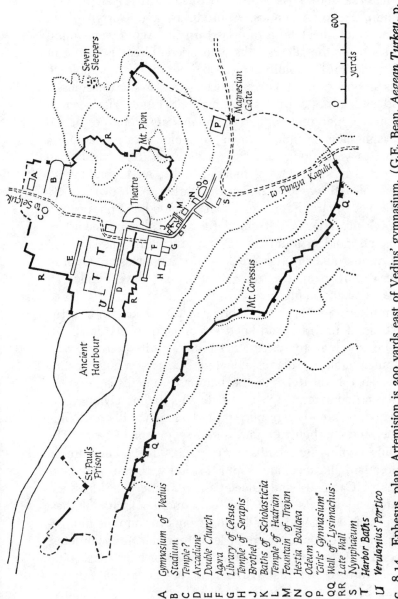

A Gymnasium of Vedius
B Stadium
C Temple?
D Arcadiane
E Double Church
F Agora
G Library of Celsus
H Temple of Serapis
J Brothel
K Baths of Scholasticia
L Temple of Hadrian
M Fountain of Trajan
N Hestia Boulaea
O Odeum
P "Girls' Gymnasium"
QQ Wall of Lysimachus-
RR Late Wall
S Nymphaeum
T Harbor Baths
U Verulanius' Portico

FIG. 8.14 Ephesus, plan. Artemision is 200 yards east of Vedius' gymnasium. (G.E. Bean, *Aegean Turkey*, p. 169. Courtesy of E. Benn, Ltd, London)

gladiatorial shows (except at Dura, and at Cyzicus, Pergamum, Perge, Aspendos, Aphrodisias, and Gortyn—there are no amphitheaters in the East). In the Agora were found the shops of the silversmiths who cried "Great is Diana of the Ephesians!" Domitian (81-96) permitted a temple to himself, on a terrace, where the excavators found the colossal head and arm (Fig. 8.15) of his cult-statue. The second-century pseudo-philosopher Apollonius at Tyana persuaded the Ephesians to pull it down. In Domitian's reign, too, a strip 650 yards long and 270 yards wide, from theater to harbor, was lined with gymnasia, and a set of baths with three colossal windows facing the harbor, each over thirty-three feet square. Exotic goods were landed at Ephesus harbor: cloth and spices from Syria and Palestine, cedar of Lebanon, golden grain from Egypt and south Russia, shimmering marble from the Greek islands, copper from Cyprus, silver from Spain, tin from Britain, and slaves skilled at cookery or at making love.

An inscription dates the Library of Celsus in 110; in it the Austrians found the lead-lined sarcophagus of its donor. Its façade is now restored. Another public-spirited citizen, with a Roman name, Verulanus, donated (124-127) a huge portico between the theater and the harbor. From the age of the Antonine emperors (138-161) date the Vedius Gymnasium, donated by another public-spirited citizen with a Roman name, and the bouleuterion, for 1400, gift of his wife. The Vedius Gymnasium baths (260 × 455 feet) compare in scale, plan, elegance, and sophistication with the huge later baths of Caracalla and Diocletian in Rome. The dressing-rooms had lockers under the seats and hooks for clothes. Statues of river-gods poured water from urns into the plunge-bath. In the basement were at least fourteen furnace-rooms, needed to heat over 10,000 square yards of floor space. The floors were so hot that bathers in the *caldarium* (steam-room) had to wear wooden clogs. The huge west windows took advantage of solar heat, as in the Forum Baths at Ostia.

FIG. 8.15 Ephesus, temple of Domitian, colossal arm. (Miltner, 1958, p. 40, by permission of F. Deuticke, Vienna)

Though archaeologists have occasionally found Greek-designed baths on purely Greek sites, for example, at Olympia, none compare in grandeur with the Roman baths of Ephesus.

A few decades after Vedius donated his baths, Ephesus was enriched, under the Severan Emperors, with a temple of Serapis opposite the Agora. The Austrians were able to reconstruct it on paper. Its columns weigh twenty-seven tons each; their capitals are the height of a man. Exotic rites were practiced here in torchlight, to the rattle of the *sistrum*.

On the hills overlooking the civic center were the houses, some with peristyle, private baths, private chapels, and frescoes, with scenes from comedy, tragedy, mythology, and daily life. All this grandeur fell before the Goths in 263. The story of the city's revival, of the "House of the Virgin," of the Council held here in 431, of the Austrian reconstruction of the sixth-century church of St. John, is fascinating, but falls outside the scope of this book.

While Corinth and Ephesus flourished as provincial capitals, Athens went on placidly as a quiet university town. Her most impressive memorial from Trajan's reign is the Philopappos Monument, on the Hill of the Muses, southwest of the Acropolis. Balanos restored it in the 'thirties, and the Italians studied it just before World War II. The Athenians built it—it is a tomb—about A.D. 116, to honor a prince of Commagene, descendant of the builder of the Nemrud Dagh tomb, C. Julius Antiochus Philopappos, who was at once a Syrian prince, a Roman dignitary, and an Athenian citizen, archon, and benefactor, a typical cosmopolitan of the Greek world under Roman sway. His tomb (Fig. 8.16, an old print) is a semicircular exedra of Pentelic marble, built to face the Parthenon; the best view of the Acropolis is from here. It has three niches for the statue of Philopappos flanked by his ancestors. Symbolic of the fusion of cultures are two inscriptions, one giving his public career in Latin, the other his princely titles in Greek.

Soon after the dedication of the Philopappos monument,

FIG. 8.16 Athens, Philopappos Monument, before restoration. (DAI, Athens)

Athens received (124/5) an Imperial visitor, the Emperor
Hadrian, whose advent was to usher in a Renaissance. The
Athenians compared him to their mythical King Theseus,
who first united Attica under Athenian rule, but as a builder
he is in the line of such historical figures as Pisistratus,
Pericles, and Lycurgus. He delighted to embellish Athens,
and she delighted to honor him. He was initiated into the
Mysteries at Eleusis, presided over the dramatic competition in the theater of Dionysus (which he adorned with
statues and new marble thrones for priests and dignitaries),
was elected archon—chief magistrate—and had a tribe named
after him. In return he built a new stretch of circuit wall,
adding 25 per cent to the city's area. One of its gates survives, with a pair of metrical inscriptions, on one side calling
Athens Theseus' city; on the other, Hadrian's. Just southeast of this gate rises Hadrian's most monumental gift to his
favorite city: the huge precinct (as big as five football fields)
and gigantic temple (173 × 359 feet) of Olympian Zeus.
Begun by Pisistratus in the sixth century B.C. (some of
his column-drums were found in 1949 in the Themistoclean
wall nearby), rebuilt by King Antiochus Epiphanes of
Syria about 174 B.C. (some of the surviving columns may
be his), and assuming its final form under Hadrian in
131/2, it has, as we saw, a long building-history. The
Hadrianic temple had 104 huge Corinthian columns, of
which fifteen are still standing (Fig. 8.17). One, felled by
a hurricane in 1852, was measured as it lay: it was sixty
feet long, the height of a five-story building. Some of the
missing ones went to the limekilns: the mortar of a mosque
in a corner of Hadrian's Library came from the columns of
Hadrian's temple. South of the Delphinion (see p. 202)
Hadrian built the Panhellenion, where he was worshiped
as Zeus and his wife Sabina as Hera: the precinct was used
as the meeting place of a Panhellenic Council instituted by
him.

Hadrian's Library, north of the Roman Agora, dates from

FIG. 8.17   Athens, Olympieion, floodlit at night, from southeast.
(Émile Séraf)

his third visit to Athens in 131/2. It was not conclusively
identified till 1919, when an English architect, M. A. Sisson,
triumphing over the complications of a site encumbered by
modern streets, houses, shops, a military barracks and prison,

and a mosque, published the definitive study (Fig. 8.18).
Stuart and Revett had thought it was the Painted Porch and
later writers had called it merely a stoa. Sisson's method
exploited literary sources, observation on the spot, and com-
parisons with similar buildings. Pausanias mentions 100 columns of Phrygian marble; Sisson was able to count exactly
that number of bases in the peristyle: twenty-two each
front and back, and twenty-eight each on the sides. The
central room on the east has two stories of recesses, com-
pensated for by buttresses on the outside. The recesses are
too shallow for statues, but just deep enough to shelve scrolls
in their containers; Sisson remembered a parallel in the
Library ("Sala dei Filosofi") of Hadrian's Villa near Tivoli.
Behind the recesses is an air space, a provision against
damp like that found in the Library of Celsus at Ephesus
and in those of Trajan in Rome, of about the same date.
There is one deeper, arched, central recess for a statue of
Athena, who as goddess of wisdom, should preside over
libraries. Sisson calculated that the four eastern rooms,
fitted with two stories of shelves round the walls and in the
middle, would hold 200,000 rolls. The building technique
proves the edifice to be of Hadrianic date: the free-standing
pedestaled columns and the architrave with only two fascias
instead of three are identical with those on Hadrian's arch
near the Olympieum, and the wall-blocks with their carefully finished edges are like those of the Olympieum's
precinct wall. The flanking rooms may have housed public
archives, but they are very grand for so humdrum a function: more probably they were used for lectures or poets'
recitations. (In that case, Sisson's calculations based on
central shelving for scrolls will have to be reduced.) Cen-
trally located, with an imposing façade, enclosed for security
and quiet in blank walls with but a single entrance, furnished with stoa, garden, and exedras, it must have been
a cool and agreeable retreat for scholars: one wonders
whether the Alexandrian Library was not like this on a
larger scale.

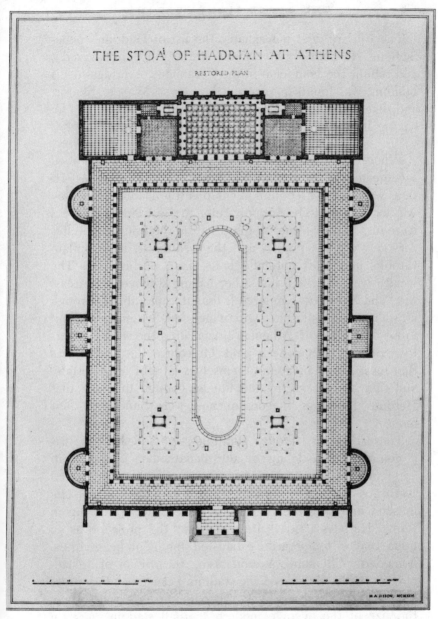

FIG. 8.18 Athens, Library of Hadrian, plan. Note 100-columned peristyle, book recesses in central room on east (at top in plan), and flanking rooms, probably for lectures. (Sisson, 1929, Pl. 21, by permission of the British School at Rome)

The Library does not exhaust the list of Hadrian's benefactions. He built a gymnasium (site as yet undiscovered),
and rebuilt the Pompeion in the Ceramicus. A bridge of his
building was found in 1950 on the Sacred Way to Eleusis,
and, like Pisistratus, he built an aqueduct. It is still in use,
having been reconditioned along with its reservoir.

When Hadrian ascended the throne in 117, a tongue-tied
seventeen-year-old student of rhetoric named Herodes Atticus was sent to greet him in camp on the Danube. The boy
was to grow up to be not only tutor to the Emperor Marcus
Aurelius, but also one of the greatest rhetoricians (Aelius
Aristides was his pupil), and the wealthiest, most philanthropic, and most cordially hated man of his time. The
wealth was inherited, his father having discovered a treasure. The hatred was inherited, too: it came about through
a provision of his father's will, which left five *minae* (about
$100) apiece to each Athenian citizen, *after* the citizen's debts
to Atticus *père* had been paid. Of course the upshot was
that most Athenians found themselves in debt to the estate,
and they were perverse and human enough to argue that
Herodes' buildings, in consequence, were built with *their*
money.

The earliest of Herodes' sumptuous gifts to his city was
a complete remodeling of the Panathenaic Stadium, in
emulation of Pisistratus the founder of the games and
Lycurgus the earlier builder. It was promised in 139/40,
finished in 143/4, the year Herodes held the consulship in
Rome. Herodes used Pentelic marble: the project was so
huge that it temporarily exhausted the Pentelic quarries.
A modern millionaire, Averoff, using the studies of archaeologists as basis, restored the stadium yet again (Fig. 8.19)
for the revived Olympics in 1896. Its capacity was 50,000,
the size of the average modern football stadium. Certain
features resemble the Coliseum at Rome: a tunnel at the
south end, possibly for wild beasts, and a grille to protect

FIG. 8.19   Athens, Stadium of Herodes Atticus, as restored for Olympics of 1896. Herms and other remains in curve are ancient.

the spectators from them. From the north there was a monumental approach by a bridge across the Ilissus. The propylon had side rooms with mosaic floors: these were probably the athletes' dressing-rooms. Herms (marble pillars surmounted by a bust) marked the turns on the track, and a Doric colonnade over thirty feet deep (missing in the modern reconstruction) crowned the whole structure. On the hill to the west Herodes built a temple to Fortune (*Tychê*, the presiding genius of the Roman, as she had been of the Hellenistic Age), a goddess to whom he owed much. The eastern hill may have held his tomb, though there is a rival claimant in the Athenian suburb of Cephissia, and a possible site on his estate near Marathon, whose entrance is inscribed "Gate of Eternal Harmony." This Herodes never achieved: his life was troubled by his inherited unpopularity, by charges of having connived at his wife's death (159/60), and of having bribed the Athenian archons (174). He was disappointed also in his son, who was said to have been so stupid that the only way he could learn his letters was to have twenty-four slaves, bearing sandwich-boards inscribed with the letters of the Greek alphabet, parade constantly in order before him.

Perhaps Herodes' mania for building was a compensation for his unhappy personal life. In 147 he undertook to provide marble seats for 7000 in the stadium at Delphi. (The splendidly sited fourth-century theater there was also restored in Roman times.) At Olympia in 153/4 he built his exedra (Fig. 8.20) to mask the end of an aqueduct. The exedra was of brick faced with marble. Its niches held twenty-four statues, utterly mediocre in technique, but they have a special room in the new Olympia Museum. Nine are of members of the imperial family, fifteen of members of his own. Rising over 100 feet high, the exedra was taller than any other building in the Altis except the temple of Zeus. In tastelessness it is hard to match: perhaps the best parallel is the colossal marble monument in Rome to Victor Emmanuel II, nicknamed "the typewriter," which also uses classical motifs in a well-meaning but moribund and derivative way. Herodes' benefactions to Corinth, possible (the odeum), and

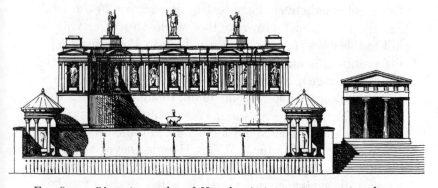

Fig. 8.20   Olympia, exedra of Herodes Atticus, reconstruction drawing. Most of the statues shown are now in the Olympia Museum. (*Olymp. Forsch.* I, Pl. 36)

FIG. 8.21 Athens, Odeum of Herodes Atticus. Note barrel-vaulted entrance, architectural backdrop and checkerboard paving of orchestra. (Greek National Tourist Bureau)

certain (Pirene remodeled), we have already mentioned. He also built an aqueduct for the city of Alexandria Troas in northwest Asia Minor.

Herodes' final gift to Athens was his roofed theater or odeum, built in 161 for 5000 people on the south slope of the Acropolis at the west end of the Stoa of Eumenes. Variously identified until the nineteenth century as the theater of Dionysus, the Areopagus, and the School of the Peripatetic Philosophers, it was excavated and finally identified by Greek archaeologists in 1848, and explored again in 1857-58. Reconstructed since World War II on a sound archaeological basis (Fig. 8.21) it is now used for summer performances of ancient Greek drama and for symphony concerts. Roman in materials—brick and *opus incertum* (fist-sized stones set irregularly in cement)—it is Greek in being built into the hillside instead of on man-made foundations. The entrances were barrel-vaulted in the Roman way; buttresses braced the walls against the strain of the cedarwood roof; the front of the stage-building (*scaenae frons*) was an architectural backdrop three stories high. The orchestra is paved in a checkerboard pattern with white and with green Carystus marble (*cipollino,* "onion-stone").

An odeum was traditionally for musical performances. Herodes was more interested in the function of his odeum as a lecture-hall, for, under imperial appointment, he was as it were Regius Professor of Rhetoric in the University of Athens. When Agrippa's odeum in the Agora was re-modeled about 150, Herodes almost certainly lectured in its auditorium, now reduced to a capacity of 500, more appro-priate for university lectures than its former size. Pairs of seated statues of philosophers, one pair for each school (Stoic, Academic, Peripatetic, and Epicurean), now adorned the new stair, and the new north porch was suitable for Peripatetic tutorials. To the north façade of this phase be-long the giant and the two colossal tritons (derived from the Parthenon west pediment) still *in situ.*

To the last half of the second century belongs a set of marble plaques, now in the Piraeus Museum next to the Hellenistic theater, near Pasha Limani, the ancient Zea har-bor. They were discovered bedded in harbor mud during dredging operations in 1931. They bear traces of fire that presumably sank a marble-laden ship bound for Rome. Like other sculpture of that period, they are classicistic, imitat-ing the style of the mid-fifth century B.C.; that they are not originals is proved by their heavy moldings, which could not possibly be fifth century; they were left rough for finish-ing when set in place in Rome. The plaques portray several subjects, each in several copies. The most interesting (Fig. 8.22) shows an Amazon of heroic size, jumping from a cliff

FIG. 8.22   Piraeus, Museum. Marble plaque found in harbor in 1931, showing Theseus and an Amazon on the Acropolis (note Ionic columns of Erechtheum North Porch, upper left), and probably derived from Phidias' rendering of the shield of Athena. (DAI, Athens)

rather than fall into the hands of a boyish Greek who pursues her. In the background is a wall, with four Ionic capitals peeping over it. When photographs of the finds were published, in bad half-tone, in the press, this wall provided one clue to the sharp eye of Hans Schrader: he saw that it was the north wall of the Athenian Acropolis; the four columns represent the north porch of the Erechtheum. He also noticed that the composition of the figures was better suited to a round than to a rectangular original, and triumphantly concluded, knowing that Theseus and the Amazons had been a subject on the shield of Phidias' statue of Athena, that the Piraeus finds imitated a Phidian original. The technique, he argued, resembles that of the Parthenon metopes but not that of the pediment or most of the frieze, which would therefore not be Phidian. Thus he turned a chance find into a controversy of great significance in the history of art.

All the buildings in the Agora and many others in Corinth and elsewhere in Greece were burnt in the Herulian sack of 267. With the details of Athens' archaeological history after that date this book, which has traced it for 1500 years, is not concerned; suffice it to say that the odeum in the Agora came into use again about 400, and served educational purposes until Justinian closed the university in 529. The discovery of an olive-press on the west side of the Agora shows what it then became: here was an untidy farmhouse on the edge of a straggling village.

For a final example of archaeological discovery illuminating the Greek world under Roman sway, we travel to the Roman frontier-post of Dura-Europus on the Euphrates 150 miles east of Palmyra. A British sapper digging trenches there in 1920 discovered the site; he reported his discovery to the Baghdad authorities while the great American Orientalist J. H. Breasted was in town. Breasted notified European archaeologists; the French under the Belgian Franz Cumont began digging in 1922-23, the workmen being members of the Foreign Legion. Excavation was resumed (1928-37) by a Yale expedition sponsored by the great economic historian of the Hellenistic and Roman worlds, M. I. Rostovtzeff. What he found was a grid-planned city (Fig. 8.23), a curious mixture of Greek, Semitic, Anatolian, and Parthian influences, going back, he discovered, to 300 B.C., and with a Roman overlay. He called it a Greco-Macedonian islet in a Semitic sea. The dry desert climate preserved wood, textiles, leather, and paper there, so that for scientific interest the finds, in quantity, quality, variety, and state of preservation, rival and sometimes exceed those of Pompeii and Delos.

FORTIFICATIONS

1. Citadel and its palace.
2. Main gate, 177/6 B.C.
3. Subsidiary gate on the desert front (main wall 65 to 18 B.C.).
4. South gate.
4a. Brick wall of the Roman Military Camp.

TEMPLES

5. Temple of Artemis-Nanaia.
6. Zeus Megistos.
7. Atargatis, A.D. 31.
8. Azzanathcona.
9. Bel (?) NW. corner, A.D. 115.
10. Zeus Kyrios, A.D. 29.
11. Aphlad, 54.
12. Gaddé, 159.
13. Zeus Theos, 114.
14. Adonis.
15. Tyche.
16. Military chapel.
17. Christian church, 232–56.
18. Synagogue, 165–200 (paintings. 243–53).

PUBLIC BUILDINGS

19. Acropolis Strategion or redoubt palace.
20. Agora.
21. Sukhs.
22. Kalm.
23. Baths.

MILITARY BUILDINGS

24. Praetorium, 211–17.
25. House of a Higher Officer.
26. Palace of the dux, after 211.
27. Mithraeum, 168–71; phase II, 240.
28. Dolichenium, 210; phase II, 251.
29. Amphitheater.
30. Barracks.

PRIVATE HOUSES

31. House of Lysias.
32. House of the Scribes.
Note: The excavated buildings are shown in plan.
   The excavated streets are shown with solid outlines.
   The unexcavated streets are shown with dotted lines.

FIG. 8.23 Dura-Europus, plan. (After Rostovtzeff, 1938, Fig. 6, by permission of the Clarendon Press, Oxford)

The excavators worked under trying conditions. In the 'twenties the journey to Dura from Beirut took four days and three nights, with the desert as the only road. (Dura was on the ancient caravan route from Antioch to Seleucia-on-the-Tigris.) Digging conditions were unsatisfactory: not only were the Bedouin poor workmen, but the job was dirty, dusty, hot, and tiring. Sandstorms were frequent; the clack of water-wheels and the cry of fox and jackal got on the nerves. The first camp was in the citadel (1 on the plan), whose arches made a dining-room and study, while its roofless towers served for kitchen and storage. There might have been hunting, for food and for diversion—there was wild boar in the tamarisk thickets, and partridge, pigeon, gazelle, and rabbit—but the French, in fear of native uprisings, confiscated all guns. The Euphrates flowed directly below the citadel (a sheer drop: part of the citadel had fallen into the river), but the path to the river was four miles long, the current was too swift for swimming, and the water unsafe for drinking. Under these conditions the patience and devotion of the Yale archaeologists, season after season, was the more remarkable and praiseworthy, and the results, as so often, made the hardships worth while.

The most interesting outcome of the Dura campaigns was to document what happened to a Greco-Macedonian town under oriental and Roman influences. Founded as a fortress-city, Dura-Europus became a caravan town, with unique oriental sukhs or bazaars, like no other Hellenistic or Roman city. The hyphenated name of the place is symbolic: Dura is Babylonian; the original Europus was a town of Macedonia, birthplace of Seleucus I, the founder of the Syrian dynasty. Very little of the Hellenistic city survives, but the walls follow the original line; the grid plan and perhaps the colonnaded main street go back to 300 B.C. The Hellenistic Agora, however (20 on the plan) was overlaid with later buildings. The ruling aristocracy tried to keep its Macedonian stock and nomenclature pure, but it was a losing battle, though Greek remained the official language. The Macedonian colonists began as landowners, but became merchants, took Levantine business partners and wives, and became Levantine themselves. The excavators found the diary of a typical businessman of Dura: he was land-agent, money-lender, merchant, and old-clothes dealer, and his partners were Iranian and Semitic. In one family the father had a Greek name, while his wife's was Semitic, and the children's Greek, Iranian, and Semitic. Palmyrene and, later, Latin occur beside Greek in inscriptions; one *graffito* is significant: it is Latin, but written in Greek letters; it records the number of hams to be served to the Roman *dux ripae* (Officer-in-Command, Euphrates). The houses begin as Macedonian peristyle types, as at Olynthus; they evolve into Babylonian ones, with stables for camels (the evidence is the mangers, set higher than they would be for horses), separate courts for men and women, and flat roofs for sleeping. The wall decoration becomes more and more like an oriental carpet: even Nemrud Dagh is more Greek (though at Dura the more palatial the house, the stronger the Greek influence). The oriental décor is Parthian in inspiration, for the Parthians took Dura in 113 B.C., and, though their policy was non-interference with the city's political, social, economic, cultural, or religious life, the excavators found no Greek buildings datable after 50 B.C., and no civic edifices such as would have served a Greek city-state. The temple of Artemis (5 on the plan) became the center of civilian worship, with a small *bouleutérion;* the temple-court served as Agora or Forum. Dura became an oriental city: its only public buildings were palaces and temples, largely to oriental gods, as the plan's legend shows (and later, under Rome, barracks). The temples are un-Greek: they stand in courts surrounded by chambers with an altar in the middle, but there is no central temple building that a Greek would recognize. The temple of Atargatis (in its second phase, dated by the Yale archaeologists in 31/2) had a small theater with reserved seats for women only. The town's aristocracy with its Greek blood came to worship Palmyrene gods, Zeus appears in Iranian dress, and other gods in Roman uniform.

An earthquake struck in 160 or 161; the citizens must have felt they had suffered another when under the Severan dynasty the Romans took over and made the city into a mere garrison-town, existing to feed and house Roman soldiers. Roman officers had little or no contact with civilians, though the petty officers probably made an occupation force's usual informal arrangements. The whole northwest quarter became a Roman armed camp, set off by a brick wall (4A), its private houses made over into barracks. It had an amphitheater (29) for gladiatorial shows, a Mithraeum (27) for the soldiers' favorite worship, a praetorium, with propylon, court, and sanctuary for the legion's standards. The Roman army's religious calendar, the *Feriale Duranum,* records oriental gods beside the deified Roman imperial family. Among the townsfolk Judaism and Christianity flourished. The evidence is a synagogue (17) of about 243, discovered by chance under a ramp near the main gate (2), and a Christian church nearby (18), made over from a private house. Its frescoes include Adam and Eve, David and Goliath, Christ walking on water, the Good Shepherd, and the three Marys at Christ's tomb. The synagogue, with its three tiers of panels illustrating the Old Testament, is restored in the Damascus Museum, the church (Fig. 8.24) in Yale's Museum of Fine Arts. Paradoxically and significantly, Christian art at Dura is much more Greek than the rest of Dura's décor, for the Christian influence came to Dura from Greek Antioch or Alexandria.

As the third century wore on, Rome, racked by domestic anarchy, grew progressively less able to protect the caravan routes, which in consequence bypassed Dura, and the town began to decline. In 256 Sapur I, King of the new Persian Sassenid dynasty, struck, and Dura fell. The excavators

Fig. 8.24   Dura-Europus, font and west wall of Christian church, reconstructed: the three Marys at Christ's tomb. (New Haven, Yale Gallery of Fine Arts)

found the mute and tragic evidence in a tunnel under the wall: some twenty Roman skeletons, armed, with money in their belts; opposite them, a single Sassanian, with a sword.

Here ends our selective survey of the Greek world under Roman sway. Its wide range, from Cyrene to Dura, has told everywhere the same story, one of a mixture of influences, Greek, Roman, and native. Greek architectural forms are usually the inspiration (as at Nemrud Dagh, Augustan Athens, Roman Corinth, and Christian Dura); the massiveness and the money are usually Roman (Baalbek, Hadrianic Athens), but Herodes Atticus was a Greek patron of architects in a tradition that goes back to the tyrants of archaic times. Against this architectural background native life went on, taking its own way, but influenced and pervaded, as the world has been ever since, by the culture that we have traced from its Neolithic beginning through Bronze Age richness, Iron Age decline, archaic lyrical strength, Periclean prime, fourth-century status quo, and Hellenistic baroque revival. This complicated, important, and fascinating story the archaeologists' spade and pen have revealed: our world owes them a great debt for so eloquently making the Greek stones speak.

ADDENDUM
(All dates approximate)

B.C.

126	Delos, Agora of Theophrastus
112	Delos, House of Poseidoniasts
after 69	Delos, Triarius' Wall
62	Nemrud Dagh, Antiochus I's tomb
50	Athens, Tower of the Winds
after 48	Eleusis, Lesser Propylaea

44   Corinth, Basilica; South Stoa (phase)
          Eleusis, Lesser Propylaea
          Athens, Roman Agora
after 31 Athens, Temple of Rome and Augustus
          Athens, Temple of Ares, reconstruction
          Corinth, Propylaea arch
15   Athens, Odeum of Agrippa
10   Athens, Gate of Athena Archegetis
4/3   Ephesus, Agora, west gate

A.D.

10   Baalbek, Temple of Jupiter (phase)
25-50   Corinth, central shops
31/2   Dura, Temple of Atargatis, Phase II
32   Palmyra, Temple of Bel, Phase I
40   Corinth, twin basilicas
41-54   Ephesus, theater (phase)
49   Philippi, St. Paul's visit
54   Ephesus, Marble Street; stadium
67   Corinth, theater (phase)
70   Palmyra, Temple of Bel, court
before 75 Gerasa, walls
76 ff.   Palmyra, Agora
81-96   Ephesus, Temple of Domitian; Harbor Baths
before 83 Gerasa, South Theater
98-117   Ephesus, theater (phase)
          Cyrene, Caesareum
100   Palmyra, Corinthian temple
          Athens, Library of Pantainos
106   Ephesus, Library of Celsus
116   Athens, Philopappos monument
120-150   Palmyra, theater; tetrapylon
120-200   Baalbek, Temple of Jupiter, Altar Court
124-127   Ephesus, Portico of Verulanius
after 129 Eleusis, Hadrianic Arch
before 130 Baalbek, Temple of Bacchus
132   Athens, Olympieum, Hadrian's Wall, Gate, Library, etc.
135   Corinth, theater, marble phase
after 136/7 Eleusis, Temple of Sabina
138-161   Ephesus, Vedius Gymnasium, Baths & Odeum
after 140/1 Eleusis, Temple of Faustina the Elder
143/4   Athens, Stadium of Herodes Atticus
147   Delphi, stadium, marble seats
148   Palmyra, "Camp of Diocletian"

150	Athens, Agora Odeum, Phase II
150-200	Piraeus, marble plaques
153/4	Olympia, Exedra of Herodes Atticus
161 ff.	Athens, Odeum of Herodes Atticus
	Eleusis, Greater Propylaea
161	Corinth Pirene, Herodes Atticus phase
163	Gerasa, North Theater
before 174	Eleusis, Temple of Artemis
174	Palmyra, Temple of Bel, Propylaea, towers
175	Corinth, Odeum
185	Corinth, Temple of Poseidon
after 185	Cyrene, Temple of Zeus, rebuilding
190	Dura, synagogue
191	Corinth, Temple of Heracles
192	Ephesus, Serapeum
200	Sardis, synagogue
211	Dura, Praetorium
211-217	Corinth, theater remodeled into arena
	Sardis, Marble Court
232	Dura, Christian church
245	Baalbek, Temple of Venus
250	Philippi, baths
256	Dura falls to Sassanians
263	Ephesus destroyed by Goths
267	Athens, Herulian sack
272	Palmyra destroyed by Valerian
370	Kenchreai, Isis panels
400	Eleusis, Mithraeum

ABBREVIATIONS

AA: Archäologischer Anzeiger
AbhBay: Abhandlungen der philosophisch-philologischen Klasse der königlich Bayerischen Akademie der Wissenschaften
AJA: American Journal of Archaeology
AM: Mitteilungen des Deutschen Archäologischen Instituts, Athenische Abteilung
AntJ: Antiquaries' Journal
ANRW: Aufstieg und Niedergang der römischen Welt
AP&P: Ancient Peoples and Places
APB: Agora Picture Books
Arch: Archaeology
ArchClass: Archeologia Classica
ArchEph: Archaiologike Ephemeris
ASAtene: Annuario della R. Scuola Archeologica di Atene
ASCS: American School of Classical Studies
BASOR: Bulletin of the American Schools of Oriental Research
BCH: Bulletin de correspondance hellénique
BdA: Bolletino d'Arte
BMMA: Bulletin of the Metropolitan Museum of Art, New York
BSA: British School at Athens, Annual
BSR: British School of Archaeology at Rome, Papers
BSRAA: Bulletin de la Société r. d'archéologie d'Alexandrie
CAH: Cambridge Ancient History
CJ: Classical Journal
DAI: Deutsches Archäologisches Institut
Delt: Archaiologikon Deltion
EI: Enciclopedia italiana
Erg: To Ergon tes Archaiologikes Hetaireias
EtCret: Études crétoises
FA: Fasti Archaeologici
FdD: Fouilles de Delphes

GRBS: Greek, Roman, and Byzantine Studies
Hdbh: Handbuch
Hesp: Hesperia
HSCP: Harvard Studies in Classical Philology
ILN: Illustrated London News
JHS: Journal of Hellenic Studies
JNES: Journal of Near Eastern Studies
MMS: Metropolitan Museum Studies
NDA: Neue deutsche Ausgrabungen, Berlin 1959
OpusArch: Opuscula Archaeologica
Prakt: Praktika tes en Athenais Archaiologikes Hetairias
ProcPS: Proceedings of the Prehistoric Society
ProcPhilSoc: Proceedings of the American Philosophical Society
RA: Revue archéologique
RE: Pauly-Wissowa, Real-Encyclopädie der klassischen Altertumswis-
    senschaft
SBWien: Sitzungsberichte der Akademie der Wissenschaften in Wien
SkrLund: Skrifter utgivna av Vetenskaps-Societeten i Lund
SMA: Studies in Mediterranean Archaeology
SPHS: Society for the Promotion of Hellenic Studies
TCI: Touring Club Italiano

BOOKS AND ARTICLES CONSULTED

CHAPTER 1: *The Aegean in Prehistory*

T. D. Atkinson *et al.*, "Excavations at Phylakopi in Melos," *SPHS Suppl. Papers* 4 (London 1904)

L. Bernabò Brea, "A Bronze Age House at Poliochni (Lemnos)," *ProcPS* 21 (1955) 144-155; *id. ILN* 231 (1957), 197-199. A new work by B. B. on Poliochni [Vol. 1, Rome 1964] had reached 4 vols. by 1976

C. W. Blegen, "Preclassical Greece," U. of Penn. Bicentennial Conference, *Studies in the Arts and Architecture* (Philadelphia 1941) 1-4

———— *et al., Troy* I-IV (Princeton 1950-58)

H. Bulle, "Orchomenos I," *AbhBay* 24 (1907)

J. L. Caskey, "The Early Helladic Period in the Argolid," *Hesp* 29 (1960) 285-303

P. Dikaios, *A Guide to the Cyprus Museum* (Nicosia 1947)

W. Dörpfeld, *Troia und Ilion* (Berlin 1902)

S. Dow, "The Greeks in the Bronze Age," (*Rapports du XIe Congrès International des Sciences Historiques* 2 (Göteborg 1960) 1-34

Sir Arthur Evans, *The Palace of Minos* I-IV (Oxford 1921-36)

Joan Evans, *Time and Chance* (London 1943)

H. Goldman, *Excavations at Eutresis in Boeotia* (Cambridge, Mass. 1931)

N. G. L. Hammond, *A History of Greece to 322 B.C.* (Oxford 1959)

E. Kunze, "Orchomenos II-III," *AbhBay* n.F. 5 (1931); 8 (1934)

W. Lamb, *Excavations at Thermi in Lesbos* (Cambridge 1936)

D. Levi, "Attività della Scuola archeologica italiana di Atene nel anno 1951," *BdA* ser. 4, 37 (1952) 320-348

F. Matz, "Die Agäis," *Hdbh der Archäologie* VI, ii (Munich 1954) 180-308

———, *Kreta, Mykene, Troia* (Stuttgart 1956) 1-41

K. Müller *et al.*, *Tiryns: die Ergebnisse der Ausgrabungen*, III-VIII (Augsburg, Munich 1930-76)

D. L. Page, *History and the Homeric Iliad* (Berkeley 1959)

J. D. S. Pendlebury, *The Archaeology of Crete* (London 1939)

———, *A Handbook to the Palace of Minos at Knossos* (London 1954)

F. Schachermeyr, *Die ältesten Kulturen Griechenlands* (Stuttgart 1955)

———, "Prähistorische Kulturen Greichenlands," *RE* (1954) Sp. 1350-1548

Chr. Tsountas, *Hai prohistorikai akropoleis Diminiou kai Sesklou* (Athens 1908)

———, "Kykladika," *ArchEph* 1898, 138-212; *ib.* 1899, 73-134

CHAPTER 2: *"Mycenae, Rich in Gold"*

Works already cited: Atkinson, Bulle, Dow, Evans, Levi, Müller, Page, Pendlebury, Schachermeyr

C. W. Blegen, "Excavations at Pylos," *AJA* 43 (1939) 557-576; 57 (1953) 59-64; 58 (1954) 27-32; 59 (1955) 31-37; 60 (1956) 95-101; 61 (1957) 129-135; 62 (1958) 175-191; 63 (1959) 121-137; 64 (1960) 153-164; 65 (1961) 152-163; 66 (1962) 145-152

——— *et al.*, *Troy IV* (Princeton 1958)

J. Chadwick, *The Decipherment of Linear B* [2] (Cambridge 1967)

F. Chapouthier *et al.*, "Fouilles executées à Mallia," *EtCret* 1 (Paris 1928); 2 (1930); 4 (1936); 6 (1942); 7 (1945); 9 (1953)

R. M. Dawkins, J. P. Droop, "Excavations at Phylakopi in Melos 1911," *BSA* 17 (1911) 1-22

W. B. Dinsmoor, *The Architecture of Ancient Greece* [3] (London 1950)

H. D Ephron, "Hygieia Tharso and Iaon: The Phaistos Disk," *HSCP* 66 (1962) 1-91

A. Furumark, "Linear A und die altkretische Sprache" (Berlin 1956) Mimeographed lecture to Arch. Gesellschaft.

G. Glotz, *The Aegean Civilization* (London 1925)

J. W. Graham, *The Cretan Palaces* (Princeton 1962)

H. B. Hawes *et al.*, *Gournia* (Philadelphia 1908)

J. Hazzidakis, "Les villas minoennes de Tylissos," *EtCret* 3 (Paris 1934)

A. W. Lawrence, *Greek Architecture* (Harmondsworth 1957) 1-82

O. Montelius, *La Grèce préclassique* I (Stockholm 1924) 134-148 (Gla)

G. E. Mylonas, *Mycenae and the Mycenaean Age* (Princeton 1966)

———, *Eleusis and the Eleusinian Mysteries* (Princeton 1961)

L. Pernier, L. Banti, *Il palazzo minoico di Festòs*, 2 vols. (Rome 1935, 1951)

———, ———, *Guida degli scavi italiani in Creta* (Rome 1947) 28-38 (H. Triada)

A. W. Persson, "The Royal Tombs at Dendra," *SkrLund* 15 (1931)

———, "New Tombs at Dendra," *ib.* 34 (1942)

D. S. Robertson, *A Handbook of Greek and Roman Architecture*[2] (Cambridge 1954)

K. Scholes, "The Cyclades in the Later Bronze Age: A Synopsis," *BSA* 51 (1956) 9-40

B. Schwartz, "The Phaistos Disk," *JNES* 18 (1959) 105-112, 222-228

M. Ventris, J. Chadwick, "Evidence for Greek Dialect in the Mycenaean Archives," *JHS* 73 (1953) 84-103

———, ———, *Documents in Mycenaean Greek*[2] (Cambridge 1973)

T. B. L. Webster, *From Mycenae to Homer* (London 1958)

CHAPTER 3: *Mycenaean Athens*, etc.

J. L. Angel, "Skeletal Material from Attica," *Hesp* 14 (1945) 279-363

J. Boardman, *The Cretan Collection in Oxford* (Oxford 1961), esp. Ch. V

O. Broneer, "A Mycenaean Fountain on the Athenian Acropolis," *Hesp* 8 (1939) 317-429

————, "Athens in the Late Bronze Age," *Antiquity* 30 (1956) 9-18

D. Burr, "A Geometric House," *Hesp* 2 (1933) 542-640

E. Buschor, "Heraion von Samos: frühe Bauten," *AM* 55 (1930) 1-99

J. M. Cook *et al.*, "Old Smyrna, 1948-1951," *BSA* 53-54 (1958-59) 1-181; *ILN* 222 (1953) 328-29

R. M. Dawkins *et al.*, "Excavations at Sparta," *BSA* 12 (1905-06) 277-479; 13 (1906-07) 1-218; 14 (1907-08) 1-158; 15 (1908-09) 1-157; 16 (1909-10) 1-67; *id.*, *Artemis Orthia* (London 1929)

V. R. d'A. Desborough, *Protogeometric Pottery* (Oxford 1952)

P. Dikaios, *op. cit.* supra, Ch. 2

H. Ephron, "The Jeson Tablet of Enkomi," *HSCP* 65 (1961) 39-107

A. Furumark, "The Settlement at Ialysos," *OpusArch* 6 (1950) 150-271

E. H. Hall, *Excavations in Eastern Crete: Vrocastro* (Philadelphia 1914)

L. B. Holland, "The Strong House of Erechtheus," *AJA* 28 (1924) 142-169

W. Kraiker, K. Kübler, *Kerameikos: Ergebnisse der Ausgrabungen* I (Berlin 1939)

Sp. Marinatos, "Le temple géometrique de Dréros," *BCH* 60 (1936) 214-285

W. R. Paton, "Excavations in Caria," *JHS* 8 (1887) 64-82

H. Payne *et al.*, *Perachora* I (Oxford 1940)

J. D. S. Pendlebury *et al.*, "Excavations in the Plain of Lasithi III, i: Karphi," *BSA* 38 (1937-38) 57-145

K. Rhomaios, "Ek tou prohistorikou Thermou," *Delt* 1 (1915) 225-279

C. F. E. Schaeffer, "Enkomi," *AJA* 52 (1948) 165-171

————, *Enkomi-Alasia* (Paris 1952)

C. G. Starr, *The Origins of Greek Civilization, 1100-650 B.C.* (New York 1961)

E. D. Townsend, "A Mycenaean Chamber Tomb under the Temple of Ares," *Hesp* 24 (1955) 187-219

J. Travlos, *Poleodomike Exelexis ton Athenon* (Athens 1960) 19-32. Eng. tr. forthcoming.

G. Welter, "Vom Nikepyrgos," *AA* 54 (1939) 2-22

S. Wide, "Gräberfunde aus Salamis," *AM* 35 (1910) 17-36

CHAPTER 4: *The Lyric Age*

P. Amandry, "La Colonne des Naxiens et le Portique des Athéniens," *FdD* II, ii (Paris 1953)

G. Ardaillon, *Les mines de Laurion dans l'antiquité* (Paris 1897)

E. Bethe, "Das archaische Delos," *Die Antike* 14 (1938) 81-119

R. M. Cook, *Greek Painted Pottery* (London 1960)

G. Dickins, *Catalogue of the Acropolis Museum* I (Cambridge 1912)

W. Dörpfeld, *Alt-Olympia*, 2 vols (Berlin 1935)

Sir J. G. Frazer, *Pausanias* 2 (London 1898) 433 ff. (Marathon mound)

A. Furtwängler, *Aegina: das Heiligtum der Aphaia*, 2 vols. (Munich 1906)

H. Gallet de Santerre, *Délos primitive et archaique* (Paris 1958)

E. Ghislanzoni, "Cirene," *EI* (1931)

R. Hampe, "Die neuen deutschen Ausgrabungen in Olympia," *Die Antike* 14 (1938) 243-248

I. T. Hill, *The Ancient City of Athens* (Cambridge, Mass. 1953), ch. 14 (Pre-Periclean Acropolis)

Fr. Hiller von Gaertringen, *Thera*, 4 vols. (Berlin 1899-1904)

R. Horn, "Kyrene," *Die Antike* 19 (1943) 163-213

J. Hulot, G. Fougères, *Sélinonte: ville, acropole, temples* (Paris 1910)

P. Kavvadias, G. Kawerau, *Die Ausgrabung der Acropolis, 1885-1890* (Athens 1908)

F. Krauss et al., *Paestum: die griechischen Tempel* 4 (Berlin 1978)

P. de La Coste-Messelière, G. de Miré, *Delphes* (Paris 1943)

G. E. Mylonas, "The Cemeteries of Eleusis and Mycenae," *ProcPhilSoc* 99 (1955) 57-67

J. V. Noble, "The Technique of Attic Vase-Painting," *AJA* 64 (1960) 307-318

H. Payne, G. M. Young, *Archaic Sculpture from the Acropolis* (London 1936)

G. Rodenwaldt, *Korkyra: archaische Bauten und Bildwerke I: Der Artemistempel: Architektur, Dachterrakotten, Inschriften* (Berlin 1940); II, *Die Bildwerke des Artemistempels* (*ib.* 1939)

C. T. Seltman, *Athens: its History and Coinage before the Persian Invasion* (Cambridge 1924)

C. P. Sestieri, *Paestum* [8] (*Itinerari dei Musei e Monumenti d'Italia,* Rome 1967)

T. L. Shear, H. A. Thompson, annual reports on excavations in the Athenian Agora (see infra, Ch. 8)

J. Travlos, *op. cit.* supra, Ch. 3, 33-46 (Archaic Athens)

G. Welter, *Aegina* (Berlin 1940)

P. Zancani-Montuoro, U. Zanotti-Bianco, *Heraion alla Foce del Sele,* 2 vols. text, 2 vols. plates (Rome 1951-54)

CHAPTER 5: *The Classical Age*

W. R. Agard, "What is 'Classical' Sculpture?," *CJ* 49 (1954) 341-349

N. Balanos, *Les monuments de l'acropole: relèvement et conservation,* 2 vols. (Paris 1938)

J. A. Bundgaard, *Mnesicles: A Greek Architect at Work* (Copenhagen 1957)

Rhys Carpenter, *The Sculpture of the Nike Temple Parapet* (Cambridge, Mass. 1929)

J. Chamoux, "L'aurige," *FdD* IV.5 (Paris 1955)

E. Curtius, F. Adler, *Olympia: Ergebnisse der Ausgrabung* I (Berlin 1897)

W. B. Dinsmoor, *op. cit.* supra, Ch. 2

———, "Observations on the Hephaisteion," *Hesp* Suppl 5 (1941)

———, "The Temple of Apollo at Bassae," *MMS* 4 (1933) 204-226

———, "The Sculptured Frieze from Bassae: A Revised Sequence," *AJA* 60 (1956) 401-452

E. N. Gardner, *Olympia, its History and Remains* (Oxford 1925)

R. Hampe, U. Jentzen, W. Wrede, *Bericht über die Ausgrabungen in Olympia* I (Berlin 1937)

I. T. Hill, *op. cit.* supra, Ch. 4, Chs. 9, 15, 16

M. B. Jameson, "A Decree of Themistocles from Troizen," *Hesp* 29 (1960) 198-223

Chr. Karouzos, "Ho Poseidon tou Artemisiou," *Delt* 13 (1930/31) 41-104

H. Kenner, *Die Fries des Tempels von Bassae-Phigalia* (Vienna 1946)

R. Koldewey, O. Puchstein, *Die griechischen Tempel in Unteritalien und Sizilien* (Berlin 1899)

F. Krauss, *op. cit.*, supra, Ch. 4.

E. Kunze, H. Schleif, *II-VI Berichte über die Ausgrabungen in Olympia* (Berlin 1938-58)

B. D. Meritt, H. T. Wade-Gery, M. F. McGregor, *The Athenian Tribute Lists*, 4 vols. (Cambridge, Mass. 1939-53)

J. Papadimitriou, "Anaskaphai en Brauroni tes Attikes," *Prakt* 1945/8, 81-90; 1949, 75-90; 1950, 173-187. See also *Erg* 1956, 25-31; 1957, 20-25; 1958; 30-39; 1960, 21-30.

J. M. Paton *et al.*, *The Erechtheum*, 2 vols. (Cambridge, Mass. 1927)

F. C. Penrose, *An Investigation of the Principles of Athenian Architecture*[2] (London 1888)

T. L. Shear, H. A. Thompson, *loc. cit.* infra, Ch. 8

A. H. Smith, "Lord Elgin and his Collection," *JHS* 36 (1916) 163-370

D. B. Thompson, "The House of Simon the Shoemaker," *Arch* 13 (1960) 239-240

J. Travlos, *op. cit.* supra, Ch. 3. Ch. 3

F. Villard, *Sicile grecque* (Paris 1955)

T. B. L. Webster, *Greek Art and Literature 530-400 B.C.* (Oxford 1939)

CHAPTER 6: *The Fourth Century*

O. Benndorf, R. Heberdey, W. Wilberg, J. Keil, *Forschungen in Ephesus*, 4 vols. (Vienna 1906-23)

C. W. Blegen, "The December Excavations at Nemea," *Art and Archaeology* 22 (1926) 127-134

———, "*Excavations at Nemea, 1926,*" *AJA* 31 (1927) 421-440

E. Bourguet, *Les ruines de Delphes* (Paris 1914)

O. Broneer, "Excavations at Isthmia," *Hesp* 22 (1953) 182-195; 24 (1955) 110-141; 27 (1958) 1-37; 28 (1959) 298-343

H. C. Butler, *Sardis* I. i, II. i (Leyden, 1922-25)

A. Defrasse, H. Lechat, *Epidaure, restauration et description des principaux monuments du sanctuaire d'Asclèpios* (Paris 1895)

W. Dörpfeld, "Die Skeuothek des Philon," *AM* 8 (1883) 147-164

G. Fougères, *Mantinée et l'Arcadie orientale* (Paris 1898)

E. A. Gardner *et al.*, "Excavations at Megalopolis, 1890-91," *SPHS Suppl. Papers* I (London 1892)

D. G. Hogarth, *British Museum Excavations at Ephesus: the Archaic Artemisia* (London 1908)

P. Kavvadias, *To hieron tou Asklepiou en Epidauroi* (Athens 1900)

H. Knackfuss, *Didyma* I, 3 vols. (Berlin 1941)

E. Kunze, "Neue Ausgrabungen in Olympia," *NDA* 263-310

M. Mayer, "Miletos," *RE* (1932), esp. Sp. 1622-1655

C. T. Newton, *A History of the Discoveries at Halicarnassus* (London 1862)

A. N. Orlandos, reports on excavation at Messene, *Erg.* 1956-60, esp. 1957, 75-80; 1958, 142-148; 1959, 110-117; 1960, 159-167

A. W. Pickard-Cambridge, *The Theater of Dionysus in Athens* (Oxford 1946); 2nd ed., D. M. Lewis, *ib.* 1962

A. Rehm, *Didyma* II (Berlin 1958) 321 ff.

G. M. A. Richter, "A Tanagra Statuette," *BMMA* 26 (1931) 18-20

D. M. Robinson, J. W. Graham, "The Hellenic House," *Excavations at Olynthus* VIII (Baltimore 1938)

E. G. S. Robinson, "The Coins from the Ephesian Artemision Reconsidered," *JHS* 71 (1951) 156-167

H. A. Thompson, R. L. Scranton, "Stoas and City Walls on the Pnyx," *Hesp* 12 (1943) 269-383

E. Vanderpool, "News Letter from Athens," *AJA* 64 (1960) 265-267 (Piraeus finds)

T. Wiegand, H. Schrader, *Priene: Ergebnisse der Ausgrabungen 1895-8* (Berlin 1904)

J. Wiesner, "Olympia," *RE* (1939) Sp. 75-174

J. T. Wood, *Discoveries at Ephesus* (London 1877)

CHAPTER 7: *The Hellenistic Age*

B. Ashmole, "Hellenistic Art," *CAH* 8 (1930) 668-708

Chr. Blinkenberg, K. F. Kinch, E. Dyggve, *Lindos, fouilles et recherches 1902-1914, 1952,* 3 vols. in 4 (Berlin and Copenhagen 1931, 1942, 1960)

E. Boehringer, "Pergamon," *NDA* 121-151 (Asklepieion)

J. Bradford, "Aerial Discoveries in Rhodes," *AntJ* 36 (1956) 57-69

E. Breccia, *Alexandrea ad Aegyptum* (Bergamo 1922)

E. Dusenbery, "A Samothracian Necropolis," *Arch* 12 (1959) 163-170

E. M. Forster, *Pharos and Pharillon* (London 1918)

———, *Alexandria: a Guide* [2] (New York 1961). First edition, 1922, by a novelist turned archaeologist

A. Gabriel, "La construction, l'attitude, et l'emplacement du Colosse de Rhodes," *BCH* 56 (1932) 331-359

L. Heuzey, H. Daumet, *Mission archéologique de Macédoine,* 2 vols. (Paris 1876). I, 175-226: Palatitsa

H. Kähler, *Der grosse Fries von Pergamon* (Berlin 1948)

J. D. Kondis, "Anaskaphikai ereunai eis ten polin tes Rhodou," *Prakt* 1951, 224-245; 1952, 547-591; 1953, 275-287; 1954, 340-360; 1955, 267-283

D. I. Lazarides, *Thasos* (Salonika 1958). Superseded by the French School's *Guide de Thasos* (Paris 1968)

K. Lehmann, *Samothrace* [4] (New York 1975); final publ., 9 vols. in 5, New York, 1958-81

R. Martin, "L'agora," *Études thasiennes* 6(1959)

M. Mellink, "Archaeology in Asia Minor." *AJA* 59 (1955) 236-37; 60 (1956) 381-82; 62 (1958) 98-99; 63 (1959) 83-84; 64 (1960) 66; 65 (1961) 48-49 (Claros)

L. Morricone, "Scavi e ricerche a Coo, 1935-43," *BdA* 35 (1950) 54-75, 219-246, 316-331

P. Petsas, "New Discoveries at Pella," *Arch* 11 (1958) 246-254

K. A. Rhomaios, "To anaktoron tes Palatitsas," *ArchEph* 1953/54 (1955) 141-150

P. Roussel, *Délos* (Paris 1925)

A. Rowe, "Excavations at Pompey's Pillar," *BSRAA* 35 (1942) 124-161

———, "Excavations at Kôm-el-Shukafa," *ib.* 3-45

P. Schazmann, *Kos* I, i: *Asklepieion* (Berlin 1932)

J. Schramm, "Der grosse Altar," *Altertümer von Pergamon* III. i (Berlin 1906)

E. Schulte, *Der Pergamon-Altar, entdeckt, beschrieben, und gezeichnet von Carl Humann* (Dortmund 1960)

E. Sjöqvist, R. Stilwell, "Excavations at Morgantina (Serra Orlando)," *AJA* 61 (1957) 151-159; 62 (1958) 158-164; 63 (1959) 169-173; 64 (1960) 125-135; 65 (1961) 277-281; 66 (1962) 135-143

H. A. Thompson, "Stoa of Attalus," *Arch* 2 (1949) 124-130; see also *Hesp* 23 (1954) 55-57; 24 (1955) 59-61; 25 (1956) 66-68; 26 (1957) 103-107

R. Vallois, *L'architecture hellénique et hellénistique à Delos* (Paris 1944)

H. Winnefeld, "Die Friese der grossen Altars," *Alt. von Perg.* III. ii (Berlin 1910)

W. Zschietzschmann, "Pergamon," *RE* (1937) Sp. 1235-1266

CHAPTER 8: *The Greek World under Roman Sway*

E. Bacon, *Digging up History* (London 1960) 80-84 (Athenian Agora)

O. Broneer, "Terracotta Lamps," *Corinth* IV. ii (Cambridge, Mass. 1930)

————, *A Guide to the Excavations of Ancient Corinth* [4] (new ed., with C. K. Williams, Athens 1969)

F. Dörner, "Die Entdeckung vom Arsameia am Nymphenfluss und die Ausgrabungen im Hierothesion des Mithradates Kallinikos von Kommagene," *NDA* 71-88

T. Goell, "The Excavation of the 'Hierothesion' of Antiochus I of Commagene on Nemrud Dagh (1953-56)," *BASOR* 147 (Oct., 1957) 4-22

P. Graindor, *Athènes sous Auguste* (Cairo 1927)

————, *Athènes sous Hadrien* (Cairo 1934)

————, *Un milliardaire antique: Hérode Atticus et sa famille* (Cairo 1930)

E. Honigmann, "Kommagene" *RE* Supplbd 4 (1924) Sp. 978-990

R. Horn, *loc. cit.* supra, Ch. 4

C. Humann, O. Puchstein, *Reisen in Kleinasien und Nordsyrien* (Berlin 1890). Nemrud Dagh.

G. Karo, "Archäologische Funde," *AA* 1931, 224-227. Piraeus plaques.

C. Kraeling, *Gerasa* (New Haven 1938)

M. Lang, C. W. J. Eliot, *The Athenian Agora: A Guide to the Excavations* (Athens 1954 and later eds.)

———, "The Athenian Citizen," *APB* 4 (Princeton 1960). Kleroteria.

D. Levi, "Missioni in Levante," *ASAtene* n.s. 19/20 (1957/58) 398-401. Cyrene

F. Miltner, *Ephesos* (Vienna 1958)

F. von Oppeln-Bronikowsky, *Archäologische Entdeckungen im 20. Jahrhundert* (Berlin 1931). Piraeus plaques.

H. Plommer, *Ancient and Classical Architecture* (London 1956)

D. M. Robinson, *Baalbek and Palmyra* (New York 1946)

H. S. Robinson, "The Tower of the Winds and the Roman Market-Place," *AJA* 47 (1943) 291-305

M. Rostovtzeff, *Caravan Cities* (Oxford 1932.). Palmyra and Dura.

———, *Dura-Europus and Its Art* (Oxford 1938)

G. Roux, *Pausanias en Corinthe* (Paris 1958)

H. C. Rutledge, "Herodes Atticus, the Greek Citizen of the World," *CJ* 56 (1960/61) 97-109

H. Schrader, "Archäologische Funde," *AA* 1931, 287-293. Piraeus plaques

R. L. Scranton, "The Lower Agora," *Corinth* I. iii (Cambridge, Mass. 1951)

T. L. Shear, annual reports on excavations in the Athenian Agora, *Hesp* 2 (1933); 4-10 (1935-41)

M. A. Sisson, "The Stoa of Hadrian at Athens," *BSR* 11 (1929) 50-72

H. A. Thompson, annual reports on excavations in the Athenian Agora, *Hesp* 16 (1947)-29 (1960)

———, "Buildings on the West Side of the Agora," *ib.* 6 (1937) 1-226

———, "The Odeion in the Athenian Agora," *ib.* 19 (1950) 31-141

———, "The Athenian Agora (A Sketch of the Evolution of its Plan)," *Acta Congressi Madvigiani* 1 (Copenhagen 1958) 341-352

C. Watzinger, "Palmyra," *RE* (1949) Sp. 262-277

S. S. Weinberg, "The Southeast Building; the Twin Basilicas," *Corinth* I. v (Princeton 1960) 35-109

T. Wiegand, *Baalbek*, 3 vols. (Berlin 1921-25)

————, *Palmyra: Ergebnisse der Expeditionen von 1902 und 1917*, 2 vols. (Berlin 1932)

ADDENDA TO LIST OF BOOKS AND ARTICLES CONSULTED

General

M. Andronikos *et al.*, eds., *Historia tou Hellenikou Ethnous*, 5 vols. in 4 (Athens 1970-73). Eng. trans., ed. Philip Sherrard (London 1974-   ). Richly illustrated

Archaeological Reports, annual supplement to *JHS*, since 1954

W. G. Biers, *Greek Archaeology* (Ithaca, N.Y. 1980). Up to date; richly illustrated

*CAH*³ vols. 1 and 2 (4 vols. in 2; Cambridge 1970-75). From prehistoric times to 1000 B.C.

R. M. and K. Cook, *Companion Guide to Southern Greece* (London 1968)

Enciclopedia di Arte Antica Classica, 7 vols. and suppl. (Rome 1958-70). Authoritative articles, well illustrated. *N.B.* Italian spelling—e.g., Atene, Festos, Pesto, Pidna, Siracusa

M. I. Finley, *Atlas of Classical Archaeology* (London 1977)

E. Kristen, W. Kraiker, *Griechenlandkunde*⁵, 2 vols. (Heidelberg 1967)

D. Leekley, R. Noyes, *Archaeological Excavations in the Greek Islands* (Park Ridge, N.J. 1975). Summaries and bibliography. See also their volume on Southern Greece (1976) and Leekley's volume on Central and Northern Greece (1980)

C. M. Robertson, *A History of Greek Art*, 2 vols. (Cambridge 1975)

S. Rossiter, ed., *Blue Guides: Greece* (London 1977). Absolutely accurate and admirable. Maps, plans

R. V. Schoder, *Ancient Greece from the Air* (New York and London 1974)

R. E. Stilwell *et al.*, *Princeton Encyclopedia of Classical Sites*. Articles, mostly by the excavators, on all post-Mycenaean sites. For caveat, see *Classical Philology* 74 (1979) 78-82. Articles from which I have derived profit: Aigina, Akragas, Amyklai, Argive Heraion, Argos, Asine, Athens, Bassai (Phygaleia), Beroia, Chaironeia, Claros, Corinth, Delos, Delphi, Dherveni, Didyma, Dodona, Dreros, Dura, Eleusis, Ephesos, Epidauros, Eretria, Foce del Sele, Gela, Gerasa, Halieis, Halikarnassos, Hieropolis (Baalbek), Iasos, Isthmia, Kalauria, Kenchreai, Keos, Kerkyra, Kos, Kydonia, Kythera, Laurion, Lemnos, Limes (Attica), Mantinea, Marathon, Megalopolis, Melos (Phylakopi), Messene, Miletos, Morgantina, Myrina, Nemea, Nemrud Dagh, Olympia, Olynthos, Orchomenos (Boeotia), Oropos, Paestum, Palmyra, Peiraieus, Perachora, Pergamon, Philippi, Priene, Prinias, Ptoion, Pydna, Rhamnous, Rhodes (incl. Ialysos, Kameiros, Lindos), Samos, Samothrace, Sardis, Segesta, Selinus, Sounion, Sparta, Syracuse, Tanagra, Tegea, Thasos, Thera, Thermon, Thorikos, Troizen, Verghina, Vouni, Xanthos.

CHAPTER 1: *The Aegean in Prehistory*

L. Bernabo Brea, *Poliochni 2* (Rome 1976)

C. W. Blegen, "Troy," (*AP&P*, London 1963)

H.-G. Buchholz, V. Karageorgis, *Prehistoric Greece and Cyprus* (London 1973). Exhaustive documentation, rich illustration

J. M. Cook, *The Troad* (Oxford 1973)

L. Dor, J. Jannoray, H. and M. van Effenterre, *Kirrha: Étude de préhistoire phocidienne* (Paris 1960)

O. Frödin, A. W. Persson, *Asine 1922-30* (Stockholm 1938)

N. G. L. Hammond, *Migrations and Invasions in Greece and Adjacent Areas* (Park Ridge, N.J. 1976). Emphasis on transhumance, and migrations from Albania and Epirus

R. Hope Simpson, "Gazetteer of Mycenaean Sites," *Studies in Mycenaean Archaeology* 52 (1979)

R. W. Hutchinson, *Prehistoric Crete* [2] (Harmondsworth 1968)

V. Karageorgis, *The Ancient Civilization of Cyprus* (New York 1969)

D. Leekley, R. Noyes, *Archaeological Excavations in the Greek Islands* (Park Ridge, N.J. 1975)

W. A. McDonald, *Progress into the Past* (New York 1967). History of Mycenaean archaeology

C. Renfrew, *The Emergence of Civilization* (London 1972). Carbon-14 dates

F. Schachermeyr, "Die ägäische Frühzeit," *SBWien* 309.1 and 2 (Vienna 1976)

K. Syriopoulos, *Pre-historia tes Peleponnesou* (Athens 1964)

Victoria Tatton-Brown, *Cyprus BC: 7000 Years of History* (London 1979). Catalogue of a British Museum exhibition

D. Theochares, *Neolithic Greece* (Athens 1973)

———, "Iolkos, Whence Sailed the Argonauts," *Arch* 11 (1958) 13-18

D. H. Trump, *The Prehistory of the Mediterranean* (New Haven 1980)

E. T. Vermeule, *The Greek Bronze Age* (Chicago 1964). Exemplary

B. Wells, "Asine II: Excavations East of the Acropolis," *Skrifter utgivna av Svenska Institutet in Athen*, 24.1.1 (Stockholm/Lund 1976)

CHAPTER 2: *"Mycenae, Rich in Gold"*

Work already cited: Vermeule

S. Alexiou et al., *Ancient Crete* (New York 1968)

P. Åström, N. Verdelis, "The Cuirass Tomb . . . at Dendra, I: The Chamber Tombs," *SMA* 4 (1977)

P. P. Betancourt, "The End of the Greek Bronze Age," *Antiquity* 50 (1976) 40-47

J. Bintliff, ed., *Mycenaean Geography: A Colloquium* (Cambridge 1977)

C. W. Blegen et al., *Pylos*, 3 vols. (Princeton 1966-73)

J. Bowman, *Travellers' Guide to Crete* (London 1974)

R. Buck, "The Middle Helladic Period," *Phoenix* 20 (1966) 193-209

G. Cadogan, *Palaces of Minoan Crete* (London 1976)

C. Davaras, *Guide to Cretan Antiquities* (Park Ridge, N.J. 1976)

O. T. P. K. Dickinson, "Origins of Mycenaean Civilization," *SMA* 49 (1977)

C. Doumas, *Thera and the Aegean World* (London 1978). Congress report; emphasis on Akrotiri and its frescoes

M. Ervin, "A Relief Pithos from Mykonos," *Archaiologikon Deltion* 18 (1963) Meletai 37-75

P. Faure, *La vie quotidienne en Crète au temps de Minos* (Paris 1973)

J. Forsdyke, "The Harvester Vase of Hagia Triada," *Journal of the Warburg and Courtauld Institute* 17 (1954) 1-9

J. W. Graham, *The Palaces of Crete* [2] (Princeton 1969)

A. Hausmann, ed., *Handbuch der Archäologie* (Munich 1969) has (pp. 234-67) a good account of Linear A by E. Grumach

S. Hiller, "Das minoische Kreta nach der Ausgrabungen des letzen Jahrzehnts," *SBWien* 330 (1977)

S. Hood, "The Minoans" (*AP&P*, London 1971)

R. Hope Simpson, "Gazetteer and Atlas of Mycenaean Sites," *Bulletin of the Institute of Classical Studies*, suppl. 16 (London 1965); with O. T. P. K. Dickinson, "Gazetteer of Aegean Civilisation in the Bronze Age," I, *Studies in Mediterranean Archaeology* 52 (1979)

S. Iakovidis, "The Present State of Research at the Citadel of Mycenae," *Institute of Archaeology Bulletin* 14 (London 1977) 99-141

S. A. Immerwahr, "Mycenaeans at Thera. Some Reflections on the Paintings from the West House," in *Greece and the Eastern Mediterranean: Studies . . . Schachermeyr* (Berlin 1977) 173-91. Admiral fresco: Mycenaean officers, Minoan crew?

U. Jentzen, ed., *Führer durch Tiryns* (Athens 1975)

P. Lehmann, ed., "A Land Called Crete," *Smith College Studies in History* 45 (1968). H. B. Hawes memorial volume; important articles by specialists

D. Levi, *Festos*, 4 vols. (Rome 1977)

C. R. Long, "The Aya Triadha Sarcophagus," *SMA* 41 (1974)

S. Marinatos, *Excavations at Thera* 1-7 (Athens 1967-76)

———, "Das Schiffsfresko von Akrotiri," in D. Gray,

"Seewesen," *Archaeologia Homerica* Ig (Göttingen 1974)

G. E. Mylonas, *Eleusis and the Eleusinian Mysteries* (Princeton 1961)

————, "Ho taphos tou Kyklou B ton Mykenon" (Athens 1973; E.T., *SMA* 7 [1964])

————, *Mycenae: Guide to Its Ruins and Its History* [6] (Athens 1977)

W. Nahm, "Zum Diskos von Phaistos: II," *Kadmos* 18 (1979) 1-25

J.-P. Olivier, "Le disque de Phaistos," *BCH* 99 (1975) 5-34

L. R. Palmer, J. Boardman, *On the Knossos Tablets* (Oxford 1963)

N. Platon, *Kato Zakro* (New York 1974)

M. R. Popham, "The Last Days of the Palace at Knossos." *SMA* 5 (1964)

N. Skouphopoulos, "Mycenaean Citadels," *SMA* 22 (1971)

Lord William Taylour, "The Mycenaeans" (*AP&P*, London 1964)

————, "New Light on Mycenaean Religion," *Antiquity* 44 (1970) 270-80

C. Tiré, H. van Effenterre, *Guide des fouilles françaises de Crète* [2] (Paris 1978)

E. T. Vermeule, "The Art of the Shaft Graves of Mycenae," *Semple Lectures,* 3rd series (Cincinnati 1975)

W. Voigtländer, *Guide to Tiryns* (Athens 1972)

A. J. B. Wace, F. H. Stubbings, *A Companion to Homer* (London 1962)

H. Wace, *Mycenae Guide* [4] (Princeton 1974)

P. Warren, "Cretan Colonies Overseas," *ProcPS* 33 (1967) 37-56

————, *Aegean Civilizations* (Oxford 1975)

A. Zois, *Vasiliki 1* (Athens 1976). Report of excavation of EM II-MM II houses near Gournia, Crete. In Greek

CHAPTER 3: *Mycenaean Athens,* etc.

Works already cited: Karageorgis, Tiré-van Effenterre

P. Alin, "Das Ende mykenäischen Fundstätten auf dem griechischen Festland," *SMA* 1 (1962)

P. Auberson, K. Schefold, *Führer durch Eretria* (Bern 1974)

G. F. Bass, "Archaeology under Water" (*AP&P*, London 1972)

L. Beschi, "Il monumento di Telemachos, fondatore dell' Asklepieion ateniese," *ASAtene*, n.s. 29/30 (1967/8) 382-436; "Contributi di topografia ateniese," 511-36

I. Beyer, *Die Tempel von Dreros und Prinias A* (Berlin 1976)

J. Boardman, "Greek Emporio: Excavations in Chios, 1952-55," *BSA* Suppl. 6 (1967)

R. A. Bryson *et al.*, "Drought and the Decline of Mycenae," *Antiquity* 43 (1974) 46-50

P. Cartledge, *Sparta and Lakonia, 1300-362 B.C.* (London & Boston 1979)

J. N. Coldstream, *Geometric Greece* (London 1977)

————, G. H. Huxley, *Kythera* (London 1977)

V. Desborough, *The Last Mycenaeans and Their Successors* (Oxford 1964)

————, *The Greek Dark Ages* (London 1972)

J. Deshayes, "Fouilles de la Deiras," *Études Peleponnésiennes* 4 (Paris 1966)

P. Dikaios, *Enkomi* 1-3 (Mainz 1969-71)

W. Fuchs, *Die Skulptur der Griechen* (Munich 1969)

B. Hayden, "A New Plan of Vrokastro," *AJA* 84 (1980) 211

R. Hope Simpson, J. F. Lazenby, "Notes from the Dodecanese III," *BSA* 68 (1973) 127-79. Mycenaean settlements on Rhodes. Good maps

S. Iakovidis, *Perati*, 3 vols. (Athens 1969-70)

S. A. Immerwahr, "The Neolithic and Bronze Age," *The Athenian Agora 13* (Princeton 1971). See also her *APB*, No. 13 (*ib.* 1973)

J. E. Jones, "Town and Country Houses of Attica in Classical Times," in H. Mussche *et al.*, *Thorikos et Laurion, Colliquium 1973* (Ghent 1975) 63-136

I. S. Mark, "The Early Architectural Phases of the Athena Nike Sanctuary," *AJA* 84 (1980) 222

R. Naumann, *Architektur Kleinasiens* [2] (Tübingen 1971)

H. Payne, T. J. Dunbabin, *Perachora 2* (Oxford 1972)

L. H. Sackett, M. R. Popham, "Lefkandi 2100-700 B.C.," *Arch* 25 (1972) 8-19

G. Säflund, *Berbati* (Stockholm 1965)

N. Sandars, "The Sea Peoples" (*AP&P*, London 1978)

G. Schmidt, *Samos 7* (Bonn 1968)

E. L. Smithson, "The Protogeometric Cemetery at Nea Ionia," *Hesp* 30 (1961) 147-78

A. M. Snodgrass, *The Dark Age of Greece* (Edinburgh 1971)

——, *Archaeology and the Rise of the Greek State* (Inaugural Lecture, Cambridge 1977)

C. G. Starr, *Economic and Social Growth of Early Greece, 800-500 B.C.* (New York 1977). Very full notes and bibliography

V. Tatton Brown, *Cyprus B.C.* (London 1979). A catalogue

R. A. Tomlinson, *Argos and the Argolid* (London 1972)

J. Travlos, *Pictorial Dictionary of Athens* (New York 1971)

B. Weiss, "The Decline of Late Bronze Age Civilization as a Possible Response to Climatic Change," Abstract, Nat'l. Center for Atmospheric Research, Boulder, Colo., May, 1979

R. F. Willetts, *The Civilization of Ancient Crete* (London 1977)

CHAPTER 4: *The Lyric Age*

Works already cited: Cartledge, Payne-Dunbabin

E. Akurgal, *Ancient Ruins of Turkey* [3] (Istanbul 1973)

B. Ashmole, N. Yalouris, *Olympia* (London 1967)

P. Aupert, *Fouilles de Delphes II: Le Stade* (Paris 1979)

B. Bergquist, *The Archaic Greek Temenos* (Lund 1967). On Artemis Orthia, Sparta

H. Berve, G. Gruben, *Greek Temples, Theatres, and Shrines* (London 1973)

J. Boardman, *Athenian Red Figure Vases: Archaic Period* (London 1975). See also his 1974 book on black figure, both richly illustrated

M. S. Brouskari, *Descriptive Catalogue of the Acropolis Museum* (Athens 1974)

P. Bruneau, J. Ducat, *Guide de Délos* (Paris 1966)

J. Ducat, "Les Kouroi du Ptoion," *Bibl. des Éc. Françaises d'Athènes et de Rome* 219 (Paris 1971)

R. Felsch, in "Chronique des fouilles," *BCH* 99 (1975) 636. On Kalapódi

S. Fleming, *Dating in Archaeology* (New York 1977). Discusses, with examples, dendrochronology, carbon 14, thermoluminescence, chemical analysis, and other techniques.

L. Giuliani, *Die archaischen Metopen von Selinunt* (Mainz 1979)

H. A. Harris, *Sport in Greece and Rome* (London 1972)

R. J. Hopper, "The Laurion Mines: A Reconsideration," *BSA* 63 (1968) 293-326

A. Invernizzi, "I frontoni del tempio di Aphaia ad Egina," *Pubblicazioni della Facoltà di Lettere, . . . U. di Torino,* 16.4 (1965)

L. H. Jeffery, *Archaic Greece* (London 1976)

H. J. Kienast, *Samos 15: Die Stadtmauer* (Bonn 1978)

C. M. Kraay, *Greek Coins* (London 1966)

J. H. Kroll, "Wappenmünzen to Gorgoneia to Owls: Some Reinterpretations of Early Athenian Coinage," *AJA* 84 (1980) 218-9

P. MacKendrick, *The North African Stones Speak* (Chapel Hill, 1980). Ch. 5, on Cyrene

A. Mallwitz, *Olympia und seine Bauten* (Munich 1972). At end, bar graph of lifetime of buildings

V. Milojčic *et al., Samos 1, 5-8, 11-12, 14-15* (Bonn 1961-78)

O. Murray, *Early Greece* (Brighton, Eng. 1980). Good on Lefkandi, Euboea

H. Mussche *et al., Thorikos 1-7* (Brussels & Ghent 1964-78)

M. Napoli, *La tomba del tuffatore* (Bari 1970).

D. Ohly, *Die Ägineten* (Munich 1976)

M. Renault, *The Praise Singer* (New York 1978). Novel with 6th-century setting

H. S. Robinson, "Corinth: The Archaic Temple," *Hesp.* 45 (1976) 224-239

G. Roux, *Delphi* (Paris 1971)

N. Sandars, "The Sea Peoples," in *Ancient Peoples and Places* series (London 1978)

T. L. Shear, Jr., "New Excavations Begun in the Athenian Agora," *Am. Sch. Class. Stud. Athens Newsletter* (Fall 1980) 2-3

A. M. Snodgrass, *Archaic Greece* (London 1980)

J. W. Sperling, "Thera and Therasia," *Ancient Greek Cities* 22 (Athens 1973)

R. Tölle, *Die antike Samos* (Mainz 1969)

J. S. Traill, "The Political Organization of Attica," *Hesp* Suppl. 14 (1975). Good maps

V. Tusa, "Due nuove metope archaiche da Selinunte," *ArchClass* 21 (1969) 153-71

R. Vallois, *L'architecture hellénique et hellénistique à Délos*, 2 vols. (Paris 1966-78)

E. T. Vermeule, "Tomba tou Skirou, Morphou, 1971," in *Mycenaeans in Eastern Mediterranean* (Symposium, Nicosia 1972)

T. B. L. Webster, *Patron and Painter in Classical Athens* (London 1972)

J. Wiseman, "The Land of the Ancient Corinthians," *SMA* 50 (1978)

W. Wurster, S. Hiller, *Alt-Ägina* 1.1, 4.1 (Mainz 1974-75)

R. E. Wycherley, *How the Greeks Built Cities* [2] (London 1967)

————, *The Stones of Athens* (Princeton 1978)

CHAPTER 5: *The Classical Age*

Works already cited: Ashmole, Wycherley

L. Bernabò Brea, section on Syracuse, *TCI Sicilia* [5] (Milan 1968) 598-642

J. S. Boersma, *Athenian Building Policy, 561/0-405/4 B.C.* (Groningen 1970)

F. Brommer, *Die Skulpturen der Parthenongiebel* (Mainz 1963); *Die Metopen*, 2 vols. (*ib.* 1967); *Der Parthenonfries*, 2 vols. (*ib.* 1977)

————, *Parthenon-Skulpturen* (*ib.* 1979). Reduces the above to one richly illustrated volume; includes discussion of cult statue

V. J. Bruno, ed., *The Parthenon* (New York 1974). An anthology. Includes E. B. Harrison on east pediment; J. Rothenberg's update of A. H. Smith on Elgin marbles

J. J. Coulton, *Ancient Greek Architects at Work* (Ithaca, N.Y. 1977)

W. B. Dinsmoor, Jr., *Guide to Sounion* (Athens 1970). See also his article on Sounion, *AJA* 70 (1974) and the critique by H. Plommer, *BSA* 71 (1976) 113-15

————, *The Propylaia to the Acropolis and Its Predecessor* I (Princeton 1979)

K. Friis, *Attic Grave Reliefs of the Classical Period* (Copenhagen 1951)

R. Griffo, *Guide . . . of Agrigento,* tr. J. B. Ward Perkins (Agrigento 1972)

M. Guido, *Sicily: An Archaeological Guide* (London 1967)

E. B. Harrison, "Alkamenes' Sculptures for the Hephaisteion," *AJA* 81 (1977) 137-78, 417-26. Suggests Hephaisteion was a building northwest of the one presently identified as H.; disproved by excavation

C. Hofkes-Brukker, *Der Bassai-fries* (Munich 1975)

G. T. W. Hooker, ed., "Parthenos and Parthenon," *Greece & Rome,* suppl. to vol. 10 (Oxford 1963). Articles by experts; plates

K. Jeppeson, "Where Was the So-Called Erechtheum?" *AJA* 83 (1979) 381-94

E. Langlotz, M. Hirmer, *The Western Greeks* (London 1967)

P. Levi, tr. & ed., *Pausanias' Description of Greece*², 2 vols. (Harmondsworth 1979). Especially valuable footnotes give archaeological updating

A. Mallwitz, "Ein Jahrhundert deutscher Ausgrabungen in Olymp," *AM* 92 (1977) 1-32

R. Martin, *L'urbanisme dans la Grèce antique*² (Paris 1974)

————, "L'Atelier Ictinos-Callicrates au temple de Bassae," *BCH* 100 (1976) 427-44

M. Napoli, *Paestum* (Novara 1970)

J. Papadimitriou, "Anaskaphai en Brauroni tes Attikes," *Erg* (1961) 20-37; (1962) 25-39; see also art. in *Scientific American* 208.6 (June, 1963) 110-120

N. D. Papahadzis, *Pausaniou Periegesis tes Hellados 2-8,* 3 vols. (Athens 1963-67)

M. Robertson, A. Frantz, *The Parthenon Frieze* (London 1975)

M.-L. Säflund, "The East Pediment of the Temple of Zeus at Olympia," *SMA* 27 (1970)

J. A. de Waele, *Akragas Graeca I* (The Hague 1971)

CHAPTER 6: *The Fourth Century*

Works already cited: Akurgal, Roux

M. Andronikos, "The Royal Graves at Vergina," *Athens Annals of Archaeology* 10 (1977) 40-72

B. Ashmole, *Architect and Sculptor in Classical Greece* (New York 1972). Authoritative on Halicarnassus

A. Bammer, *Architektur des jüngeren Artemision von Ephesos* (Wiesbaden 1972)

G. E. Bean, *Aegean Turkey* (London & New York 1966), 190-96 (on Claros)

O. Broneer, *Isthmia* 1-3 (Princeton 1971-77)

A. Burford, *The Greek Temple Builders at Epidauros* (Liverpool 1969)

H. Calvet, P. Roesch, "Les Sarapeia de Tanagra," *RA* (1966) 297-332

S. Charitonidis *et al.*, "Les mosaïques de la Maison du Menandre à Mytilène," *Antike Kunst*, Beiheft 6 (Basel 1970)

J. Fontenrose, *The Delphic Oracle* (Berkeley 1978)

C. H. Greenewalt, Jr., "Archaeological Research at Sardis in 1979," *AJA* 84 (1980) 209

G. Gruben, "Das archaïsche Didymaion," *Jahrb. deutsch. arch. Inst.* 78 (1963) 78-182

J. H. Hicks, "Acanthus and the Date of the Acanthus Column at Delphi," *AJA* 84 (1980) 213

R. A. Higgins, *Greek Terracotta Figures* (London 1963)

B. H. Hill, L. T. Lands, C. K. Williams, *The Temple of Zeus at Nemea* (Princeton 1966)

G. Kleiner, *Die Ruinen von Milet* (Berlin 1968)

D. Papaconstantinou-Diamantourou, *Pella* 1 (Athens 1971). In Greek. Air views, details of pebble mosaics, plans, maps

H. W. Parke, *Greek Oracles* (London 1967)

P. M. Petsas, "Pella," *SMA* 14 (1964)

———, "Pella, Alexander the Great's Capital," Institute for Balkan Studies 182 (Salonika 1978)

J. Pouilloux, G. Roux, *Enigmes à Delphes* (Paris 1963)

F. Salviat, *Guide de Thasos* (Paris 1968)

M. Schede, *Die Ruinen von Priene*[2] (Berlin 1964)

A. Stewart, *Skopas of Paros* (Park Ridge, N.J. 1977). Skopas at Tegea, Epidauros, Samothrace

G. B. Waywell, *The Free-Standing Sculpture of the Mausoleum at Halicarnassus* (London 1978)

F. E. Winter, *Greek Fortifications* (Toronto 1971)

———, "Toward a Chronology of the Later Artemision at Ephesus," *AJA* 84 (1980) 241

CHAPTER 7: *The Hellenistic Age*

Works already cited: Akurgal, Bean, Bruneau-Ducat, Salviat

M. Bell, III, "The City Plan of Morgantina," *AJA* 84 (1980) 195

K. H. Berger, *Der Aufstand der Giganten* (Berlin 1963)

J. J. Coulton, *Architectural Development of the Greek Stoa* (Oxford 1976)

S. Dakaris, "Das Taubenorakel von Dodona und das Totenorakel der Ephyra," *Antike Kunst,* Beiheft 1 (1963) 35-54

L. Durrell, *Reflections on a Marine Venus* (London 1953). About Rhodes

E. Dyggve, *Le sanctuaire d'Athana Lindia et l'architecture lindienne* (Berlin 1960). See J. D. Kondis' critique, *Gnomon* 35 (1963) 392-404 (no new plans, amateurish photos)

A. M. Fallico, on Morgantina, TCI *Sicilia,* 542-45

P. M. Fraser, *Ptolemaic Alexandria,* 3 vols. (Oxford 1972)

E. Giouri, *Ho Krateros tou Derveniou* (Athens 1978). Superb plates. In Greek

N. G. L. Hammond, *Epirus* (Oxford 1967). Index *s.v.* Dodona

————, " 'Philip's Tomb' in Its Historical Context," *GRBS* 19 (1978) 331-50, supports identification of Vergina tomb as Philip's

G. M. A. Hanfmann, *Archaeological Exploration of Sardis,* 4 vols. (Cambridge, Mass. 1971-78)

————, *From Croesus to Constantine* (Ann Arbor 1975)

C. M. Havelock, *Hellenistic Art* (London 1971)

H. Kähler, *Pergamon* (Berlin 1961)

P. W. Lehmann, "The So-called Tomb of Philip II: A Different Interpretation," *AJA* 84 (1980) 527-31

E. Melas, *Temples and Sanctuaries of Ancient Greece* (London 1973)

K. Ninou, ed., *Treasures of Ancient Macedonia* (Salonika 1978). Catalogue of an exhibition

Ph. Petsas, *Ho Taphos tôn Lefkadiôn* (Athens 1966)

C. M. Robertson, "Greek Mosaics," *JHS* 85 (1965) 72-89. Pebble-type: Olynthus, Pella, Alexandria

G. Roux, "L'architecture de l'Argolide," *Bibliothèque des-*

Écoles françaises d'Athènes et de Rome 199 (Paris 1961)

B. Schlüter, K. Pohler, *Pergamon: Topographische Karte, 1:25,000* (Vienna 1973)

S. M. Sherwin-White, "Ancient Cos," *Hypomnemata* 51 (Göttingen 1978)

E. Sjöqvist, *Sicily and the Greeks* (Ann Arbor 1973)

V. M. Strocka, *Piräusreliefs und Parthenosschilde* (Berlin 1967)

CHAPTER 8: *The Greek World under Roman Sway*

Antike Welt Sondernummer (1975) 3-89. On Nemrud Dagh. Superb color and b. and w. photographs

M. Garlikowski, *Le temple palmyrénien* (Warsaw 1973)

D. J. Geagan, "Roman Athens," *ANRW* 7.1 (Berlin 1979) 371-437. Full bibliography

G. M. A. Hanfmann, *Letters from Sardis* (Cambridge, Mass. 1972)

C. Hopkins, *The Discovery of Dura-Europus,* ed. B. Goldman (New Haven 1979)

L. Ibrahim *et al., Kenchreai 2: Panels of Opus Sectile in Glass* (Leiden 1976)

K. Michalowsky, *Palmyra,* 5 vols. (Warsaw 1960-66)

R. Scranton *et al., Kenchreai 1: Topography and Architecture* (Leiden 1978)

D. B. Small, "A Proposal for the Reuse of the Tower of the Winds," *AJA* 84 (1980) 97-99

H. A. Thompson, R. E. Wycherley, *Agora XIV: The Historical Shape and Uses of an Ancient City Center* (Princeton 1972)

J. B. Ward Perkins (with Axel Boëthius), *Etruscan and Roman Architecture* (Harmondsworth 1971) 417-20 (Baalbek); 453-57 (Palmyra)

J. R. Wiseman, "Corinth and Rome," *ANRW* 7.1 (Berlin 1979) 228-67, 438-548. New plans, reconstructions, photographs. Includes Isthmia

INDEX